AF528874

Guarding INDIA'S Integrity

A Proactive Governor Speaks

Some of our Learned Authors

General S Padmanabhan; General Shankar Roy Chowdhury; General Deepak Kapoor; Air Chief Marshal FH Major; Admiral Arun Prakash; Dr. A. Sivathanu Pillai, DRDO; Dr. R.K. Tewari, Scientist; Parvez Dewan, IAS; N Vittal, IAS; PK Agrawal, IAS; Sudhir S Baloeria, IAS; NS Sisodia, IAS; Dhirender Singh, IAS; Yogendra Narain, IAS; G Sundaram, IAS; JK. Bagchi, IAS; K Sankaran Nair, IP; DC Nath, IPS; Maloy Krishna Dhar, IPS; BR Lall, IPS; PC Dogra, IPS; DC Pathak, IPS; Dr. S Subramanian, IPS; R.K. Ohri, IPS; SR Arun, IPS; Birbal Nath, IPS; VN Rai, IPS; AP Maheshwari, IPS; VK Agarwal, IRS; Virendra Gupta, IFS; Lt Gen SK Sinha;Lt Gen Raj Kadyan; Lt Gen HB Kala; Lt Gen Arjun Ray; Lt Gen Amitav Mukherji, Lt Gen CK Kapur; Lt. Gen. NS Narahari; Lt. Gen. Chandra Shekhar; Lt Gen ML Chibber; Lt. Gen. Ashok Joshi; Lt Gen S Pattabhiraman; Maj. Gen. Nilendra Kumar; Maj. Gen. Vinod Saighal; Maj Gen VK Singh; Maj Gen Samay Ram; Maj Gen VK Shrivastava, Maj Gen SV Thapliyal, Maj Gen Dipankar Banerjee; Maj Gen Y Behl; Air Marshal SR Deshpande; Air Vice Marshal AK Tiwary; Air Vice Marshal Samir K Sen; Air Cmde (Dr.) CN Ghosh; Air Cmde NB Singh; Arvind Gupta, IFS; Ambassador Kishan S Rana, IFS; Ambessador Prem K Budhwar; Cmde Ranjit B Rai; Cdr. Alok Bansal; VK Singal, IRS; Sudha Raman; Carlos Ramirez-Faria; Brig Yash Mohan, VSM; Brig. Kim Yadav; Brig. DK Khullar; Brig Trigunesh Mukherjee; Brig Suryanarayan; Brig HK Kar; Brig. MS Patial; Brig. Parmodh Sarin; Brig. RP Singh; Brig. Jaspal Singh; Col. PK Gautam; Col. MN Gulati; Col. MS Jaswal; Col. Anil Shorey; Col. Anil Bhatt; Anuj Dhar, Journalist; Sapna Gupta; Prakash Nanda, Journalist; Ranjit Kumar; Vijay Naik, Journalist; Nirendra Dev, Journalist and many more.

Guarding INDIA'S Integrity

A Proactive Governor Speaks

Lt Gen (Retd) SK Sinha, PVSM

Former

Governor: Jammu and Kashmir
Governor: Assam
Acting Governor: Arunachal Pradesh
Acting Governor: West Bengal
India's Ambassador: Nepal
Vice Chief: Indian Army
GOC-in-C: Western Command

Foreword by

Dr. APJ Abdul Kalam & Shri IK Gujral
Former President of India | Former Prime Minister of India

Manas Publications
New Delhi-110002 (INDIA)

MANAS PUBLICATIONS
(We Convert Fighters into Writers)
(Publishers, Library Suppliers, Importers & Exporters)
4402/5-A, Ansari Road (Opp. HDFC Bank)
Darya Ganj, New Delhi - 110 002 (India)
Phones: Off.: 011-23260783, 23265523, Res.: 011-23842660
E-mail: manaspublications@gmail.com
manaspublications@yahoo.com
Website: www.manaspublications.in

2nd Impression 2012

ISBN 978-81-7049-348-8

Rs. 595/-

Designed at
Manas Publications

Printed in India at
RK Print Services, Delhi
and published by Mrs Suman Lata for
Manas Publications, 4402/5-A,
Ansari Road, (Opp HDFC Bank),
Darya Ganj, New Delhi - 110002 (INDIA)

CONTENTS

Dedicated to my Parents
to whom I owe
so much

Foreword

I am happy to write a foreword for the book "Guarding India's Integrity". General Sinha, wherever he took over as Governor, brought a linkage between the culture of the State and the heroic deeds of historic leaders who gave pride to the States. General Sinha has contributed in a unique way to give an action oriented Governorship during his tenure as Governor of Assam for six years and as Governor of Jammu and Kashmir for five years.

During his tenure as Governor, Assam, General Sinha evolved a systemic approach for promoting peace to the society. In Jammu and Kashmir, his approach to win the hearts and minds of the people through *Kashmiriyat* was definitely making an impact. General Sinha had seen *Kashmiriyat* in action in 1947. At a time when the entire region was engulfed in communal violence during the partition, surprisingly there was no communal violence in the valley. Srinagar reverberated to the slogan of "Hamlewar Khabardar - Hum Kashmiri Hindu Muslim Sikh Tayyar". General Sinha declared that he would do his best to promote *Kashmiriyat* which stood for amity and brotherhood cutting across religious divide. I could see this spirit in General Sinha during my visit to Jammu and Kashmir. He travelled with me, he walked with me and participated in all the events which included prayers at the Mata Vaishno Devi Temple, where Goddesses Maha Kali, Maha Lakshmi and Maha Saraswati are venerated. The Hazratbal shrine on the banks of Dal Lake which houses the holy relic of the Prophet inspired me and gave me divine feelings. Gompa (Budhist Monastery) at Leh, where I met venerable Kushok Bakula Rinpoche who was recognized by the 13th Dalai Lama as a reincarnation of Bakula Arhat. Gurudwara Shri Patthar Sahib, where the stone thrown by the jealous demon on Guru Nanak Devji is believed to have turned into wax. In all these places we both prayed for righteousness in the heart of the people, harmony in the homes, order in the state and the nation leading to peace in the world.

General Sinha has highlighted his last fortnight in J&K, before his relinquishing office, which became turbulent. However, the passage of the time healed the wounds and demonstrated to the world, the power of democracy in J&K through large voter turn out in December 2008 elections. The election result definitely reveals that people's power is truly mighty.

General Sinha had an opportunity to interact with four Chief Ministers during eleven years of his Governorship and he has been frank in describing the typical relationship he had with the Chief Ministers. This work can definitely become an interesting case study for constitutional experts and students of political science.

APJ Abdul Kalam

Foreword

I take great pleasure in writing this Foreword to Gen. Sinha's book - 'Guarding India's Integrity'. Many books have been written about the insurgencies in Assam and the J&K - fields of the author's focused attention. The author's contribution in meeting challenges there remain fresh in the memory of a grateful Nation. As a seasoned strategist, the General has first made a deep study of the history and cultural ethos of the State and then proceeded with needed firmness to tackle the issues.

I have experienced several incarnations of the author but reading his last book: 'A Governor's Musings' revealed to me some unfamiliar aspects of his personality. I now saw in him a remarkable politician, historian and an Essayist. While writing this Foreword, I recall some of his essays in his last book.

Our friendship began when Government of the time had stood in the way of his well deserved ascendance to the top of his chosen calling—soldiery. Amidst the widely spread public protests, late Madhu Mehta - a remarkable public man, thought of voicing this uneasiness in various parts of the country. He invited Gen. Sinha and me to join his band wagon. Both of us accompanied Madhu to various cities and towns of the country to rouse the public protests against the widely spread corruption.

In his last book, Gen. Sinha has undertaken the task of educating the public about some historic issues that have left a lasting impression on the Nation's psyche.

A very pertinent issue that had conditioned the memories of several generations is the 'three wars of Panipat'. Having lived most of my life near the war fields of Panipat, where several fateful wars were fought, I often used to wonder why the generations of warriors had so often chosen this spot for their clashes. Even in ancient times, the Mahabharat was fought by the Aryan tribes on this spot. Much later I learnt from the writings of a German scholar that the geography of the vast area of the Indo-Gangetic plains was full of thick forests that were impenetrable. An invader could either be resisted on his crossing the fast flowing Sindh River near Atock or where the forests were thin near Panipat. Gen. Sinha's perceptive mind elucidated details of the battle scenes that I quoted in my recently published small book: 'Scrap Book of a Prime Minister', I had quoted some of his essays on the 'three wars of Panipat'. While vividly describing scene of the first war of Panipat, Gen. Sinha says, "*On reaching Sirhind, Babar learnt that Ibrahim Lodhi was moving out to contest his advance. Hamid Khan, the Governor of Hissar was advancing from Hissar and Ibrahim Lodhi was marching with a large force from Delhi towards Panipat. Babar decided to deal with these forces before they could effect a junction. He advanced to Ambala and detached a select body of troops under his son Humayun together with some experienced commanders to deal with Hamid Khan. Humayun's contingent had a sharp and quick engagement with Hamid Khan's force and dispersed it. Hamid Khan fled and Humayun brought back 100 prisoners and 7 to 8 elephants as trophies*". Reading this episode with a scholar's touch, Gen. Sinha gave the history of 'civil-military relations' in the 19th century and in the contemporary era. An anecdote that was of interest to me was about Gen. Zorawar Singh who came back to Jammu after his victories in Chitral. Raja Gulab Singh, the ruler of Jammu, held a darbar to honour him where the noted General vowed his loyalty to his sovereign and announced that hence forth he would not draw any salary in service of his mentor and he lived up to it. How different it sounded the contemporary era ridden with the 'Pay-Commissions' of all sorts.

My relations with Gen. Sinha have seen many fields of his activity. Prime Minister V.P. Singh and myself as his Foreign Minister, had appointed him as Ambassador to Kathmandu when the Indo-Nepal relations were at very low point. He skillfully got them back to its pristine glory. I had later watched him in action as a Governor of Assam but unfortunately I could not travel to Jammu or Kashmir when he was Governor of the problem ridden State.

As he says, as a seasoned strategist, he would treat his civil appointments with the similar skills by first formulating a strategy based on his study of the history and cultural ethos of the State. Describing his tasks as Governor in Assam, he says in the book, *"I made a deep study of the causes of the people's alienation when otherwise they are so friendly. In the medieval period at least for 600 years, Assam had repulsed repeated invasions by the rulers of Delhi. While rest of India was being ruled by the Delhi Sultans and Mughal Emperors, Assam had remained independent. The British annexed Assam in early nineteenth century and made it a part of Bengal Presidency. Its separate identity and culture got engulfed by the new dispensation. With the British came Bengalis who were exposed to English education for some time. They occupied all the subordinate official positions in the administration and constituted the new intelligentsia in terms of teachers, doctors, lawyers and clerks. Bengali was made the State language, which also became the medium of instruction at schools. Assamese language was not officially recognized"*. This gave him the gen of the Assam problem that he dealt with skill and human touch.

There are many quotable quotes in the book that I would leave to the readers for discovery.

I am sure the book will facilitate the readers understanding of some complex issues that still besiege Assam and J&K.

I.K. GUJRAL
Former Prime Minister

By the same author

* A Governor's Musings: Soldier Statesman Speaks
* Changing India: Straight from the Heart
* Operation Rescue
* Of Matters Military
* Veer Kuer Singh
* A Soldier Recalls
* Patliputra: Past to Present

INTRODUCTION

During my tenure as Ambassador to Nepal, I completed writing my autobiography. It was published soon after my return to India, under the title, *A Soldier Recalls*. I was pleasantly surprised to find that the response to my book was so positive. I received laudatory letters from numerous friends. The reviews of the book published in several newspapers and magazines were very favourable. There was not a single adverse criticism. This was a source of great satisfaction to me. I had closed the active phase of my life in service of the Nation, on a high note, much beyond any legitimate expectation that I could entertain. I felt beholden.

Six years earlier, when I resigned from the Army, having been denied the top position, I had felt overwhelmed by the unprecedented support and sympathy across the board for me, from top political leaders, the Press and countless common people. The issue was also debated in the Parliament. Yet I confess that I was disappointed at being denied the opportunity to close my career of forty years in the Army without achieving my legitimate due. My feelings on my return from Nepal were significantly different in this regard. I had immense satisfaction that my humble efforts had received much more recognition than I deserved. In an unprecedented gesture, the King and the Queen came to our residence at Kathmandu, on the eve of our departure. The Prime Minister of India stated that I had been the cornerstone for the remarkable success in achieving cordial Indo-Nepal relations. The Prime Minister of Nepal wrote, "We will always remember General Sinha. He was a true friend of Nepal. We will miss him. He was as much India's Ambassador to Nepal as Nepal's Ambassador to India". I could not in my wildest dreams have visualized this overgenerous appreciation. It was unique for a soldier in our country to receive such encomium, in the field of diplomacy.

On my return home, I found myself in great demand for giving lectures at various institutions like colleges, universities, Rotary Clubs, Lions Clubs and other public fora. During the first few months, I was busy travelling all over the country giving talks on Indo-Nepal relations. My dear friend, the late Shri Madhu Mehta, President of the Hindustani Andolan, an NGO based in Mumbai, organized a public reception in my honour in Delhi. Shri A P Venkateswaran, a distinguished former foreign secretary presided over this function. There were several eminent national personalities who spoke at this meeting. They were late Shri Dharam Vira, former governor of West Bengal, Shri I K Gujral, former external affairs minister, who later became Prime Minister, Justice H R Khanna, the well-known former Judge of the Supreme Court, and Shri Arun Shourie, the reputed journalist, who later attained distinction as a Union cabinet minister. They all made very laudatory references to me. A special message from the Prime Minister of Nepal on the lines of what he had written earlier, as quoted by me in the preceding paragraph, was read out at the meeting. I could not ask for greater honour to be bestowed upon me for my humble effort. The International Friendship Society organized a function at Royal Bengal Hotel in Kolkata, where I was awarded the 1990 Vijay Shree Award "for enriching human life and outstanding attainments". I felt overwhelmed by such generous appreciation for my contribution in Nepal. I could now say to myself with a great amount of satisfaction that I had been able to close the active chapter of my life in service of the Nation, on a high note. Destiny had indeed been too kind to me.

Subsequent to my resigning from the Army, I had been given a diplomatic assignment in Nepal, after an interlude of six years. This was almost like a soldier on completing his Colour Service proceeding on Reserve and being recalled to serve in a crisis. This is referred to as Recalled to Colours, in the Army. I was recalled to service of the Nation after two interludes, first as Ambassador to Nepal and on the second occasion as Governor of Assam and thereafter of Jammu and Kashmir. In my two gubernatorial assignments, I was associated with guarding India's integrity against secessionist forces, supported by our hostile neighbours.

As I wrote in the previous volume of my autobiography, on my return from Nepal, I felt I was in the twilight zone of fading away and faded away. Later events proved me wrong. There was now a second interlude of another six years in my life before I was again Recalled to Colours. Inscrutable are the ways of Providence. This book is a continuation of my previous autobiography, *A Soldier Recalls*. It covers the period of my second interlude followed by my tenure as Governor of Assam for six years and thereafter as Governor of Jammu and Kashmir for five years. With the Independence of India in sight in 1946 Sir Fredrick Burrows Governor of Bengal asked Mahatma Gandhi as to what would like a Governor to do, the Mahatma replied, "Nothing". I could not follow this advice meant for a British Governor. I was Governor of Assam for six years followed by Governor of Jammu and Kashmir for five years. During this period I also served two short tenures each as Governor of West Bengal and Arunachal Pradesh. Eleven continuous years as a Governor was a record. Assam and Jammu and Kashmir are the two most sensitive states from the point of view of national security. Governors are constitutional appointments in which the holders of that high office are virtually required to live in a gilded cage and perform only ceremonial duties. I did not relish the idea of living in the ivory tower of a Raj Bhavan and function like the proverbial monkey—see no evil, hear no evil and speak no evil. Governors in militancy affected States have an onerous responsibility in contributing towards guarding national integrity and sovereignty. With my army background and long experience of handling insurgency during my army career, I took active interest in counter-insurgency operations. I was proactive in carrying out my duties within the role prescribed for a governor in our Constitution. In both my gubernatorial assignments, I also had additional assignments—Chairman of North East Council when I was in Assam and Chairman of two Shrine Boards in Jammu and Kashmir. These carried executive responsibilities, entailing management of budgets, running into hundreds of crores.

I had my share of success and failure as governor in two very sensitive states. Failures were not on account of any lack of effort on my part. I have tried to record these as objectively as possible.

In conclusion, I would like to place on record my gratitude to Shri A K Koul, who as in the case of my previous two books, so willingly and efficiently typed and retyped drafts of the first part of this book, and to Lance Naik, Lekh Bahadur of my battalion who did the same for the remaining part of the book.

SK Sinha

IMPORTANT COMMENTS

Lt General (Retd) SK Sinha has served in Jammu & Kashmir in various capacities in the Indian Army since independence. He was at the forefront of action against the Kabaili raiders in 1947. He was recently Governor of the State and did commendable work towards Kashmiriyat. His book discloses many facts that are unknown to the common people.

Farooq Abdullah

Member-Rajya Sabha and
former Chief Minister of Jammu & Kashmir

Guarding India's Integrity by Lt Gen SK Sinha, PVSM (Retd.) is not just the autobiography of a distinguished soldier, diplomat and governor. For the people of Assam, it is the saga of a Governor who far outshone all his predecessors in being not just the titular head of state, but a Governor who served the State brilliantly and with deep commitment to its people for six glorious and eventful years from 1997 to 2003. He sought to rebuild the psychological alienation that crept in between Assam and the Indian heartland. In striving to serve the State to the best of his ability, he proved to be the most proactive Governor the country has ever seen. I am sure, the book will have many interested readers all over the world, especially in Assam.

DN Bezboruah

former President, Editor Guilds of India

1 INTERLUDE

It was nice to be back home after a successful and satisfying tenure in Nepal. I looked forward to a period of relaxed life, with no official commitment or tension. I could now devote more time to my family. Yet, I did not want to cut myself off from society and lead the retired life of a recluse. In this, I could do no better than follow in the footsteps of my father. Although he had retired from official position some thirty years ago, he continued to lead a very active life till the last. He spent a lot of time doing honorary social work and also in yoga and prayers. He was the President of the Bihar Relief Committee, Chairman of the Mahavir Temple Trust, President of the State Branch of the Divine Life Society, an active Free Mason, Chairman of Gyan Niketan, a flourishing public school with 2000 boys on its rolls, and so on. He was leading a very regulated life. I recall that much against my wishes when he was well past ninety, he had undertaken a journey to Palamu, some 400 km from Patna, to oversee the functioning of free kitchens, that the Bihar Relief Committee was running there during a drought. I would try to persuade him not to strain himself so much as his age. He would insist that if he did not keep working as he was doing, he would not remain physically fit. He believed in leading a very purposeful life, even in retirement. Looking back to those days, now that I too am old, I realize how right my father was. I have been emulating him in my own way and have been leading a busy and active life. My children remonstrate with me and want me to go easy. I give them the same reply which my father used to give me.

My father had built a special room for me adjacent to my bedroom in the house that he had constructed on Boring Canal

Road in Patna, named Alakh Raj after his parents. I found this room very convenient. I had furnished it with all my army memorabilia and my books. This was my work place. Having been an early riser all my life, I used to start my day at dawn and put in two to three hours of work, while my father was doing his prayers and Yoga. I would join him for breakfast at nine every morning. Thereafter, he would go to his office and I would engage myself in my study room or in various social and political activities.

I had given up writing articles for newspapers while I was Ambassador to Nepal. I resumed writing. Some 300 articles written by me appeared in the Edit pages of various national newspapers. I wrote three books during this period. Besides this, I also undertook other commitments. I accepted to become the National Vice President of Lok Swaraj Aandolan started by Madhu Mehta from Mumbai and also the President of the Bihar Unit of that organisation. I became the Convenor of INTACH (Indian National Trust for Art, Culture and Heritage) in Bihar, Convenor of the Vivekananda Kendra for Bihar and President of the Patna Golf Club. My wife often complained that my tempo of activities remained as high in my retirement as during my army career.

Our family having lived in Patna for several generations, we had a large circle of relations and family friends. I grew up in Patna and there were a few friends from my school and college days, notably Bepin Beharee Sinha, who had been a minister in Bihar, Sachitanand Sinha who had retired as additional chief electoral officer of Bihar, and Nityanand Singh who had retired as IG Police. My father also had a large circle of friends. Due to my participation in public life, I developed contacts with national leaders of different political parties. To name some of them, Atal Behari Vajpayee, L K Advani, V P Singh, Ram Krishna Hegde, Raj Mohan Gandhi, Shatrughan Sinha, Karpoori Thakur, Ajit Singh and so on. They all visited our house. I became intimate with Devendra Prasad Singh, a freedom fighter and an associate of Jayaprakash Narayan. He was ten years older than me and a highly respected senior citizen of Patna. He was fully supportive of my non-party political activities. There was also my brother-in-law, K N Sahaya, the husband of my wife's elder sister. He too was nearly ten years older than me and had always been very indulgent towards me. A towering personality, he was a prominent public figure of Patna. He was Mayor of Patna for a record period of seven years. He was also President of All India Mayors Association and had been made the vice-president of World Mayors Conference in Morocco. He gave me valuable support in all my public activities. He was a frequent visitor to our house. With a host of people coming to see either my father or me everyday, our house had become a hub of activity. People would remark that we were a unique father-son duo, so active in our retirement.

2

All my children were living abroad. The three daughters were settled, one in Spain and two in the USA. My son being in the Foreign Service, was posted in diplomatic missions abroad. Just before we had gone to Nepal, we had been abroad on a two-month holiday. I had persuaded my father to accompany us. Two of my brothers, Jyoti and Pranu, were in Paris and London respectively, and my son was in Rome. One of my young nephews studying in Paris would say that the Sinha family had captured the Golden Triangle of Europe–London, Paris and Rome. Along with my father, his younger brother and my uncle, with his wife, accompanied us. It was a most enjoyable family holiday of two months in Europe and America. We managed to visit my brothers at London and Paris, our eldest daughter at Valencia in Spain, my son in Rome and the two younger daughters living in New York and Binghamton in the USA. Our younger grandson, Vinayak, was born in Rome, the elder boy, Ambuj, having been born in Saudi Arabia, three years earlier. The two other grandchildren from our eldest daughter, Anjali and Rahul, were fast growing up. They were not only very affectionate but looked after us very well, when we visited our daughter staying in Germany. Many friends remarked that we were indeed a good example of the Indian joint family.

After return from Nepal, my wife and I again made trips to our children in Europe and America in 1991, 1995 and in 1997. My brother, Pranu, was in Air India and he could give free tickets to his blood relations. I took full advantage of that facility. My wife's elder brother had also been a Senior Executive in Air India. She also could take advantage of this facility for some time while he was in service. In 1991, we had gone to Germany instead of Spain because our daughter and son-in-law were staying there on an assignment. Our son with his family drove up from Rome and we spent a holiday together in Germany. I had been to Germany some 40 years earlier, when it was still recovering from the ravages of the Second World War. Germany had now made remarkable progress and become the leading economic power of Europe. The unification of East and West Germany was taking place. Our son and daughter took us round to various places like the Hohenzollern Castle, Alsace Lorraine, the Black Forest, Munich, Frankfurt, Nuremberg, Stuttgart, Baden Baden and Strasbourg. We saw the impressive building of the European Parliament. We felt sorry that our subcontinent had not been able to emulate the European example. A decade later when I became Governor of Jammu and Kashmir, I started ardently advocating the European Union model as a solution to the Kashmir problem. I was much impressed by the sense of discipline of the German people. They are so punctilious about cleanliness. Even public toilets at railway stations are kept scrupulously clean, the like of which I had not seen in any other country. In the USA, we spent our time visiting places of tourist interest in New York and the pretty countryside of the New England States. We would return from our foreign trips fully reinvigorated and I would resume my normal activities in Patna.

3

The new Prime Minister of Nepal, G P Koirala, came on a visit to India on the invitation of Chandrashekhar, the then Prime Minister of our country. I got a telephone call from the Military Secretary to the President of India conveying the President's desire that I attend the banquet at Rashtrapati Bhavan in honour of the Nepalese Prime Minister. It was gracious of the President to have thought of me for the occasion. I had known G P Koirala even before I was appointed ambassador to Nepal. His elder brother, B P Koirala, who was the first elected Prime Minister of Nepal was revered as the Father of Democracy in that country. He had lived in exile in Patna in the early Forties when I was a college student. He had also participated in our freedom struggle and gone to jail during the Quit India Movement. He was a neighbour and a good friend of my uncle. I used to meet him in those days. Later, his son, Shashank and my son were classmates at St Xavier's, Patna. The Koirala family was very close to my friend, Devendra Prasad Singh. G P Koirala used to come and stay with him in Patna and they would come to my house. My contact with the Koiralas and the Nepal Congress stood me in good stead when I was ambassador to Nepal. I was only too happy to respond to the invitation for the banquet at Rashtrapati Bhavan. I have never travelled such a long distance, from Patna to Delhi, just to attend a banquet and that too in retirement, at my own expense. President Venkataraman thanked me for coming all the way to Delhi for the occasion. I told him that I still considered myself a soldier and it was a great honour for me to comply with the wishes of my Supreme Commander. However, I could not but recall my farewell call on him in 1983 when he was the Defence Minister and I had resigned from the Army. It had been such a cold and unpleasant experience. At that time he had warned me not to join politics. That was hardly the occasion for giving me such unsolicited advice. I had gone to him on a courtesy farewell call at the end of my forty years' service in the Army. The fact that I was not even offered a cup of tea during that farewell call was adversely commented upon in the Press. A lot of water had flown down the Yamuna since then. At the banquet he was graciousness personified. G P Koirala was of course very warm. I met several ministers, senior political leaders and top officials at the banquet. For the first time I met Rajiv Gandhi who was then no longer prime minister. I had no opportunity to talk to him. However, he appeared to be a well-mannered young man. Unfortunately, not long after, he was assassinated.

After his visit to Delhi, G P Koirala came to Patna. When I was in Nepal, I had taken the initiative to have the Bank Road in Patna, where B P Koirala had lived in the Forties, named after him. I had accompanied the then Nepalese Prime Minister K P Bhattarai from Kathmandu to Patna for the function organised to rename that road. I had also floated the proposal for his life-size statue to be installed there. The statue was ready and his brother G P Koirala, now Prime Minister of Nepal, had been invited to unveil it. It was, indeed, strange that the Government of Bihar chose to ignore me and did not extend the courtesy of inviting me for the function. I was reminded of how General Douglas MacArthur, the maker of modern Japan, was ignored after his retirement in the USA, when the Japanese Peace Treaty was signed in that country. It is not unusual in public life for people to have a short memory and my home State, Bihar, is in a class by itself. I was hoping that during the tenure of G P Koirala in Nepal and of Chandrashekhar in India, Indo-Nepal relations would improve further because Chandrashekhar had been very close to the Koirala family for a long time. This did not happen. Our government took a rather rigid stand on the Bara Pani Hydel Project on the UP-Nepal border. This added fuel to the anti-India sentiments amongst the intelligentsia of Kathmandu. After the short tenure of Chandrashekhar as Prime Minister, not much was achieved in terms of raising the level of cordiality between the two countries. Later, there was an unfortunate sharp decline in the security scenario in that country with widespread Maoist violence. The King and his entire family were massacred in the Palace. And after a decade of civil war, monarchy came to an end in Nepal.

4

After leaving the Army and before I was given the assignment in Nepal, from 1983 to 1989, I had deliberately kept away from the Army, except for being associated as a member of the Executive Committee of the United Services Institution (USI) at Delhi. Both while in the Army and after, I maintained close links with the USI. A dear friend of mine, who had dedicated his life to the USI, Colonel Pyara Lal, had been the Director of USI for decades. He had rendered yeoman service to that institution. The several crore USI complex, built on Rao Tula Ram Marg in New Delhi, is a tribute to his vision. Alas, he passed away before the building complex came up and the USI got established there. His successor, Maj Gen S C Sinha, was also a very dear friend of mine. We were commissioned together from the Officers Training School at Belgaum in 1944 and had served together at several places in our army career. In fact, due to a common surname and with almost identical initials, we often got mistaken for each other. He also did very commendable work for the USI for a decade, ably nurturing it at its new location. A few years back he too passed away. My reason for maintaining distance from the Army during the early years of my retirement was obvious. In view of the circumstances in which I had resigned from the Army and the controversy connected with it, I felt that I would be embarrassing the authorities and undermining discipline, if I kept in touch with the Army. However, with the passage of time, old memories of my supersession faded and circumstances had also changed drastically. During my tenure in Nepal, I had several army officers on my staff. I also had to interact with Army Headquarters in New Delhi. There are over a hundred thousand Gorkha ex-servicemen in Nepal and over a hundred thousand serving Gorkha personnel in our army, paramilitary and police. The Indian embassy in Nepal looks after the welfare of the families of these serving personnel; it disburses pension of ex-servicemen. No Indian embassy in any country has as many army officers on its staff as in Nepal. Although my association with the Army had got revived, through my assignment in Nepal, it was a pleasant surprise for me when I was invited to deliver the Field Marshal Cariappa Memorial Lecture at Delhi, organised by Army Headquarters. This prestigious memorial lecture has become a major annual army event in New Delhi. Field Marshal Manekshaw was very appropriately invited to deliver the first memorial lecture, the previous year. The fact that I was invited to deliver the second memorial lecture, when there were several retired army chiefs around, had a special meaning for me. It showed that the Army had not forgotten me. It gave me a feeling of being vindicated. It also gave me an opportunity to pay my tribute to a great General whom I had admired so much and whom I had the privilege to serve as his Staff Officer. Much later, when I was Governor of Jammu and Kashmir, I was invited to deliver the Admiral Katari Memorial Lecture. Katari like Cariappa had been the first Indian Chief of his Service. Soon after I relinquished the appointment of Governor of Jammu and Kashmir, Manekshaw passed away and I was invited to deliver the first Field Marshal Manekshaw Memorial Lecture.

I chose, "Indian Army Before and After Independence and its role in Nation Building" as my topic for the Cariappa Memorial Lecture. I addressed a large gathering for this lecture at the Air Force Auditorium in Delhi. This included several ministers, diplomats, political leaders and serving and retired defence officers. It was a good occasion for me to highlight the great contribution made by the Army through the centuries, in the service of the Nation. Since we had won our Independence primarily as a result of a non-violent freedom struggle led by the Father of the Nation, there is little awareness among our people of the contribution made by the Army towards Independence and thereafter in Nation building and preserving our democratic polity.

No doubt the British conquered India with the help of both their own army and the Indian Army, the latter comprising Indian soldiers led by British officers. Yet, it would be unfair to dub the Indian Army of that period as a mercenary army which some people are inclined to do. In the 18th century when the present Indian Army came to be raised, there was little awareness in the country of our national identity. The Indian soldier volunteered to serve in the army because he considered soldiering an honourable profession. Although serving a foreign master, he remained loyal to the three Ns — *Naam, Namak* and *Nishan* (Name, Salt and Flag). *Naam* stood for his family and community, *Namak* for the Government to which he had sworn loyalty, and *Nishan* for the regimental flag. He may not have been motivated by any nationalist feelings but he was not guided by any mercenary consideration either. He did not serve only to earn money or to offer his service to the highest bidder. Thus, it would be unfair to describe the Indian soldier of that period as a mercenary. Serving his British masters loyally, he contributed to the establishment of the British Empire in India and also to extending that Empire to various parts of Asia and Africa. When the British got involved in the First and the Second World Wars, the Indian Army played an important role, fighting for the British. It may be recalled that Mahatma Gandhi had raised a corps of stretcher bearers, and served the British during the Boer War for which he had been awarded the Kaiser-e-Hind medal. He had stood by the British in the First World War, and had encouraged recruitment to the Army. The gallantry of the Indian solidier and its appreciation the world over, became a source of national pride for our people. Circumstances had changed in the Second World War. The Mahatma had now called for a boycott of the war effort. Yet many Indians joined the Army, some even hoping that this may help in getting rid of the British. Churchill paid a tribute to the contribution made by the over two million Indian Army in the Second World War. He referred to it as the largest volunteer army known to history. The gallant performance of the Indian soldiers in the two World Wars drew the admiration of the world. It was also a matter of pride for the Indian people.

The 1857 Uprising, called the Great Mutiny by the British and referred to as the First War of Independence by Indians, was primarily a movement of the Army. Although the Uprising got mercilessly quelled by the British, it lit the spark of nationalism within the country and became a source of inspiration for later generations. Our freedom struggle was no doubt unique. For the first time in the history of mankind, non-violence was used as a political weapon. It was primarily through this unique approach of the Mahatma, that we were able to wrest independence from the mightiest Empire known to history. However, three events from our freedom struggle connected with the Indian Army need to be recounted. First, under the orders of Brigadier General Dyer, Indian soldiers had opened fire on an unarmed crowd hemmed in from all sides at Jallianwallah Bagh. This aroused widespread indignation and resentment against the British, as no other event had done. Second was a converse of Jallianwallah Bagh during the Civil Disobedience Movement of 1930, when the Garhwali soldiers refused to open fire on the unarmed Khudai Khidmatgars at Peshawar. The third was the role played by the prisoners from the Indian Army under the custody of the Japanese in Malaya in 1942. They joined the Indian National Army (INA), led by Netaji Subhash Chandra Bose, in large numbers. The military impact of the INA may not have been great, but its psychological and political impact was tremendous. The Viceroy, Lord Wavell, wrote to the Secretary of State for India on 20 August, 1945', "This is the first occasion in which an anti-British politician had acquired a hold over a substantial number of men in the Indian Army and the consequences are quite incalculable." Field Marshal Auchinleck, the Commander-in-Chief of the Indian Army, had ordered the court martial of three officers from the Indian army who had held senior positions in the INA. They were Shah Nawaz, Sehgal and Dhillon — a Muslim, a Hindu and a Sikh. Thus, he inadvertently reinforced nationalist feelings by unifying the three major communities on this issue. He had miscalculated. He thought that an open trial of these officers, highlighting the atrocities committed by them, would arouse anti-INA feelings among the Indian people. This did not happen. On the contrary, these trials aroused nationalist feelings and popular support for the INA. There was a ground swell of support in the country for them. A massive patriotic fervour swept the country and the Independence movement received a tremendous fillip. Soon after, there was the Naval mutiny at Bombay and Karachi. This shook the foundations of the British Empire in India.

Popular support for the INA not only among the people but also within the Army and the outbreak of the Naval Mutiny convinced the British Government that they could not now rely on the Indian Army to uphold their imperial rule. After the Second World War, an economically and militarily exhausted Britain was in no position to maintain a strong British military presence in India. The British decided to quit India. Thus, the Army complemented the Mahatma's call for the British to quit this country. Earl Atlee, who was the British Prime Minister in 1947, on a visit to India in 1956, told the Governor of West Bengal that their decision to withdraw from India was taken on account of a host of reasons and one of the most important was the realisation that the loyalty of the Indian Army had been undermined. The 1857 Uprising had laid the foundation of our freedom struggle by igniting the spark of nationalism and the Naval Mutiny of 1946 proved to be the last straw for the British. The wheel had turned full circle. The Indian Army which had played an important role in the establishment of British rule over India also played a significant role in ensuring the demise of British imperial rule over India.

I quoted a statement by Mahatma Gandhi about the Indian Army, published in the *Harijan* on April 21, 1946. He had said "Uptil now they were employed in indiscriminate firing on us. Today, they must plough the land, dig wells, clean latrines and do every other constructive work they can, and thus turn the peoples' hatred of them into love." Another significant statement about the Indian army at that time was the one made by Lord Wavell, the outgoing Viceroy. In his farewell speech on March 21, 1947 he said "I believe that the stability of the Indian army may perhaps be the deciding factor in the future of India." This turned out to be a prophetic statement. In the chaos of the Partition Riots when the civil administration had collapsed in North India, the Army was the only effective instrument available to the Government to restore order.

The Army's role during Partition and in ensuring the integrity of the country in Junagadh, Kashmir, Hyderabad and later Goa, endeared it to the people of the country. Without undertaking any constructive work as visualised by the Mahatma, overnight the Army became the most popular instrument of the government with the people of the country. The transformation from a colonial to a national army was complete. I recounted the role played by the Army in the defence of the country during the wars of 1947–48, 1962, 1965 and 1971. The 1999 Kargil War took place later. I also brought out that by remaining totally apolitical the Army has been sustaining our democratic polity. It has been the only apolitical army of the Third World and also unlike some of the armies of the West, no Cromwell or Bonaparte had ever risen from its ranks. Besides, the Army has been playing a significant role in two other areas. It has always risen splendidly to alleviate the sufferings of the people during natural and man–made calamities. Its personnel, drawn from all parts of the country, have been a living symbol of our national unity.

I have summarized the main points made by me during the Cariappa Memorial Lecture. I felt I was fortunate in having an opportunity to portray the unique role of the Indian Army, which has not received due recognition among our people. I was happy to get an opportunity to pay my tribute to the institution in which I served for 40 years and to which I owe so much. As stated earlier, it gave me immense satisfaction to find that 13 years after I left the Army, I had not been forgotten by the Army, and given the great honour of being invited to deliver the second Field Marshal Cariappa Memorial Lecture. This enabled me to pay my homage to the memory of the Father of the modern Indian Army. I had served on his staff and had the good fortune of closely interacting with him and learning much from him.

I had addressed the audience extempore for nearly one and a half hour. Subsequently, my speech, which had been recorded, was duly published. I was glad to find that there was great appreciation for my speech in the Press and by the audience, many of whom came up to me after the talk to express their overgenerous appreciation. Some even wrote letters to me. Shri L K Advani, who later became the Deputy Prime Minister, wrote: "Though delivered by you extempore, it was a masterly presentation of the subject". The British High Commissioner, Sir David Gore-Booth wrote: "I was sorry to have to rush away after your Carriapa Memorial Lecture (though I did manage to grasp your hand just in front of L K Advani). There seem to be national days everyday in Delhi and 26th October was no exception (Austria). I would like to say that I thought your lecture was a *tour de force* in terms of both delivery and content. I was particularly struck by your brave and entirely justified concluding remarks. I feel I can say this because you were equally frank about the British. I congratulate you." Air Marshal K C Carriapa, the son of Field Marshal Carriapa wrote to me "There is so much of and about my father that I know very little. This is in part perhaps due to the vast age difference between us and in part because I really spent such little time with him. It is only now that one receives nuggets of information given to some insight into him, his character and his vision. Your address has added to this slowly growing unwritten file case. In fact, I have been asked to put together anecdotes but I have demurred each time saying I never really knew my father. Perhaps, I will after some time. It was such a great pleasure meeting you ... To me, you have been a legend of whom I have heard so much — then to meet you in the flesh and blood more than I had conjured in my mind's eye."

5

My son, Yash, got posted to New Delhi in early 1992. It was good for him to get this posting after his foreign tenures in Egypt, Saudi Arabia and Italy. I welcomed this because during my frequent visits to Delhi, I could now spend some time with him and my two grandsons, Ambuj and Vinayak, of whom I am so fond, as all grandfathers are. In fact, his being in Delhi became an added reason for me to make my visits to the capital more frequent. Initially, he was posted as deputy secretary in the Ministry of Defence. I found this interesting for two reasons. Bepin Joshi was a Brigadier on my Staff when I was commanding a Corps at Chandimandir. My son had competed for the IAS while I was at Chandimandir. I had simultaneously been promoted and appointed Army Commander. At a farewell party hosted by me, Joshi had told my son, whose results had just come out, that in the IAS people got quick promotions and soon he will be a deputy secretary in the Ministry of Defence, trying to boss over Brigadiers. My son had replied that he had grown up in olive green (Army) environment and a Brigadier would always be an uncle to him. This had amused Joshi. He told me that my son was very diplomatic and he would do well in the Foreign Service. A few weeks later he got into the Indian Foreign Service (IFS) which was his first choice. After about ten years, Joshi was now the Army Chief and my son a deputy secretary in the Ministry of Defence. There was also another aspect to this. For decades, I had been championing the crying need to rationalise our higher defence organisation. I had been critical of the bureaucratic stranglehold on our defence set-up on the plea of supremacy of the Civil. I had been urging that as in all democracies, there should be direct interaction between the professionals and the political executives, in the Ministry of Defence without the civil servant functioning as a middleman between them and, in the process, exercising authority without expertise and without accountability. I had also been urging that officers from the Foreign Service should preferably be posted to the Ministry of Defence which was exclusively manned by officers from the IAS. I maintained that the appointment of defence secretary should be held by an IFS officer and the defence ministry should be manned primarily by IFS officers. An IFS officer with experience of having served in embassies abroad, particularly in our neighbouring countries like China and Pakistan, would be an asset in the Ministry of Defence. Defence policy and foreign policy are two sides of the same coin. Close interaction between IFS and defence service officers would be very advantageous. In our set-up, IAS Officers with no background of foreign policy or knowledge of defence matters serve in the Ministry of Defence. They are not in a position to make any meaningful contribution. My view has been that it is as incongruous to have an IAS officer serving as defence secretary as it would be to have an IFS officer posted as home secretary. It was indeed, a coincidence that the first officer from the IFS to be posted to the Ministry of Defence was none other than my own son. However, he did not stay in the Defence Ministry for long as his parent ministry wanted him on the Pakistan Desk in that ministry. From his career point of view, it was better that he should be doing a tenure in his parent ministry, particularly on the Pakistan Desk. Anyway, this was the beginning of an arrangement whereby an IFS officer now serves in the Ministry of Defence. Not much progress has been made in this regard beyond upgrading the appointment of the IFS officer in that ministry from deputy secretary to joint secretary. To this day, only one IFS Officer serves on deputation with the Ministry of Defence.

Soon after Bepin Joshi had taken over as Army Chief, he came on a tour to Patna and called at my house. He sought my advice on matters of personnel management in the Army. He requested me to function as a consultant and also promised remuneration. I told him that I had been working on personnel matters of the Army for a long time and also, of course, when I held the appointment of Adjutant General. The latter is the Army's Chief of Personnel. I was not very optimistic about any radical changes being allowed in the personnel policy of the Army. The civilian bureaucracy was so well entrenched in seats of power, that it would not allow any worthwhile changes to be made. Basically, the requirement had been to provide a long career for both officers and personnel below officer rank in the Army. A soldier in the Army retired in his thirties, when he is in the prime of youth and most of the officers retire many years earlier than their civilian counterparts, at a time when their family commitments, with growing children are at their peak. I had made out a plan for lateral movement of soldiers after 15 years of service in the Army to paramilitary forces and other departments. This arrangement could effect a saving of thousands of crores to the Government as pensions to soldiers for up to 20 years or more, would not be required to be paid during the period of their re-employment. There would also be savings in training costs. A similar plan for the officer cadre could be worked out, which would not only ensure a youthful profile in the Army but a more contented officer cadre. I had worked on these issues during my stint as Adjutant General at Army Headquarters. I agreed to work on this again for the Army and told Bepin that I would do so in an honorary capacity. All that I needed was a skeleton staff, secretarial assistance and transport during my visits to Delhi. He readily agreed to this arrangement. I had a comprehensive paper produced on the subject and Bepin was very enthusiastic about getting it accepted by the Government. Unfortunately, he died suddenly on the golf course and, as I feared, all my efforts proved to be nothing more than love's labour lost. Nearly twenty years later, the Sixth Pay Commission came out with this recommendation. I do not know to what extent this updated recommendation will be allowed to be implemented.

About this time my grandson, Ambuj, then about six years old, fell ill and the doctors discovered that he had a congenital kidney problem. He had an extra half kidney which was on top of one of his kidneys and this had to be removed. This required complicated surgery. We thought of taking him abroad but, ultimately, decided to have the operation performed in Delhi at the All India Institute of Medical Sciences. A competent and confident surgeon was available and in Delhi we had all the family support for the boy. Interestingly, Ambuj created no problems and went through the numerous tests and hospitalisation quite cheerfully. I recall that before being taken into the operation theatre, he told us that all those who loved him must also get an operation done on their stomach. I assured him that I will get myself operated after his operation. God was merciful and his operation, which lasted several hours, was successful. I was in an adjacent room, all the time, waiting to hear the results of the operation. Those were the most agonising moments of my life. After he came out of the hospital, true to my promise, I had my gallbladder operation performed, which I had been delaying for a long time.

6

Madhu Mehta, a Bombay based industrialist, had become a good friend of mine. He drafted me into his Hindustani Andolan movement which was designed to get individuals not committed to any political party on a common platform to work for the society and promote moral values in politics. One did not have to pay any membership fee to join Hindustani Aandolan. Madhu had at one time been very active in politics. He was the general secretary of the Swatantra Party under the chairmanship of C Rajagopalachari. The aims and objectives of the Hindustani Aandolan appealed to me and I became a member of that organisation. When I stood for elections as an independent candidate to the Parliament in 1984, Madhu, with a team of workers, had come to Patna to campaign for me.

Madhu Mehta now thought of organising the Lok Swaraj Andolan with a view to becoming proactive in politics in an independent capacity. As against there being no membership fee for Hindustani Andolan, membership fee was duly prescribed for the Lok Swaraj Andolan and a Constitution was drawn up for it. The Andolan was registered with the Election Commission and obtained an election symbol. The idea behind starting the Lok Swaraj Andolan was to get eminent people with a clean image to join politics without being identified with any political party. The aim was to have a group of such people in Parliament who may project views on issues without any party bias, and influence decisions in Parliament. They were not to accept any office in Government. Such selfless politicians would raise the level of politics and contribute to clean politics in the country sans corruption, crime, nepotism, and sectarianism. He requested me to be the national vice-president of this Andolan and also its State President in Bihar. I accepted his invitation. He managed to draw a whole lot of very eminent people to participate in the activities of the Andolan. This included distinquished personalities like I K Gujral, Ram Krishna Hegde, Arun Shourie, B K Nehru, Air Chief Marshal (later Marshal of the Air Force) Arjan Singh, Rajmohan Gandhi, MN Buch and so on. We toured the country and held meetings under the banner of Lok Swaraj Andolan in Mumbai, Delhi, Chennai, Lucknow, Kolkata, Ahmedabad, Patna and other cities. There was a good response from the intelligentsia for this movement. However, it was essentially an elite club, debating issues of importance in auditoriums. Although we received encouraging response from students, our movement could never become a mass movement, which in any case was not our objective. We had a limited aim, of promoting values and good people's participation in the democratic process, which should not be left exclusively to professional politicians.

We organised a three-day People's Parliament in Delhi. There were various burning issues which were discussed in this Parliament, without any bias for any political party. The idea was to work out constructive road maps in political, economic, security and social spheres with the help of experts in different fields, who were not affiliated to any political party and had no vested interest. The quality of debate was of a very high order. It was a tribute to the organising genius of Madhu that he could collect such a distinguished assemblage from all parts of the country. We discussed a lot of subjects like constitutional reforms, electoral laws, foreign policy, national security, industrial policy, educational system, urban development, agriculture and so on. On each of these subjects, resolutions drafted by acknowledged experts in their respective fields were presented and debated. Proceedings of the People's Parliament with its recommendations were prepared and we went in a delegation to President Venkataraman in Rashtrapati Bhavan to present them to him. A copy of the proceedings was also sent to the Prime Minister. Our effort received a good coverage in the Press and we felt amply rewarded. At the State level in Bihar, I organised a People's Assembly on the same lines, where we discussed aspects affecting our State. It provided a good opportunity for the intelligentsia in Patna, who were not in any political party, to participate in the deliberations of the People's Assembly. At the end of the session, we presented a copy of our report to the

Governor and forwarded a copy to the Chief Minister. These well-meaning moves were primarily designed to assist the Government and improve the quality of governance in the country.

I also organised public meetings in Patna on various issues for which we invited leading personalities in the country. Ram Krishna Hegde talked on clean politics, T N Seshan on the conduct of elections, Maulana Wahid-ud-Din on communal harmony, Rajmohan Gandhi on moral values and B K Nehru on Constitutional reforms. These meetings were well attended and generated a lot of interest. The otherwise marginalised intelligentsia in the public life of Bihar was enthused and happy to participate in discussions on these issues.

The Lok Swaraj Andolan put up candidates for elections from Gujrat and I was asked to campaign for them. I had done so for Rajmohan Gandhi in Amethi constituency and for V P Singh in Allahabad constituency. Rajmohan Gandhi had stood against Rajiv Gandhi and both had excellent family credentials in politics. Rajmohan is the grandson of Mahatma Gandhi on his father's side and of C Rajagopalachari on his mother's side. Rajiv Gandhi was the grandson of Jawaharlal Nehru and son of Indira Gandhi. Apart from ancestry, Rajmohan had an excellent record of social work in the Moral Rearmament Movement and had been a journalist of repute. He had also authored several books. Besides his family claim, Rajiv Gandhi had little to commend himself other than having been a co-pilot in Indian Airlines. Yet Rajiv Gandhi won hands down and Rajmohan Gandhi lost by a big margin. Earlier, he had lost in an election to the Parliament from Jabalpur. I felt saddened that the India of today had ignored a brilliant progeny of the Father of the Nation. V P Singh managed to win with a convincing margin in Allahabad and later went on to become the Prime Minister. I also campaigned for I K Gujral in Patna where I found myself in the company of Lalu Prasad Yadav who I had always opposed. I realised the validity of the adage that politics makes strange bedfellows. My task in campaigning for Lok Swaraj Andolan candidates in Gujrat was not easy. I found it difficult to mobilise the support of the people on the basis of moral values. All the candidates I campaigned for, lost at the hustings. However, it was a good experience for me to tour Gujrat. I travelled over one thousand kilometres by car and was much impressed to see the quality of roads in that State. I did not come across any potholes on the roads and this was so different from conditions in Bihar, where you cannot travel a few hundred yards on any road without encountering potholes. The level of development in the State was way ahead of what is seen in the "Bimaru" States (Bihar, Madhya Pradesh, Rajasthan and Uttar Pradesh), particularly my home State of Bihar. The heartland States of the country have been lagging far behind in terms of both development and governance, with Bihar at the bottom.

During my tour of Gujrat, I had occasion to visit the simple Patel Memorial Museum at the Sardar's native village of Karamsat, not far from Vadodra. Despite the Sardar's outstanding role during the Freedom Struggle and after Independence, in integrating over 500 Indian Princely States with the Indian Union, successive Congress Governments at the Centre have not bothered to put up any memorial for him anywhere. They are concerned only about the Nehru dynasty. At the Sardar's village, the local people have put up a memorial for him. This was in his ancestral house. An eternal lamp burns in the room in which he was born. The oil and wick for this lamp are provided by the villagers. The house is a double-storey building with several small rooms. Hundreds of photographs of the Sardar at various stages of his life have been put up on the walls in the rooms. In the forecourt of the house there are two marble bust statues of the two brothers, Vithalbhai Patel and Vallabhbhai Patel. I learnt that the father of these two great national leaders was Jhaverbhai Patel who had fought alongside the Rani of Jhansi in the 1857 Uprising. When the Rani attained martyrdom in battle at Gwalior, Jhaverbhai was wounded and taken a prisoner. He spent several years in jail at Indore. After being released, he had returned to his village, where he built his house and his two great sons were born. I enquired from the guide at the museum as to whether the Sardar had any other property of his own. He had been a flourishing Barrister at Ahmedabad, when he joined the Freedom Movement. I thought he may have acquired a house in Ahmedabad. I was told that the only immovable property owned by Sardar Patel was the house in his village which he had inherited from his father. The guide added that when the Sardar died, his bank balance was only Rs. 287/-. I was deeply moved. Here was a man who had been the Treasurer of the Congress Party for 30 years and, who as Deputy Prime Minister, dealt with more than 500 Maharajas and Nawabs. This included the Nizam of Hyderabad who, in his time, was supposed to be one of the richest men in the world, second only to the Emperor of Japan. Can one think of a better example of honesty and integrity in public life? How different were our stalwarts of the Freedom Movement from the present generation of politicians. None of the progenies of Sardar Patel was given any office of profit in the Government, nor catapulted to high position in the Congress Party. This was in sharp contrast to the Nehru family in the Congress. This dynastic syndrome has now spread to quite a few political parties of the country.

It was about this time that the Government of India woke up after over four decades to announce a posthumous Bharat Ratna for the Sardar. He should have been given this award in his lifetime like Nehru and others or soon after his death. Giving him this award after so many years of his death was almost belittling his great achievements in the service of the Nation. His stature like that of Mahatma Gandhi had become above Bharat Ratna. To add insult to injury, Patel's name was Number 2 in the Government Notification announcing this award, with Rajiv Gandhi's name in the first place. Perhaps, it was thought that Rajiv Gandhi having been the Prime Minister, should take precedence over Sardar Patel, who had only been a Deputy Prime Minister. I could not make out whether this was an act of revolting sycophancy or of the bureaucracy's limited vision. It is a pity that the Sardar's grandson chose to accept this award at an investiture ceremony in Rashtrapati Bhavan when the descendents of Netaji Subhash Chandra Bose, rightly declined to accept this posthumous award for their great ancestor. The inordinate delay in showing any official recognition for either the Sardar or Netaji was perhaps due to a feeling that this may detract from all the adulation being lavished on the Nehru dynasty. The fact that there were differences between Nehru and these two leaders of equal eminence, should not have allowed to be the determining factor in this. During my tour in Gujrat I came across a few people who were bitter about this. They mentioned that Jawaharlal Nehru did not have the magnanimity to attend the funeral of two of his lifetime colleagues in the Freedom Movement with whom he had differences, Sardar Patel and Dr. Rajendra Prasad. In this respect his daughter, Indira Gandhi had done better in attending the funeral of Jayaprakash Narayan who had opposed her and had even got her dislodged from power.

7

I was invited to be the Chief Guest at the annual function of Maharana Pratap College at Gorakhpur. I was impressed with the manner in which this function was organized. The Mahant of Gorakhnath Temple was my host and it was a pleasure to stay at his well-appointed campus and to be served all the choicest vegetarian delicacies. A Kavi Sammelan was organized as part of the celebrations. It was a well-attended popular event. However, I got scared by the depth of feeling on the issue of the Babri Masjid at Ayodhya. This controversy had been simmering for some time but I had not paid much attention to it. At the Kavi Sammelan, one poet after another recited poems lamenting the fact that while India had become free, Maryada Purushotam Ram was being kept behind bars in a mosque. I could see that the audience got emotionally very surcharged during the function. I felt that this did not augur well for communal harmony in the country. The sooner an amicable solution to this dispute was found, the better it would be for our country.

Not long after, Rajiv Gandhi decided to have the doors of the Babri Masjid opened. No doubt this was welcomed by the people who could now go and offer prayers to Ram Lalla, inside the mosque. Rajiv Gandhi also accorded permission for Shilanyas (laying of foundation stone) for a Ram Mandir near the Babri Masjid. This generated enthusiasm among Hindu activists. They started collecting bricks with 'Jai Shri Ram' written on them. Large numbers of such bricks were collected from all States in the country. Nepal, the only other Hindu majority country, also agreed to send bricks but with a difference. The bricks from Nepal had 'Jai Shri Sitaram' written on them. Sita was born at Janakpur, which is now in Nepal, on the border with Bihar. The brick collection exercise aroused emotions among the masses and this began to be exploited by politicians. It was also sharpening the divide between Hindus and Muslims. I felt concerned about these developments. They gave me visions of the events leading to 1947.

The growing dispute regarding the Babri Masjid had snowballed into a major national issue. My wife comes from a village not far from Ayodhya. When I used to go to the village of my in-laws, I often had occasion to visit the Babri Masjid, which used to be a deserted place with not many people taking notice of it. Animals grazed on its grounds. Unfortunately, with the issue getting politicized, it became the most important controversy on the national stage.

While I was Ambassador in Nepal, I found that the Sita Temple at Janakpur, a popular pilgrimage site for Hindus from all over India, showed beginnings of becoming a major controversy. A hundred years earlier, the Maharani of Kutch had the present building of the temple constructed. Most of the masons employed were Muslims from Rajasthan. Some of these workers had settled down on land close to the temple. In course of time, this had developed into a village with a fairly large habitation. They constructed a mosque in the village which is fairly close to the temple. A loudspeaker had recently been installed at the mosque for calling the faithful to prayer. The noise of the loudspeaker interfered with the rituals in the temple. This was resented by the local Hindu population and they were demanding that this mosque and the Muslim habitation be shifted to another location, some distance away from the Janaki Temple. The local Muslims were opposed to this. I found that the staff of the Pakistan Embassy at Kathmandu was taking undue interest in the matter and its officials had been frequently visiting Janakpur. I tried to persuade the Nepalese authorities to bring an end to this controversy by allowing the mosque and the Muslim village to continue at their locations. To assuage Hindu feelings, the Muslims should be persuaded not to use loudspeakers at the mosque. After all the loudspeaker was a modern invention and in the old days there were no loudspeakers at the mosque. This suggestion was agreed to and I am glad that the controversy in Nepal was nipped in the bud and not allowed to get out of hand like the controversy at Ayodhya.

On my return to Patna from Gorakhpur, I tried to go into the history of the Ayodhya dispute. There was no historical evidence for the fact that Lord Ram was born at that specific site. Religion is a matter of faith and it is difficult to substantiate religious beliefs on the basis of historical evidence. Since the dawn of history, Hindus have believed that Lord Ram was born at Ayodhya. There is no need to question that belief. The same consideration should apply to other religions as well. The Christians believe in the immaculate conception by Virgin Mary and the Muslims believe that God revealed the Holy Qoran to the Prophet who recorded it. It will be most inappropriate for the people of other faiths to question the veracity of these beliefs. Instead of questioning them, they should show respect for those beliefs. Such understanding is necessary for developing a harmonious pluralistic society.

Insofar as the Babri Masjid was concerned, the Hindus maintained that there used to be a big Ram Temple at Ayodhya which was destroyed by Babar and a mosque was built at that site. There may well have been a large Ram Temple at Ayodhya. For thousands of years, Ayodhya has been a sacred pilgrimage site for

Hindus as it is associated with the birth of Lord Ram. However, there was no historical evidence of a temple having been destroyed by Babar and a mosque built at that site. Babar's memoirs are known to be very accurate and detailed. After the battles of Panipat and Kanva, Babar had continued his march of conquest to the East. He advanced to Ayodhya and beyond. Details of his campaigns are found in the *Babarnama*, but unfortunately the pages of the original manuscript dealing with his campaign around Ayodhya, are missing. Thus, we cannot ascertain about the facts regarding the destruction of the Ram Temple at Ayodhya from the *Babarnama*. However, there is no denying the fact that during the medieval period, thousands of Hindu temples were destroyed in India and mosques built at those sites. The temples at Somnath, Kashi and Mathura, all very sacred places of Hindu pilgrimage, had suffered that fate. This, of course, is no justification for the present generation to demand removal or destruction of mosques at those sites. In the modern day and age, we must learn to coexist harmoniously and respect each other's sentiments. Any attempt to rewrite the past can only have disastrous consequences as indeed the unfortunate subsequent developments at Ayodhya amply demonstrated.

Whereas the Hindus allege that a Ram Temple was destroyed by Baqi, a general of Babar and a mosque was built at that site, the Muslims dispute this, maintaining that no Ram Temple was destroyed to build the mosque. This dispute had been going on for centuries. It is said that the Mughal Emperor, Akbar, worked out a compromise allowing the Hindus to have a *chabutra* (platform) within the precincts of the mosque to enable them to offer prayers to Lord Ram. This practice was subsequently discontinued after Akbar. During the reign of Wajid Ali Shah of Awadh, there was tension in Ayodhya on this account. The practice of Hindus being allowed to offer prayers at *Ram Chabutra* was revived. European travellers who had visited Ayodhya in the 17th and 18th centuries wrote about this dispute in their accounts. The District Gazetteer of Ayodhya published by the British in the 19th century refers to the dispute regarding the Babri Masjid. The Uprising of 1857 saw close cooperation between the Hindus and the Muslims and prayers continued to be offered at *Ram Chabutra*. In 1930 there was a communal riot as a result of which two domes of the mosque got damaged. The British Government imposed a collective fine on the Hindus and had the domes repaired.

No doubt there was a long history connected with the Babri Masjid dispute, but it had remained a local issue. The rest of the country did not take any interest in it and most people were not even aware of it. In 1949, the District Magistrate of Ayodhya allowed some people to surreptitiously install the idol of Ram Lalla inside the mosque, when the doors of the mosque were supposed to be closed and a police guard posted there. It was given out by some Hindus that the idol of Ram Lalla had on its own emerged from the bowels of the Earth. This led to great excitement among the Hindus. They started visiting the mosque in large numbers for "Darshan". The Muslims understandably contested the canard that had been spread. They justifiably maintained that the idol had been installed surreptitiously and it was not a supernatural event. The administration had two options to resolve the dispute. It could have had the idols removed or could persuade the Muslims to respect Hindu sentiments. As a gesture of goodwill, they could be persuaded to hand over the mosque, lying in disuse for years, to the Hindus. Had Jawaharlal Nehru got the idol removed, the Hindus would have reconciled themselves to his decision. Similarly, in the wake of Partition and the guilty feeling among Muslims at that time, they could be persuaded to agree to the mosque being handed over. Jawaharlal was too staunchly secular to consider the latter alternative and he could not take a hard decision. He chose the easy course of putting the ball in a court of law. He wanted the conflict to be resolved through a judicial verdict. Half a century had elapsed since then and yet a legal solution was nowhere in sight. This compounded matters.

About the same time that the Ram Lalla idol had got installed at Ayodhya, a famous temple in West India had got restored. At the initiative of Sardar Patel, the Somnath temple, which had been destroyed by Mahmud Ghazni, was rebuilt. Jawaharlal Nehru was opposed to this being done and particularly to the participation of the State in it. Sardar Patel rightly decided that no Government funds would be used in the restoration of that temple. However he invited the President, Dr Rajendra Prasad to inaugurate the temple. Nehru was opposed to the President's participation in the function but the President ignored his advice.

I feared that the Babri Masjid dispute might snowball into another disaster of 1947 dimension. I felt that it was the duty of the sober elements from both communities to work out a compromise which would satisfy both and be mutually acceptable. This could not be done because the extremists on both sides were not prepared to accept any compromise. The Hindus were ill-advised to rake up this old dispute, making it a political issue and arousing emotions. The Muslims, on the other hand were adamant in their stand and were not ready to yield any ground. They argued with some justification that if they agreed to give up their stand, then that may become the tip of the iceberg, opening a Pandora's Box. The Hindu demand for restoration of temples and removal of mosques built at or near those sites, particularly at Kashi and Mathura, would gain momentum. Instead of being a silent spectator to the downslide of relations between the two communities on this highly controversial and emotive issue, I tried in my humble way, to put forward a compromise solution. I wrote articles on this subject and under the aegis of Lok Swaraj Andolan, propagated my views. I found that my effort was like swimming against a massive tide. Yet I felt that it was worth striving to help in resolving the issue.

Although there was no convincing historical evidence of Lord Ram having been born at a specific site in Ayodhya, the fact remains that the Hindus, for centuries, fervently believed that the Lord was born at that site. Had the Muslims shown magnanimity and agreed to handing over the disputed site to the Hindus, it would have had a tremendous impact in fostering communal harmony. The Hindus could have been made to give a written guarantee that there would be no further agitation for removal of any mosque or restoration of any temple. A Ram temple at that site had special religious significance for the Hindus. There was nothing very special about the mosque at Ayodhya. No doubt, all mosques are sacred buildings but the Babri Masjid was not in the same category as the sacred Shrines at Mecca, Madina or Ajmer Shareef. Muslims argued that all mosques were equally sacred and the Babri Masjid could not be given up. This was too rigid a stand. It ignored what has been happening in different countries. In Saudi Arabia, there was an instance of a mosque being demolished to allow straightening of a road. In Pakistan, when the Mangla Dam was constructed, several mosques got submerged in water. In India, a great number of mosques after Partition fell into disuse and disappeared. The solution that I had thought of was on the pattern of what I had found during my visit to my son in Egypt in the early Eighties. When the Aswan Dam was to be constructed, it was realized that the ancient Pharaoh temple of Ramses-II would get submerged in water. It was a world heritage building of great importance, which had to be preserved. Using modern technology, the ancient temple, thousands of years old, was lifted without any damage to its structure and reinstalled at another site. I suggested a similar solution to be worked out at Ayodhya. Both Hindus and Muslims cooperating with each other could have had the mosque lifted from its foundations and moved to an alternative site which could have been beautified with improvements and landscaping on a magnificent scale. A grand Hindu temple could then be constructed at the disputed site. Both Hindus and Muslims could be persuaded to cooperate in the two endeavours. I am afraid, there were very few takers for this suggestion. My article on the subject in the *Indian Express* drew adverse reactions. It was argued by fundamentalists that not only a mosque but the land on which a mosque stood was holy and my suggestion was a sacrilege. Anyway, I realised that both communities had an uncompromising stand and they were not prepared to see reason or do anything to prevent the downslide into chaos and anarchy. The extremists on both sides remained adamant and the politicians from both communities had a field day.

On 6 December 1992, much to my horror and surprise, I saw on the television the domes of the Babri Masjid being demolished. It was most unfortunate that some misguided and fanatic Hindus committed this totally indefensible act of vandalism. They not only gravely hurt the feelings of the Muslims but also that of a vast majority of Hindus. I was dismayed and disillusioned. These vandals had acted in a manner totally contrary to the traditions of religious tolerance which has been the cornerstone of Hinduism through the centuries. No matter what others may have done in the past, this behaviour could not be justified. My thoughts went back to that great warrior, Chhatrapati Shivaji. In an age when thousands of Hindu temples were being destroyed by religious fanatics, he gave a shining example of respect for other religions. His Army never destroyed any mosque. He showed due reverence for the Holy Qoran. Whenever his troops found a copy of the Holy Book, he had it handed over with reverence to Islamic clerics. He always showed respect and consideration for them. In those days conquerors would treat women as prize of war to which they had a legitimate right. After his troops had captured Kalyan, the Maratha Sardars took the daughter-in-law of the Muslim governor to the Maratha capital. This young lady was one of the prettiest women of her time. The Sardars brought her as a prize for Shivaji and presented her to him in his Court. On seeing her stunning beauty, Shivaji spoke to her. "If my mother had been half as pretty as you, I would not have been so ugly as I am." Thereafter he ordered the lady to be returned with due honour and respect to her family. No wonder even the enemies of Shivaji admired his moral stature and he became a symbol of Hindu renaissance.

As stated earlier, the Ayodhya dispute had remained a local affair and the country as a whole had been oblivious of it. Unfortunately, in the Eighties, this issue got politicised and it snowballed into the most explosive dispute in the country. Our vote-seeking politicians of all hues — secular, saffron and green — found it a convenient issue to exploit for their selfish gains. The dispute continues to be kept alive by them, much to the detriment of our national interests.

I had seen the Partition holocaust of 1947 from close quarters. For two months I was travelling in the Viceroy's special train given to Lt Gen Sir Dudley Russell for use as a mobile headquarters. We were ten staff officers in this skeleton headquarters and I was the only Indian amongst them. We were completely self-contained on the train for accommodation, offices, escort, vehicles, intercommunication and so on. We travelled in this train between Delhi and Lahore during those momentous days. The gory scenes which I witnessed at that time, were the worst spectacles of human barbarity and brutality that I have ever seen. One million people had been killed and twenty million had been uprooted. It was one of the greatest human tragedies in the history of mankind. Before Partition, we had never visualised such a disastrous course of events. I had hoped that the dispute between the Congress and the Muslim League would ultimately get sorted out and the country would not get partitioned. Perhaps, with a little give and take on both sides, starting from the Lucknow Pact of 1916 or during the formation of popular Governments in the Provinces in 1937, particularly in United Provinces (Uttar Pradesh), the holocaust of 1947 could have been avoided. At one stage the Mahatma had even pleaded that for the country to remain united, Mohammed Ali Jinnah be appointed Prime Minister of India. Things did not work out that way. And the two new Dominions had to pay a very heavy price in human lives and suffering. Unfortunately, more than half a century after Partition, we continue to suffer from its ill effects, with numerous innocent people getting killed.

In destroying the Babri Masjid, the Hindu vandals had been very unfaithful to long cherished and admired traditions of their community. The destruction of thousands of Hindu temples in the medieval age cannot be any justification for the destruction of any mosque in the modern age. It was argued by some that the several-hundred-years-old functioning Hindu temple at Ramana in Dhaka in Bangladesh had been destroyed in the Seventies, without any murmur anywhere. Further, along with ethnic cleansing of Kashmiri Pandits from the Valley, numerous Hindu temples were destroyed in Kashmir before the destruction of Babri Masjid. The secular brigade's reaction to the plight of Kashmiri Pandits and the destruction of Hindu temples was of thundering silence. They were much obsessed by the fear of being labelled as communal. They wore their secularism on their sleeves, adopting an anti-Hindu outlook, to prove their secular credentials. When the priceless statues of the Buddha at Bamiyan in Afghanistan were destroyed by the Taliban, they either maintained mute or even tried to provide a fig-leaf of justification for it by comparing it with what had happened at Ayodhya. The Bamiyan statues were the largest statues in the world and were a rare world heritage of thousands of years. They were destroyed by artillery bombardment with the operation lasting a few days in the full glare of the world. It was puerile to compare this deliberate act of State vandalism with the action of a berserk mob at Ayodhya. Only a diseased mind could do so.

Religious fundamentalism of both the majority or the minority community should be condemned with equal vehemence. Selective condemnation of only the majority community as practised by our secular brigade, adds fuel to the fundamentalism of both communities. The RSS was found practising Hindu fundamentalism but they did not have much following. They were considered part of a lunatic fringe. With selective secularism practised by many politicians and even the intelligentsia not engaged in politics, and the phenomenal growth of fundamentalism in our neighbouring countries, Hindu fundamentalism grew by leaps and bounds. Besides the RSS, other organizations like Vishwa Hindu Parishad (VHP) and the Bajrang Dal mushroomed. All this culminated in the tragedy at Ayodhya. I have narrated these facts not to provide any defence for the condemnable demolition of the mosque but to promote a better understanding of that tragedy. Little could I then realize that some years later, I would get embroiled in a communal imbroglio started by some religious fundamentalists.

The demolition of the Babri Masjid brought about a chain of most unfortunate events. In Pakistan, some of the few remaining temples left there were destroyed with bulldozers and mobs, led by ministers and other dignitaries. In Bangladesh also, similar retaliatory action took place and riots broke out. There was widespread communal violence in our country in which a large number of people got killed. There was serial bombing in Mumbai, in which several hundred people lost their lives. Even the great tragedy of the large scale killings in Gujrat in 2001 was sparked off by the gruesome burning of the train at Godhra of people returning from Ayodhya. All this chain of unfortunate incidents was almost a repeat of what had happened at the time of Partition. Luckily, the Governments in different States in the decade following the sacrilege at Ayodhya, managed to control the situation and not allow it to get totally out of hand as had happened in 1947. It must be mentioned that the State Government in Gujrat failed to take due action for the first couple of days to control the violence unleashed against the minority community, but other State Governments ensured that this violence did not spread. Later, the Gujrat Government prevented the outbreak of riots when the Akshardham Temple was attacked and many innocent people killed.

Politicians have been trying to take advantage of the situation by continuously harping on the Ayodhya tragedy. This has continued for over a decade now. However, I give full credit to the Hindu electorate who expressed its abhorrence for the demolition of the Babri Masjid during the Assembly elections in the following year. The BJP, which was regarded as being associated with this demolition, got routed in the Assembly elections in the Hindu heartland States of Uttar Pradesh and Madhya Pradesh. Yet the hope that political exploitation of the Ayodhya tragedy would die down continues to remain unrealised.

Soon after the demolition of the Babri Masjid on 6 December 1992, I took the initiative in Bihar to undertake some damage control. I held informal meetings with several Hindu and Muslim friends. I proposed that the best way of reducing the highly charged communal atmosphere would be for the Central Government to take immediate action in the matter. The Muslims had been saying that the Holy Qoran does not allow destruction of any place of worship of another religion. In fact it is categorically stated in the Qoran, that prayers offered at a place of worship of another religion, are not acceptable to Allah. The Hindus maintained that a large Ram temple at that site had been destroyed by Babar and a mosque built there. There was no convincing archaeological evidence in support of this contention. I proposed that the Archaeological Department should carry out immediate televised excavation at the site in the presence of leaders from both communities. If no archaeological evidence was found of a Hindu temple at that site, the Hindus and Muslims together should rebuild the Babri Masjid and the Hindus may be allowed to build a large Ram temple at another site in Ayodhya. On the other hand, if archaeological evidence revealed a destroyed Hindu temple, then the Hindus should be allowed to build a Ram temple there and both Hindus and Muslims should build a grand mosque in Ayodhya at another site. This formula found acceptance amongst quite a few apolitical intelligentsia of both communities. We submitted a memorandum suggesting this solution to the then Prime Minister, P V Narasimha Rao. The memorandum was signed by some eminent Hindus, Muslims and Christians of Patna. Amongst the Muslims, notable signatories were Justice Wasim Ahmed, former Judge of Patna High Court and S Q Rizvi, former Director General of Police of Bihar. We did not associate any political leaders with our memorandum. I went to Delhi and sought a meeting with Prime Minister Narasimha Rao. He was good enough to grant me an audience, but unfortunately, no result came out of our effort. Our formula drew no response and the Babri Masjid has remained an albatross round the neck of our Nation, with disastrous consequences.

A few months later, Madhu Mehta got in touch with Maulana Waheed-ud-Din, an Islamic scholar based at Delhi. His learned articles in English are frequently published in newspapers and he is a person with very liberal views. He agreed to tour with us to different States and address audiences under the banner of the Lok Swaraj Andolan to help in resolving the Babri Masjid dispute. He had a formula of his own. He advocated that Muslims should forget one and Hindus should forget two. He meant that Muslims should give up their stand on Babri Masjid and Hindus should give up their stand on Kashi and Mathura. This effort also did not yield much result. Controversy and litigation has been continuing on this dispute. Many years later, Allahabad High Court directed the Archaeological Department to carry out an excavation at the site to determine if a Hindu temple had existed there. Extensive digging was carried out for several months and evidence was found of existence of a Hindu temple at that site. Its report was submitted to the High Court but its veracity has been challenged and a solution is still nowhere in sight. Had the digging been done immediately after the demolition in December 1992 and in full view of the people on the television, it is possible that on the basis of evidence quickly unearthed at that time, an amicable solution could have been found. The long delay in doing so has not helped matters and has given an excuse for levelling allegations of manipulation. Be that as it may, this dispute continues to fester and one does not know when it will get finally resolved.

8

I grew up as a child in Patna in my ancestral home only a couple of kilometers from the ruins of ancient Patliputra. As a child I used to roam in those ruins, drawing inspiration from the exploits of the great Mauryas. I was inspired more by Chandragupta Maurya, than his world-famous grandson, Ashoka, whom H G Wells in his book *Outline of World History*, has eulogised as the greatest ruler in the history of mankind. My fascination for Chandragupta Maurya grew from the fact that over two thousand years ago, he had liberated Punjab from Greek rule and later defeated the world conquering Greek Army under Alexander's successor Selucus, that invaded India. As a result of this victory, he had annexed Afghanistan. At a time when we in India were under British rule, it was an understandable ambition for a growing young Indian boy to dream of getting rid of foreign rule and aspire to be a citizen of an Independent Nation. Along with this patriotic urge, there was also a regional pride in the history of Bihar. Till a generation earlier, Bihar, during British rule, had even lost its separate identity and had been made a part of Bengal. The effect of this was that Bengalis dominated all intellectual pursuits in Bihar like the medical profession, the legal profession, government service, educational institutions and so on. I did not suffer from any regional parochialism but there was a natural desire that Bihar and the indigenous people of the State should progress and flourish.

As a young man, I lived to see India become independent. It was a most welcome dawn even though it was marred by the communal holocaust of 1947. As a Major in the Army operating between Delhi and Lahore, I had witnessed those gory and chilling sights from close quarters. Nevertheless, as time passed, particularly during the first one and a half decades after Independence, I had developed a feel good outlook. I felt both mesmerised and proud of the leadership provided by Jawaharlal Nehru to the Nation. He was my icon from my student days. Independent India had come out to be highly regarded in the world. We may not have had much military or economic strength but we certainly had a universally regarded great moral stature. Jawaharlal Nehru was recognized as a leading world statesman. Within the country, my home State, Bihar, had been doing well. Nehru had sent for an American expert on Public Administration, Appleby, from the USA, to advise on governance in India. He toured all the States of India in the mid-fifties and submitted his report in which he referred to Bihar as the best administered State in the country. All this was music to my ears and a feeling of fulfillment of my childhood dreams. However, as I started approaching middle age, a certain amount of disillusionment started setting in. Nehru's mishandling of the country's China policy and the great humiliation that he brought about on the Nation in 1962, eroded my great regard for him. He ceased to be the icon of my young days. Simultaneously, in Bihar a great degeneration set in. This decline was very rapid. From being considered one of the top States of the country, Bihar hit the bottom and became a byword for backwardness and everything bad. It almost became an object of ridicule in the country. After I quit the Army and returned to Patna, I tried to analyse the reason for our State's decline. I came to the conclusion that casteism,corruption and lack of pride in our glorious past were the main reasons for our pathetic condition.

So far as casteism is concerned, it would not be out of place to mention two incidents affecting me personally. They may be trivial but they showed the ridiculous extent to which the State had sunk. I had a carbine given to me by the Army. I held a licence for it for 20 years. The licence used to get renewed every three years. Even in my retirement in Patna, the licence had been renewed three times. When I sent my chauffeur to the office of the district magistrate to have the licence renewed, I landed in difficulties. For three months or more my licence was kept in that office on some pretext or the other and was not being renewed. I spoke on the telephone to the magistrate dealing with arms licences and later to the District Magistrate, but beyond being told that the matter was being looked into, nothing happened. I spoke to the Commissioner and later to the Secretary to the Governor who was a friend of mine. They all assured me that the licence would be renewed and yet nothing happened. It was strange that a person who had served for 40 years in the Army and had been its Vice Chief and also had been India's Ambassador to Nepal, was being denied renewal of his arms licence. I came to know through unofficial sources that the reason for my licence not being renewed was that the new unwritten policy in the State in Lalu Yadav's regime, was to issue a licence or renew it only for the backward castes and minorities. The upper castes were to be denied this facility. I could not imagine that casteism could be taken to such an absurd extent. I filed a petition in the High Court. The District Magistrate of Patna was asked to submit an affidavit. I am glad that within a week of this, my licence duly renewed, was delivered at my residence. Afterwards, I again happened to hold high public office and my licence was getting periodically renewed in a matter of minutes.

There was another incident which showed how the cancerous disease of casteism had affected our State. I saw a programme on the 1857 Uprising on Doordarshan. It was a good attempt to depict the history of that great struggle but I was unhappy to find that the great legendary military hero of that war, Veer Kuer Singh, found no mention in that programme. He was 80 years old when he took up arms against the British and he was the only leader of the revolutionaries who had repeatedly defeated the British in battle. I felt that this great omission was like making a presentation of the Ramayan with no mention of Hanuman in it. The K P Jaiswal Research Institute at Patna invited me to deliver a lecture on Veer Kuer Singh on his Victory Day of April 23, which is celebrated every year in Bihar. That was the day on which in his last battle, Veer Kuer Singh had decisively defeated a British Force. He died soon after that great victory. I did a little research on him and made a presentation of my assessment of his military leadership. The office bearers of this leading research institute in Bihar requested me to write a book on Kuer Singh. I readily accepted to do so without seeking any honorarium. However, I wanted the Institute to provide me secretarial support and to reimburse me for expenses to be incurred in going for research to the National Archives at Delhi and the National Library in Kolkata. They were enthusiastic about this and said that there would be no difficulty in doing so. The matter was taken up by the Institute with the State Government and for months nothing happened. I was later told unofficially that since Kuer Singh was not from a backward caste, the Government was not supportive of the project. It so happened that I had to go to Delhi and there I was asked to preside over a function organized by the United Services Institute of India. An American professor had come from the USA and he delivered a lecture on American military history. At the end of his talk, in my presidential address, I made a mention of some of the instances of the American Civil War and of the achievements of General Douglas MacArthur. After the lecture, I had tea with the chief guest and the dignitaries who had come for the function. Dr Ravindra Kumar, the Chairman of the Indian Council of Historical Research was appreciative of the points made by me in my presidential address. I told him that during many years of my army career, when I used to be a lone officer with my troops in pickets on the hills in Kashmir, I had spent a lot of time studying military history. I also told him how I had not been able to work on a project for writing a book on Veer Kuer Singh. He responded enthusiastically and said that he would get me a senior fellowship of a couple of lakhs from the Indian Council of Historical Research to write a book on Kuer Singh. The rules required that anyone getting a senior fellowship should have a good academic record with a Ph.D or at least a postgraduate degree and preferably some years of teaching experience in a university. I had no postgraduate degree and I had never been a teacher in any university. However, after retirement, I was a Visiting Professor on Military History in Pune University for a couple of years. Dr. Ravindra Kumar assured me that he would get the Council to make an exception in my case and get me a senior fellowship. He was true to his word and I got a fellowship of Rs 2 lakhs for this project. I did research at the National Archives in Delhi and at the National Library in Kolkata. Thereafter I went to London where I carried out research at the India Office Library. There, I found a lot of useful material for my project. I was lucky that my daughter Minnie, who has a Ph.D. in Indian History and who was then a professor in Southern Illinois University at Carbondale, was in London, working on her project. She was living in a two bedroom flat meant for the faculty at Imperial College. My wife and I stayed with her and she showed me the ropes in the India Office Library. This was of great help. My son-in-law Clem, who is a professor of English, got me interesting material from the records of the Royal Artillery of the British Army at Woolwich. I thus managed to complete the assignment that I had got from the Indian Council of Historical Research. My book on Kuer Singh was published both in English and in Hindi. The publisher organized a good function for the release of the book at India International Centre in Delhi. Shri Atal Behari Vajpayee who was then the Leader of the Opposition in the Parliament, graciously agreed to release the book. I had good personal relations with him and he had visited my house in Patna. He was very generous in his speech. The book sold fairly well outside Bihar My publisher was surprised at the apathy of people in Bihar towards my book. All his efforts to get this book acquired for the libraries of educational institutions in Bihar turned out to be futile. Possibly the caste factor again prevailed.

I undertook to write a book on Veer Kuer Singh with two motives. I wanted to instil a sense of pride amongst the people of Bihar in their past. I also wanted to send a message in the highly caste ridden society of the State that my admiration for Kuer Singh, transcended any caste consideration. Kuer Singh was a Rajput. I am afraid I did not achieve much success in achieving my aims. The response to my book in Bihar was lukewarm. Some favourable response for this book in Bihar came mostly from individual Rajputs. I was, however, happy that at the national level, there were favourable reviews of this book. I received a letter from a British author in London who frequently writes on Indian History, expressing his appreciation.

Undeterred by the lack of adequate response to my book on Kuer Singh in Bihar, I continued to take other measures to hark back to the past glory of the State. I was invited to deliver the Dr Sachchitanand Sinha Memorial Lecture at Patna. Dr Sinha was one of the creators of modern Bihar. He was in the vanguard of the movement for separating Bihar from Bengal and it becoming a separate province. He was also the first pro tem President of the Constituent Assembly, before Dr. Rajendra Prasad succeeded him. I chose to speak about the martial traditions of Bihar, because Biharis were considered non-martial in the North. It was here that Lord Buddha had gained enlightenment, Lord Mahavira had founded the Jain religion, Mahatma Gandhi had started his non-violent movement for India's freedom and Jayaprakash Narayan through peaceful agitation restored democracy which had been derailed during the Emergency. These were all non-martial achievements. After the 1857 Uprising, the British had stopped recruiting soldiers from Bihar in the Indian Army because they had played a leading role in that great Revolution. Biharis were declared non-martial achievements. I recall that when I joined the Army during the Second World War, very few Biharis had entered the officer cadre of the Army. At a time when the strength of Indian officers in the Army had gone up to 12,000, there were perhaps about two dozen officers from Bihar in the Army. In 1972 when I was promoted to the rank of major general, the Press in Bihar hailed my appointment stating that I was the first Bihari general officer of the Indian Army. This was more a matter of regret than pride for me. Punjab, whose population was less than a quarter of Bihar, had a general from almost every village and certainly dozens from every district of that State. This only underscored how much the State had fallen from its martial eminence. Hence I chose to highlight Bihar's past martial achievements in my Sachchitanand Sinha Memorial Lecture.

In my talk on military traditions of Bihar, I recounted the contribution made by the State to the military glory of our nation. In the ancient period of our history, military leaders from Bihar had defeated world conquering armies of that period. Chandragupta Maurya under the guidance of his mentor Chanakya had helped in engineering the mutiny in Alexander's great Army on the banks of the Beas. He subsequently, on Alexander's retreat from India, liberated Punjab and threw out the Greek garrisons left behind by him. Later, Alexander's successor, Selucus Nikator invaded India. Chandragupta decisively defeated him in the Battle of Indus in 310 B.C. and annexed Afghanistan to his Empire. Chandragupta, the Second, of the Gupta Dynasty, defeated the Scythians called Sakas in India, who had introduced horse-archery and had conquered large parts of Asia. He had earned the title of Sakahari (Destroyer of Sakas). Prince Asumitra of the Sunga dynasty defeated the later Greeks led by Menander. Prince Skandagupta defeated the Hun invaders in 458 B.C. The Huns had conquered several countries both in Asia and Europe. Rome was known to have quailed before Attilla, the notorious Hun. In the medieval period, Sher Shah from Bihar, defeated Humayun forcing him into exile. He established his rule over the whole of North India and in a short period of five years before he died, he had great achievements to his credit. He laid the foundation of secular rule in the country. He devised an effective and just revenue system and also constructed the famous Grand Trunk Road from Gaur in Bengal to Peshawar in the West. Sher Shah became a role model for Akbar when he ascended the Mughal throne. When the British came to India, it was primarily with soldiers from Bihar under British leadership that they conquered North India. And again it was the soldiers from Bihar who were in the vanguard of the 1857 Uprising. The martial tradition of Bihar over the centuries has been unique and is a matter of justifiable pride for the people of Bihar. My lecture underscored this fact.

I started a movement for renaming Patna as Patliputra. No city in the country has such a long and glorious history. Lord Buddha had witnessed the construction of this city as ordered by King Ajatshatru. The Enlightened One had forecast that it would become one of the greatest cities of the world. Patliputra was the capital of India for nearly one thousand years. The Greek Ambassador at Patliputra, Megasthenes, in the fourth century BC in his book, *Indica*, has referred to Patliputra as the greatest city of the world. Fahien, the Chinese pilgrim who came 700 years later, wrote about this city in very glowing terms. He said that the city was far too beautiful to have been constructed by human hands. Gods must have descended from Heaven to construct this city. I obtained one lakh signatures from the citizens of the city for restoring its old and glorious name. I presented it to the Mayor of Patna. This was a couple of years before Madras became Chennai and Calcutta, Kolkata. In our memorandum, we had stated that several cities in the country and abroad had been renamed like Varanasi for Benares, Vishakapatnam for Vizagapatnam, Vadodara for Baroda, Thiruvananthapuram for Trivandrum and abroad, Jakarta for Batavia, Beijing for Peking and so on. No city in the world had greater justification for being restored its old and glorious name than Patna. I also pointed out the emotional attachment of the people of the city for the name of Patliputra. One had only to open the telephone directory of Patna to find hundreds of telephone connections of various institutions, shops, colonies, roads, hotels, enterprises with a Patliputra prefix. The Patna Municipal Corporation unanimously approved our memorandum, a copy of which we also presented to the Governor. The Congress government in the State led by Shri Bindeshwari Dubey considered the proposal. This was unanimously approved by the State's Council of Ministers. The State Government forwarded its recommendation in this regard to the Government of India. I interacted with Rajiv Gandhi, the then Prime Minister. He responded favourably. Unfortunately, soon after, the Babri Masjid dispute erupted. Some Leftist and Muslim historians opposed the move on the ground that renaming Patna as Patliputra would give a fillip to Hindu fundamentalism. There was no religious connotation whatsoever in the proposal to revive the name of Patliputra. In the hey days of Patliputra, it was the capital of a Buddhist Emperor. Some people believe that the name Patna was derived from Patan Devi, the Hindu deity whose ancient temple is in the city. Unfortunately, our effort to get Patna renamed Patliputra got stuck in a political quagmire and was shelved.

Along with the proposal to rename Patna as Patliputra, I had also put forward various suggestions for the beautification of the city. I had suggested a road along the bank of the Ganga from Digha to Supaul. This river front road could be like the Marine Drive in Mumbai. Some portion of the proposed road was already in existence. Since Patliputra was a river port and much of the traffic in the old days was river based, I felt that the erection of a Civilization Gate (Sabhyata Dwar) leading to the river, at a suitable place would be a good idea. This Gate could be something like the Gateway of India at Mumbai or India Gate in New Delhi. There could be large murals on this Gate depicting past events like Prince Mahendra and Princess Sanghamitra, children of Ashoka the Great, setting out by boat from Pataliputra as Buddhist monks to spread Buddhism in Sri Lanka. The arrival of Magasthenes the Greek Ambassador in Patliputra and of Fahien, the Chinese pilgrim could also be shown. I further proposed that parks be developed in certain areas of the city. None of these proposals received any serious consideration by the Government. Undeterred by this and undaunted by the proposal to rename the city being thrown into limbo, I tried to continue with my endeavours with our limited resources. We started a Green Patna Movement and developed some parks on the Boring Canal Road. I also organized a movement for clearing garbage in the city on the pattern of what was being done in Bangalore. We procured cycle rickshaws mounting a wooden dust-bin with tin lining inside. As a small beginning, I had 24 such cycle rickshaws prepared and issued to responsible people known to me in different areas. The idea was to have these rickshaws go from house to house in their given area of operations, to collect garbage. The house owner was required to contribute Rs. 20/- per month for this service. With the amount so collected, the emoluments of the rickshaw driver and expense on the maintenance of the rickshaw could be met. These rickshaw drivers were required to dump the garbage at nominated places in the city from where the Municipal Corporation would collect and dispose it. My brother-in-law, K N Sahaya, who was the Mayor of Patna, extended full cooperation. I contacted some banks in Patna, notably the State Bank of India and got donations from them, with the help of which we were able to buy rickshaws and fabricate the dustbins fitted to them. This effort was much appreciated by the people . However, it did not prove long lasting and the fervour for it died down after some time. I happened to leave Patna for assignments outside the State and, I am afraid, the movement fizzled out.

I conceived a mega plan to project the glorious past of the city in an entertaining manner. I decided to organize Patliputra Mahotsav (Festival) on a grand scale. It was to be a food festival-cummini exhibition and carnival. I organized it on the extensive grounds of New Patna Club under the banner of INTACH, of which I was the Convenor at Patna. My problem was that we had no funds with our branch of INTACH and its central organization at Delhi could not give us any financial assistance. I collected a group of young enthusiastic people who liked my idea and went all out to give it a concrete shape. Among the many who assisted me in this project were Dr R S Akhauri, Rajendra Pratap Singh, Mahasweta Maharathi, Mohan Saran, Kanak Saran, V P Sinha and a few others.

I tried my hand at producing a documentary film on the history of Patliputra. I made use of local talent for this. A young and keen film producer, Pranav Sahi, extended full cooperation to us, undertaking to produce this film at concessional rates and on credit. Based on material and ideas provided by me and in close cooperation with us, he produced a good documentary film of 40 minutes. The film started with the commencement of the construction of Patliputra in 487 BC. The film covers two sagas: it begins in the year 487 BC when Lord Buddha visited Patliputra at the time of its construction. And, the film ended with the unfurling of our national flag in 1947 on the dawn of Independence. This documentary covered all the major historical events connected with the city during the previous 2500 years. We showed the film at the festival and it became a major attraction. The film was shown in the club hall with overflowing audience, two to three times a day. We had five elaborately constructed food stalls. The pandals had Mauryan, Greek, Chinese, Mughal and British architecture. The cuisine, the dress of waiters and taped music in the stall corresponded to the relevant culture. In front of each stall, we had a large cut-out of a personality connected with it who had had association with the city. Chanakya's cut-out was in front of the Mauryan pandal. The cut out of Magasthenes, the Greek Ambassador, was in front of the Greek pandal. The cut-out of Fahien, the Chinese pilgrim who had visited the city, was in front of the Chinese pandal. Prince Azim Shah, the grandson of Aurangzeb, had been the Mughal Viceroy at Patna. His cut-out was in front of the Mughal pandal. Job Charnock's cut-out was in front of the British pandal. He had been the East India Company's agent at Patna for 16 years in the eighteenth century before he left and founded the city of Calcutta. These food stalls were a great hit and did brisk business. We also had a mini carnival at the festival site where people could play games of skill and buy souvenirs and other goods from stalls. We invited Shri K R Narayanan, the then Vice President of India to this function and he graciously accepted our invitation. At the last moment he had to cancel his visit due to sudden illness. The Governor inaugurated the festival.

The Patliputra Mahotsav was indeed a mega event and drew much appreciation from the people. Our team worked splendidly and in a most dedicated manner. We spent several lakhs over organizing this festival but I am glad that after meeting all the expenditure, we could have a net profit of Rs. 3 lakhs which we credited to Patna INTACH funds to further the objectives of the organization to preserve art, culture and history. I had the satisfaction that we could so demonstratively and effectively provide both entertainment and a glimpse of the city's glorious past.

During my visit to Manisha, our youngest daughter at Sturbridge in Massachusetts on the East Coast of the USA in 1995, I was surprised to receive an invitation to address the Rand Corporation at Los Angeles on the West Coast. They wanted me to speak on India's Kashmir Policy. The Rand Corporation is a leading security think tank in the USA, funded by both the State Department and the CIA. I was told that very few Indians had been invited to lecture at that Institution. So far, I was the only serving or retired army officer from India to be invited to speak at that institution. The subject being sensitive, I was hesitant to accept this invitation. I told them that my wife and I were holidaying with our daughter and we would find it difficult to afford travelling to the West Coast. I also told them that much as I would like to visit the West Coast. I may not be able to accept the invitation. The USA is a country of continental dimension and flight time from the East Coast to the West Coast is six hours non-stop. They promptly replied saying that they would pay for air travel for both me and my wife and arrange accommodation for us in a good hotel for a weekend besides paying an honorarium for my lecture. They suggested that I deliver my talk on Friday, stay over for the weekend in Los Angeles and return on Monday. Their offer was very tempting but I still had reservations. I wondered how they knew about me and my association with Kashmir. I did not hold any official position at that time and I did not have to take any permission from our Government for accepting this invitation. Yet, I thought it would be prudent to take the concurrence of the Indian Ambassador at Washington, Dr Sidharth Shankar Ray. I had known him when he was a minister in Indira Gandhi's Cabinet in the Seventies and had also met him lately, when he had come to Patna before taking up his present assignment. His response was positive. He felt that I should avail of this opportunity to put across the Indian point of view on the subject. I asked for guidelines or talking points so that I did not express views contrary to what our Embassy might have been projecting. I was told that some material would be sent to me but they felt that I knew all about the subject and I did not need any briefing or guidelines. In the event, I did not get any material from the Embassy. I decided to go to Los Angeles with my wife and to bat on my own.

We were received at the airport and taken to Santa Monica Hotel near the Hollywood Film city. There were a few film personalities staying in the Hotel. The West Coast is certainly a pretty area with lovely beaches. The roads with six lanes of traffic are wider than in other States. California is called the Golden Gate State.

I addressed a group of some 200 research scholars at the Rand Corporation. The audience comprised mostly American scholars as also a large number from NATO countries. There was no one from either India or Pakistan. I spoke for two hours including an hour's question and answer session. I was grilled with a number of searching questions. I recalled my association with Kashmir starting from 27th October, 1947 when the Indian Army got inducted into that State on the Maharaja acceding to the Indian Union. As a young Major, when the British officers of the Indian Army had departed or were departing, I had to shoulder responsibility much beyond my rank or experience. I was an Operations Staff Officer in a skeleton headquarters of ten officers under Lt Gen Sir Dudley Russell. We were assigned the task of conducting military operations in the State. The British Government had placed an embargo on British Officers from either Indian or Pakistan Army going to J&K. In about two months our headquarters got fully Indianised. Initially, being the only Indian officer in our headquarters and also being an Operations Staff officer, I had to visit Kashmir frequently. I was associated with the planning and conduct of operations in that theatre for the entire period of the first Indo-Pak War of 1947-48. In the beginning, the odds were loaded heavily against us. The enemy had captured Baramulla, a mere 30 miles from the capital city of Srinagar. There were no obstacles nor anyone to offer resistance along the tarmac road from Baramulla to Srinagar. The tribal raiders led by Pakistan army officers busied themselves with plunder, rape and pillage in the beautiful township of Baramulla, well known for its fruit orchards. They totally devastated the township, molested the nuns in the convent, nurses in the hospitals and took away hundreds of young Kashmiri girls.

The situation was very critical. We had to rush troops to Srinagar, self-contained with logistics for six months of winter isolation. Srinagar had a fair-weather grass airfield in those days, which would become unusable after a couple of weeks with the onset of snow in November. The road to Srinagar went over the Pir Panjal Range across the 9000 feet high Banihal Pass. The Pass would get blocked with snow by mid-November cutting off road communication for nearly six months till May, when the snow would melt. There was no Banihal Tunnel in those days. All Dakota aircraft in India of private airlines with mostly European pilots, were requisitioned and made available to us for organizing the airlift from Delhi to Srinagar. I was made in-charge of this operation. About fifty Dakotas could be mustered. We made each aircraft do two sorties a day. At times, aircraft had to be sent from Delhi to distant places like Kanpur, Jabalpur and Pune to collect urgently needed stores and ammunition and fly them to Srinagar. We flew in some 800 sorties in 15 days. It was a miracle that this task was accomplished without any mishap. The weather over the Pir Panjal is often turbulent and the low ceiling height of Dakotas posed difficulties. The Dakota was a sturdy aircraft but unlike modern aircraft, it could not fly above the weather. The landing facilities at Srinagar airfield were primitive with no night landing arrangements. Between the landing of one aircraft and the next, a few minutes had to elapse for the dust to settle down. Despite these stupendous difficulties, it was amazing that this task was successfully completed without any mishap. It was a tribute to the skill and dedication of the pilots who, as I have stated earlier, were mostly European, We removed the cushioned seats in the Dakotas to increase their payload. Troops were made to sit on the floor of the aircraft. The seating capacity in the aircraft was increased from about 20 to 30. The then Governor-General of India, Lord Mountbatten wrote "In my long experience of war, I have not come across another instance of such a massive airlift organized at such short notice and so successfully." Looking back at what we were able to achieve, I feel that during my 40 years of service in the Army, this was perhaps the most important contribution I had made for a national cause. This was at a time when I was a young officer, not even 22 years old.

With our backs to the wall, we managed to save Srinagar and fought a decisive battle at Shalatang on the outskirts of the city. We advanced and liberated Baramulla by 7 November, 1947. I saw the ghastly scenes of a devastated Baramulla. It was a strange Jehad launched by Pakistan in which the victims at Baramulla were mostly their own co-religionists.

Our Headquarters was now fully Indianised with Lt Gen Sir Dudley Russell being replaced by Lt Gen K M Cariappa and all the British officers in the Headquarters going back to their country. We established our Tactical Headquarters at Jammu to conduct operations in the theatre. As Operations Staff Officer, I invariably accompanied the Army Commander to the front in all the regions of the State. After the ceasefire on Ist January 1949, I went to the conference convened by the UN Commission for India and Pakistan (UNCIP) to delineate the Cease Fire Line. I was appointed the Secretary of the Indian delegation. We interacted for ten days with the members of the UNCIP and a high powered Pakistan delegation, led by a senior British General. After ten days of meetings and discussions, an agreement was reached on the ceasefire line which was subsequently, jointly delineated on the ground. Thereafter during my Army career I had served for a period of over 10 years at intervals in all the three regions of the State – Jammu, Kashmir and Ladakh. I may have impressed my audience with my long personal association with Jammu and Kashmir, but I do not know if I did so, with my views. The mindset of the people in the West from the early days of the Cold War had been so much in consonance with the views of their most friendly non-NATO ally, Pakistan. Undeterred, I gave them a brief survey of the course of military operations in Kashmir in the three Indo-Pak Wars of 1947–48, 1965 and 1971. Having lost in all these wars, Pakistan had formulated a new strategy. Assisted by the abundance of petrodollars from some Arab countries and with the fundamentalist fallout from the Iranian Revolution, Pakistan had launched a low intensity conflict since 1989. This ongoing conflict was a mix of insurgency, terrorism and proxy war. In the process, it is a pity that the liberal Sufi Islam tradition of the older generation of Kashmiri Muslims got subverted and replaced by a fundamentalist Wahabi Islam outlook among the young generation in Kashmir. Their strategy was to inflict a thousand cuts on India, bleeding her to death and forcing her to abandon Kashmir. The Indian Army was valiantly fighting an invisible enemy and there was no question of it yielding to the evil designs of the terrorists. MacArthur had rightly said in the early Fifties that he was fighting communism in Asia on the battlefield while in Europe people were trying to do so verbally. Similarly, it could be said that India was fighting terrorism in Kashmir while the Big Powers remained insensitive to the threat posed by the fundamentalists and their perverted concept of Jihad, manifesting itself in deadly terrorism. All this was of course before September 11, 2001 when the USA woke up to the threat of international terrorism and later got stuck in the Iraqi quagmire. This was also much before the terrorist explosions in Madrid and London, and before Russia's involvement with the fundamentalists in Chechnya.

I found my audience very interested in various aspects of the Kashmir problem. Their questions pertained mostly to political aspects. They contended that India had been partitioned on the basis of religion and the Muslim majority areas had become the State of Pakistan. Kashmir was a Muslim majority State and should in all fairness be made a part of Pakistan. This was typical of the Western thinking on the subject. I had to go into the history of Partition to correct their fallacious view and disabuse their mind of wrong notions. I pointed out that before 15 August 1947, India comprised two separate political entities. The first was known as British India, consisting of eleven provinces directly administered by the British Government of India. The second entity which the British called Native India, comprised some five hundred odd Princely States, ruled by Maharajas and Nawabs. As per the Indian Independence Act, 1947 passed by the British Parliament, the basis for determining the future of these two entities was to be different.

The Governor-General and Viceroy of India had a dual role. In his former capacity he was the supreme authority in the country, directly administering the provinces. The erstwhile British India consisting of the eleven provinces was to be partitioned on the basis of religion. Although the Congress was opposed to the two nation theory, it had to accept Partition but it stuck to its secular ideology. Today, there are more Muslims in India than in Pakistan. The Viceroy, as his designation indicated, represented the British Sovereign. As the representative of the Paramount Power, he dealt with the Princely States who had entered into treaties with the British Sovereign in the previous centuries, surrendering foreign relations and defence, but retaining full control of internal administration of their States. With the decision to quit India, the British were abrogating their treaty obligations with the rulers of the States. After the lapse of paramountcy, a State could accede to either India or Pakistan. Except for the very few large States, Independence was not a viable option and even for those States not a realistic course. Of course geographical contiguity was an important factor that had to be taken into account. This virtually ruled out the possibility of Hyderabad merging with Pakistan, but the case of Jammu and Kashmir was different. It had borders with both India and Pakistan.

The State Congress parties of the Princely States were affiliated to the Indian National Congress during the freedom struggle. The Congress had taken the stand that the future of the States should be decided by the people of those States. On the other hand, Jinnah and the Muslim League wanted that the decision about the future of the States be left to their rulers, conforming to the provisions of the Independence Act. There was a sinister design behind this stand.

There was not much difficulty in deciding the future of most of the Princely States but two major States, Hyderabad and Jammu and Kashmir, posed a problem. Hyderabad had a Muslim ruler with over 90 percent Hindu population. It was the richest and the largest Princely State of India. However, it was landlocked by Indian territory all round and it was not contiguous with Pakistan. On the basis of the Independence Act, the Nizam had to decide the future of his State. Jinnah hoped that the Nizam would either opt for Independence or accede to Pakistan. He even tried to ensure the accession of Jodhpur and Jaisalmer to Pakistan on the basis of the decision of their Hindu rulers and despite their 90 percent Hindu population. He gave these two Maharajas blank sheets of paper and asked them to write down their conditions for acceding to Pakistan. He assured them that he would accept those conditions. Better sense prevailed on these Maharajas and they were not tempted to join Pakistan. Insofar as Jammu & Kashmir was concerned, the situation here was the reverse of Hyderabad. The State had a Hindu ruler and a Muslim majority population but, non-Muslims, mostly Hindus, constituted about 30 percent of the population of the State. Jinnah hoped that through tribal invasion he would get the Maharaja to accede to Pakistan. The Maharaja chose to opt for the Indian Union. The Instrument of Accession signed by the Maharaja of Jammu and Kashmir made that State an integral part of India. In the event, Jinnah could neither get Hyderabad nor Jammu and Kashmir. He succeeded in getting only a moth-eaten Pakistan as the two provinces of Bengal and Punjab were also partitioned along with the country, on the basis of religion. Jinnah was ill-advised by his Generals to invade Kashmir on 22 October. This allowed the Indian Army sufficient time to intervene at the invitation of the Maharaja. Had he delayed this invasion by two weeks, the valley would have got cut off from the rest of India both by road and air, due to snow, for the next six months. This would have ruled out any intervention by India and Pakistan would have had enough time to annex Kashmir and consolidate its position .

I had to answer several questions pertaining to plebiscite. I was asked why India after having accepted the holding of plebiscite dragged its feet and had not allowed this process to be completed. My reply was that as per the UNCIP Resolution of 13 August 1948, accepted by both India and Pakistan, the Kashmir problem was to be resolved in three stages. First, ceasefire and delineation of the ceasefire line. Second, withdrawal of all Pakistani forces from the State of Jammu and Kashmir. Pakistan failed to honour its commitment in this regard and failed to withdraw its forces from Pakistan Occupied Kashmir. Their reason for not doing so was perhaps the fact that the tribal invasion launched by them in 1947 had led to a lot of atrocities over the Kashmiri people. While the memory of those atrocities was fresh in people's minds and while Sheikh Mohammad Abdullah, the towering Kashmiri leader with wide popular support was around, the prospects of Pakistan winning the plebiscite were bleak. Thus, Pakistan did not withdraw its forces and we could not proceed to the third stage of Plebiscite. If Plebiscite could not be held in the State, the responsibility for that lay squarely with Pakistan and not India.

Another question raised was about the right of self-determination. I tried to explain that the citizens of a sovereign country do not need any right of self-determination. The way in which the local population had assisted the Army, both during 1947–48 War and during the 1965 War, had made it abundantly clear where their sympathy lay. In 1947–48 the people had been victims of acts of brutality of Pakistani tribals. The Kashmiri people assisted the Army in fighting the raiders. In 1965, Pakistan launched another invasion of Kashmir with code name Operation Gibraltar. Several thousand Pakistani infiltrators were sent to Kashmir. They hoped that this would ignite an uprising amongst the Kashmiri people and Pakistan Army could then move into the State to deliver the *coup de grace*. The Indian Forces would be evicted from the State and Kashmir would become part of Pakistan. This plan had been made at the instance of Zulfikar Ali Bhutto, the then Pakistan foreign minister in the Cabinet of Ayub Khan. Unfortunately for Pakistan, the people of Kashmir did not cooperate as anticipated and their ambitious plan failed. Recalling the operations in Kashmir of that period, I stated that our success in locating the infiltrators and then hounding them out of the State was in a large measure due to the support we received from the people of Kashmir. They gave information to the Army and also acted as guides. In giving us this valuable assistance, they exercised their right of self-determination in as convincing a manner as they could have in a referendum. General Musa, the then Commander-in-Chief of the Pakistan Army, in his book, *My Version,* has admitted that their invasion of 1965 failed, because the people of Kashmir did not support them. Thus both in 1947–48 and in 1965, the Kashmiri people had unmistakably showed their preference for India. I was then grilled on the fact that democracy is a game of numbers and a majority of the Kashmiri people either wanted to merge with Pakistan or become independent. They asserted that very few wanted to remain with India. In my reply, I said that from my experience and knowledge from 1947–48 and after, I knew fully well that the vast majority of the people of Kashmir wanted to remain with India till militancy erupted in 1989 fuelled by an international wave of religious fundamentalism. I had not been to Kashmir for the last few years and I could not vouch for the current ground situation there. Even if what the questioner maintained was correct, there was no reason why India should withdraw from Kashmir. No doubt, democracy is a game of numbers but fundamental values override any majority opinion. I quoted an example from American history. Abraham Lincoln was one of the greatest democrats of all times. He attached great importance to the concept of individual freedom and abolition of slavery. The Southern States, with the majority support of their people, wanted to continue with slavery. They also had the constitutional right to secede from the Union. Lincoln did not accept the majority opinion of the South, nor did he allow the Southern States to secede. He launched a long drawn American Civil War in which the American people suffered more casualties than their combined total casualties in the two World Wars, the Korean War and the Vietnam War. Similarly, we in India fervently believe in the concept of secularism. We cannot sacrifice secularism at the altar of the game of numbers in a democracy. If Kashmir was now to secede from India to conform to the pernicious two nation theory, which had led to the great and unprecedented holocaust of 1947, we may only be repeating that most unfortunate tragedy. We cannot allow the revival of that theory in Kashmir as this will have a disastrous effect in the rest of India. There are over 150 million Muslims in India which is more than the total population of Pakistan. For the sake of some 5 million Kashmiri Muslims, we could not sacrifice the interest of 150 million other Muslims of India.

I went on to bring out that terrorism and religious fundamentalism are grave threats to the civilized world. There is a

University of Terrorism at Peshawar and its graduates have been very active not only in Kashmir but also in other parts of the world. A Pakistani was involved in the explosion at the World Trade Centre in New York in 1993, Pakistanis were also behind the serial blasts in Mumbai 1993 in which over 300 people were killed. During the hostage crises in Kashmir, nationals of USA, UK and France had been their victims. History has not known of an incident when the boundaries of a Nation State had been changed as a result of terrorism. If this is allowed to happen in Kashmir, it will be a great tragedy for the world as a whole. It would give a fillip to the efforts of terrorists to achieve their goals through their nefarious and barbaric acts. I said all this long before the terrorist attack on the World Trade Centre in New York and the Pentagon in Washington on September 11, 2001.

On the issue of the violation of human rights by the Indian Army in Kashmir, I said that their record was infinitely better than various foreign armies. I referred to the Pakistan Army's flagrant violation of human rights in erstwhile East Pakistan in 1971 and later during the Baluch uprising in their country, from 1973 to 1977. They had used artillery and helicopter gunships against the Baluchis. General Tikka Khan, the Pakistan Army Chief was called the 'Butcher of Baluchistan'. The American record in Vietnam was even worse. America's violation of human rights in Afghanistan and Iraq, particularly the latter which shocked the conscience of the civilized world and its own people, had not taken place till then. Most of the allegations of violation of human rights by the Indian Army were either totally false or highly exaggerated. In some cases where allegations were found to be true, the army had taken severe disciplinary action against the offenders. It is surprising that human rights activists, who continuously harp on excesses by Security Forces, maintain a dumb silence with regard to the much worse violations of human rights by the terrorists.

I do not know if I managed to bring about any change in the mindset of the audience I was addressing, but I had the satisfaction of putting across my views in an unambiguous and emphatic manner. Later, I sent a synopsis of my talk at the Rand Corporation to our Ambassador at Washington for record. I got a feedback from his staff that my presentation at Los Angeles was much appreciated.

The local Press had reported my talk at the Rand Corporation. A few members of the Indian community settled in California got in touch with me and organized functions for me. SIVA (Society of

Indian Veterans Association) of California comprising former officers from Indian Defence Services, engaged in different civil vocations, invited me to address them, followed by a dinner hosted in my honour. One of them, a retired Major from the Parachute Regiment of the Indian Army was the Security Officer at the famous Getty Museum at Los Angeles. He personally took us round the museum, including areas not normally open to the public. The breathtaking collection at the museum was beyond my imagination. During the long weekend that my wife and I spent at Los Angeles, we toured extensively by road and saw the beautiful landscape and the wonderful beaches. We also visited Disneyland, a fantastic amusement park for children. We missed our grandchildren when we went around the place. However, I am glad that a few years later my son got posted to the Permanent Mission of India at the UN in New York. He took the children to the Disney World at Orlando and also the amusement park in Los Angeles. They enjoyed their visit to that place much more than their grandparents.

During my stay in the USA in that year, I was also invited to the Bihari Association at New Jersey for a talk. I readily accepted the invitation and took advantage of the occasion by showing them the documentary film on the history of Patna which was made for the Patliputra Mahotsav. The cassettes of this film sold like hot cakes and I received generous donations from many Biharis in the USA for INTACH Patna.

While in the USA, I heard the sad news of my dear friend Madhu Mehta suddenly passing away when he was on a visit to his son in the Philippines. It was a great loss to the Lok Sawaraj Andolan that he had started. He was the life and soul of the organisation. On my return to India, I went to Bombay to offer my condolence to his family. I suggested that either his widow or his son should take over the presidentship of the Lok Swaraj Andolan, as the President should be someone located in Mumbai where we had the central organisational setup and the facility to mobilize resources for our activities.

My wife and I also took the opportunity of going to Goa which we had not visited earlier. I had been a cadet at Officers Training School, Belgaum in 1944 and I had then wanted to go to Goa for a holiday. I could not do so at that time because it was then Portuguese territory and I did not have a passport or visa to go there. Goa adjoins Belgaum and I always felt sad to have missed the opportunity of going there. However, more than half a century later, my wife and I managed to spend a short holiday in Goa. We enjoyed the hospitality extended to us by my friends in the Army Signal Corps, which has its Centre there. We were made very comfortable in their Officers Mess. Thereafter, we also went on a pilgrimage to Badrinath in the Himalayas, where again my army connections were of great help. Army Engineers in Border Roads, went all out to help us and were very hospitable. This made the pilgrimage ever so easy for us. The Army is a great brotherhood and old bonds stand one in good stead without getting dimmed by the passage of time.

We had some anxious times in India on return from the USA. Two of my younger brothers fell seriously ill, one after the other. Sunny, who was a general manager at TISCO in Jamshedpur, suffered a head injury. This caused serious complications after a few days. I had to rush to Jamshedpur and we flew him out to Delhi in a special aircraft provided by TISCO. He was operated upon at All India Institute of Medical Sciences where after a while, he fully recovered. My other brother, Jyoti, was posted as a Commissioner in the Cabinet Secretariat at Calcutta. He suffered a serious heart attack and was hospitalized for some time. I went over to Calcutta to be with him. He gradually recovered. While in Calcutta, I happened to meet Lt. Gen. Jameel Mehmood who was the Army Commander in the East. I had known him for a long time. He had been a Brigadier in my Command when I was Army Commander in the West. Jameel came from a distinguished family of Hyderabad. He told me that he was very concerned about the influx of Bangladeshis into India, particularly to Bengal and Assam. This was rapidly changing the demography of those States. He had been repeatedly cautioning the Chief Ministers of the two States, Jyoti Basu and Hiteshwar Saikia, of the danger from this influx. He went to the extent of telling them that if this influx was not stopped, we would have to redraw our boundaries in the East. I was impressed by his patriotic concern but there was little I could do in the matter. Some politicians attach more importance to vote bank politics than national security. Jameel died in a helicopter crash, a few months later. I did not then know that one day, I would get intimately involved in dealing with the unabated influx of illegal migrants from Bangladesh into Assam. However, the concern shown by Jameel made me aware of the seriousness of this problem. In a somewhat similar manner, a few years earlier, when I was in the USA, I had received letters from retired Gorkha soldiers redirected to me there. They informed me of how they were suffering on account of the "economic blockade by India". Salt and kerosene had become scarce in their homes in Nepal. What they called "blockade" was the Trade and Transit Treaty between the two countries, being allowed to lapse. On my way back to India I broke journey with my brother Pranu at London. He was then serving with Air India and posted in London. I went to a dinner with him where I met a couple of well-to-do Nepalese working in London. They were happy to talk to me in Nepali but were bitter against India for the economic hardships being suffered by Nepal on account of the non-renewal of the Trade and Transit Treaty. Not long after my return home, to my surprise, I was appointed the Indian Ambassador to Nepal and had a lot to do with resolving the problem. Destiny has its own ways. Both in the case of "blockade" of Nepal and illegal migration into Assam, destiny propelled me into a position in which I could make significant contributions.

A year after my return to Patna, I was asked by my friends in Mumbai to take over as National President of the Lok Swaraj Andolan. I had reservations about this because it was difficult to function in that capacity from Patna when the Central Organisation was at Mumbai. Madhu Mehta had good contacts and had a marked ability for raising funds, which I did not have. I tried to do my best but, I am afraid I could see that the Andolan had lost its old momentum which it had acquired under the dynamic leadership of Madhu. Undeterred, I persisted in my efforts to keep the Andolan alive, but I could see that it was a losing game.

A few months later, my wife and I proceeded to the USA again in 1997. Our youngest daughter, Manisha, was expecting her first child and we went for her delivery. Soon after our arrival, our grandson, Sheel, was born. By God's grace, our family had been growing. We now were blessed with five grandchildren.

While I was in the USA, there was a change of Government in India. My friend I K Gujral became the Prime Minister. I sent him a congratulatory message, which he acknowledged warmly. His son in the USA contacted me and told me that his father wanted the support of his friends like me to help him in shouldering his onerous responsibilities. I did not attach much significance to what he told me but I mentioned to him that on return to India, I would certainly go and meet his father in Delhi.

We had a misfortune in the family, while I was in the USA. I lost my youngest sister Chitralekha at Patna and this was a big blow to my father. I hurried back home from the USA. While passing through Delhi, I tried to contact Gujral, but he was out of town and I could not stay back in Delhi because I wanted to get back to Patna soon to be with my father. He had stoically faced the tragic loss of his youngest child.

I picked up the threads of the normal routine of my life at Patna. I had no idea that I would soon be reaching the end of my second interlude of retirement and would be again called upon to shoulder responsibilities in the service of the Nation. Inscrutable are the ways of Providence.

2 MISSION ASSAM

One morning in late August 1997, while I was working in my study at my home in Patna, I received a telephone call from Delhi. The caller at the other end said that the Prime Minister would like to speak to me. I was surprised to receive this call. At first, I thought that it could be to enquire why I had not met him at Delhi on my way back from the USA. I had conveyed to his son that I would be doing so. For a moment, another thought crossed my mind. This call could be related to my article recently published in the *Statesman* regarding the CBI Joint Director, U K Biswas. He had sought army help to arrest the Chief Minister, Lalu Prasad Yadav. The High Court had given verbal instructions to that effect but Biswas could not get the police or the paramilitary to execute the direction. I had pointed out in my article that the army does not normally get involved in arresting people which is the task of the police. The local military authorities had rightly declined to comply with the request of Biswas. However, there are abnormal occasions when it may not be possible to adhere to the normal procedure. I quoted what had happened in Allahabad High Court some time earlier. The ruling party in UP had called for a Bandh against the demand for Uttarakhand breaking away from UP and becoming a separate State. The political workers of the party had been forcing people to observe a Bandh. Shopkeepers were made to close their shops. Schools were also forced to close down. The Bandh activists found the High Court functioning. They went inside, forcing the lawyers to suspend work. They even went into the chamber of the Chief Justice and broke the furniture there. It was alleged that some policemen had accompanied the goons and were not making any attempt to stop them. They were even encouraging them to commit their depredations. The situation was critical and demanded immediate action. The Chief Justice rang up the Military Commander in the nearby Cantonment and asked for military help. A company of the army was immediately rushed to the High Court and the vandals were dispersed. Legally, assistance from the army to restore peace is required to be requisitioned by the State Government or the senior magistrate at the scene of the incident, and not by a Chief Justice. Notwithstanding this, no one criticized the Chief Justice for summoning the army, nor the army for promptly responding and saving an ugly situation from getting worse. I had tried to bring out that Biswas may have acted in a manner not prescribed by law but he should not be penalized for what he had done, because he was facing a very abnormal situation and had acted in good faith. This article had created a lot of controversy and knowing that Lalu Yadav had become a political ally of Gujral, I thought the latter had possibly rung up in that connection.

Soon, Gujral was on the line and he told me that Assam was burning and he wanted me to take over as Governor of the State forthwith. I was taken aback by this most unexpected proposition. I told him that I required some time to think over the matter saying that my wife and I were living with my 94 year old father and looking after him. There was no one in the house to take care of him and we could not go to Assam, leaving him alone. Gujral stated that this should not be a problem for me. Guwahati has a medical college with all the necessary facilities for health care. My father would be better looked after in Guwahati than in Patna. Gujral emphasized that the situation in Assam was very critical and said that he could not give me more than 24 hours to make up my mind. He also expressed surprise at my hesitation in undertaking a gubernatorial assignment, when others intensely lobby to be appointed as governors.

I informed my father about my conversation with Gujral. He was enthusiastic about my accepting the offer of the Prime Minister. He said that he would accompany me to Guwahati but would not stay there permanently. He was still very active looking after a few NGOs and did not want to give up doing work. We worked out a compromise, whereby he could stay with us for half the time and the remaining half he could stay in Patna, with my brothers and sisters taking turns at being with him. Once we had agreed upon this, it became easy for me to respond positively to the Prime Minister's offer. I made up my mind to accept the offer, particularly when I found my father so keen about it. He reminded me that earlier in 1989 when V P Singh had offered me governorship of

Jammu and Kashmir, he had been keen to witness my swearing-in as a governor. That offer had been changed at the last minute to Ambassador in Nepal. Although he was then happy at my going to Nepal, he would have been happier to see me as governor. In his young days he had for a short while been ADC to a British Governor in Bihar. Due to his proficiency in sports, particularly Polo and Tennis, he was frequently invited to the Government House (called Raj Bhavan after Independence). This had given him the opportunity to interact with successive governors socially. However, some friends, including my own uncle, had doubts about the wisdom of my taking up the challenge in Assam. They pointed out that in our Constitution, a governor was only a constitutional head and did not have any executive powers. I may not be able to do much in Assam and it may turn out to be a frustrating experience. I also had some reservations on that score but my mind was made up. I decided to take the plunge.

2

Having decided to accept the Prime Minister's offer, I rang back his office later in the day, asking his staff to convey my acceptance to him and also inform him that I would be reaching Delhi two days later. In the intervening period, I decided to go to Mumbai to attend the wedding of my nephew, Gautam, the son of my sister. I did not realize that news travels so fast. The radio and the television carried the news of my appointment that evening, while I was on my way from Patna to Mumbai. At Mumbai airport I picked up a book, "Strangers of the Mist," by the reputed Assamese journalist, Sanjoy Hazarika. I found this book very interesting. It gave me an excellent background to the Assam problem.

I had not left my contact number at Mumbai with my wife. She had stayed back in Patna to be with my father. She had the time of her life answering numerous telephone calls from friends and relatives. There were also calls for me from the President's Secretariat and the Prime Minister's office. My wife complained to me later that she had never in her life answered so many telephone calls. By next morning, friends and relatives started pouring into our house to congratulate me. They met my father and my wife and expressed their happiness at my being appointed as Governor of Assam. By the time I arrived at Mumbai, the news of my appointment had reached there and was the topic of conversation at my nephew's wedding.

After the wedding, I flew to Delhi and contacted the Prime Minister's Office. I was invited for breakfast at his house. I was overwhelmed by his friendliness and generous hospitality. The fact that he was now the Prime Minister had not brought about any change in his attitude. We had worked together in the Hindustani Andolan and for one of its functions, he had come to Patna and to my house. Thereafter, I had occasion to work with him officially when I was Ambassador in Nepal and he was the External Affairs Minister. He stood for the Parliament from Patna Constituency in 1992 and I had actively supported him. He came to my house for meetings that I organized for him. Thus, there was an old bond of friendship between us. I found that this had in no way changed. I recalled that in 1990, I had accompanied the Prime Minister of Nepal to Delhi. At a crucial stage of the Indo-Nepal talks, I had gone to the PM's house for breakfast along with the PM of Nepal. V P Singh was the PM at that time. Gujral was then the External Affairs Minister and was also present at that breakfast meeting. The impasse in Indo-Nepal relations got resolved at that meeting. I reminded Gujral about that. I also mentioned that his house had old memories for me. I had lived in that house when I was the Vice Chief of the Army. At that time Indira Gandhi was the Prime Minister. She was living close by at Safdarjung Road. After her assassination, my successor had to vacate the house, because Rajiv Gandhi decided to move into it. Mrs Gujral very graciously offered to show me round the house to see what changes had been made. There was no change in the basic structure, although the inside of the house had been given a facelift and had much better furnishings.

Gujral told me that I had been chosen for a tough assignment and he was hopeful that I would be successful in meeting the challenge. He wanted me to meet Sita Ram Kesri, the then President of the Indian National Congress, which was the mainstay of the Government, supporting it from outside. He also wanted me to meet Atal Behari Vajpayee, the then Leader of the Opposition. Thereafter, he suggested that I should get myself updated in the Ministry of Home Affairs, with the current situation in Assam.

After breakfast, I went to meet Sita Ram Kesri who had been duly rung up by the Prime Minister's staff. When I arrived at his house, I saw hundreds of people on the lawn in front of his house and many crowding in his sitting room. On being told of my arrival, Kesri took me to his bedroom where he sat on his bed and I was given a chair. He told me that for a politician, the only place in his house where he could have meaningful conversation was his bedroom and, therefore he had got me there. I noticed that he was chewing "pan" and there was a spittoon near his bed, something very common among the gentry in Bihar. He told me that he knew my grandfather and had met my father several times. He had visited my ancestral home at Danapur in Patna on many occasions. Our house was barely two kms from his house. I had never met Kesri before but I had heard of him and seen his pictures in newspapers and on television. He spoke to me in Bihari dialect and told me that as a Bihari he was both happy and proud that I was going to Assam. He and the Nation expected much from me. I assured him that I would do my best and that the appointment had come as a complete surprise to me. He insisted on my having 'lassi' with him and some typically Bihari sweets. That was the first and last time that I met Kesri. He impressed me as a grass root politician with no airs about him. His way of talking and living was typically Bihari. It reminded me of my childhood days.

From Kesri's house I proceeded to the residence of Vajpayee. He heartily welcomed me. I had been interacting with Vajpayee for some time. Soon after I resigned from the army in 1983, he as the President of the BJP, and Choudhary Charan Singh as the President of Dalit Mazdoor Kissan Party (DMKP), had formed a democratic alliance. They invited me to address the Opposition MPs in Mavlankar Hall, near the Parliament. I was asked to speak on Threats to National Security. That was the time when Indira Gandhi was trying to project that a war with Pakistan was imminent. She was wanting to cash in on the threat syndrome and garner votes for the coming parliamentary elections. I gave my professional assessment in my address. I brought out that threat of war with Pakistan was ever present but there was no imminent threat as such at that time. My analysis suited the Opposition. After my address, in his concluding remarks Vajpayee stated that I did not want to join "Rajniti" but I would have to join "Rashtraniti". Translated into English these two words would mean party politics and national politics respectively. He was interrupted by a member of the audience saying, "After hearing the General I now realize what great injustice had been done to Bihar, by the Government not appointing him the Army Chief". Vajpayee corrected him saying that it was not an injustice to Bihar but an injustice to India. This had been the beginning of my close association with Vajpayee. A few months later, he invited me as a guest speaker to the BJP's National Convention at Pune to speak on National Security and Party Politics. I hesitated to accept his invitation because I was not wanting to join any political party, nor did I want to get identified with any party. He assured me that he was inviting me as a professional to speak on the subject and it did not mean that I had to join his party. The previous year M C Chagla had been so invited at the BJP Annual Convention and he had spoken as a specialist on Independence of the Judiciary. I felt reassured and I accepted his invitation to the Pune Convention. Our contacts had continued over the years and we had been meeting often. He had also come to my house in Patna. He did me the favour of releasing my book on Veer Kuer Singh at a function organized by my publishers at India International Centre in Delhi. I was very grateful to him for his laudatory remarks about me at that function. Thus, it was a pleasure meeting Vajpayee again. He expressed his happiness at my being sent to Assam. He added that it was in the Nation's interest that I should go there and I was the right man for the difficult assignment. I told him that the confidence being reposed in me by Gujral, Kesri and him made my task both easy and difficult. I could count on the support of the top leadership of the country, cutting across party lines, which would certainly facilitate my working. I felt overwhelmed by the confidence they had in me. I also told Vajpayee that at times I feared I may not be able to measure up to the challenge and fulfill the trust being reposed in me. Vajpayee laughingly assured me that there was no risk of that. Knowing me as he did, he was confident that I would succeed. That was a morale booster for me.

3

My association with Assam had started in 1945 when I was only 19 years of age. I had been commissioned in the 9th Jat Regiment and was posted to 6/9 JAT at Palasbari in Guwahati. After Independence, the Regiment dropped its 9th numeral and it became the Jat Regiment with my Battalion redesignated as 6 JAT. It had been an exciting experience for me to set out in life on my own, at a time when the War had reached the eastern fringes of Assam. Only a few months earlier, the Japanese invasion of Assam had been foiled and they were in retreat from Assam to Burma, now called Myanmar. My Battalion was training in the hills and jungles near Palasbari, to move into Burma to pursue the retreating Japanese into Siam, now Thailand.

My train journey from our Regimental Centre at Bareilly to Guwahati was interesting. I travelled on the broad gauge to Calcutta and thence to Parbatipur, now in Bangladesh. From Parbatipur, I travelled on the metre guage to Amingaon on the northern bank of the Brahmaputra. I crossed the river to Pandu in a railway streamer. A senior subaltern had come in a truck to receive me. He was a British officer who had risen from the ranks. He was a rough and over-bearing person. He shouted at me asking me to get into the rear of the truck. I had to travel standing in the body of the vehicle to the battalion location which was about half an hour's distance from Pandu. Palasbari was a typical Assamese village on the river bank. There was plenty of open space near the village. The battalion was living in tents and I had a small 40 pounder tent for myself. There were 16 officers in the battalion and I was the junior most amongst them. We were four Indian officers, the remaining twelve being British. Amongst the Indian officers, two were Muslims, one Christian and I was the only Hindu. This created a problem for me because in the Officers Mess, beef was the staple diet, which everyone partook of. The mess secretary and the senior officers were not very considerate. There used to be no dish in lieu of beef for me. I used to get food for myself from the Men's Cook House, which I ate in my tent before going to the Officers Mess to go through the ritual of eating boiled vegetables. At times, I felt friendless. I used to roam in the neighbouring villages. It was Bihu season and there used to be a lot of singing and dancing in the villages. The villagers were very friendly and hospitable. I used to be given eatables, particularly sweets which I liked very much. This was the beginning of my love for Assam and the Assamese people. Little could I then foresee how in the years to come, this association would flower into a deep emotional attachment. After a couple of months, I moved with my battalion to Burma.

My second tenure in Assam was more than a decade later in the Fifties when I was a company commander in the rank of Major. Naga rebellion had just started. Naga Hills District (now Nagaland) was then part of Assam. Thereafter, in the late Sixties, I served as a Brigade Commander for a couple of years combating Naga militancy. In the Seventies, as a Major General I commanded a Division in the Brahmaputra Valley. Later still, as Chief of Military Intelligence at Delhi and subsequently as Vice Chief of the Army, I was associated with tackling insurgency in the North East. I saw the beginning of the Students Movement in Assam which ultimately led to the eruption of the ULFA (United Liberation Front of Assam) militancy in the Brahmaputra Valley. I was now going back to Assam in 1997 as the Governor of that State, when militancy was at its peak.

I had found Sanjoy Hazarika's book, "Strangers of the Mist", very absorbing and also very useful. This book starts with the problem of influx of Bangladeshis into Assam. This demographic threat had been a matter of very grave concern to the Assamese people. Sanjoy quoted Myron Weiner, a noted authority on migration. The latter in his book *Sons of the Soil: Migration and Ethnic Conflict in India.* "Had Assam's population increased at the same rate as the rest of India from 1901 to 1971 (130%), her population would now be 7.6 million rather than 15 million...Between 1961 and 1971, the population of Assam increased by 34.7 percent as against 24.7 percent of the rest of India". Sharifa Begum, researcher of the Institute of Development Studies at Dhaka, in her research paper had stated that 5 million Bangladeshi nationals had crossed into India from 1951 to 1974. Since the vast majority of Bangladeshis who had come, were Muslims and the majority population of Assam is of Hindus, this migration acquired a communal dimension, causing tension. Of course, the migration was taking place not because of any religious considerations but due to economic compulsions. In 1991, the per capita income in Bangladesh was 170 US dollars which was half of the per capita income of Assam. Sixty percent of the population of Bangladesh was below the poverty line. The density of population in Bangladesh was the highest in the world. It was 969 per sq. km. The population growth rate in Bangladesh was 2.2 percent per year and every year, millions of people got displaced due to recurring floods. Given these circumstances, a large scale influx of Bangladeshis into Assam was inevitable. This was compounded by the vote bank politics pursued by some political parties. And it was the large scale influx of illegal migrants from Bangladesh which had been the root cause for insurgency in Assam.

I was given a detailed briefing in the Ministry of Home Affairs. I was also briefed in the Intelligence Bureau, Research & Analysis Wing and Army Headquarters. Militancy started in Assam in the late Seventies in the wake of the Students Movement against the influx of Bangladeshis. I was the Vice Chief of the Army when the students movement was at its peak. Trouble began with the updating of the voters list in Mangaldoi in April 1979. During the revision of electoral rolls of that constituency, 70,000 complaints were registered against illegal migrants. A tribunal was set up and it upheld 45,000 complaints out of a total electorate of six lakhs. These statistics stunned the Assamese people and provided fuel for the anti-foreigners movement, launched by the students. Two muslim ministers of the Assam Government, Zaheer-ul-Islam and Ghulam Usmani resigned protesting against the deletion of the names of illegal migrants. This provoked a strong reaction from AASU (All Assam Students Union). The spark of statewide unrest got ignited at Mangaldoi, which in the nineteenth century had witnessed the start of a strong peasant movement against the British and in the mid-twentieth century, the language riots against the Bengalis.

About this time, Shakdhar, the Chief Election Commissioner, addressing a conference of State Chief Electoral Officers stated, "In one State (Assam) the population in 1971 recorded an increase as high as 34.98 per-cent over the 1961 figures and this increase was attributed to the influx of a very large number of persons from the neighbouring countries. The influx has become a regular feature. I think it may not be a wrong assessment to make, on the basis of the increase of 34.98 per cent between the two censuses, that the increase that is likely to be recorded in the 1991 census would be more than 100 per cent over the 1961 census. In other words a stage would reach when the State would have to reckon with the foreign nationals who may probably constitute a sizeable percentage, if not the majority of the population of the State. Another disturbing factor in this regard is the demand made by the political parties for the inclusion in the electoral rolls of the names of such migrants who are not Indian citizens, without even questioning and properly determining their citizenship status".

The statement of the Chief Election Commissioner and the detection of the names of such a large number of illegal migrants in the voters' list of Mangaldoi constituency, aroused great resentment among the people. It led to widespread agitation among the people of Assam. Prafulla Kumar Mohanta, the President of AASU, issued a statement, "We demand our constitutional rights that foreigners be deported and detected to save Assam and the Assamese people". The student movement adopted the slogan: "No detection, no revision, no election". Indira Gandhi was determined to force an election on the Assamese people using the disputed voters' list. There was now open confrontation between the Government and the people. I had personal experience of the Quit India Movement of 1942 when I was a student. That movement was the strongest in Bihar. Yet I found that the Students' Movement in Assam of 1983 was more widespread than what I had seen of the 1942 movement in Bihar. When a call would be given by AASU for Janata Black Out, lights remained switched off in the entire State. Similarly, when a call was given to boycott passenger trains, the trains would run empty. After the third Arab-Israel War of 1973, the Arabs had effectively used oil as a weapon to pressurize the Western Nations and extract a much increased price for black gold. The Assamese also used the oil weapon by stopping the flow of oil out of Assam and starving the oil refinery at Barauni. At that time off shore oil had not come into much use and Assam was the main source of oil in India. AASU received support from all segments of Assamese society. Assam started burning.

Indira Gandhi remained adamant about holding elections. The electoral exercise became bizarre and farcical. Polling booths were effectively boycotted and the voter turn out was less than 3%, lowest in the history of elections in India. About this time, the tragedy of the Nellie massacre took place. That area is dominated by the Lalung Tribe who had lost their land to Bangladeshi immigrants. They were illiterate and were made to give thumb impressions on the sale documents which they did not quite understand. When they found that they had been cheated out of their land and were reduced to penury, they became very resentful. These immigrants made it known that they would vote in the coming election. This caused great tension. To make matters worse, rumours spread that these Muslim immigrants had been molesting tribal women. The Lalung Tribe decided to attack the Bangladeshi immigrants from three directions, with armed gangs of 2000 from each side. The Bangladeshi immigrants were taken by surprise and for five hours killing of men, women and children continued in a most merciless manner. In one day, more than 1700 people were killed. This was the worst pogrom on a single day in Independent India. The final toll of killings at Nellie, was 3000-4000.

The Congress ministry that came to power under the leadership of Hiteshwar Saikia as a result of the farcical election of 1983, lacked legitimacy. The Students' Movement against the Government continued with increased intensity. After the assassination of Indira Gandhi, Rajiv Gandhi became the Prime Minister. An accord was signed between the Government of India and the AASU in which it was agreed to hold fresh elections in Assam. In these elections, the AASU, which had formed a political party named AGP, won with a thumping majority. Simultaneously, ULFA, another offshoot of the Students' Movement, continued its violent activities, with the aim of securing the secession of Assam from the Indian Union.

In 1985, when the first AGP Government came to power, ULFA was allowed to function as a parallel government. Their writ not only ran in the countryside but also in the State secretariat. An intelligence agency described it as easily one of the most efficient money gathering extremist machines in India. They demanded money from the managers of tea gardens, the business community and even government servants. People were asked to deposit money demanded by ULFA with officers of the State Government like deputy commissioners and police officers to be handed over by them to ULFA. There was a great demoralization in the State Police. The lower ranks of the police began associating themselves with ULFA. The State home minister described ULFA as "from among us". There were 133 cases of murder by ULFA activists in the State, but no action was taken nor FIR recorded. The Commissioner Jorhat Division was assassinated in his office and so was a superintendent of police in Dibrugarh. The ire of ULFA was also directed against non-Assamese people and extortion of money was taking place on a mind boggling scale. They demanded Rs.14 million @ Rs. 2 per kg of tea produced from the Hindustan Lever Tea Garden in Doomdooma. Besides, Brooke Bond and Lipton were asked to cough up 5 percent of their net profit. The principals of Hindustan Lever, Unilever in London, took up the matter with the Indian High Commissioner who in turn made a reference to the Government of India. Chandra Shekhar was then the Prime Minister. He decided to strike. A little used airfield near Doomdooma Tea Gardens was used to secretly fly out the staff and families of Tea gardens in a Boeing aircraft of RAW. Next day, the State Government was dismissed and President's rule imposed in Assam. The Army was called out. It launched 'Operation Bajrang' to liquidate the ULFA militants. Although the latter suffered casualties, the bulk of them managed to get away, the top leaders escaping to Bangladesh. After a few months of counter-insurgency operations by the army, it was decided to hold elections in Assam and send the army back to barracks.

The AGP, during its first tenure of five years, lost popular support due to rampant corruption and bad governance. A leading literary figure of Assam, Hemen Borogohain, wrote, "I do not mean to say that all politicians before them were saints and only the AGP politicians are a bunch of rogues but they frightened us by their arrogance, intolerance, bad manners and disrespect of our age-old values". Matters got further compounded for AGP because of the quarrel between their two top leaders, Prafulla Kumar Mohanta and Bhrigu Phuken. The results of the 1991 elections were disastrous for the AGP. It was reduced to a small minority and the Congress, under Hiteshwar Saikia, was back in power.

Hiteshwar Saikia was a shrewd politician. He managed to organize the surrender of 3500 militants. Each surrenderee was given Rs. 2 lakh and allowed to retain his weapon. Some were given PSOs (Personal Security Officers). These surrendered militants, called SULFA, indulged in various antisocial activities and became very unpopular with the people. They continued extortionist activities but were useful in dealing with the ULFA militants. The army was again called out to tackle militancy in Assam and 'Operation Rhino' was launched. The Corps Commander, Lt Gen Ajai Singh, had kept a tag of militant activities and had organized a good intelligence network during Operation Bajrang. Thus, when the army undertook Operation Rhino, it was able to inflict heavy attrition on the militants and the situation improved markedly.

After five years of Congress rule in Assam under Hiteshwar Saikia, elections were held again in 1996. Hiteshwar Saikia died on the eve of this election and Prafulla Kumar Mohanta managed to win the election by a slender majority with the help of a few coalition partners. In its election manifesto, the AGP had made three commitments. They had announced that the army would be returned to barracks, the black laws like Armed Forces Special Powers Act, 1958 and Disturbed Areas Act, 1990 would be repealed and the people of Assam would be given the right of self-determination. The militants had supported Mohanta in this election but when they found that he could not redeem these promises they turned against him.

Large scale violence broke out in Assam. There was an attempt on the Chief Minister's life and he had a narrow escape. In the city of Guwahati, in two separate incidents, an Inspector General of Police and a Brigadier had been killed. Two Colonels paying obeisance inside Kamakhya Temple were shot. Similarly, some soldiers and officers were killed inside Krishna Temple at Tezpur. There were explosions on the Brahmaputra Mail and the North-East Express, killing a few hundred passengers. There was ethnic violence between Bodos and Adivasis in which 700 people were killed. Two lakh refugees, mostly Adivasis, were forced to take shelter in refugee camps. The Chief Secretary and the Director General of Police of Assam had both fled away and new incumbents were posted in their place. I was also told that there was an old CBI case of corruption against the Chief Minister but I did not attach much importance to that because that was nothing very unusual about modern day politicians.

The situation in Assam was indeed very grim. Gujral was very right when he had told me that Assam was burning and I must go there forthwith. Having updated myself with all this information, I met the Home Minister, Indrajeet Gupta and the Home Secretary. The former appeared receptive to my suggestion of the Army coordinating security operations of the paramilitary and the Police. The situation appeared ripe for President's rule. However, I felt that it should be the last option. Casually talking to the Home Secretary, I mentioned that in 1947 when there was complete breakdown of law and order in Delhi and Punjab, I had to put up an operational map showing locations of army units for a Cabinet meeting at Governor General's House (later re-designated as Rashtrapati Bhavan). Mountbattern had been requested to return from Simla to Delhi. Though only a constitutional Head of State, he used to preside over the emergency meetings of the Cabinet attended by Nehru and Patel. Abnormal situations required abnormal solutions. My intention behind mentioning this was that in Assam, if possible, we could evolve a solution short of President's rule. The Home Secretary appeared to have been intrigued by my loud thinking on these lines. However, soon, I heard from different sources that in the ministry of home affairs there was a feeling that being an army officer, I was not aware of the niceties of a democratic Constitution. I ignored the insinuation. No one in authority took any notice of it.

Before leaving Delhi, I decided to call on Shri L P Singh, one of the most distinguished civil servants of India who had served as Governor of Assam in the Seventies. When he was a young ICS officer in Bihar, my grandfather was the police chief of the province and when he became chief secretary of Bihar, my father was the police chief of the State. My father and he were good friends. I used to call him uncle and both he and his wife were always very kind to me. Shri L P Singh was interested in military history and when I used to go home on leave to Patna, we often had discussions on that subject. He had written the Foreword to my book on Veer Kuer Singh, which was released by Atal Behari Vajpayee at India International Centre, a couple of years earlier. I went to his house in Vasant Vihar in New Delhi to seek his blessings and got guidance from him. He was delighted that I was going to Assam and we spent some time discusing Assam. He gave me useful advice. We discussed the role of a governor in our set-up. He remarked that he was happy that I was following in his footsteps.

After having been a very distinguished home secretary, he had been denied the top appointment of Cabinet secretary for political reasons. He received due recognition after retirement. He was appointed Ambassador in Nepal and then Governor of Assam. Having missed out on getting the top appointment in my Service like him, I had also been appointed Ambassador to Nepal. And now again, like him I was going as Governor of Assam buoyed by his blessings and advice. I was now ready to proceed to Assam.

4

After a fruitful visit to Delhi, I came back to Patna for a couple of days before departing for Guwahati. I was glad that the news of my appointment as Governor of Assam had been welcomed not only in Bihar but all over the country. I received a couple of hundred letters and telegrams felicitating me and sending me good wishes for success in a challenging assignment, in the interest of the Nation. Many of those who had written to me were not known to me. It only showed how our people are guided by patriotic feelings. The ongoing militancy both in Assam and Jammu and Kashmir had been a source of grave concern to our people all over the country.

There was, however, one discordant note. The President of the State unit of RJD, the ruling party of Lalu Prasad Yadav in Bihar, issued a statement about my appointment in Assam. He expressed his unhappiness at the Government of India deciding to send me to such a sensitive appointment. He alleged that I was a member of the BJP and that I came from a family of traitors. Indubitably, I had close friendly relations with the two top BJP leaders, Vajpayee and Advani, but I was never a member of their party, nor for that matter, any political party. His accusation that I was from a family of traitors was absurd. It was totally false and malicious. He alleged that in 1942 my father was the Senior Superintendent of Police of Patna. To please the British rulers, he had ordered firing on the unarmed crowd of students in front of Patna Secretariat. As a result of this firing, seven students were killed. After Independence, a Martyrs' Memorial comprising bronze statues of the seven martyred students had been put up in front of the Secretariat. In August 1942, my father was some 300 km away from Patna serving as Superintendent of Police of Purnea. And Purnea had the unique distinction of being the only district in North Bihar where the army or the police had not opened fire on political demonstrators during the 1942 movement. My father had, through tactical intervention, managed to disperse agitating crowds in Purnea without using force. He had returned a contingent of British troops that had been sent to the district saying that he was confident of maintaining order in his district without any help from the army. When he left Purnea, the following year, the president of the district Congress Committee and British planters plus other distinguished citizens had presented him with a set of golf clubs in recognition of his service during the 1942 movement. This presentation had been made after obtaining due approval of the Bihar Government. A number of people issued Press statements and wrote letters to the Editor of the concerned newspaper pointing out how false and mischievous was the accusation made by the President of the State RJD. Some had written that they were present at the secretariat in Patna and had seen that the firing had been ordered by the British district magistrate and fire had been opened by British soldiers. Some others wrote that they had been in Purnea and had personal knowledge of how my father had managed to deal with grave situations on a couple of occasions without opening fire. My second brother was very upset at the accusation made against the family and he filed a defamation suit in the court. Our legal procedures are so slow that for a couple of years hardly any progress was made in the case. Hearings kept getting adjourned and my poor brother who had filed the case passed away due to illness. We decided not to pursue the case.

Other than the lone instance of the false and mischievous allegation against me and my family, my appointment was hailed in the Press and by the people. However, there was apprehension in some newspapers of Assam. They expressed fear about a military man being sent as governor to impose military rule in the State. I had encountered a similar situation when I had gone to Nepal as Ambassador. The Kathmandu Press had expressed hostile views saying that for the first time a military man had been sent as Ambassador to Nepal. This was indicative of India's militaristic ambition to establish hegemony over Nepal. It took me some time to make the Nepal Press realize that their fears were totally unfounded. Similarly, I hoped that I would be able to win over the Assamese people and put at rest their fears on this account.

My son, Yash, was posted as a Consular at the Indian Embassy in Pakistan. He was keen to attend my swearing-in-ceremony at Guwahati. He telephoned me that he had managed some work at Delhi and would take a couple of days off to come to Patna and then proceed with me to Guwahati. I was delighted at the prospect of his being present for the function. My father was accompanying me and my wife to Guwahati and so was one of my sisters, Padma. The Governor of Bihar, Dr A R Kidwai, had very kindly responded to my request and arranged for the Bihar State aircraft to be made available to me for going from Patna to Guwahati. There was no direct commercial flight from Patna to Guwahati. Travelling by the State plane, we could avoid breaking journey for a night at Kolkata.

There were a few farewell functions at Patna for me. A large crowd of friends, including many army officers from the Cantonment, gathered at Patna Airport to bid us farewell. People remarked that it would be a unique instance at Guwahati for a governor to be sworn-in, in the presence of both his father and his son. Pranab Sahi who had at my instance, produced the documentary film on the history of Patliputra, volunteered to film my departure at Patna while Debashiah Sharma, the Special Officer at Raj Bhavan, Guwahati, complemented this by doing the same at Guwahati. Thus a complete documentary film was prepared of my departure from Patna, and arrival at Guwahati as also of the swearing-in ceremony. This became an interesting record fo. our family. My three daughters abroad, Meena, Minnie and Manisha were each sent a copy of this film.

The Gods of weather were kind. Despite the monsoon being at its peak, 1st September, 1997 was a nice and clear day. We took off by the Bihar Government plane form Patna to Guwahati carrying the good wishes of numerous friends for my success in my task of national importance.

5

We landed at Guwahati airport as scheduled, on a bright morning on 1 September, 1997. Elaborate arrangements had been made for my reception. The Chief Minister and his entire Cabinet, some prominent citizens and senior civil and military officers were there to welcome me. There was a smart Guard of Honour of the State Police at the airport which gave me the General Salute. I had not yet been sworn in as Governor and as such could not be given the National Salute. After inspecting the Guard and meeting the dignitaries who had come to receive me, I proceeded by car to Raj Bhavan. There was a long cavalcade of cars with escorts and members of the staff following me. The Raj Bhavan is half an hour's drive from the airport with the road going along the southern bank of the mighty Brahmaputra river. It was the monsoon season and the water level in the river was high. I could not help but recall how 52 years earlier, I had travelled on the same road standing in the back of a military truck on my way to join my battalion at Palasbari, which is not far from the airport. A lot had changed in the past over half a century, when I first came to Assam in 1945. I could not at that time in my wildest dreams ever imagine that I would one day be taking over as the Governor of the State and travel with such protocol trappings.

My father, who was then 94 years of age, had come with me and travelled in the same car. I could see the emotion on his face. Being a father myself, I could realise what his feelings were. Many years later destiny bestowed a similar good fortune on me when my son became an ambassador and also began being addressed as "His Excellency" while I was Governor of Jammu and Kashmir. As we passed the hill close to the road on which the Kamakhya Temple is located, in a choking voice my father said how blessed he was that he would now have the great good fortune to pay obeisance at that sacred Temple. He was beholden to the Lord. My father was well travelled both in India and abroad but that was the first time he had come to Assam. He had offered prayers at all the major Hindu pilgrimage sites except Kamakhya.

Shri L P Singh was right when he had told me of the beautiful location of the Raj Bhavan at Guwahati. In the Seventies when Meghalaya separated from Assam, he was Governor of both Assam and Meghalaya. Shillong was the capital of undivided Assam and had a beautiful Raj Bhavan from the British days. It was a chateau type building with extensive grounds. As Governor, he used to stay at Shillong and visit the new capital of Assam at Guwahati, off and on. Initially, he had a suite of rooms permanently reserved in the Circuit House for himself but found the arrangement unsatisfactory. A new capital had to be built for Assam and the place selected for it was Chandrapur, some 20 kms from Guwahati. Indira Gandhi had laid the foundation stone for the new capital at that place but work on this project had not started for one reason or the other. As a temporary measure, the State Secretariat was housed in the Tea Warehouse buildings at Dispur. Alterations were made to the buildings to meet their new role. Shri L P Singh had selected a very good site on top of a hill for a temporary Raj Bhavan, which could be used by the Governor, till the capital complex came up at Chandrapur. Although the site was excellent with a very commanding view of the Brahmaputra and the hills in the neighbourhood, the Raj Bhavan was a very modest building. I was disappointed by its layout and furnishings. This was now to be my residence for the next six years. During that period, we had an earthquake which damaged the building with cracks in walls, an outbreak of fire in one of the bedrooms which was completely gutted but luckily the fire was brought under control. We also had a visitation by a python of large size which was caught and sent to Guwahati Zoo.

My swearing-in was to be on the same day I arrived at Guwahati, in the Darbar Hall. The large tin shed, modestly furnished, was an apology for a Darbar Hall. The State Government had enquired if I would like any personal guests to be invited for the function. I had suggested that the Commandant of my Regimental Centre at Shillong be invited and so should Ajit, my cousin, who was then a manager in a tea garden. The protocol for swearing-in was well observed with a guard of honour first giving me the General Salute before the swearing-in and subsequently giving the National Salute after I had taken the oath of office. The Chief Justice administered the oath to me. The Chief Minister chose to make a speech welcoming me. Normally, no speeches are made at such functions. I had occasion to be sworn-in twice each as Governor in Bengal and Arunachal Pradesh for short periods, once again in Assam for my second term and much later as Governor of Jammu and Kashmir, but on none of these occasions were any speeches made. As the Chief Minister had spoken, I thought it appropriate to respond. I stated that it was a homecoming for me because I had first come to Assam over half a century earlier and had served four tenures in different ranks at different points of time in the State. I had happy memories of the warm hospitality and friendliness of the people of the State, particularly during Bihu. It was a matter of grave concern that the people of that beautiful State had been suffering the ravages of widespread violence for several years. I mentioned that I had come from the land of the Buddha and had brought a replica of the peace stupa at Rajgir with me. I earnestly hoped that during my tenure, winds of peace and prosperity would once again start blowing in the State. I made a special reference to the great personalities of Assam whom I called our national heroes. In this context, I mentioned the names of Mahapurush Shrimant Shankardev, the patron saint of Assam, Lachit Borphukan, the great military leader of the seventeenth century and Lokpriya Gopinath Bordoloi, the first Chief Minister of the State. After the swearing-in function, we adjourned for tea and I interacted with a large number of guests who had come for the function. The reaction to my impromptu speech was very favourable. I felt that although the normal protocol for the occasion had been violated by the speeches, I had made a good beginning. Some people remarked how fortunate I was to have both my father and my son present at the function. The army officers were understandably happy that one of their fraternity had taken over as the Head of the State. The Commandant of my regimental centre invited me to visit the centre at Shillong as the men would be very happy to welcome a regimental officer as a governor. Shillong is about 3-hour drive by road from Guwahati. I told him that I would soon visit the Centre.

My first priority on taking over as Governor was to visit some of the flood affected districts. I visited Tezpur, which was reeling under the effects of flood and the army was doing extensive flood relief work. After I had gone round the worst affected areas, I returned to the Circuit House at Tezpur, where press correspondents were waiting for me. I was asked if I had come to impose President's rule in Assam and my reply was that I had not come to replace the State Government but to assist it in whatever way I could do so. They asked me as to when the army would be returned to barracks. Largely due to the propaganda unleashed by the militants, the people were not too well disposed towards the Army. I replied that at a time when Assam was suffering so much due to floods and the army was going all out to provide succour to the people, I was surprised at being asked that question. Surely no one would like the army to stop all the relief work it was doing. My first tour on taking over as Governor went off well although I did read comments in some newspapers of my having gone on a tour unaccompanied by any minister. It was also said that I appeared to be a proactive governor. I was determined not to confine myself to the ivory tower in Raj Bhavan, performing only ceremonial functions. I intended to go all out to serve the people and help the State Government at a time of grave crisis. I also went round some army units in Tezpur and expressed my appreciation for the excellent work they were doing. This was good for their morale.

While visiting the flood affected areas of Guwahati district, I happened to visit the village of Palasbari, close to the airfield. The old village had been washed away by the Brahmaputra over the years. A new Palasbari had sprung up, not far from the old site which now lay in the bed of the river. Our camp in 1945 had been in a large open space close to the old village. This area had been encroached upon considerably and a lot of buildings and trees had come up, making it difficult to recognize the site. Luckily, I met an old villager who told me that during the Second World War, he had worked with the MES (Military Engineering Service) at Guwahati and had been associated with the construction of a military camp near Palasbari. He guided me to a few spots where the remnants of brick hard standings for tents and kitchen could still be traced. It made me feel very nostalgic. I recalled the old days when I had lived in that camp.

5

I took a day off to visit my regimental centre at Shillong, in response to the invitation extended to me by the Commandant. I was overwhelmed by the warm welcome given to me during this visit. For a soldier, a regimental centre is his professional home. I had served in the regiment for nearly 40 years and many of the Gorkha soldiers were second or third generation members of their family serving in the regiment. I had known the grandfather and father of a few of them. I was given a guard of honour on my arrival. It was the same parade ground where I had been given a farewell guard of honour 14 years ago when I had resigned from the Army and had laid down the office of the Colonel of the Regiment. The holder of that office is looked up to as a father figure in the regiment. I remembered that at the farewell function in 1983, there was a pall of gloom. There was a feeling that the regiment had been unfairly deprived of the opportunity of having one of its officers taking over as the Chief of the Army. I had been the Vice Chief of the Army at that time and the unexpected decision of the Government not to give me the top job had caused much controversy. This was reflected both in the Press and the Parliament. The atmosphere now was entirely different. The officers and men of the regiment were very happy that one of them had become the Governor of Assam. For the first time in the 150-year old history of the regiment, a guard of honour presented a National Salute to its erstwhile Regimental Officer. As these thoughts crossed my mind, I felt emotionally overwhelmed while taking the salute. The officers at the centre told me that this was the first occasion of a Gorkha officer having taken over as Governor and also perhaps the first occasion when an officer of our army on retirement, had the privilege of being appointed both Ambassador and Governor. I acknowledged their felicitation with due humility. I was most fortunate in having got much greater recognition than I deserved.

I spent two very relaxed and enjoyable days at the regimental centre. I addressed a special Sainik Sammelan of officers and men of the regiment. I told them how much I owed to the regiment and the strong bond between us would exist for ever. The Commandant mentioned that I had become a legend for the regiment and my achievements would always be a source of great pride for the officers and men of the regiment. He wanted to have a museum built in the regiment to house all my memorabilia which would inspire the present and future generations of soldiers of the regiment. I readily agreed to this. I presented my uniforms comprising both barethea suit and my green patrols to the museum. Besides, I presented various trophies and important mementos. These included the Japanese *samurai sword* presented to me in Burma by a Japanese officer after he had surrendered. I had then been the Adjutant of a Japanese Prisoner of War Camp. There was a signed photograph of Their Majesties the King and Queen of Nepal along with the Crown Prince, the Crown Princess and the young Prince in a golden frame. The King of Nepal is hailed as an incarnation of Lord Vishnu and is highly revered amongst the Nepalese. Almost all the soldiers of my regiment hail from Nepal. The credentials presented by me to the King and his response accepting them, suitably framed with the Royal Insignia, and carrying his signature, was given by me to the museum. Much later events changed. The aura of kingship in Nepal was gone and monarchy terminated. At the time of my departure from Nepal, the Prime Minister had presented me the national Insignia of that country of a mythical flying Lion in brass. I also handed this over to the museum. These artifacts were of great significance for the Nepalese soldiers. There were numerous other mementos of my army career which I handed over to the regiment. These included all my car flags from a Brigade Commander to an Army Commander, of Senior Staff Officer at Army Headquarters, of Principal Staff Officer at Army Headquarters, of Vice-Chief of Army Staff, of Colonel of 5 Gorkha Rifles and of Colonel Commandant of the Intelligence Corps. Besides the Army car flags, there were also the National car flags of ambassador and governor. These were tastefully arranged on a circular wooden platform. It looked very elegant and impressive. All the formation signs worn by me on my arm in my uniform were put together in rows of wooden shields on a wooden board. The parchment signed by the President awarding me the

PVSM was framed and displayed in the Museum. A copy of each of the five books that I had written till then was put in a showcase. A framed Warrant of Appointment issued by the President of India, appointing me as Governor of Assam was also put up on the wall. Besides, there were numerous other mementos that I had acquired during my army and civil career. The room got filled with all this memorabilia. Later, when there were many more mementos presented to me as Governor of Assam and as Governor of Jammu and Kashmir I had them all sent to the Centre. The regiment did me the great honour of having a separate new building constructed called General Sinha Museum, to house all my memorabilia.

There was a social evening in the officers mess where they had put up my oil painting in uniform on the wall as Colonel of the Regiment. I also attended a Bara Khana with the soldiers who had put up a nice cultural programme for me. They forced me to join them in Nepalese dancing and were thrilled to find that despite my age, I could dance in step with them and sing old Nepalese tunes.

It was a very memorable visit to the regimental centre for me and I returned to Guwahati fully relaxed and rejuvenated to face the challenges before me in Assam.

5

There were four important issues that I had to address on priority. First, imposition of President's rule; second, the strategy for resolving the Assam problem; third, the unabated influx of illegal migrants from Bangladesh; fourth, the chief minister's involvement in the Letter of Credit (LoC) Scam.

After the briefings I had received in Delhi, I was inclined not to go in for President's rule. The Prime Minister had suggested to me in Delhi that I could have KPS Gill as my advisor. Gill was a police officer of the Assam cadre who had served for many years in the State. He had the reputation of being a go getter who could produce results. He was sent on deputation to Punjab as DGP of that State. He had played a stellar role in restoring peace and normalcy in that State. He had deservedly received due recognition for his outstanding achievement in Punjab and had become a national hero. I told the Prime Minister that I would make up my mind after going to Assam and studying the situation on the ground. He told me that even if President's rule was not imposed, I could still have Gill as security advisor in Assam. I replied that having served many years both in Assam and Punjab and knowing the characteristics of the people in the two States, I felt that Assam should be tackled in a different manner from Punjab.

On arrival at Guwahati, I found it a dead city. A sense of fear gripped the people and they did not like to venture out of their houses after sunset. The traditional "At Home" was not being held in the afternoon on Independence and Republic Days at Raj Bhavan. It was feared that guests returning after the function to their houses in the evening, would not be safe. I gave much thought to the issue of imposing President's rule. I interacted with army and civilian officials as also with some prominent non-officials. The more I thought of the problem, the more I felt that imposing President's rule in the long term may turn out to be counter-productive. No doubt it could achieve quick results but these may not be long lasting. The people's alienation with Delhi would get accentuated. They would feel that they had been forced to yield to Central dictates. On the other hand even if quick results in restoring normalcy were not achieved, the fact that democracy functioned in the State and the issue was seen to be resolved by its own people, would have a more lasting effect. As for the rough approach adopted by the Police in Punjab, I felt that the people of Assam should be handled differently keeping in view their sensitivities. My mind was made up and I told the Prime Minister that neither President's rule nor a security advisor was required in Assam.

I may mention an interesting report that I received, when rumours were rife about President's rule being imposed in the State. During the spell of President's rule in the early Nineties there were allegations of corruption against an officer of the Raj Bhavan staff who later quit the service. My Special Officer in Raj Bhavan was Debashish Sharma. I found him very loyal and highly intelligent. He was educated at Delhi before competing into the State Administrative Service. One day he told me that a known moneybag of the State who had considerable political clout had rung him up to tell him that President's rule was being imposed shortly. He also told him that they could now have a good time as there would be plenty of opportunity to make money. This only strengthened my resolve not to go for President's rule. During my six years as Governor I never met this moneybag nor did he ever make any attempt to meet me.

6

Having decided not to go for President's rule, I started formulating my strategy for tackling militancy in the State. I had had many years of experience of dealing with insurgency in the North East. My battalion, 3/5 Gorkha Rifles, was one of the first two units to be inducted to combat Naga rebellion that broke out in 1956. I was a company commander in my battalion. In the Sixties I had served as a brigade commander for over two years actively associated with counter-insurgency operations when Naga gangs were returning with weapons from Yunan province in China through North Burma to Nagaland and Manipur. There was no General Staff training manual on counter- insurgency in the army. Towards the end of my tenure as brigade commander, I was asked to draft a manual for the army. Apart from the experience I had gained in dealing with insurgency, I made extensive study of British counter-insurgency operations in Malaya and American in Vietnam. The draft prepared by me was accepted by Army Headquarters and was published as a General Staff training manual. Subsequently, I commanded a Division in Assam in the early Seventies and thereafter I served as Director of Military Intelligence at Army Headquarters for nearly three years. In the latter appointment I was closely connected with our counter-insurgency efforts in Nagaland, Manipur, Mizoram and Tripura. This long exposure to insurgency stood me in good stead as Governor in planning a strategy to combat militancy in Assam.

I evolved a three-pronged strategy for Assam—unified command, economic development and psychological initiatives. For the third prong of this strategy, I was averse to using the commonly accepted terminology of psychological warfare. I thought that the nomenclature, psychological warfare was inappropriate when we were dealing with our own nationals. I chose instead, psychological initiatives, to bring about an attitudinal change among the people and to get them back to the national mainstream.

Not long after I took over as Governor, Gujral came on a visit to Guwahati and stayed with me. I briefed him of my assessment of the situation in Assam and my proposed strategy at a meeting in my office attended by the Chief Minister and senior civil and military officials. I had developed very cordial relations with Prafulla Kumar Mohanta, the Chief Minister. He showed regard for my age and experience. He had no objection to my assuming a pro-active role in dealing with insurgency. He felt that with me as

Governor, the Army could be relied upon to give maximum support to the State Government. Gujral approved of the strategy spelt out by me.

Unity of command is a fundamental requirement for the conduct of counter-insurgency operations. Security forces of all countries in the world combating insurgency have this arrangement. We had been engaged in counter-insurgency operations in the North East for over forty years but had failed to establish a joint command under the senior Army officer. The army had been advocating this for several years but the Government had inhibitions in accepting this necessity. It was argued that such arrangement would mean imposing martial law and handing over control to the army which was not acceptable in a democracy. This only reflected confused thinking. Whereas overall control of policy and governance should remain with the civil administration, it was desirable that the coordination of security operations of the army, the paramilitary and the police be done by one commander. The senior army officer with his expertise and resources was in the best position to carry out this task. This was the accepted practice all over the world. Somehow, we had not been able to work out this arrangement in the North East. Apart from the inhibitions of the civil administration, there were also ego hassles and turf wars among different elements of the security forces. Thus there was a tendency for the Army, the paramilitary and the police to function more as competing than complementary forces. At long last in 1997, the Government of India accepted the need for unity of command and this greatly facilitated the conduct of counter-insurgency operations in Assam. I took personal interest in ensuring the smooth functioning of this arrangement. There were some inevitable hiccups and teething problems which had to be addressed. At one stage, I had to get the Chief Minister to even transfer the DGP of the State from his appointment because he had been creating hassles in the smooth functioning of the unified command.

We evolved a good organizational structure for the unified command in Assam. We wanted a civilian to chair the apex committee, which was called the Strategy Group. The Chief Minister declined to preside over this group for political reasons. We, therefore, gave that role to the Chief Secretary. I was keen that there should be a civilian at the head to project the right image and counter any allegation of imposing army rule. The senior army officer, the heads of police, paramilitary, intelligence agencies and some civil officials of the secretariat were members of this group.

My secretary, who was coordinating psychological initiatives under my directions, also attended the meetings of the Strategy Group. This group laid down the broad strategy for the conduct of operations. There were also two sub-groups: the Operations Group and the Intelligence Group. The Operations Group was headed by the senior army officer with heads of police, paramilitary and Intelligence agencies as its members. This group planned, coordinated and monitored the operations of all elements of the security forces. The Intelligence Group was chaired by the head of the State CID with the local heads of Central Intelligence agencies (RAW & IB) and Military Intelligence as members. This ensured coordinated intelligence functioning and intelligence assessments. Besides this organizational set-up, we also had district committees. The deputy commissioner, the army representative, normally a brigade commander, the SP and Intelligence officers operating in the district were members of this committee. Other local officials were co-opted to attend its meetings on as required basis. There were protocol hassles. The army maintained that a brigade commander had a higher status than a deputy commissioner and had reservations about the latter presiding over the district committees. We got over the difficulty by meetings being held alternately in the DC's office and at Brigade Headquarters and chaired alternately by the two.

The unified command set up by us, was highly successful and achieved very good results. The ULFA and other militant groups had their camps across the border in Bhutan. Our forces could not cross the border and strike their sanctuaries from which they carried out hit and run raids. The King of Bhutan was assuring us that he would in course of time eliminate the militant camps, if he failed to persuade them to quit. He was also wanting help in terms of funds, weapons and other facilities to be able to take on these camps. This went on for the nearly six years that I was governor in Assam. I kept pressing Delhi at the highest level to allow us to send forces to carry out strikes against these camps and even told the authorities that the King was leading us up the garden path. My recommendation was not being accepted by Delhi because of two reasons. First, we did not want to upset the King who had been a most friendly and trusted ally. Our relations with Bhutan had always been very cordial and Bhutan had always supported India on all issues in various international fora. In fact, we had problems in our relations with all our neighbouring countries except Bhutan. The second consideration which weighed heavily with Delhi was that they did not want to get embroiled in fighting militancy in Bhutan and open a new front. The fears on this account were unfounded. I was only advocating a strike in Bhutan with troops pulling out in a day or two, without remaining there for any length of time. A few months after I left Assam, the King ultimately undertook a highly successful military operation against the militant camps assisted by the Indian Army sealing the border in our territory to catch fleeing militants. In retrospect I realized that I was wrong and Delhi was right in turning down my recommendation. Similarly, I was also wrong in my assessment of the King's intentions. However, the fact remains that had we on our own acted or got the King to do so earlier, we could have saved the casualties which both security forces and civilians suffered at the hands of militants. There were some exasperating moments which used to upset me a lot. In this connection I would like to mention one such incident on the border with Bhutan.

This was an occasion when I felt that our forbearance crossed all limits. On the night of 26/27 October 2002 a few militants from Bhutan came across to Dadgiri village on our side very near to the border. Some Hindi speaking villagers were picked up from their houses and lined up against the wall on the border. Twenty-one of these helpless people were shot in cold blood and 10 injured. Barely 20 yards from this site was an entry gate into Bhutan with two searchlights on it. A Bhutan Police Sentry was supposed to be on guard at the gate. Another twenty yards from the gate was a Bhutan Police barrack, housing a platoon. On the fateful night, the sentry was not present on duty, the two searchlights were not functioning and the policemen in their barracks were asleep. Obviously, the policemen had either connived or were too scared to do anything. I decided to visit Dadgiri. The helipad was some 20 kilometers from the village and the track to that place went through a thick jungle in which militants were reported to be moving freely. The civil administration was against my visiting the village for security reasons. The army was not too happy either at my going there but I got them to take special measures to sanitise the track. I felt that my going to the village would be good for the morale of the local people. They were happy to see me there. I announced compensation for the victims, establishment of a police post near the village and other relief measures like water pumps and so on. This went down very well with the local people. I also walked across into Bhutan territory and asked the Bhutanese police to call their officer. Soon a superintendent of police and a subdivisional officer arrived. They were apologetic about what had happened. They assured me that they would not allow such a thing to happen again. I asked them to convey my personal regards to the King whom I had known for some time. Thirty years earlier I was commanding a division in Assam and the King, then about 18 years old had visited us. His 16-year old sister who was the finance minister of Bhutan had accompanied him. The King was fond of games, particularly football. We organized a football match between the army team and the Bhutan team of which the King was the captain. He was playing as the centre forward for his team. We ensured that the Bhutan team won and the King scored a few goals. This thrilled him. I had also met him at Delhi earlier. I wanted the local Bhutanese officials to know of my old association with the King so that it imposed a degree of caution among them. On my return to Guwahati I sent a detailed report of this incident to the Government of India recommending a joint Indo-Bhutan inquiry. Those found negligent of their duties in failing to prevent the massacre should be punished and suitable follow-up action taken. I do not know if New Delhi took up this matter with the Government of Bhutan but at the ground level no action was taken in the matter. I have highlighted this incident to underscore the difficulties we faced in dealing with militants holed up in Bhutan.

7

The second prong of our strategy was economic development. Insurgency thrives in economically backward regions with a large population of unemployed youth. Poor governance is another contributory factor. Assam had more than the normal share of both. We had to address these issues vigorously. Apart from ensuring availability of funds, their proper utilization had also to be ensured. A governor can do little about all this. That lies in the domain of the State Government. However, at the personal level I tried to help the government. The financial health of the State Government was not too good. It relied heavily on overdrafts and grants from the Centre. There were occasions when it faced acute crisis and funds were not available to even pay the salaries of government officials. I had known Yashwant Sinha for a long time. He was the Union Finance Minister. We had been family friends. At the request of the Chief Minister, I would exploit the old personal connection to get his support and bail out the State Government.

On one of my tours to Dhubri, I found some farmers using improvised shallow bamboo tube wells for cultivating their fields.

The water-table in the Brahmaputra Valley is high and shallow tube wells are quite effective. Plots of land with shallow tube wells had crops growing but those without, were lying fallow. Assam was dependent upon the monsoon for cultivation and used to have only one crop a year. Much of that crop got damaged due to the perennial floods every year. The Green Revolution had transformed the agriculture scenario in the rest of India. Assam had been left out of the orbit of this revolution. Up to 1947, Assam had been self-sufficient in rice, which is the staple food of the Assamese people. After 1947, with exploding population and a large influx of migrants from Bangladesh, it had become a rice deficit State. Seeing the success of improvised shallow tube wells, I thought a proper shallow tube well with water pump would produce better results. I proposed that we install one lakh shallow tube wells in Assam. Most people I spoke to felt that it was a hare-brained idea and not practicable. They pointed out that it would involve huge expenditure and the State Government was not in a position to provide any funds for it. They raised doubts about the availability of one lakh water pumps in the country in a short time-frame. They pointed out that the Assamese farmer was lazy and would not be able to take advantage of the scheme. The cultivators I had seen at Dhubri were Bangladeshi immigrants who are hard working. They were very sceptical about our ability to implement this grandiose scheme. I discussed this scheme with Chief Minister Prafulla Mohanta. He was supportive of the idea, provided the Government of India could provide the necessary funds. Chandra Mohan Patwari, the Agriculture Minister was enthusiastic about the scheme. He told me that in his previous tenure as minister, he had set up Farm Management Committees in rural areas, which functioned like cooperatives. These committees could be dovetailed into our scheme.

The total cost of one shallow tube well including boring, water pump and pipes came to about Rs. 22,000. We decided that instead of giving these pumps free to the farmers, we should make them stakeholders for the sake of better care and maintenance. Two-thirds of the amount should be provided by the Government of India as grant or soft loan and one-third should be the contribution of the cultivators through the Farm Management Committees. I discussed this project with Yashwant Sinha and K C Pant. The latter was Deputy Chairman of the Planning Commission. Both were receptive and agreed in principle to support the scheme. One-third each was to be provided by the Government of India as outright grant and as soft loan from NABARD for one lakh shallow tube wells. This worked out to about Rs. 150 crores. The remaining one-third would be the contribution of the farmers.

To convince the Finance Minister about the feasibility of this project I invited him to Guwahati and promised to show him a demonstration of the functioning of shallow tube wells. I chose a 1000 acre open land on Alaboi Plains on the outskirts of Guwahati. A small high ground in the middle provided a good viewpoint. I had twelve shallow tube wells at suitable intervals installed all around. At each site we earmarked some local farmers trained to operate the shallow tube wells, to interact with the visitors. At a given signal all the twelve shallow tube wells would start and it would look like mini fountains throwing up water. We had made elaborate arrangements for the demonstration in typical Army style. Alaboi Plains is associated with the military history of Assam. In 1671 during the one year long siege of Guwahati by the Mughal Army of Aurangzeb, the Ahom King of Assam insisted that his General, Lachit Borphukan should move out of his defensive fortress in the low hills surrounding Guwahati and engage the Mughal cavalry in battle on Alaboi Plains. Lachit was loath to do so because his small ponies were no match for the Turkish horses of the Mughals. At the insistence of the King, Lachit had to carry out his suicidal order. The inevitable happened. The Assamese suffered a disastrous defeat. Seveal thousands were killed. Lachit withdrew into his defences and later in a naval engagement won a decisive victory over the Mughal Army on the waters of the Brahmaputra in the battle of Saraighat. The Mughal forces retreated and withdrew from Assam. Through the shallow tube well demonstration on the same Alaboi Plains, I was now wanting to bring about an agricultural victory for Assam.

The day before I was to take Yashwant to see the demonstration, we had a very heavy premonsoon shower. The entire area of the demonstration site became very slushy and a quagmire of mud. Vehicles could not move to the viewpoint or the twelve shallow tube well sites. I mobilized army resources and had PSP (perforated steel plates) and duck boards laid to develop vehicle tracks. We went up to near the chosen site for the demonstration in cars on the tarmac road and thereafter travelled in 4×4 army jongas over the improvised tracks. I personally drove the jonga with Yashwant sitting by my side. This must have been the one and only occasion when a governor drove the Union finance minister in an army jonga. Yashwant was very impressed with the demonstration. He readily agreed to sanction the funds required for the project.

It was a Herculean task to implement the scheme of installing one lakh shallow tube wells all over the Brahmaputra Valley in one year. The dynamic Agriculture Minister went all out to complete the task. A team of dedicated officers assisted him to do so. I was personally monitoring the progress in carrying out this work. I would get weekly progress reports for each district. I also frequently toured the districts, often accompanied by the Agriculture Minister. On my visits to districts, I would not give previous notice of the shallow tube well site that I would be visiting. On arrival in the district I would tell the district authorities the site which I wanted to visit. This ensured that the local officials had to be prepared for my visit to all the sites in their district and could not get away with returns on paper without actual work on the ground. I was told that it was a common practice to send such false progress reports in different States, particularly in Bihar. Sometimes, I would even get independent checks on the ground carried out by army formations and units deployed in the area. All this ensured that the scheme was duly implemented on the ground.

After we completed installing one lakh shallow tube wells and they became operational, Assam from a rice deficit State became a rice surplus State. Production of paddy increased by 11.53 percent and the rabi crops by 6.93 percent. Annual income generated for an individual farmer varied from Rs 51,000 to Rs 1 lakh. This became a great success story. The Planning Commission wrote very favourably about it in its Annual Report. The Prime Minister spoke to me and complimented me for it. Officials from different States came to Assam to see the functioning of our shallow tube wells.

I would make it a point during my tours to visit villages with lush green paddy fields during the non-monsoon season, when previously the cultivable land used to remain fallow for lack of water for irrigation. These visits gave me great personal satisfaction and a great sense of achievement. Often when interacting with the villagers I would be told by the village elders that they had not seen a governor before nor had they seen crops growing in the fields during the non-monsoon period. Assam had now had its own Green Revolution. The world renowned agriculture scientist, Swaminathan who had been the Father of the Green Revolution in India, came on a visit to Assam. He was much impressed by what we had achieved. He gave us useful tips to improve the quality of rice being produced by us. He also invited me to his unique research centre and laboratory at Chennai. I found the visit most educative. We also sent some of our agriculture officers and farmers to this leading research centre in the world for training.

9

The third prong of my strategy was psychological initiatives designed to win the hearts and minds of the people. As per the standard practice for counter-insurgency operations, the army had a civic action programme to earn the goodwill of the people. This included a host of activities like holding medical camps, building roads, renovating schools and temples, developing play grounds, arranging vocational training for youth and so on. Some of the schemes evolved were innovative and were much appreciated. All this activity was part of what the army called Operation Samaritan. I got funds allocated for this operation increased substantially and its span of activities enlarged considerably. I often used to inaugurate some of these projects. However, I felt that this was not enough. I also felt that there was a need for me to identify myself with the people and touch their emotional chords. Such an approach had never before been tried out in counter-insurgency operations. I was not sure as to how far I would succeed. I had no example to guide me. Anyway, I fired my first salvos for this crusade by taking up issues which would touch the emotional chords of the people.

One of the first things I did on taking over as Governor was to give a new look to the Raj Bhavan. Apart from refurbishing the austere Raj Bhavan, I tried to give it an Assamese ambience. Two cannons used by the great Assamese military hero, Lachit Borphukan, in the battle of Saraighat, were taken from the museum, and placed at the gate of Raj Bhavan. A replica of his iron victory pillar in the museum was made and placed in the foyer of Raj Bhavan, and so was a large imaginary painting designed by me of his decisive victory at the famous battle of Saraighat. This painting became popular in Assam with its copy on display at various places. I also got local artists to produce a stunning large painting of Bihu dance which was greatly admired. The sitting room of the Raj Bhavan was decorated with this painting. The traditional "Horai" and "Jhapi" plus a whole lot of Assamese artifacts were prominently displayed. Proper livery was introduced for the Raj Bhavan staff. All this was done on a war footing. Within a month, the Raj Bhavan acquired a noticeably different look. Visitors were impressed by all this and were appreciative of my attempt to give an Assamese orientation to the residence of Assam's Head of State. This was only the beginning. A year or so later, I undertook a very ambitious venture adding a complete new wing to the Raj Bhavan making it one of the prettiest in the country. I will discuss its details later.

Soon after I took over as Governor of Assam, the Indian Council of Historical Research held a national seminar at Guwahati. I was invited to inaugurate this meet. I utilised the occasion to convey a message to the people of Assam that I felt strongly about the neglect of Assam. In my inaugural address, I stated that historians had neglected Assam but history had not done so. Our history text books talk about the Indus Valley, the Ganges Valley and Cauvery Valley civilizations but hardly make any reference to the Brahmaputra Valley civilization. They tell us about our great military heroes like Rana Pratap and Shivaji but make no mention of an equally great hero, Lachit Borphukan of Assam. I also had a dig at the separatists who claimed that the Assamese were a separate Nation. They argued that Assam had never been part of the Indian State nor was it ever ruled from Delhi, till the British occupied Assam after the treaty of Yankaboo in 1826. I pointed out that in the ancient period Kamrup (old name of Assam) was part of the Gupta Empire as inscribed in the Iron Pillar of Samudragupta at Allahabad. Bhaskarvarman the great ruler of Assam and a contemporary of Harshavardhan ruled over present Bangladesh, West Bengal and North Bihar. Hieun Tsang the Chinese traveller visited the capitals of both Harshavardhan and Bhaskarvarman. He referred to the latter as the Emperor of Eastern India. The two rulers had very cordial relations with each other. However, it is true that neither during the Sultanate nor the Mughal periods was Assam ruled from Delhi but that did not mean that Assam had ceased to be a part of India. It had always been part of the Indian civilization State. I added that whereas all regions of India from Kashmir to Kerala and NWFP to Bengal had succumbed to foreign invasions and had adopted Persian as their official language, Assam was one State that had repeatedly defeated invading forces. At the dawn of the Sultanate era, Bakhtiyar Khilji who had conquered Bihar and Bengal, and had destroyed the famous Nalanda University, was defeated by King Prithu at Kamrup at Konai Borso Sil near Guwahati. This was inscribed on stones at that site and corroborated by the account left by Minhas, the chronicler of Bakhtiyar Khilji, in *Tabakat-i-Nasiri*. Again at the height of Mughal imperial power, the nearly one lakh Army of Aurangzeb was decisively defeated by Lachit Borphukan at the battle of Saraighat at Guwahati. In the medieval period, Sanskrit remained the official language in the State unlike all other States which had adopted Persian. In this respect, Assam was more Indian than the rest of India. I announced that my ambition was to make the people of Assam proud of their past and the rest of India proud of Assam. I concluded my address with the salutation Joi Ai Assom, Jai Hind.

The former in Assamese means victory to Mother Assam. My address was widely reported in the Press and had a good impact on the intelligentsia of Assam. It was music to their ears.

There is a place called Vashista in Guwahati on a small stream in the midst of a large clump of trees. This place has the ambience of an Ashram. It is believed that Guru Vashista of the Ramayan had his Ashram there. I had it developed as a tourist spot. My wife and I proceeded on a pilgrimage to Dwarka. On arrival there, I first visited the temple of Rukmini, the consort of Lord Krishna. All over India, we have Radha Krishna temples but there is hardly any Rukmini temple anywhere. During my visit to the Rukmini Temple, I was asked a stage managed question by the Press, whether we would also be visiting the main temple of Lord Krishna. I replied that we would definitely go there but before doing so I had decided to first visit the Rukmini temple. Rukmini was from Sadiya in Assam and as Governor of Assam, I felt I must first pay obeisance at her temple before doing so at the temple of Lord Krishna. This was duly reported in the Assamese Press. My purpose behind developing Vashista in Guwahati and my pilgrimage to Dwarka, was to underscore the fact that from the dawn of history, Assam had been part of the Indian civilization. This was to counter the propaganda of the militants about Assamese being a separate Nation.

Militants and separatists projecting the concept "Swadhin Assam" were trying to re-read, reinterpret and recreate history to build their theory of Assamese being a saparate Nation amalgamated with British India through treachery and fraud. My effort was to rebut this and bring out that Assam had always been an inseparable part of India.

There are three highly revered icons of the Assamese people. They are Mahapurush Shrimant Shankardev, Veer Lachit Borphukan and Lokpriya Gopi Nath Bordoloi. Each excelled in his own sphere but little was known about them outside Assam. I decided to promote awareness about them in the whole country.

Shankardev was one of the great social and religious reformers of the fifteenth century during the Bhakti era in our country. Great religious reformers had emerged in different parts of the country like Chaitanya Mahaprabhu, Sant Tukaram, Kabir, Tulsidas and so on. They preached in the regional languages bringing religion closer to the masses. They translated Hindu scriptures from Sanskrit to the regional languages. Shankardev was unique in many ways.

A physically strong person who could swim across the mighty Brahmaputra even during floods; he lived up to the ripe old age of 115. He was a multifaceted genius. He is regarded as the father of Assamese literature. He organized drama shows which he directed and also acted in them. He composed lyrics and dances. He was also a great social reformer and was the only Hindu religious reformer of his time, who tried to break the shackles of the caste system. As a result of his legacy, today caste is not so important a factor in Assamese society. Unlike all other States in India where elections are fought on caste basis, caste is not of much consequence during elections in Assam. Shankardev established Sattras and Namghars, the former being a monastery and the latter a community hall open to people of all castes and creeds. Even today Sattras and Namghars dominate the Assam rural scene. He had been on long pilgrimages to distant parts of the country and showed his patriotic sentiments by often referring to India as Bharat Punyabhoomi. I tried to highlight these aspects of the Mahapursh on various occasions. I had a documentary film prepared on him which was televised on Doordarshan. I got the army to give a facelift to his Ashram at Madhupur where he spent his last days in the adjacent district of Cooch Behar in West Bengal. I also had a big painting of Shankardev put up in the Raj Bhavan Durbar Hall. This provided the backdrop for all important functions like the swearing-in of Governors, Chief Ministers and Chief Justices. At first, I had thought of having a statue of Shankardev prepared and installed in Raj Bhavan like the statue of Gautam Buddha in Ashoka Hall at Rashtrapati Bhavan but I discovered that his followers object to his statues being made but had no objection to his pictures being painted. The interest shown by me in the teachings of this patron saint of Assam was liked by the people of the State. I was greatly honoured when three years after I left Assam and was serving as Governor of Jammu and Kashmir, I was invited to inaugurate a seminar on Shankardev's philosophy at Delhi. Numerous Sattradhikars and intellectuals of Assam had come to Delhi for this function. The audience at the seminar looked like a mini-Assam in Delhi. The aim of the seminar was to propagate Shankardev's teachings all over the country. The people from Assam at that seminar were happy to find me amongst them and I, of course, was even happier to be with them.

Lachit Borphukan is the most popular military hero of Assam. A great military leader, he served his King most loyally. The Mughals had occupied Guwahati. The capital of Assam was then at

Sibsagar in Upper Assam. The King commissioned Lachit to expel the Mughals from Guwahati. He conducted a brilliant campaign liberating Guwahati and taking the Mughal Governor a prisoner in 1669. An iron victory pillar was put up at Guwahati to commemorate Lachit's victory. The inscription on the pillar recounted his exploit. This pillar is now in the museum at Guwahati. As mentioned earlier, I had a replica of this pillar installed in Raj Bhavan.

The following year Aurangzeb launched an invasion of Assam to avenge the defeat suffered by his Army at Guwahati. The invading forces comprised: cavalry, infantry, guns and a large flotilla of boats. Anticipating retaliatory action by Mughals with all their military might, Lachit organized an impregnable defence of Guwahati taking full advantage of the terrain. His cavalry based on Assamese ponies was no match in quality or in numbers to the Turkish Cavalry of the Mughals. I studied Lachit's deployment for the defence of Guwahati on the ground from the record of his dispositions. He used the ground skillfully to deny the Mughals their great advantage of an irresistible cavalry. The siege of Guwahati lasted for over a year. Several Mughal attempts to breach Lachit's defences were foiled. During the last phase, Lachit won a decisive naval victory in the battle of Saraighat in 1671 on the waters of the Brahmaputra. The Mughal Army was in full retreat. Guwahati was saved and Lower Assam, under occupation of the Mughals was liberated. It was by all standards a great and decisive victory. I studied Lachit's campaign in detail and wrote a booklet on his military leadership. I delivered a talk on Lachit at Guwahati University. Another talk on Lachit by me was arranged by some Assamese scholars at Delhi. The then Vice-President of India, Krishna Kant presided at the meeting. The meeting at Delhi was a big success with a large audience of Assamese people in Delhi attending the lecture. I had a documentary film prepared on Lachit which was televised on Doordarshan. As Chancellor of Guwahati University I introduced an annual Lachit Memorial Lecture at Guwahati University. I used to invite leading personalities of the country to deliver this lecture. The first lecture was delivered by Dr A P J Abdul Kalam. Lachit Borphukan Park with a water tank close to it was developed as a showpiece of the city. A replica of Lachit's victory pillar was placed in the park and a bronze plaque depicting the battle of Saraighat was prepared and attached to the pedestal of his equestrian statue. We started having a colourful function to celebrate Lachit Divas (birthday of Lachit) at the park every year. The Chief Minister and I followed by various dignitaries would place wreaths at the statue. A military guard of honour presented arms. This used to be followed by a public meeting and screening of the documentary film on Lachit. He had died soon after the battle of Saraighat. His grave at Sibsagar was in a state of neglect. We gave a facelift to that site and the track to it was macadamised. Besides, I arranged for his bronze statue to be installed at National Defence Academy Khadakvasla, Pune. The statue was unveiled by me and we instituted a Lachit Gold Medal for the best cadet in officer-like qualities, passing out from the Academy. I also gave a talk to the cadets at the Academy on Lachit's military leadership. The people of Assam were very appreciative of what I had done to project their popular hero at the national level. The ULFA complained that I had hijacked their hero !

Lokpriya Gopinath Bordoloi was the first Prime Minster of Assam before Independence. After Independence, this designation was changed to Chief Minster. A leading Congressman of the freedom struggle, he had led the independence movement in Assam. As the head of the government, he had made a great contribution to the administration and development of Assam after Independence. In 1946, the Cabinet Mission had come to India and presented its Grouping Plan. This catered for Hindu majority provinces to be in Group A and Muslim majority provinces in Group B, but United Bengal with its Muslim majority and Assam with its Hindu majority were placed in Group C. Provinces had the option to opt out of a Group after ten years. The Grouping Plan was accepted both by the Congress and the Muslim League. Bordoloi saw this as a stepping stone to the partition of India. He was very concerned about Assam which had been grouped with Bengal. The latter's population was ten times more than that of Assam. He feared that Assam would get swamped by Bengal in Group C and eventually become a part of East Pakistan. Nehru tried to persuade Bordoloi to accept the Grouping Plan for preserving the unity of India and to prevent Partition. He told Bordoloi that if the Grouping Plan was found unsatisfactory for Assam, it could opt out of it after ten years. Bordoloi was adamant. He said that there would be no Assam left after ten years. He raised a standard of revolt against the Congress High Command on this issue. Luckily for him, Mahatma Gandhi supported his stand. The Grouping Plan was shelved. The people of Assam hailed Bordoloi as their saviour. As a member of the Constituent Assembly and Chairman of the Committee dealing with the North East he drafted the Sixth Schedule which met the aspirations of the Christian tribals of the region. He became very popular among the tribal population of Assam. There was a fear that these tribals may opt out of India and along with the tribals of North Burma, and become a Crown Colony as envisaged in the Coupland Plan formulated by a British civil servant by that name. Bordoloi died in 1950. He had been an icon of the people of Assam but unfortunately Delhi had hardly done anything to recognize the great contribution he had made in the service of the Nation. There was only a few-hundred-yards-long bye-road in Chanakyapuri at New Delhi named after him. I may mention my maternal grandfather's association with Bordoloi at the Gaya Congress in 1920 before I was born. My grandfather was the Chairman of the reception committee of that famous conference and my mother had commanded the guard of honour of the Girl Volunteers at that conference. In 1945, when I was posted to Assam as a young army officer, my grandfather had suggested that I meet Bordoloi but realizing that it would be imprudent for an army officer to do so, he changed his mind and told me not to make any attempt to meet him. On arrival at Guwahati airport as Governor of Assam in 1997, I remembered Bordoloi and decided that one of my first acts would be to get the airport named after that great man. I discussed the matter with the State Government and they were enthusiastic about the idea. The bureaucracy raised hurdles but I managed to persuade the Minister of Civil Aviation to accept the proposal. It took nearly a year to get the sanction of the Central Cabinet. The Borjhar Airpot at Guwahati was renamed Lokpriya Gopinath Bordoloi Airport. On seeing this announcement in the newspapers his widow, Surabala Bordoloi, then in her nineties, wrote a charming letter to me. I was thrilled to receive this letter which I reproduce below:-

Surabala Bordoloi

Gopinath Bhavan
Ulubari Guwahati
1 Sep. 98

My dear Sinhaji,

The renaming of Borjhar Airport has been the subject of much discussion over the years with successive governments making unfulfilled promises.

It was always my dream to have the airport named after my late husband, Lokapriya Gopinath Bordoloi. Now this has become a reality. This is solely due to your untiring and sincere efforts in getting the approval of the Central Government for renaming of the airport. It is likely that without your presence here, and as Governor of Assam, the matter would have still been between the covers of a file.

I, on behalf of my family and all the patriotic people of Assam, offer my sincere thanks and gratitude to you in your laudable efforts. We shall always remain indebted to you, and remember you with love and kindness.

Please accept my sincere and kind regards.

Thanking you once again,

I am,

Very truly yours,

Sd/- Surabala Bordoloi

The Honourable
Lt Gen (Retd) S K Sinha
Governor of Assam
Raj Bhavan
Guwahati

A function was held at Guwahati airport for naming the airport after Bordoloi. We had a marble statue of Bordoloi installed at the airport which I unveiled. In my speech, I mentioned some anecdotes from the life of Bordoloi. He had studied at Scottish Church College Kolkata in the early years of the twentieth century. My paternal grandfather had also studied in that college and was a few years senior to him. I had learnt from my grandfather how the students at that college had hailed Japan's stunning victory over Czarist Russia in 1905. This victory of an Asian country over a mighty European power had inspired students of his generation and many joined the independence movement. Mrs Bordoloi was also invited for the function and sat on the dais with me. She was very happy to find that I had studied the life of her husband and had recounted some of his achievements in my speech at that function. On my part I was much struck by her charm and grace. She became a mother figure to me. I was invited by the Assamese society in Kolkata to speak on Bordoloi. I was delighted to accept the invitation. We also got a documentary film made on Bordoloi which was telecast by Doordarshan.

I decided to take up the case for a posthumous award of Bharat Ratna to Gopinath Bordoloi. It was an uphill task to get this approved. There had been some controversy about the award of Bharat Ratna after it had been posthumously conferred upon M G Ramchandran. A committee under the then Vice-President K R Narayanan had been constituted to examine the policy for giving these awards. It had recommended that Bharat Ratna should nct be awarded to anyone posthumously. Narayanan was now the President of India. I spoke to Prime Minister Inder Gujral and tried to convince him that this award to Bordoloi, as proposed by me, was in national interest. He saw my point but said that in view of the recommendation of the Narayanan Committee it would be difficult to get the President to approve my proposal, contrary to the recommendation of that Committee. However, he told me to speak to President Narayanan and find out his reaction. He also added that the quota for this award for 1999 had already been filled and no additional name could be considered for that year. I met the President and pleaded the case before him. On my stressing the importance of the proposal for winning over the people of Assam, I was happy to find that he was prepared to have an open mind on the issue. He wanted me to discuss this matter with the new Prime Minister. Vajpayee had now taken over as Prime Minister. I spoke to him. He pointed out his difficulties. Apparently his coalition partners were also lobbying for posthumous Bharat Ratnas for their erstwhile leaders. Naveen Patnaik, Chief Minister of Orissa, was reported to be wanting a posthumous Bharat Ratna for his father, Biju Patnaik. Similarly, Chandra Babu Naidu wanted this award to be given posthumously to his father-in-law, N.T. Rama Rao. The bureaucracy was totally opposed to a posthumous Bharat Ratna being given to anyone as they felt that it would open a Pandora's box. They even told the Prime Minister that I had only a one-point agenda for Assam and that was a Bharat Ratna to Gopinath Bordoloi. Undeterred I kept persisting with Vajpayee. I said I had no personal or family interest in making the recommendation. I was doing so in national interest as I was convinced that it would have a tremendous impact in Assam. Ultimately, Vajpayee saw my point and assured me that he would take up the matter. After some time, one day he very kindly rang me up to say that a posthumous award of Bharat Ratna to Bordoloi had been approved. I immediately informed my Chief Minister Prafulla Mohanta and he conveyed this information to Mrs Bordoloi. Within hours Mrs Bordoloi with her two sons, Robin and Bolin came to Raj Bhavan to personally thank me. The 92 year old lady in a wheelchair had tears in her eyes. I was overwhelmed and spontaneously touched her feet seeking her blessings. My wife followed suit. It was an emotional meeting and we all had sweets to celebrate the occasion. The following day, all the newspapers in Assam, carried the news of Bordoloi being awarded the Bharat Ratna prominently on their front pages. It had an electrifying effect among the people of Assam. Their feeling that New Delhi had been neglecting Assam and discriminating against the State was duly countered. I now proposed that a life size bronze statue of Bordoloi be installed in the Lok Sabha at Delhi. This was readily agreed to. A 11 foot-high bronze statue of Bordoloi was installed in the Lok Sabha and it was unveiled by Vajpayee. I attended this function along with members of the Bordoloi family.

My efforts to project the three great icons of Assam, Mahapurush Shrimant Shankardev, Veer Lachit Borphukan and Lokpriya Gopinath Bordoloi, as our national heroes, had certainly borne fruit. This touched the emotional chords of the people of Assam and endeared me to them. I had done all this not for any personal reason to build any constituency for myself. I had no political ambitions and there was no question of my seeking any electoral gains. I had done so because of my deep attachment for the people of Assam and also because I strongly felt that it was in our national interest to get the alienated people of Assam into the national mainstream. However, all this was only the icing on the cake. The baking of the cake was achieved by my taking up the burning issue of the unabated influx of illegal migrants from Bangladesh. This had been the main cause for the outbreak of militancy in Assam and I was determined to take up this matter with all my energy and dedication. The fact that in doing so, I may be disturbing a hornet's nest did not deter me from addressing this problem, which posed a threat not only to the identity of the people of Assam but also to our national security.

10

The large influx of population from Bangladesh into Assam was the root issue behind the students' movement in Assam and concurrently the eruption of ULFA militancy in the State. The two worked in tandem. Since this was the core issue behind insurgency in the State, I carried out an indepth study of the problem. I also toured the entire length of the Assam-Bangladesh border both by road and speed boat on the waters of the Brahmaputra. I interacted with the people on the border and was alarmed to see the large scale change in the dress of the people in these areas, revealing their Bangladesh identity. I also met various officials and public leaders in Guwahati to get their views. All this took me about a year. I decided to send a report to the President of India on this subject. The Union Home Minister, Shri Indrajeet Gupta had told the Parliament on 6 May 1997 that there were 10 million illegal Bangladeshi immigrants in India. Intelligence agencies estimated that some 4 million of these were in Assam.

Illegal migration from Bangladesh into Assam had to be viewed against the backdrop of past history, present realities and future dangers. Migration into Assam had been taking place from the dawn of history. However large scale movements started with the utilization of cultivable land for the tea industry. It was now necessary to clear forests to grow food. Mr S C Mullan ICS, Census Superintendent of Assam in 1931 wrote, "Probably the most important event in the Province during the last 25 years — an event, moreover, which seems likely to alter permanently the whole future of Assam and to destroy more surely than did the Burmese invaders of 1829, the whole structure of Assamese culture and civilization — has been the invasion of a vast horde of land-hungry Bengali immigrants mostly Muslims from the districts of East Bengal and in particular Mymensingh... . The only thing I can compare is the mass movement of a large body of ants...it is sad but by no means improbable that in another thirty years, Sibsagar district will be the only part of Assam in which an Assamese will find himself at home." In the Forties, the Muslim League had come up with its demand for partition. The Muslim League Ministry of Sir Sadaulla Khan in Assam started making concerted efforts to encourage the migration of Bengali Muslims on the plea of promoting the "Grow More Food" campaign of the Government of India during the Second World War. Lord Wavell, the then Viceroy, in his book "Viceroy's Journal", wrote that Sir Mohammad Sadaulla's Ministry was trying "to increase the immigration into the uncultivable Government lands under the slogan of "Grow More Food" but what they are really after, is "Grow More Muslims."

After Partition the large scale movement of population from erstwhile East Pakistan acquired an international dimension. Initially, it was a refugee movement of mostly Bengali Hindus who had got uprooted from their homes in East Pakistan. There was a long history of Bengali-Assamese differences. When Assam was incorporated by the British in their Empire, it was initially made a part of Bengal Presidency. Bengalis had taken to English education much earlier. Along with British rule came an army of Bengali officials at lower levels of the administration. Bengalis also dominated the legal, medical, and teaching professions in Assam. Bengali was made the medium of instruction replacing Assamese language. The Assamese agitated against this. In 1884 Assam was detached from Bengal and the Assamese language became the medium of instruction in schools. However, Bengali domination in lower levels of bureaucracy as well as various professions continued. Against this backdrop, the large scale influx of Bengali refugees from East Pakistan caused tension in Assam. This led to language riots in Assam, as a result of which the influx of Hindu refugees ceased. They continued to seek shelter in other States of India particularly in West Bengal. The Hindu population of East Pakistan had been 27% in 1947. It had now come down to less than 10%. The influx of Bengali Muslims from East Pakistan continued. They were mostly farmers and labourers. The Congress Party in Assam and the Communist Party in Bengal were encouraging their migration as part of their vote bank politics. In the late Sixties, B K Nehru, the then Governor of Assam and B.P. Chaliha, the then Chief Minister of Assam were much concerned about this influx. B K Nehru was a cousin of Indira Gandhi, the then Prime Minister and Chaliha a veteran Congressman of the old generation. Their credentials could not be questioned. They took up this issue with the Congress High Command at Delhi which was then dominated by three Assamese — Dev Kant Barua, of India is Indira and Indira is India fame, Fakhruddin Ali Ahmed and Moinul Haque Chowdhary. The latter had been Private Secretary to Jinnah before 1947. This coterie did not allow any effective measures to be taken against illegal migrants. Their strategy for ensuring Congress victory in perpetuity in Assam was to mobilize the support of Ali and Coolie. Ali stood for Bangladeshi immigrants and Coolie for tea labour, who were all non-Assamese. B K Nehru in his autobiography, "Nice Guys Finish Second", wrote on illegal migration from East Bengal, "Efforts were made from time to time by the Government of Assam to evict these illegal migrants but they were always frustrated by Delhi. One such effort was made during my time with my full support. What happened was that Messrs Fakhruddin Ali Ahmed (later President of India), Moinul Haque Choudhary (later Industry Minister of India) and DK Barua (later President of the Congress Party) raised a hue and cry at Delhi saying that atrocities were being committed on the Indian Muslims. The cry was heard and acted upon. The East Bengal Muslim was the main vote bank of the Congress Party in Assam. Chaliha coming as he did from the days of the freedom struggle was governed by the values of that time. He placed the national interests above those of the party. But the High Command thought otherwise. Chaliha was ordered to stop the nonsense forthwith. This was of course welcomed by the Government of Pakistan. It had always pretended as Bangladesh does now that there was never any migration from its territory to Assam. In this statement there is as much truth as there is in Pakistani denial about its direct involvement with terrorism in Kashmir."

In 1993 I had been to Kolkata, when I happened to meet the then Eastern Army Commander, Lt Gen Jameel Mahmood. I had known him when I was Western Army Commander in the early Eighties during my Army career. At that time he was one of my brigade commanders. He told me that he was very concerned about the unabated influx of illegal migrants from Bangladesh into Assam and Bengal. As a nationalist, he felt it was his duty to apprise Hiteshwar Saikia and Jyoti Basu, the then chief ministers of the two states, of the danger posed by this influx. He had told them if this was not stopped, the boundaries of India would have to be redrawn in the North East. Neither had taken any notice of what he had told them. I told him that I much appreciated the action taken by him but as a private individual there was nothing that I could do about it. Little could I then imagine that one day I would be Governor of Assam and would have to address this problem. Unfortunately, not long after, Jameel died in a helicopter crash. During my research I found that Jameel had taken up this issue at the Civil and Military conference at his headquarters on 3 March 1993 and had also sent a long paper on "Illegal Migration" to Army Headquarters. I quote some extracts from this paper entitled, "Influx of Illegal Migrants from Bangladesh into India" : "The ethnic Assamese population is already reduced to 47 percent. Out of 24 districts of Assam, 16 districts are already affected. The Congress (I) Governments in Assam and Tripura and CPM in West Bengal shield the illegal immigrants due to their need for vote banks. It is not far-fetched to visualize a Kashmir-like situation arising in another five to ten years, wherein Bangladesh egged on by Pakistan, may fight a proxy war and cause a serious national security problem."

The Illegal Migration (Determination by Tribunal) Act 1983, commonly referred to as IMDT ACT, was passed by the Congress Government at the Centre, ostensibly to detect and deport illegal migrants from Bangladesh into Assam. In reality it was a clever ploy to promote illegal migration in pursuit of the ruling party's unabashed pursuit of vote bank politics. Abolition of this Act was one of the main demands of the Assamese people who had been agitating against the unabated influx of Bangladeshis into Assam. The provisions of this Act, to say the least, were bizarre. This Act applied to Bangladeshi immigrants in Assam only and not in the neighbouring State of West Bengal or any other State in the country. Migration into all States other than Assam was governed by the Foreigners Act. There were many aspects of the IMDT Act which made the process of detection and deportation infructuous. Whereas in the case of Foreigners Act the onus of proof was on the individual to establish his claim for Indian citizenship, in the case of the IMDT Act 1983, it was for the State to establish that a particular individual was not an Indian citizen. The procedure laid down for invoking the IMDT Act was that two individuals living within a radius of 3 kilometers of a suspected illegal migrant's place of residence, should file a complaint at a police station with a deposit of Rs. 25. Later the stipulation regarding the distance of three kilometers was relaxed and anyone residing in the area of the police station concerned could lodge this complaint and the deposit amount was reduced from Rs. 25 to Rs. 10. The illegal migrants generally would reside in areas dominated by people of the same origin. A person complaining against an illegal migrant ran the risk of retaliation by them. The police had no authority to arrest or search an illegal migrant. It could investigate and prepare the case for a decision by a district tribunal. Normally, once the police started investigation, the suspected illegal migrant would go underground and would not be traceable. Even if this did not happen and the police could obtain conviction by the district tribunal, the convicted person had to be given 30 days to appeal to a State tribunal. During this period there was no provision for him to be arrested. He thus had ample opportunity again to go underground and become untraceable. No wonder that during the 15 years that the IMDT Act had been in operation, when millions of illegal migrants were reported to have come into Assam, only 9,599 illegal migrants had been identified and out of these only 1454 could be deported. For all one knows, even among these 1454, many may have re-entered Assam. And for this exercise in futility, the Government of India had set up a huge machinery of a State tribunal and 16 district tribunals and a force of 4000 border policemen.

Various census statistics confirmed the large presence of Bangladeshi illegal migrants in Assam. Forty of the 123 Assembly constituencies seats were now dominated by these illegal migrants. On 10 April 1992, Hiteshwar Saikia, the then Chief Minister of Assam had declared in the State Assembly that there were 3 million illegal Bangladeshi migrants in Assam. The MLAs supporting these illegal migrants threatened to withdraw their support from the Saikia Government. This would have led to the fall of the Government. Thus, two days later Saikia had no compunction in issuing a statement that there were no illegal Bangladeshi immigrants in Assam. In four out of 23 districts of Assam, these immigrants were now in a majority and in two other districts they constituted nearly 50 percent of the population and soon would become a majority. Three of these districts, Dhubri, Goalpara and Barpeta in Lower Assam were close to the strategic narrow Siliguri corridor connecting the North East land mass with the rest of the country. With the growth of international Islamic fundamentalism and Bangladesh declaring itself an Islamic Republic, the threat to our narrow land link to North East had become great. This was particularly so in the light of assertions by responsible Pakistani and Bangladeshi leaders at different points of time. Zulfikar Ali Bhutto in his book "Myths of Independence" wrote, "It would be wrong to think that Kashmir is the only dispute that divides India and Pakistan, though undoubtedly the most significant. One at least is nearly as important as that of Kashmir are some districts of India adjacent to East Pakistan. To these, Pakistan has very good claims." Even a pro-India leader like Sheikh Mujibur Rahman in his book *Eastern Pakistan: Its Population and Economics* observed, "Because Eastern Pakistan must have sufficient land for its expansion and because Assam has abundant forests and natural resources, coal, petroleum etc, Eastern Pakistan must include Assam to be financially and economically strong." Leading intellectuals in Bangladesh had been making out a case for "lebensraum" (living space) for their country. No matter how friendly our relations with Bangladesh, we can ill-afford to ignore its demographic expansion into Assam and the threat that this poses not only to the identity of the Assamese people but also to the security of the Nation.

I was aghast to find that various measures to check infiltration were either non-existent or woefully inadequate. It was decided to have border fencing in Assam in 1985 even after 13 years this was not complete. In 1998 I found that fencing on the border was still not complete. Compared to Punjab, where fencing was completed in 2 years, the quality of fencing in Assam was very poor. Observation towers and lighting had been provided in Punjab In Assam, Observation Towers were confined to a small sector in Dhubri with no towers elsewhere nor lighting in any part of the border. There was no fencing on Indo-Bangladesh border in the neighbouring States of West Bengal, Meghalya, Mizoram and Tripura. Further, a large portion of Assam/Bangladesh border is riverine patrolled by speedboats and country boats with outboard motors. The deployment of BSF on the ground in Assam was much thinner than in Punjab.

After research and extensive tours of the border, I submitted a 42- page printed special report to the President of India. I personally presented this report to him on 8 November 1998 during his visit to Guwahati with the following covering letter:-

> "Large scale illegal migration from East Pakistan/Bangladesh over several decades has been altering the demographic complexion of this State. It poses a grave threat both to the identity of the Assamese people and to our national security. Successive governments at the Centre and in the State have not adequately met this challenge.
>
> As Governor of Assam, I feel it is my bounden duty to the Nation and the State I have sworn to serve, to place before you this report on the dangers arising from the continuing silent demographic invasion. I have also formulated my recommendations for dealing with this issue of vital importance. I earnestly hope that this matter will receive due consideration and suitable action taken to avert the great danger that has been building up for some time."

I sent copies of my report to the Prime Minister, the Home Minister and the Chief Minister of Assam. I had several discussions with Prafulla Kumar Mohanta, the then Chief Minister of the State. He fully agreed with my views. After all he had led the students' movement in Assam and their main demand was to put a stop to this illegal migration. However, he did not want to openly support me because he was heading a coalition government and his party had only a wafer thin majority. Abdul Mujib Majumdar who had drafted the IMDT Act when he was a member of the Congress Party was now with another party, which was part of Mohanta's coalition government. He was a minister in the cabinet and bitterly opposed the repeal of the IMDT Act. My report to the President got leaked to the Press. Every newspaper in Assam, brought out the entire report in full in a few parts. It took the Assamese people by storm and I started being referred to as "Our Man in Raj Bhavan". No one in any official position had taken a stand supporting their point of view in such a manner. My stock rose sky high among the Assamese people.

I recommended a host of measures like effective border fencing, floating border police posts in the riverine sector, strengthening BSF deployment, photo identity cards for our nationals in border districts, updating of the national register for citizens and above all the repeal of the IMDT Act. The latter was the most sensitive part of the report. The Bangladeshi immigrants and the many among minority community, bitterly opposed my recommendation for repealing the IMDT Act. The Congress party which then constituted the main opposition joined the chorus denouncing me for the sake of its vote bank. My effigy was burnt at a few places by some Bangladeshi immigrants and their sympathisers.

Congress MPs and MLAs from Assam petitioned the President of India, asking for my recall. They were up in arms against me for raising an old issue and thereby arousing communal passions. They even questioned the propriety of my sending a report to the President. Apparently, they did not know that a governor is required to send a monthly report to the President with a copy to the Prime Minister on the affairs of the State. There was nothing wrong in my sending a special report to the President. However, privately many Congress leaders including legislators met me and told me that they were fully with me on the recommendation that I had made regarding the repeal of the IMDT Act but for political reasons they had to protest against my report. Besides the Congress, the Assam Muslim Students Union and the United Minority Front also appealed to the President to recall me from Assam. The Chief Minister Prafulla Kumar Mohanta fully supported my views but chose not to issue any statement. However, a cabinet minister in the State Government, Abdul Mujib Majumdar reacted strongly. He dubbed me a BJP agent. I ignored the unbecoming language used by my minister against his Head of the State. Despite all the sound and fury of some people, the vast majority of the people of the State were enthusiastically supportive of my report.

I was flooded with letters from various people in the State congratulating me on the stand taken by me. It was most encouraging to find that some leading Assamese Muslims also supported my stand. One of the most distinguished academics of Assam, Professor Ashraf Ali, who had been the Principal of Assam's most prestigious educational institution, the Cotton College, and who had retired as the Director, Public Instruction of the State, many years ago, wrote to me. I reproduce his letter:

To

The Most Respected Lt Gen (Retd) Sri S K Sinha,
Governor of Assam, Raj Bhavan, Guwahati.

Respected Sir,

In my lifetime I had the opportunity to come in personal contact with many governors from Syed Fazal Ali, late L P Singh, late B K Nehru, Sri Durga Das, Sri Loknath Misra and a few others. I have never seen an active governor (of Assam) like you. I am happy that true to your constitutional responsibility and obligation, you move about to all parts of Assam and assess the general situation as well as problems faced by the downtrodden people of Assam.

It is a fact that none but you have the courage, initiative and dash to bring Sri Sri Sankar Dev as well as our beloved political leader late Gopi Nath Bordoloi to the limelight and making Borjhar an international airport after the name of G.N. Bordoloi. Lachit Borphukan Park at Jalukbari is your other achievement. Whatever politicians say, kindly tackle the problem of infiltration and protect Assam (nay India) from Pak and Bangladeshi intruders.

With deepest regards.

Yours Sincerely,

Ashraf

The above letter showed that right thinking Muslims in Assam recognised the threat posed by illegal migrants and had no communal bias unlike Congress politicians guided by vote bank considerations and also unlike the communal elements within the community. It would not be out of place to quote the views of another very eminent educationist Dr H K Barpujari, the leading historian of Assam and former President of Indian Council of Historical Research: "The Governor has rendered a yeoman service to the State by forcefully and boldly projecting the problem..... No person holding a high office has rendered such service to the State after Gopinath Bordoloi, the first Chief Minister of Assam who saved the State from being merged into erstwhile East Pakistan." The Assam Sahitya Sabha congratulated me, `for displaying deep understanding of not only the foreigner's problem but also the Assamese psyche'. Dr. Nagendra Saikia, the President of Assam Sahitya Sabha wrote that nobody of my stature had tried to gauge the gravity of the problem of the Assamese mind so realistically. The demands, protests and the fears of the Assamese people have got the most powerful projection in his report. He congratulated me on my bold and realistic step to try to save Assam and thereby the sovereignty of India.

Besides the above laudatory comments there were various meetings held in Assam of eminent citizens, bar councils, academicians and political parties, acclaiming my report and the stand taken by me. Several letters to the Editors in newspapers appeared in support of me. Some of the editorials in newspapers were equally laudatory as follows:

North East Times

"The pertinent point is that—who then is a true Assamese. Lt Gen (Retd) S K Sinha is a true Assamese for he has the genuine interest of the Assamese people at heart. While his report may not save the future generations, it will surely be remembered as a historical document compiled by a man who really tried to do his job very well which is a rare phenomenon in these times. Kudos to you Governor, and thank you."

Assam Tribune

"The Assam Governor Lt Gen (Retd) S K Sinha has done a yeoman service to Assam in particular and the Nation in general by apprising President K R Narayanan of the grave problem created by continuous influx of immigrants........ Given this background about the influx which has increased from year to year, Governor Sinha's communication to the President is timely and a warning to all concerned — the Centre, the Assam Government and political parties..... Time is running out and it is for all concerned who sincerely desire to preserve Assam's integrity against illegal migration of people from the neighbouring country to heed the Governor's warning after he has realistically assessed the alarming problem."

The Sentinel

"Given the political implications of the continuing large scale infiltration of Bangladeshi nationals into Assam, Governor Sinha could have either turned a blind eye on the problem (as his predecessors had chosen to do) or undertake an in-depth study of the problem and, being alarmed at the gravity of the present situation, prepare a well researched memorandum on the subject for the President of India — as he chose to do..... Coming to the memorandum itself, one must hail it as one of the most well researched albeit concise works on the subject in recent times.........the marshalling of known facts and the analysis provided by him makes the document a collector's item."

Dainik Asom

"The Assam Governor has done a commendable service to Assam by apprising the President about the present

> situation of the influx of foreigners into Assam. We should be proud of the fact that someone amidst us is concerned about this grave situation. Although a non-Assamese, the Governor is concerned about the problem faced by the Assamese people."
>
> ***Ajir Batori***
>
> "Every patriotic and concerned Assamese individual is supporting the Governor's decision and hopes that the Governor would lead us in the last battle of Saraighat."

When I submitted my report to the President, the United Front Government led by I K Gujral was in power at the Centre. Soon thereafter the NDA Government led by Atal Behari Vajpayee came to power. The BJP was fully supportive of my recommendation to repeal the IMDT Act. In fact this had been one of their demands for a long time. The repeal of this Act was now included in the President's Address to the Parliament. I discussed this matter with L K Advani who was the Home Minister. He told me that the Government was keen to repeal the IMDT Act but it did not have the required majority to get the Bill passed in the Rajya Sabha. He was toying with the idea of having this done through an ordinance but this did not work out. Possibly, BJP could not carry its allies in NDA with it on this issue.

A Public Interest Litigation (PIL) was filed by All Assam Students Union in the Supreme Court. The State Government was asked to file an affidavit. In consultation with the Chief Minister I had the Advocate General file an affidavit recommending repeal of the IMDT Act. After some years in 2006 when I had left Assam, the Supreme Court gave the welcome verdict striking down this Act. The judgment quoted extensively from my report to the President. This was a vindication of the stand taken by me. I was flooded with letters, telegrams and telephone calls from Assam thanking me for the contribution that I had made in this happy outcome. However, their jubilation was short-lived. The Congress party was now in power both at the Centre and in the State. They found a way to get things back to square one. Although the IMDT Act had gone they had amendments introduced in the Foreigners Act with a special provision in the case of Assam for Bangladeshi immigrants. There is no logic in having a separate set of rules for these foreigners in Assam from what obtains in other States of the country. This brought back the IMDT Act from the back door.

B K Nehru's observation about the party's interest being paramount and above the nation's interest was proved correct.

11

During my briefing in Delhi, in late August 1997, prior to my taking over as Governor of Assam, I came to know that a corruption case was being investigated by the CBI against Chief Minister Prafulla Kumar Mohanta. I did not enquire about the details of the case and decided to deal with it on its merits, when it came to me. A 300-page report along with draft charge sheet, seeking my sanction to prosecute the Chief Minister was presented to me by the CBI on 30 December 1997.

I studied the case made out by the CBI in great detail and within five days wrote back to them asking for 13 additional documents and seeking clarification on 24 specific points. The CBI took some two weeks to send me the required answers. In the meanwhile, there was a tirade in some sections of the Press against me for delay in according sanction to prosecute the Chief Minister. I realized that if I accorded sanction as sought by the CBI, the Chief Minister would be required to resign and this could lead to political instability in the State. Considering that the State was in the throes of an ongoing insurgency, it was in our national interest to avoid political instability in the State. Apart from the Congress Party, which was in the Opposition in the State clamouring for immediate action against the Chief Minister, there were people within his party, including some cabinet ministers who were keen on P K Mohanta being made to quit so that they could replace him as Chief Minister. Bhrigu Phuken who had been one of Mohanta's closest colleagues in the party and had been the Home Minister in the previous Mohanta government and now had broken up with him, came to see me a few times. He was obviously trying to cultivate me so that the way could be cleared for his becoming the Chief Minister. There was much speculation in the Press. It was being said that the CBI was the premier investigating agency in the country and it had recommended the prosecution of the Chief Minister. I should immediately give the required sanction. A Press correspondent accosted me in Delhi and enquired as to why I was delaying matters. I told him that as Governor I was not a rubber stamp of the CBI. I had to study the facts of the case presented to me and satisfy myself that a *prima facie* case had been made out against the Chief Minister, before according sanction for his prosecution. Within five days, I had completed the initial examination of the voluminous report of the CBI and had sought certain clarifications. I was told that no governor had ever rejected the recommendation of the country's premier investigating agency. My reply was that I would be guided strictly by the provisions of the law and not by past precedents. In any case the three instances of corruption cases against chief ministers known to me of Antulay, Jayalalitha and Lalu Prasad Yadav, in which CBI had recommended prosecution, were kept by respective governors for months and years before according sanction. I had no intention of following their example. I assured the Press that I would be taking a decision in the case of Prafulla Kumar Mohanta within a fortnight or so.

I was disappointed at the quality of investigation by the CBI. The presentation of the report was also sub-standard. The CBI sent me the documents and clarifications I had asked for except in regard to two documents. I came to know that there was a divided opinion within the CBI about the culpability of the Chief Minister. The initial investigating officer had concluded that a criminal case could not be made out and the Additional Solicitor General's legal opinion conformed to that investigation report. I wanted to examine these documents but the CBI declined to make them available saying that the final investigation report had already been made available to me and there was no need for the preliminary report being sent to me. As for the views of the Additional Solicitor General, they were only legal advice during the course of the investigation and not a legal opinion as such.

I could not seek any legal opinion in Assam with regard to the case involving the Chief Minister. In normal circumstances, I could have sought the legal opinion of the Advocate General of the State. However, since he was an appointee of the ruling party liable to be changed with the change of the party in power, I felt that his opinion may not be unbiased. I decided to seek the advice of Ashok Desai, the Attorney General of India. I went to Delhi and sought a meeting with him. He was very nice but expressed his inability to give me legal advice in the case. He said that at a later stage the case could come up in Supreme Court and he would be called upon to give his views. Any advice given by him at this stage may embarrass him in dealing with the case subsequently. I saw his point of view. However, he was good enough to give me some half a dozen case rulings of the Supreme Court and High Courts, which laid down categorically that the sanctioning authority had to fully satisfy itself that a *prima facie* case had been made against an alleged accused, before according sanction for prosecution. Although these rulings were relevant and helpful, they did not fully meet my requirement. I wanted to be assured that my thinking in the case of Prafulla Mohanta was on the right lines. I decided to take the legal opinion of some legal luminaries. I had known Justice H R Khanna, a retired Judge of the Supreme Court. We had worked together in the Hindustani Andolan, a NGO for promoting clean politics. I also met Justice JS Verma who had just retired as Chief Justice of India. He had been a student at PC Banerjee Hostel in Allahabad University with my younger brother. I had once met him at Allahabad in those days. I decided to seek their opinion informally. I discussed the case with them and gave them a synopsis together with my tentative conclusions. They were good enough to go through the papers and when I met them again after a couple of days, they told me that they agreed with my views. Justice Verma even said that if he had been in my position, he would not have sanctioned the prosecution on the basis of the evidence gathered by the CBI. Their views gave me a lot of strength in dealing with this high profile case which could involve me in a major controversy. Matters were complicated by the fact that the CBI had submitted a charge sheet for the prosecution of Prafulla Mohanta, the then serving Chief Minister and Shri Nakul Das, former minister for animal husbandry and veterinary. Both were alleged to be involved in what had come to be known as LoC (Letter of Credit) scam. The two were from different political parties. Mohanta was from Assam Gan Parishad and Das from the Congress Party. Mohanta's involvement was during the period that he was Chief Minister in his first term and had continued while he was an Opposition MLA. In the case of Nakul Das, he had been involved when he was minister in the Congress government after Mohanta's first term as Chief Minister. The main accused in both cases was one RP Borah but there was no connection between the cases of Mohanta and Nakul Das. In the case of the latter, evidence, including documentary and circumstantial, was available to establish his culpability but in the case of Mohanta, such evidence was lacking. I was inclined to sanction the prosecution of Nakul Das but withhold it in the case of Mohanta because I was convinced that a *prima facie* case had not been made out against him. I realized that my sanctioning prosecution against one and not against the other would be misinterpreted and I could be accused of bias. I decided that I would act according to my conscience and be prepared to face any consequence. I had to take a hard decision and I chose not to flinch from it.

During this period, the Director CBI, R C Sharma visited Guwahati and became the unfortunate victim of a strange accident.

He had gone inside the Indian Airlines aircraft at Guwahati airport. After the ladder of the aircraft had been removed and before the door was closed, he went up to the door to communicate with someone on the tarmac. In that process he fell down from the aircraft on the tarmac, suffering severe injuries. He was a heavily built person. A stretcher was soon brought to evacuate him but the stretcher broke under his weight. An ambulance vehicle was sent for to take him to the hospital. On the way to the hospital, the ambulance broke down and another ambulance was summoned which took some time to arrive. He had suffered a severe spinal injury. After a few days, he was shifted from Guwahati Hospital to the All India Medical Institute in Delhi. He remained hospitalized in Delhi for nearly a year and thereafter he retired from the service. Rumours started floating in Guwahati that Mohanta had invoked evil spirits. It was said that R C Sharma had become a victim of Black Magic.

After my meeting with Chief Justice Verma and Justice Khanna, I sent for the new CBI Director, Kartikeyan, to discuss Mohanta's case with him. Kartikeyan told me that he had recently taken over as Director and he was not aware of the details of the case. I briefed him about my thinking in the case of Mohanta and Nakul Das and the tentative conclusions that I had reached. I also told him that if in the next one week his staff sent me additional evidence or material, I was prepared to examine that with an open mind and, if convinced, change my views. I received no further communication from the CBI After the stipulated one week, I decided to announce my decision. I wrote both to the President and the Prime Minister apprising them of my decision. The Gujral Government had lost its majority in the Parliament and fresh Parliamentary elections had been announced. The Prime Minister was in Jalandhar for election campaigning. He rang me up from Jalandhar to say that I had taken a very bold decision. I also received a telephone call from M S Gill, the Chief Election Commissioner, whom I had not met before. He told me that only a General could have taken such a bold and hard decision. Mohanta, on hearing of my decision was, of course, overjoyed and expressed his deep gratitude.

It was not incumbent upon me to issue a speaking order while rejecting the CBI's recommendation for the prosecution of Mohanta. A one line order refusing to grant permission for prosecution would have met the legal requirement. Given the circumstances of the case, I felt that for the sake of transparency and to meet the requirements of healthy democratic functioning, I should issue a speaking order analyzing the evidence and giving the reasons behind my decision.

Five charges had been levelled against Mohanta. These were: First, Rs 40 lacs had been paid to Mohanta by R P Borah for the 1991 Assembly election; second, R P Borah had purchased air ticket for Mohanta at a cost of Rs 4350 for travel between Guwahati and Delhi; third, RP Borah had purchased 2000 bundles of CI sheets to be distributed in the Nagaon constituency of Mohanta during the 1991 election; fourth, Mohanta had ordered R P Borah to prepare drafts for Rs 26 lacs for distribution to various institutions; and fifth, Mohanta had entered into a conspiracy with R P Borah to defraud the government of Rs 48.1 crores. I examined each of these charges and did not find sufficient evidence to establish a *prima facie* case made in respect of any charge.

RP Borah was the main accused in the whole case, who was a businessman and also a member of the AGP which was the ruling party when the LoC scam had started. The first charge that he had paid Rs 40 lacs as bribe to Mohanta had no documentary, oral or circumstantial evidence. This charge had been made out on the basis of a verbal accusation by Borah. This was supported by another witness who had stated that Borah had told him that he had given that bribe to Mohanta. The latter's statement was a mere hearsay and could not be admitted as evidence. During investigation of the case by CBI, Borah had stated that he had paid Rs. 40 lacs to Mohanta. After the CBI report was submitted to me and when I had raised certain queries, Borah changed his statement, saying that he had paid Rs 4 crore to Mohanta and not Rs 40 lacs. This only showed that he could not be treated as a reliable witness. I enquired if the CBI had carried out any investigation to find out if Mohanta's income was disproportionate to his known sources of income. The CBI replied that they had not done so because that was not part of the terms of reference for investigation of the case. This was indeed very surprising. In the case of the other accused Nakul Das, a former Congress minister, the CBI had not only submitted oral and documentary evidence of misappropriation of Rs. 48.81 crores but also evidence of the minister, having acquired assets disproportionate to his known source of income. The cases of Mohanta and of Nakul Das were not at par. I had therefore taken different decisions in these two cases.

The other four charges against Mohanta were frivolous. Borah had bought eight air tickets from Guwahati to Delhi for AGP party members including one for Mohanta for Rs 4350. There was no evidence to establish that the tickets had been handed over personally to Mohanta. Borah was a financier of the AGP and it is a common practice for tickets being bought by a political party for its members attending party meetings. The allegation of 2000 bundles of CI sheets being sent to Mohanta's constituency was not fully substantiated. It was not proved that Mohanta had any knowledge of this nor what had happened to these bundles of CI sheets. They appeared to have disappeared mysteriously. It was also alleged that when Mohanta was the Chief Minister, bank drafts of Rs 26 lacs had been distributed to various NGOs at a public meeting by the deputy commissioner in his presence. This did not establish any culpability on the part of Mohanta. The last charge that Mohanta had entered into criminal conspiracy to defraud the government also lacked credible evidence. Although the CBI had alleged that Mohanta and his colleagues had intimate relations with Borah, in his statement on record Borah stated, "I was not very much known to Shri P K Mohanta".

Given the circumstances of the case and the flimsy evidence made by the CBI against Mohanta, I was convinced that the CBI had failed to establish a *prima facie* case of criminal culpability of Mohanta. I had to act according to my conscience. The several rulings of the Supreme Court and High Courts in various cases of corruption given to me by the Attorney General had established unambiguously that the sanctioning authority must apply his mind and be convinced that a *prima facie* case existed before giving sanction for prosecution. One Supreme Court judgment read, "The sanctioning authority should know the facts of the case and apply its mind to the relevant facts before according sanction to prosecute a public servant. The duty of granting sanction can hardly be imagined to have been properly discharged by merely putting one's signature on a ready-made sanction presented by the Police".

Apart from informing the President and the Prime Minister, and issuing a formal speaking order rejecting the recommendation of the CBI to prosecute Mohanta, I also got my Secretary to issue a Press Release stating my rejection of the CBI's recommendation with reasons for my doing so. Understandably, this caused a big furore and I was in the eye of a storm generated on this account. It became a major national controversy. Some Opposition MPs from Assam submitted a memorandum calling for my recall. Newspapers with leanings towards the Opposition, wrote editorials criticising me. A leading newspaper from Patna, my home town, which closed down after a couple of years, was very critical of me. It accused me of double standards by exonerating Mohanta but according sanction to prosecute Nakul Das. I was accused of anti-Congress bias. It was even said that I was taking my revenge against the Congress because when it was in power at New Delhi, it had superseded me for the appointment of Army Chief leading to my resigning from the Army, some 15 years earlier. I was accused of toeing the line of the United Front (UF) Government in power at New Delhi of which Mohanta's party was a constituent. The fact that the UF Government had lost its majority in the Parliament and fresh elections had been announced at the time when I took a decision on this case was ignored. I was also accused of acting more as a judge than a sanctioning authority for prosecution. My credentials to sit in judgement over the report of the premier investigating agency of the country were questioned. This was the first time a governor had rejected the recommendation of the CBI. A former military officer could not claim the competence to do so. I was also told that the CBI hierarchy was very upset with my decision.

My father was in Patna and he was worried about all the controversy raised in the Press. He brought forward his plans to visit me and came over to Guwahati. In 1947 when he was in the Intelligence Bureau at Delhi, he had been asked to hold charge of the Special Police Establishment (previous designation of one CBI). After a few months, one of his colleagues and close friend, Kohli, took charge of the SPE and he was designated Director CBI. When my father came to Guwahati, I explained the circumstances of the case to him and he felt relieved saying that he was happy I had taken a bold and correct decision. However, he also mentioned that he was one of the founding fathers of the CBI, at the time of Independence. The organisation had been set up to provide professionalism of a high order in the investigation of important cases. He was surprised how standards had fallen in police investigation and regretted that his own son had been forced to take a stand against an organisation which he had helped to build.

A Public Interest Litigation was filed by parties opposed to Mohanta in Guwahati High Court. It came to me as a great relief that after a year, the judicial verdict not only fully supported the decision that I had taken but the judgment also examined the arguments in the speaking order issued by me and concurred with my views. At one time I was thinking that if the High Court gave an adverse judgment, I should resign, as that would be the only honourable course open to me. The necessity for that did not arise. An appeal was made by the petitioner to the Supreme Court but the latter declined to admit the case.

The controversy over the LoC scam did not completely die in spite of the judicial verdict. Elections to the State Assembly were held a little later in 2000. The State Congress Party had included in its election manifesto that on coming to power it would reopen the case. It so happened that Mohanta and his party lost the election and the Congress came back to power. Tarun Gogoi, a lawyer himself, tried to argue that the Constitution had provided specific circumstances in which a governor could act at his own discretion. Mohanta's case did not fall in that category. My acting on my own in this case without the advice of the council of ministers was violative of the provisions of the Constitution. I pointed out that it made little sense for me to seek the advice of the council of ministers in a case in which allegation had been levelled against the Chief Minster. The Governors of Maharashtra, Tamil Nadu and Bihar had not sought the advice of their council of ministers while sanctioning the prosecution of their chief ministers — Antulay, Jayalalithaa and Lalu Prasad Yadav. Another point raised by Tarun Gogoi also lacked validity. He tried to assert that in the case of Mohanta, he was alleged to have been involved in corruption as a MLA and the sanctioning authority for prosecution should have been the Speaker of the State Legislative Assembly and not the Governor. This view also got rejected. The allegation against Mohanta covered the period when he was both the Chief Minister and later an Opposition MLA. Moreover, there is no provision in law for the Speaker's sanction to be obtained for prosecuting a legislator for any act by him outside the precinct of the legislature. In such cases, the Speaker had only to be apprised of any proceedings initiated against a legislator.

Thus ended the controversy over my decision to refuse sanction for the prosecution of Chief Minster P K Mohanta. It was indeed a very hard decision that I had taken and the long drawn controversy over it as also the personal attacks against me had caused me worries. Anyway the adage that all is well that ends well, proved right in this instance.

I must add that my decision, led to most cordial relations with Mohanta, who continued to be the Chief Minister for some time. I never interfered with the functioning of the government but I had the benefit of the government's whole hearted support in tackling insurgency in the State. This was in national interest. However, I hasten to add that this consideration had in no way influenced me in taking the decision that I had taken. I had even stated in my order that although Mohanta's criminal culpability could not be proved, he could not escape moral and political responsibility for the Scam. He was chief minister holding the finance portfolio when the State exchequer had been defrauded of several crores.

12

Soon after I took over as Governor of Assam, my name got dragged into another controversy which figured prominently in all the national newspapers. It was about the nexus between ULFA and Tata Tea, the leading business house of our country. It had been common practice for ULFA and other militant organizations of Assam to extort money from business houses.

It was believed that, Tata Tea had avoided paying extortion money by carrying out affirmative action for the local people. They had set up a hospital in Upper Assam for the people and were doing other philanthropic work. They claimed that they had never paid any money to any militant organization. In 1997 it came to light that Pranati Deka, the Social Secretary of ULFA and the wife of an important leader of that organization, was pregnant and had gone to Mumbai for her delivery. She had been admitted in a leading hospital and some of her friends and family members who had accompanied her had been put up in a five-star hotel at Mumbai. It was alleged that the Tatas had picked up the bills for her trip to Mumbai and also treatment and hotel accommodation. Besides, it was reported that some underground ULFA leaders had been put up in Tata Guest House at Kolkata. It was also reported that some Tata officials had gone to Bangkok where they had met ULFA leaders. The police had collected enough evidence to prosecute Tata officials for assisting the ULFA. All this was anti-national activity. It was one thing to pay extortion money under duress but another to lend such support to a terrorist organization indulging in anti-national activities. Two senior executives of Tata Tea, Managing Director Krishna Kumar and Executive Director Saeed Kidwai had been interrogated by the police. After interrogation they had obtained anticipatory bail.

Mohanta decided to take a tough stand. This was also an opportunity for him to show that he had now changed and would not allow a soft approach towards the militants or those helping them.

Senior Tata Tea officials accused in the case wanted to meet me at Guwahati. I felt it was not proper for me to meet them as the case was subjudice I should not be seen to be interfering. Subsequently, when I was in Delhi, I was approached for a meeting with Ratan Tata I had heard that he had already met the Chief Minister and there was little that I could do in the matter. A few of my friends who met me at Delhi mentioned to me that the Tatas were innocent and they were being unnecessarily dragged into a legal case. I told them that the law should be allowed to take its course and if they were innocent, their stand should get vindicated in court. L K Advani came to see me at J&K House in Delhi with a bouquet of flowers to congratulate me on taking over as Governor of Assam. We had known each other for a long time. It was a kind and friendly gesture on his part but it was reported in some newspapers that he had come to see me to plead for the Tatas. The BJP spokesperson rebutted the allegation. I confirmed that Advani's visit was a personal one and was in no way connected with the Tata Tea case.

My younger brother, Sunny, who had retired as a senior executive in the Tatas was worried about the repercussions of my stand. His son was serving with the Tatas and he felt that he may be penalized by his bosses. I told him that we should have confidence in the Supreme Power to look after us. One has to do one's duty and not worry about the result. Luckily, this did not in any way affect my nephew in his career with the Tatas.

A few weeks later I was surprised to see a front page report in the *Indian Express* of the taped conversation between Field Marshal Manekshaw and Nusli Wadia, the business tycoon of Mumbai and a friend of Ratan Tata. The verbatim conversation reported in the Press involved me in the case. Manekshaw was reported to have told Wadia that he had spoken to me about the case and had dispatched a letter to me by courier. He also told Wadia that I was a friend whom he had known for long. He had spoken to me that Tatas were his "Jatwalas" (of his caste) and I should help them. He further stated that I had assured him that I would help in the case and he should not tell anyone anything about it. This was red hot news for the Press and all the newspapers carried it prominently in their editions. This put me in a very embarrassing position. Tongues could wag accusing me of undue interference with the process of law and some may even accuse me of taking bribes from the big business house. It was imperative that I immediately contradict this news falsely implicating me. It was painful for me to do so because of my long association with Manekshaw and my great personal regard for him. He was the most distinguished officer of our Army.

A whole lot of Press correspondents wanted to meet me to find out what had transpired between Manekshaw and me. I categorically denied meeting or speaking to Manekshaw about the Tata Tea case. I had received no letter from him. The last I had met him was at Mumbai airport, on the day my appointment as Governor of Assam had been announced. On that occasion he had enquired how my family was and what I had gone to Mumbai for. I also told the Press that I had known the Field Marshal for half a century having first served with him in 1946 when he was a Lt Col and I was a Captain. Thereafter, I had served under him in different capacities on five different occasions. I always had the highest regard for him and I respected him as the most distinguished officer of our Army. I said that to me the taped conversation appeared to be fraudulent. It talked of Manekshaw's caste and his interest in the Tata case on that account. Such an approach was totally contrary to the ethos and tradition of the Indian Army, where caste consideration did not prevail. This only confirmed that the tapes were not genuine. My contradiction was carried in all the newspapers and this put an end to the controversy involving me in this case. Manekshaw never issued any statement on this issue.

Intelligence Agencies played the tape of Manekshaw's conversation with Nusli Wadia to me. I recognised Manekshaw's voice. The tape appeared genuine. It seems that as part of his usual light hearted banter Manekshaw had spoken to Nusli Wadia on the telephone without realizing its implications. He may have meant to contact me later but either forgot to do so or decided against doing so. I am glad I managed to extricate myself from this controversy.

Ram Jethmalani, the famous criminal lawyer who had supported Mohanta during the student movement in Assam of the Eighties wrote an open letter to Mohanta with regard to the Tata Tea case which appeared in the Press. Jethmalani's daughter, also a lawyer, was defending the Tatas in the case. Mohanta sent him a strong open reply which also came out in the Press. Many controversial aspects of the case appeared in the Press. It was claimed that the top Tata officials had gone to Bangkok at the instance of an intelligence agency to establish contact with ULFA leaders. The point about the breach of the right of privacy by unauthorisedly tapping telephone conversations was raised. This high profile case continued in court for some time and I lost track of it.

Pranati Deka, whose treatment for ordinary delivery in a Mumbai hospital had given a lead to the police in this case, was sent to jail with her small baby. The court granted her bail on humanitarian grounds and she went to her village home. The police failed to ensure proper vigilance on her. She jumped bail and again went underground. I sent for the police chief and he could not give me any satisfactory explanation for the negligence by the police. This was not the first time that Pranati Deka had jumped bail. I expressed my displeasure to the police chief.

13

While I was in Assam I suffered four family tragedies in quick succession. They were heart-rending.

My brother Sunny was three years younger to me but I always felt a special sense of responsibility for him. Our mother had died when he was only a few months old. My father married again after some time and we now had a mother who was always kind to us. Yet I felt that it was my duty to take special care of Sunny. He duly responded by showing me great respect despite the difference of only three years between us. As children we never quarrelled and he would always do what I told him. On completing his education he joined Burmah Shell as a covenanted executive while I was still a Major in the Army leading an austere and hard life. His lifestyle was much higher than mine and I felt almost a "parental pride" in seeing him do so well in life. When Burmah Shell got nationalized, Sunny decided to join TISCO at Jamshedpur and rose to be a general manager, before he retired from there. We were all shocked to learn that he was suffering from an advanced stage of cancer of the liver. It was all very sudden. We tried various specialists in Delhi and contacted doctors in Mumbai and London but they all felt that nothing could be done at that late stage to cure him of the foul disease. It was a great blow for all of us. Sunny used to be in pain, particularly when he walked or even drove in a car. He had taken the turn of events very well. He said that he would spend some time with his daughter at Delhi and son at Kolkata. Thereafter he would like to be with me at Guwahati awaiting the end. He came to me at Guwahati where our father was also staying. We decided to contact the Tibetan doctor of the Dalai Lama and got him to treat my brother. This treatment did him a world of good. His pain had disappeared and he was near normal. I even took him to Delhi to attend a wedding in the family. Everyone was so happy to see him recovered and the doctor who had treated him at Delhi was pleasantly surprised.

We returned to Guwahati after the wedding at Delhi. My father and I had to go to Patna for the inauguration of the Cancer

Hospital there by the Dalai Lama. My father was the President of the NGO, which had put up that hospital. Sunny was perfectly alright when we left and till lunch time the next day. In the afternoon he suddenly developed acute pain in his stomach. My wife sent for the doctor and he was immediately rushed to the hospital. By the time he reached the hospital he was in coma from which he never recovered. I returned to Guwahati the next day to find him still in coma in the ICU at the hospital. The following morning he passed away. It was a great blow for my father and me. I went to the hospital to bring home my dear brother's body. The State Cabinet was in session. When they heard of my brother's demise, the Chief Minister and all the cabinet ministers came to the hospital to condole with me. Such show of sympathy in moments of distress provides relief. My nephew and niece immediately came to Guwahati. Due to the very disturbed security situation at that time, the police was deployed for my security on the road up to the cremation ground and at the ground itself. My consolation was that my brother did not suffer much agony for long in his last moments. Normally, patients suffering from such a disease live in lingering agony for a considerable time till the end. With security deployment and special arrangements, Sunny's last journey was befitting that of a Head of a State.

After my brother's demise, in a matter of a couple of months or so, we had two tragedies in quick succession in the family. I had been very close to my brother-in-law, K N Sahaya, the husband of my wife's elder sister. When I had quit the Army and returned to Patna, he was the Mayor of Patna. He gave me invaluable support in all my social and political activities. He had fallen ill and was in bad health. He came to Guwahati for a month. He passed away soon after his return to Patna.

The next casualty in the family was my uncle, Colonel Sahai, married to my father's youngest sister. He was a brilliant scholar of history and an excellent Shikari. I had much in common with him. He was suffering from Alzheimer's leading to loss of memory. He also came to us at Guwahati for a few weeks and soon after returning to Delhi, he passed away.

I felt broken by these three tragedies one after another. My wife insisted that we take a break and go on a holiday to our children in the USA. Winter was approaching and my father who was now about 97 years old used to feel the cold a lot. We decided that he should go to one of my younger brothers Pranu, serving with Air India in Mumbai. The winter is very mild in Mumbai and we thought my father would find the climate there more congenial. My brother took him to Mumbai while we proceeded on a month's holiday to the USA. My father expressed concern at my being away from him for so long but appreciated that I needed a break and spend sometime with each of my three children in the USA. My father was perfectly alright, both physically and mentally, when we parted. Little I could then imagine that it was the last time I would be seeing him in good health.

While I was in the USA, my father suffered a chest infection and had to be hospitalized in Mumbai for a few days. He came out of the hospital and was recovering. On return from the USA I had to go straight to Guwahati for an important engagement. My father was due to proceed to Patna shortly, accompanied by my younger sister Amrita who lived in Patna. I had planned to go to meet him at Patna and then take him with me to Guwahati but that was not to be. On his way back from Mumbai to Patna via Delhi he broke journey at Delhi to spend some time with my other sister, Padma. On the day following his arrival in Delhi, he suddenly collapsed in the morning after breakfast. He was taken to the nearest hospital and admitted for treatment. He was in coma. I rushed from Guwahati to Delhi and so did my three brothers from their respective locations where they were serving. A day or two after my arrival in Delhi he regained consciousness for a short time and I had the satisfaction of interacting with him very briefly. We shifted him to the All India Medical Institute and the best possible treatment was given to him. All his sons and daughters were now at Delhi and we did not leave anything wanting in care for him but we realized we were fighting against heavy odds. Not seeing much hope of recovery we decided after a couple of weeks to shift him to Patna. He was on a ventilator and had to be taken to Patna in a special aircraft which was arranged by my brother Jyoti while I got the army to provide us a doctor, a medical attendant and a ventilator for the journey. I had to go for a day to Guwahati to address the State Assembly after which I joined the family at Patna where he was admitted in a local hospital for a couple of days. It had been my father's wish that he would like to die in Patna. To respect his wish we had moved him to Patna. After a few days in hospital we realized that there was no chance of recovery. We shifted him to his house on the morning of 15 March 2000. He was still unconscious but for a brief moment recovered and we could see that he was happy to be in his own bedroom in his house. That afternoon he passed away while all his children were with him, leaving us all very disconsolate.

Being the eldest it fell upon me to perform all the funeral rituals. My father believed in orthodox Hindu rituals which last for 13 days. I had seen him perform those rituals meticulously when my grandfather had passed away some 25 years earlier. I was determined to go through all the arduous rituals; sleeping on the ground in a separate room, going to the Ganges for a bath every morning, eating special food cooked separately for me, wearing no stitched clothes and so on. I was 75 years old then but I am glad I had the strength to perform all the rituals without any difficulty and with great devotion, as my last duty towards my departed father. He passed away when I had myself attained a ripe old age. Yet I felt orphaned without him and a feeling of emptiness in not having a father to look for guidance and paternal affection. Being the eldest among his children I now decided to play the role of the head of the family for my brothers and sisters.

We were overwhelmed with the outpouring of sympathy and condolence from numerous friends and relations. My father had led a full life up to the age of 97, and was very active till the last few weeks. The newspapers referred to his demise as the passing away of the Grand Old Man of Bihar, who had become a legend in his lifetime. In a condolence letter to me, President Narayanan very aptly wrote, "I am very sad to hear of the demise of your distinguished father. He lived a full life and has made the final crossing with spiritual and intellectual fulfillment. For the family this is a moment of irreparable loss and bereavement. I send my sincere condolence to you and to other members of the family and pray for the repose of the departed soul". The first top leader to telephone me from Delhi within almost minutes of my father's demise was L K Advani, the then Deputy Prime Minister, who had been close to me. The Governor of Bihar and a whole lot of top leaders and officials came to our house to place wreaths on his body. The Bihar Police Association of British Officers in London passed a condolence resolution for him. Kenny, one of the British officers who had served under him and whom I had known when I was a student in college, was the secretary of the association in England. He wrote an affectionate letter of sympathy to me. Chief Minister Prafulla Mohanta, with his wife and two ministers came all the way from Guwahati to Patna to condole with us. I was deeply much touched by their very kind gesture.

My father had been very active in social circles of Patna throughout his life. After retirement from the police for nearly 40 years he was associated with various NGO's as their president. He was president of the Bihar Relief Committee for 20 years. He had succeeded Loknayak Jayaprakash Narayan after his death. Even at the age of 94 he would go to Palamu some 300 kilometers from Patna to supervise the running of free kitchens during the drought. As President of the Mahavir Sansthan Trust he was associated with putting up a magnificent Mahavir Temple in Patna, which is perhaps the biggest Hanuman Temple in the country. He was associated with the setting up of a Cancer Hospital in Patna by that Trust, which was inaugurated by the Dalai Lama. Today, that has become a leading cancer hospital in Eastern India. He was also chairman of a public school, Gyan Niketan, which is a leading institution of its kind in Patna, with over 2000 students. Being a keen sportsman in his youth he continued with his interest in sports. The Mithilesh Sports Stadium in Patna named after him is a tribute to his contribution in sports. He had also been the president of the Patna Golf Club and the Bankipore Club. He was very active in the social life of Patna and was much sought after at social functions. During the marriage season he would not hesitate to attend three or four wedding functions in one evening. His age commanded great respect in society and people were much impressed by his energy, punctuality and turn out. Throughout his life he was very particular about his dress and he was often referred to as one of the best dressed men in town. A documentary film on his life was telecast on Patna Doordarshan as a tribute to his memory.

The State Government decided to give my father a State funeral. The State police went all out to make necessary arrangements. My father had served in the Bihar police for 35 years and had risen to be its Chief for a record period of nine years. He had been the first Indian to command the Bihar Mounted Police in 1943. A troop of horse with riders in their ceremonial uniform came to escort my father's cortege to the cremation ground where a Police guard of honour did the honours. A whole lot of police officers, army officers from Danapur Cantt and various dignitaries were present at the funeral. Many people told me that my father was an outstanding personality who had enriched the State by his contribution in various fields. He believed both in style and substance. We bid him a befitting farewell. I was fully aware that nothing is permanent in life and end is inevitable for everyone. Yet the parting then as now, has been very painful. I owed such a lot to him and realized that the void left after his demise can never be filled.

13

Soon after I had taken over as Governor of Assam, the then Prime Minister, IK Gujral had visited Guwahati and had stayed with me. He had come with his family and staff. He had remarked that I had the smallest Raj Bhavan in the country. I added that it was also the most austere and I would try to rectify its shortcomings.

After a while, President Narayanan came to us. That was the time I took the opportunity of briefing him about illegal migration from Bangladesh. Mrs Narayanan was of Burmese origin. I found much in common with her talking about various places in Burma (now Myanmar). I had served in that country during the Second World War. She was much impressed by my memory and my knowledge of the geography of her country of origin. The two VIP guest rooms in Raj Bhavan were on the first floor. She had some knee problem and was not too comfortable going up the steps to the first floor. She preferred to spend the afternoon with my wife on the ground floor verandah adjacent to our bedroom. Soon after the visit of the President, I had a lift installed in Raj Bhavan. Its installation took a few months. It became an asset when we had elderly visitors staying at Raj Bhavan.

Our next important visitor was Vajpayee who had recently taken over as Prime Minister. I invited him to visit Assam and suggested that his first tour after taking over as Prime Minister should be to Assam. I said that it would be a step towards removing the feeling among the people of Assam about being neglected by Delhi. I reminded him that he and his party had supported the students' movement in Assam and his visit to the State would be a much appreciated gesture. Vajpayee accepted my suggestion. We received his tour programme which catered for his coming by special Air Force aircraft to Guwahati. He was to proceed in a helicopter from the airport to Jogighopa to inaugurate the railway bridge over the Brahmaputra. Thereafter he was to return to Guwahati airport and go back to Delhi. I urged his staff to cater for a night halt at Guwahati but they did not agree saying that he would have to undertake a 40 minute drive by road through the city from the airport to Raj Bhavan and that was a security risk. I assured them that full security measures would be taken as had been done for Gujral's visit a couple of months earlier. Yet they were not convinced. I then spoke to Vajpayee and got him to accept my suggestion overruling his staff. I have found that the

Prime Minister's security staff are paranoid about security. I had heard that when Narasimha Rao had gone to the USA, prior to his visit, his Chief Security Officer wanted to check the runway at JFK airport to ensure that there was no explosive buried under it. With aircraft landing every minute at that airport it was an absurd idea to check the runway for buried explosive. The Prime Minister's security chief was carrying a loaded pistol which was not permitted. The Americans noted this and asked him to hand over his pistol. He protested but ultimately complied handing over the loaded weapon pointing towards the American officer without proving that it was unloaded. The Americans detained him for pointing a loaded weapon towards a person. The matter was later resolved. I cannot vouch for the veracity of this story but on numerous occasions when prime ministers have been visiting me, I have found the security staff coming out with some weird ideas. Anyway, I was happy that I had been able to persuade Vajpayee to stay for the night at Raj Bhavan. This was during the Bihu festival, when Assamese people organise "Bihu tolis" for singing and dancing. I decided to take the Prime Minister to the Bihu toli at Judge's ground in the city. I got the Army and the Police to provide extra security and man all the buildings surrounding the open ground. The Prime Minister's security staff was aghast when they heard of my plan but the Prime Minister was willing and even liked the idea. At the insistence of his security staff I agreed that the Prime Minister should depart from the site before dark. We adjusted the programme and took him there an hour before sunset. I had special Moonga silk dress in Assamese style including jacket and turban made both for him and myself. We turned up at the Bihu toli to tremendous applause from the people. The Prime Minister's gesture was much appreciated by the audience. The newspapers wrote that this was the first time in over 50 years of Independence that a Prime Minister had participated in the Bihu festival and that too in Assamese dress. The Chief Minister received us at the function and was taken by surprise seeing us dressed in typical Assamese style while he himself was in his usual bushshirt and trousers. So far as I was concerned, the visit of the Prime Minsiter to the Bihu toli was a part of my numerous psychological initiatives to win the hearts and minds of the people.

Sonia Gandhi had recently come out of her seclusion and become active in politics. She had taken over as the President of the Congress Party and was coming to Guwahati in connection with the forthcoming parliamentary election. Some senior Congress leaders were to accompany her. The State Congress Party wrote to my staff requesting that Sonia Gandhi be accommodated in Raj Bhavan for security reasons and the Congress Party would pay for her stay. My staff recommended to me that since she was coming for party work and she held no official position (she became Leader of the Opposition after the election), it would not be appropriate for us to put her up in Raj Bhavan. I was also told that when Indira Gandhi had come for the AICC meeting as Prime Minister, she had stayed in Brahmaputra Hotel where necessary security arrangements were made. I overruled my staff saying that even if Sonia Gandhi held no official position, being the widow of a Prime Minister, she should be accommodated in Raj Bhavan. Moreover, with the ongoing militancy at Assam which was not there in the time of Indira Gandhi and her being in Z plus security category, it was only right that she stayed in Raj Bhavan. However, other Congress leaders coming with her could not be accommodated in Raj Bhavan. There should also be no political or party meeting in Raj Bhavan. As for payment for her stay in Raj Bhavan, the question of any payment did not arise. Raj Bhavan was not a hotel. People staying in Raj Bhavan were guests of the Governor.

Sonia Gandhi arrived in the afternoon and I met her over tea in the Raj Bhavan sitting room. This was the first time that I was meeting her. After tea, she was to go to a public meeting organized by her party. People had not assembled for the meeting and she started getting messages to wait till there was a large gathering. Our meeting which was supposed to be for a few minutes lasted for well over an hour with just the two of us in the room. I talked to her about the weather but one could not do so for long. I tried to talk to her about Italy where I had been recently. My son was posted in our Embassy there. She changed the conversation and it was obvious that she did not want to talk about Italy. I found her reticent and not too self-confident. Of course, subsequently when I met her, I found she had changed and become self-confident. This was but natural. It reminded me of her mother-in-law Indira Gandhi who had come to Imphal soon after she had taken over as Prime Minister. I was then in command of the Army formation deployed in Manipur. I had occasion to interact with her when she arrived and over lunch at the residence of the Lieutenant Governor. She went to a public meeting which turned violent with Meite agitators brickbatting and firing shots. She had to come away from the meeting without addressing it. The army was called out to restore order. I was summoned by the Lieutenant Governor who wanted the army to take over protection of Raj Nivas and her security. I saw her from the verandah where I was with the Lieutenant Governor. She looked agitated and not too self-confident. The same Indira Gandhi had become the Iron Lady by 1971 and led the Nation to a great victory. During my meeting with Sonia Gandhi there were awkward pauses. I decided to talk about her children and her face lit up, particularly when talking about her son. At that time, the Press was reporting that her daughter, Priyanka, who had the traits of her grandmother (Indira Gandhi), and was more charismatic, would be her heir in the Congress. After my conversation with Sonia Gandhi, I came to the conclusion that she would like to have Rahul and not Priyanka as her successor.

King Gyanendra of Nepal with his wife and a large entourage of civil and army officers came to Guwahati. The King had come on a pilgrimage to Kamakhya temple in Guwahati. This was not long after the previous King and his elder brother Birendra, had been assassinated, along with his entire family. When I was Ambassador in Nepal, I was quite close to King Birendra. I had a hand in persuading him to come to terms with democracy in Nepal and in giving a boost to Indo-Nepal relations. During my stay in Nepal, I had met King Gyanendra a few times at social functions. At that time I did not have the faintest idea that one day he would be the King of Nepal. The previous King had two sons and a daughter who preceded him in line of succession to the throne.

King Gyanendra had come to Guwahati as a guest of the Government of India, in a special IAF Boeing aircraft. The Chief Minister and I received him on the tarmac at the airport. He warmly shook my hand and spoke to me in Nepali, reminding me of our meetings in Nepal and stated how happy he was to meet me in Guwahati. I hosted a banquet in his honour. King Birendra had presented me with his family group photograph, all in their ceremonial dress. I had the photograph framed and hung in the foyer of Raj Bhavan above the table on which the Visitors' Book was placed. As the officials accompanying the King arrived, they noticed King Birendra's family group picture. Each of them stopped before the photograph and bowed before it with reverence. The Nepalese revered the King as an incarnation of Lord Vishnu and King Birendra was a highly regarded monarch. King Gyanendra was the last to arrive. I escorted him through the foyer to the sitting room. Perhaps he had missed seeing his brother's family group photograph. During the banquet both the King and the Queen were very gracious. They much appreciated all the Nepalese music that I had arranged for the band to play. After the banquet the King was escorted by my ADC to sign the Visitors' Book. As he sat down to dc so, I noticed that he saw his brother's family group photograph through the corner of his eye while signing the Visitors' Book. He then quickly got up and thanked me for the banquet before departing. I found it strange that he had nothing to say about his brother's picture. The following day I had a long meeting with him before he left Guwahati for Delhi. We first discussed the insurgency situation in Assam and what we were doing to bring about a mind change among the people. We then discussed the increasing Maoist violence in Nepal. I told the King that in 1990 I had advised his brother to come to terms with democracy otherwise the non-violent movement for democracy could turn violent and the demand for constitutional monarchy may become a demand for a Republic. King Gyanendra pointed out that in 1990 there was no Maoist violence. He was of the view that the Maoists had to be tackled militarily for which the Royal Nepal Army had to be strengthened. There was need for a strong and stable Government which could deal with the situation firmly. I realised that his mind was made up. I felt that his views boded ill for Nepal. Later events in Nepal proved my fears right. Monarchy ended in Nepal and Gyanendra was dethroned.

I had a number of ambassadors of different countries visiting me in Guwahati. Having been an ambassador myself, I realized that the purpose of their visit was to assess the situation in a troubled region and keep their governments informed. I found interaction with Robert Blackwill, the American Ambassador, interesting. He was well-informed and talked to me at length about insurgency and the situation in Assam. He was appreciative of our success in containing violence and winning the hearts and minds of the people. He felt that our psychological initiatives were unique and were achieving remarkable results. He also wanted my view on the Kashmir problem which we also discussed at length. On his return to Delhi, he wrote a warm letter to me saying, "It was a profound pleasure to visit the Raj Bhavan, and to share some of your remarkable experiences. One of our great statesmen, Dean Acheson coined a phrase which has become part of our history — 'present at the time of creation' (referring to the post-war international system) — which I think you may quite rightly claim for yourself in the Indian context. Your insights into Assam's future were very valuable to me as well." He concluded his letter thanking me for his "unforgettable visit to the North East". Not long after Blackwill returned to his country, and the newspapers reported that he had joined the power coterie of the US President, George Bush.

A month or so after Blackwill's visit three faculty members of the Asia-Pacific Centre for Security Studies in Hawaii came to see me. The meeting had been arranged at the request of the Consulate General of the US and our Ministry of External Affairs had given the necessary clearance for it. The three faculty members were Professor Dr Robert Wirsing, Associate Professor Herman Finley and Assistant Professor, Dr Christopher Jasparro. Dr Wirsing, a specialist in Indo-Pak affairs, had undertaken 30 visits to India and Pakistan. He had held assignments in Pakistan universities and had interacted with different Pakistani military establishments. He had also had an assignment with Baroda University in India and had interacted with other institutions in India connected with security and international affairs. He had appeared before the US Congress to depose on US security interests in South Asia. He was a member of a New York based Kashmir Study Group. He had authored a book, *The Kashmir Dispute at Fifty: Charting Paths to Peace*. He certainly had formidable credentials and good knowledge of Kashmir.

Dr Wirsing and his team held discussions with me for nearly two hours during which they made copious notes. I gave them my views on Kashmir. During our meeting it came out that in 1994, I had addressed the Rand Corporation at Los Angeles on India's Kashmir policy. I felt that Dr Wirsing appeared to have a bias for Pakistan on the Kashmir issue. I was forthright in projecting my viewpoint on Kashmir. He listened attentively with an open mind. At the end of the meeting, he told me that I had apprised him of certain aspects of the Kashmir problem which he was not aware of. He also told me that he would be writing another book on Kashmir shortly in which he would incorporate some of my views. Our meeting took place on 9 September 2001. A little later on that day the twin towers in New York came crumbling down. The world changed suddenly after that catastrophic event. I do not know if Dr Wirsing wrote a book on Kashmir and if so, whether he incorporated any of my views. Anyway, I found my interaction with him intellectually stimulating.

14

The golden anniversary of our wedding was in 1999. All our four children who were in the USA planned a big function for us in New York with family and friends. They had booked an expensive hotel for the function and our stay. I had obtained sanction from the President to proceed on a month's leave to the USA. In the meantime Vajpayee Government lost the confidence vote in the Parliament and a fresh election was to be held. Advani telephoned me saying that the term of the Governor of Arunachal Pradesh, Mata Prasad, had expired and according to convention, a caretaker government could not appoint a governor. A new Governor would have to be appointed by the next government. He wanted me to hold additional charge of Arunachal Pradesh for the interim period. He also told me that he was aware of my leave having been sanctioned by the President but it would be nice if I could postpone my leave, till after the coming elections. I agreed to do so. Apart from meeting the need for a stop-gap governor in Arunachal Pradesh, I felt my presence in Assam during the Parliamentary elections was necessary. Our children were disappointed at our not being able to go to the USA to be with them, as planned. It also cost them a tidy amount to cancel the reservations.

It so happened that I was at Kokrajhar along with my wife on the day of our golden anniversary. 6 JAT, the battalion in which I had been commissioned during the Second World War and with which I had served in Burma was also at Kokrajhar. Unknown to me, the Commanding Officer of the battalion had got to know about our golden anniversary. He invited me to visit the battalion which I agreed to do. I was surprised to find that he had made special arrangements to felicitate us on the occasion. He presented me a ceremonial "hooka" huble-buble. Jats are very fond of smoking a "hooka". In battle, F echelon trucks carrying the ammunition replenishment would also bring a "hooka". My wife too was given a token present. I felt overwhelmed by this kind gesture. Officers and soldiers of a battalion in the army, consider themselves as part of one large family. Hence, if we could not be with our children for our golden anniversary, we had the satisfaction of spending that day with the battalion.

I was sworn in as Governor of Arunachal Pradesh at Itanagar. Arunachal Pradesh is a recently constituted State. Its Raj Bhavan is modern and neatly designed with plenty of grounds. Its first occupant, Col Raja, had taken great interest in developing the Raj Bhavan. During my tenure of a little over three months, the Darbar Hall was under construction. The following year, I again acted as Governor of Arunachal, as the governor proceeded on one month's leave. By then, the Darbar Hall was ready and my second swearing-in took place in that Hall. It was nice to have a small golf course in the Raj Bhavan grounds and I made full use of it. There was also a helipad at Raj Bhavan. At Guwahati, the airport, the helipad and the golf course were about half an hour's distance from Raj Bhavan.

Mithi was the Chief Minister of the State. He had recently replaced Apang in a political coup in which Apang had lost his majority in the Assembly. Apang had been the longest serving chief minister in the country. He was now the Leader of the Opposition. Though Apang and Mithi were hostile to each other, I had cordial relations with both. A year or so later, Apang bounced back to power in Arunachal. Tribal laws permit polygamy. The State was governed by tribal laws and not by the country's civil code. I was amused to find that many of my ministers had more than one wife, and some three to four!

The draft of the governor's monthly report to the President put up to me by my staff, had a paragraph on the boundary dispute between Arunachal and Assam criticising the latter. This dispute had been lingering since the creation of the new State of Arunachal Pradesh. As I was also the Governor of Assam, it was incongruous for me to be critical of that State. I decided to organize a meeting of both chief ministers at Itanagar under my chairmanship. The case had been in the Supreme Court and had been subjudice for some time. Pending a verdict of the Supreme Court, I got the two chief ministers to agree to a working formula for resolving disputes arising from day-to-day incidents. We constituted joint committees of revenue and police officials at tehsil, subdivision and district level to deal with incidents and cases in disputed areas. This arrangement proved to be satisfactory.

Tucked in the Himalayas, Arunachal Pradesh abounds with scenic beauty, like Kashmir in the North. The difference lies in the fact that the people of Arunachal have had little interaction with the outside world. In fact, the several tribes in the State lived in isolation from each other in their respective areas flanked with mountain ridges running from North to South. Lateral surface communications are poor and even the North-South roads from Assam to Arunachal are neither adequate nor in a good condition. There is no airfield in Arunachal and air connectivity is provided by a commercial helicopter service. The heliport is about half an hour's drive from the State capital. Itanagar is at a height and often gets covered in cloud making regular helicopter services difficult.

Therefore, the heliport has been developed at a lower height, some distance away from Itanagar.

During my tenure as Governor of Arunachal, I toured extensively, going to all the districts. I had been to Bomdila — Tawang, the battle zone of the 1962 war, during my army career. As Governor of Arunachal, I decided to go there to see the developments that had taken place in that area. My wife had not been there and was keen to visit the place. There was also a personal reason for her wanting to go there. When we got married in 1949, my wife joined me at Amritsar soon after. In fact, that was her first exposure to army life. I was the Brigade Major at Amritsar. There were two young officers, viz. Capt Trilok Nath and Lt Pant with me in the headquarters. The Brigade Major in the neighbouring brigade at Gurdaspur was Major Brahmanand Avasthy. We were good friends. We and our families often used to meet. All these three officers were from the Rajput Regiment. In 1962, Brahma was commanding the battalion, Trilok was the second-in-command and Pant was the adjutant. All the three got killed in that war and a memorial had been put up for them. We placed wreaths at their memorial in Bomdila. There is also a nice war memorial at Tawang for all our heroes who got martyred in that war. We visited the Tawang monastery which is very impressive. The multi-storey wooden structure constructed several centuries ago has no nails joining various wooden pieces. It is a marvel of engineering. The vegetable dye used for old paintings inside the monastery makes them look fresh. We found several young Lamas learning by rote the scriptures written on leaves, bound in wooden covers.

We also had the opportunity to see all the good work being done by the Ramakrishna Mission in Arunachal Pradesh. We visited a well-appointed hospital run by the mission at Itanagar and schools at Ziro and Khondsa. We were much impressed to see tribal girls and boys attending Sanskrit classes in the latter school. We saw the school assembly saying prayers collectively in faultless Sanskrit. Unlike the tribals in the North East, the tribals in Arunachal are mostly Hindus. At Daparijo, we found extensive paddy fields combined with fish farms in the shallow water in those fields. We were taken to a typical tribal hut on stilts. We were entertained to a meal cooked in the hollow of a bamboo comprising rice, egg, and fish. The food had a bamboo flavour and was tasty.

Once, when we were returning to Itanagar by helicopter from the forward areas, we ran into very foul weather. It was one of the most bumpy and harrowing helicopter rides that we ever had. Itanagar and the entire region was covered in thick clouds and the pilot kept hovering for a long time to find an opening through the clouds to descend. He was running out of fuel. He took a chance and did an almost blind landing through the clouds and we landed on a football ground of a school about 50 miles from Itanagar. The school authorities and children were very surprised to see us land. We waited at the school for our cars from Itanagar to come and fetch us.

My friend Virendra Shah was Governor of West Bengal. He and his wife had done a lot to renovate and improve the historic Raj Bhavan at Kolkata. He had to go on long leave to the USA in two successive years. On both those occasions I was asked to hold additional charge of West Bengal. Thus, besides being Governor of Assam, I had occasion to act as Governor of Arunachal Pradesh and West Bengal and twice in each case.

The swearing-in function as Governor of West Bengal was very impressive. I was escorted by mounted police in ceremonial dress. Policemen with lances flanked my path on the wide flight of steps. In the Durbar Hall I sat on the silver *howda* (throne like seat on an elephant) of Tipu Sultan with a thick velvet curtain draped from golden Ashoka Lions on the top.

The British had ruled India from Kolkata for over 150 years and from Delhi for 36 years. The Raj Bhavan at Kolkata has more history connected with the British Raj than the Rashtrapati Bhavan at Delhi. Its history goes back to 1799 when Marquis Wellesley, the then Governor General of India, started its construction on the pattern of Keddleston Castle in England, and shifted his residence from Barrackpur to Kolkata. Successive Viceroys and Governors General lived in this huge building comprising hundreds of rooms from that time till 1911, when the capital shifted from Kolkata to Delhi. Among the Viceroys who did a tremendous lot for giving the building a facelift was Lord Curzon. It was a coincidence that he was from the Keddleston family. One of Curzon's contributions which is still there is the group of marble statues of the ten Caesars that he got installed in the foyer. He fancied himself a Roman Pro-Consul on a civilizing mission and holding the scales of justice. He was a workaholic and had earned the jibe, "I am a very superior person; I am George Nathniel Curzon".

The Raj Bhavan of Kolkata has extensive grounds in the heart of the city. A well laid-out garden with small water bodies, a mini nine-hole golf course, tennis courts, and a swimming pool in its huge enclosed compound. Living in that mansion and roaming on its grounds, one can be oblivious of the fact that one is in the heart of one of the largest cities of the world. During the period I spent in that Raj Bhavan, I tried to explore various parts of it. The Governor's office is a huge room overlooking a portion of the garden. It was from this room that British Viceroys and Governors General had functioned taking momentous decisions, which influenced the course of history. I recalled that as a student at the university I had learnt that the Viceroy of India was the most powerful man in the world. This was particularly so before modern communication systems like the telegraph, telephone, internet, or television were invented. We learnt that the President of America ruled but not reigned, the King of England reigned but not ruled, the Viceroy of India both ruled and reigned. Often, sitting in that historical room, I recalled some of the momentous events of history. Marquis Wellesley must have briefed his younger brother Arthur Wellesley in that room about the campaign against Tipu Sultan of Srirangapatnam. Later in recognition of the latter's distinguished role in that siege, he appointed him the Military Governor of Mysore. That set Arthur Wellesley on the course to become the Duke of Wellington, more than a decade later. The British would refer to him after the Battle of Waterloo in which he defeated Napoleon, as the World's Conqueror's Conqueror ! It must have been from that room that William Bentinck must have approved of Macaulay's famous note on introduction of English education. Dalhousie must have evolved his Doctrine of Lapse from that room and implemented it with vigour. This led to the Great Uprising of 1857 which Canning was at pains to douse. So many decisions on wars must have been taken in that room, some within the country and some outside. I have in my mind the Mysore Wars, the Maratha Wars, the Sikh Wars and the Gorkha Wars. As for wars beyond India's borders, these were the Burma Wars, Afghan Wars, the Expedition to Tibet and the campaign in China during the Boxer Rebellion. Apart from wars there were other numerous momentous decisions that must have been taken from that room like the preservation of ancient monuments, plans to rival the Taj Mahal in architectural beauty by having the magnificent Victoria Memorial constructed in Kolkata, the decision to partition Bengal in 1905 and so on. I used to feel overweighed with a sense of history, functioning from that room.

The mini-museum at Raj Bhavan has some rare items like the coach of Warren Hastings. This horse-driven coach looks like an oversize hand rickshaw of our time. There are several other items in the Raj Bhavan reminding one of old history like Tipu Sultan's silver couch, a Silver Pagoda from Beijing, the gong of the King of Burma and so on. The Raj Bhavan Library has a very large collection of old documents written in long hand during the pre-typewriter era. I found several such notes written by Curzon. A research scholar will find many documents of interest to him.

There had been several members of British royalty and world leaders who had visited the Raj Bhavan at Kolkata. Among the members of the British royalty were the then Prince of Wales in the late nineteenth century who later became King Edward VII, King George V in 1911 and another Prince of Wales in 1920 who after ascending the throne as King Edward VIII, abdicated for his love. I read an interesting account of the visit of Lt Gen Arthur MacArthur, Governor General designate of Philippines accompanied by his son and ADC Capt Douglas MacArthur in the early twentieth century. The son was later to become a legendary figure in the Second World War and the unique Pro-Consul of Japan thereafter. The father son duo were visiting various Governors General in the world to see how they functioned and their style of living. They had visited the Japanese Governor General in Manchuria, the French in Saigon, the Dutch in Batavia (now Jakarta), the British in Singapore, Kolkata and Cairo. The style of functioning and living of the Viceroy in India, impressed Lt Gen Arthur MacArthur the most and he tried to adopt them as Governor General of the Philippines in his Government House at Manila. Besides these foreign visitors a whole lot of Indian dignitaries also had been visiting the Viceroy's House at Kolkata. These included Ram Mohan Roy, Rabindranath Tagore, Surendra Nath Banerjee and Mahatma Gandhi. Their pictures are in the Raj Bhavan.

I was attracted by a room in the Raj Bhavan which I was told was used as the chamber for the meeting of the Bengal Council. The room has a seating arrangement for some 30 people organized in a semi-circular manner with a podium in the centre. Prior to the 1909 Morley Minto Reforms, the British had instituted a Bengal Council for the Bengal Presidency. The members of the Council were elected by the local bodies; viz. municipalities and district boards. The Bengal Presidency of those days included the present States of Assam, Arunachal, Meghalaya, Nagaland, Mizoram, West Bengal, Bihar, Jharkhand and Orissa, besides now the foreign countries of Bangladesh and Myanmar. My great-grandfather Honourable Gajadhar Prasad had been elected as a member of that Council. He was the sole member from Bihar in that Council. India had certainly changed a lot from the time of my great-grandfather. He died within a couple of years of my birth and I have no recollection of him. I do not suppose he could have ever imagined that one of his progency would be living as the Head of the State in that huge building, reflecting the grandeur of British imperial power. His progeny now constitute a very large number. I invited all the members of our extended family and family friends in Kolkata to a banquet at Raj Bhavan.

I learnt of many anecdotes connected with the present Raj Bhavan building. Lord Amherst, one of the Governors General who lived in that building in the nineteenth century, liked that a liveried *Chaprasi* should precede him announcing his arrival when he moved from one room to another. Perhaps he had heard of the Mughal style of announcing the arrival of the Emperor. The Amherst University in the USA was started by him and is named after him. My daughter, Manisha, has been teaching at that university for the last ten years. There is another anecdote connected with the visit of a Duchess from England in the early twentieth century, when Lord Curzon was the reigning Viceroy. A banquet had been hosted by the Viceroy during her visit. An Indian High Court Judge, perhaps the first Indian elevated to the Bench, had been invited to the banquet. It was rare in those days for an Indian to be invited to a banquet at the Viceroy's House. The practice in those days was for ladies to be escorted to the banquet hall on the arm of a gentleman, who would be sitting next to her at the table. The ADC told the Duchess that the Indian gentleman would be escorting her to the dining room. She said, "Good heavens, no. I refuse to go on the arm of a Nigger. He gives me the creeps." The Indian Judge was of a very dark complexion and the Duchess had never before interacted with any Indian gentleman. When Lady Curzon was informed of this, she told the ADC to convey to the Duchess that in that case there would be no place for her on the Viceroy's table and dinner would be served to her in her bedroom. The Duchess reluctantly agreed to go with the Indian Judge keeping at a distance and touching his arm with her little finger. At dinner, when the Judge tried to cut the quail with his knife and fork, it slipped from his plate and landed on the lap of the Duchess who screamed. The Judge had a sense of humour. He said that the quail was so well cooked in Her Excellency's kitchen that it still had life in it and avoided damaging a lady's dress. It had landed on the serviette of the Duchess. There was laughter at the table and this little incident passed off without any hassle. Another anecdote relates to a missing diamond top of a Vicerene. It was felt that it had perhaps been stolen. The police was asked to investigate the case. The British superintendent of police in charge of security was investigating the case but was not making headway. An old sub-inspector came up to him and said that he had found some clues but to complete his investigation he would require the other diamond top. This was duly made available to him. A few days later he reported that the missing diamond top had been found. A sweeper had stolen it. The sub-inspector had got a duplicate diamond top made by a jeweller and it was duly given to the Vicerene who was very happy. The sweeper had confessed and he was dismissed. The sub-inspector was awarded the title of Khan Saheb. A couple of months later, the Vicerene found that her missing top was in one of her drawers. The poor sweeper was reinstated and the sub-inspector removed.

While I was acting as Governor of West Bengal, I had to address the State Assembly at the start of the budget session. I had had no problem doing so in the Assam Legislature. The odd MLA would raise a placard or there would be one or two occasions, when some members would mildly interrupt my speech to express dissent. I knew that governors in some States, particularly in my home State of Bihar, had a tough time on such occasions. The previous year when Virendra Shah had gone to the State Legislature, he was almost roughed up by some Opposition legislators and his shirt had got torn. He was not allowed to speak as the Opposition kept shouting. He left his written speech on the Speaker's table and came out of the Assembly to find that the Opposition MLAs were sitting on the roof and bonnet of his car. He walked back from the Assembly to the nearby Raj Bhavan. Having heard about what had happened on the previous occasion, I tried to have foolproof arrangements for my security. Policemen or weapons are not allowed inside the legislature. Unarmed marshals working under the directions of the Speaker are required to assist in maintaining order inside the legislature. I asked the Speaker to nominate some policemen in civilian dress to function as marshals for the opening day of the budget session. The DG Police was told by me to detail some physically tough policemen for this role. I wanted them to form a ring round me as I entered the Assembly Hall and walked to the podium. As for my car outside, I instructed them to have an armed guard to prevent anyone coming near it. This arrangement worked. As I entered the Assembly Hall there was some mild shouting and the throwing of a few harmless paper balls towards me. I reached the podium without any physical interruption. However, as I got up to deliver my address there was much shouting from the Opposition benches and I could not proceed with my address. The Speaker appeared helpless and the Chief Minister sitting in the front row of the Treasury Bench looked embarrassed. I spoke loudly placing the printed script on the Speaker's table, saying that it may be treated as read. The band played the National Anthem but the shouting continued unabated. I walked out with the marshals forming a ring around me and got into my car in the porch to return to Raj Bhavan. I managed to ensure that neither did anyone tear my clothes nor did I have to walk from the State Assembly to Raj Bhavan. I never faced such a situation while delivering my budget speech to the State legislature as governor for eleven years in two militancy affected States.

As I was leaving the State Assembly, Budhadeb Bhattacharya, the Chief Minister, apologized to me for the rowdyism in the Assembly. I found him always courteous and correct in my interaction with him. When he was Home Minister of West Bengal, I had submitted my much talked of report to the President on illegal migration from Bangladesh. West Bengal is equally, if not more, affected by this problem. The Congress and the CPM for vote bank politics had been encouraging this influx. In fact there were reports that the Communists in Bengal were helping illegal migrants to get ration cards, and on that basis, getting their names included in the voters' list. Given this background, I was pleasantly surprised to read in the newspapers one day that Budhadeb Bhattacharya as Home Minister of West Bengal expressed concern over the change in the demographic profile of the population in border areas of West Bengal, due to illegal migration. Later, when he was Chief Minister of West Bengal, I interacted with him as Governor in Kolkata. He came to Guwahati for a party meeting. He called on me at Raj Bhavan as a courtesy gesture. While at Guwahati he spoke to the Press and mentioned that there had been an alarming increase in Madarsas in the border areas of Assam. I was told by some people that there were rumours that I had influenced his thinking. The politburo of his party contradicted his statement and Budhadeb had to state that the Press had misquoted him.

While I was in Kolkata, I read in the newspapers that the famous Bengali writer, Anada Shankar Roy, had been felicitated on his 99th birthday. I asked my staff to arrange for me to visit him. He readily agreed to receive me. There was a reason for my wanting to meet him. He had been a brilliant student of Patna College, where a generation later, I had also studied. He and my father were in the same class and were good friends. My father often used to talk about him. Patna University was founded in 1917 and he was the first student to get a First Class First in English in BA (Honours) in 1925, before I was born. He had also got a First Class First in MA. His record had remained unbeaten when I graduated eighteen years later in 1943. He and my father sat for the ICS and the IP examinations respectively. In those days the ICS and the IP examinations were held separately. The ICS examination was held at the all India level and the IP examination at the provincial level. About six vacancies were available in the ICS and only one vacancy in IP in each province, every year. Neither he nor my father were selected in their first attempt. Both Anada Shankar Roy and my father narrowly missed competing. The following year they took their examinations again. and both successfully competed for their respective service. The remarkable thing about Anada Shankar Roy was that after writing his examination the following year, he told my father and his friends with great self-confidence that he would stand first in the country. When the results were announced he was found to have got the top place. He got into the ICS and was absorbed in the judicial stream of his service. However his real claim to fame was as a Bengali writer. He wrote several books in Bengali and also a few in English. He became a legendary figure of his time as a Bengali writer. I had never met Anada Shankar Roy. I thought that while I was acting Governor of West Bengal I must pay my respects to him. He was happy to meet me and was very warm recalling his association with my father, who had passed away two years earlier. He presented me with a copy of his latest book in English of selected short stories. I enjoyed reading it. I got a glimpse of his genius from his book. One of the things he told me about my father was that even as a student, he was always very well dressed and his shoes always used to be shining. This was so true of my father till his last days.

I had heard a lot about the Raj Bhavan at Darjeeling. During the British days, the Viceroy used to move from Kolkata to Shimla for the summer. After 1911, he moved from Delhi to Shimla. The Governor of Bengal used to move to Darjeeling for his summer resort. The Raj Bhavan at Darjeeling is still being maintained in all its grandeur. I had been to Darjeeling a few times but I had not seen the Raj Bhavan there nor travelled on the narrow gauge train from Siliguri to Darjeeling. The Darjeeling Himalayan Railway constructed in the nineteenth century was considered an engineering marvel of its time. It has now been declared a world heritage. I decided to go on tour to Darjeeling. My wife and I flew from Kolkata to Siliguri and from there took the "toy train" to Darjeeling. The Darjeeling Himalayan Railway is now part of the North East Frontier Railway. As Governor I was entitled to travel by a special train. The General Manager of the North East Frontier Railway organized a special train for me with a saloon and travelled in the train with us. The Raj Bhavan at Darjeeling is an imposing building with a blue dome. It has marvellous Burma teak panelling and staircase. From the bedroom, one gets a wonderful view of the snow covered Kanchanjunga. I also managed a round of golf at the six-hole mini golf course in the Raj Bhavan grounds.

Although it meant added responsibility and additional work, I was happy to have the opportunity of holding additional charge twice each as Governor of Arunachal Pradesh and of West Bengal. The former provided an excellent sojourn in the beautiful Himalayas and the latter a *tour-de-force* through history.

15

The North Eastern Council (NEC) was set up after the 1971 war by an act of Parliament for coordinating economic development of the seven North East States. It was a mini planning commission for the region comprising the seven States of the North East. All the seven governors and the seven chief ministers were members of the NEC. A governor nominated by the President functioned as the Chairman of the Council. The first meeting of the Council was held at Shillong in 1972 under the chairmanship of Indira Gandhi. It was boycotted by the Chief Minister of Nagaland. It so happened that none of the annual meetings had the presence of all members of the Council. In 1997 when I took over as Governor of Assam, the governors were to be dropped from membership of the Council. The chief ministers resented the presence of governors in this Council, maintaining that the latter were constitutional functionaries and should not be called upon to take part in taking executive decisions. The latter was the domain of the chief ministers and one of them should be the chairman of the Council. I was given to understand that an amendment was on its way and soon the governors would cease to be members of the Council. In view of this, I had kept away from meetings of the Council in my first two years as governor and my chief minister or one of the ministers used to attend the Council meetings. Moreover, for the first two years, I was too involved in tackling militancy in Assam. In 1999 Prime Minister Vajpayee spoke to me and wanted me to put more life into the functioning of the Council. He also said that the governors would continue to be members of the Council. The Council needed inputs from individuals without any regional or political bias. The governors were well suited to contribute to the functioning of the Council uninhibited by political or regional considerations.

Now that I was made the Chairman of the NEC, I decided to get actively involved in its functioning. I held this appointment for the next four years while I was Governor of Assam. The NEC had a secretariat of some 200 officers and clerks functioning under a secretary who was a senior IAS officer and of the rank of secretary in the Government of India. It had been undertaking several projects for the region and had been receiving annual budget allocations of about 350 crores from the Planning Commission. I was briefed by the secretary of the Council about the various ongoing projects. I found that the office accommodation for the secretariat at Shillong was very unsatisfactory. One of the first decisions I took was to have a proper building for it in Shillong. Various alternatives were considered and ultimately we decided to buy land from a private party. We built a modern secretariat building and an auditorium. We also built a guest house to accommodate visitors coming to NEC headquarters at Shillong. We had also acquired a plot of land at Chanakyapuri in New Delhi. We decided to have a NEC guest house also in New Delhi. This was necessary because our staff had to visit Delhi frequently for meetings and discussions with various ministries in the Government of India and with the Planning Commission. I believe that satisfactory working and living conditions promote efficiency. The NEC secretariat at Shillong cost Rs. 24 crores and the NEC guest house at Delhi another 5 crores.

K C Pant, the then Deputy Chairman of the Planning Commission was very helpful. I had interacted with him earlier for our one lakh shallow tube wells in Assam. The success of that scheme had established my credibility with him. Like chief ministers pleading for development funds for their States before the Planning Commission, I had to do that for the NEC. Despite opposition from the staff, K C Pant agreed to a hike of Rs. 100 crores for NEC budget which got raised to 450 crores. This was a good start. Later, I got the budget allocation raised further to over Rs. 500 crores.

To make the NEC more vibrant, I felt I must get all the members to attend the Council meetings and hold two meetings a year. For the first time in 2000 we had all the fourteen members present for the Council meeting. I invited the then Deputy Prime Minister, L K Advani, to address the Council meeting. The last time a senior member of the Central Cabinet had addressed the Council meeting was when Indira Gandhi had inaugurated the NEC. In 2002, it was decided to make the Governor and the Chief Minister of Sikkim associate members, pending the inclusion of Sikkim in the Council. We now had sixteen members/associate members.

The chief ministers understandably made bids for their respective States and it was often difficult to get them all on board on various issues. Their conflict of interests had to be reconciled. I had to use all my tact at the meetings and behind the scenes to work out a consensus. The governors were easier to tackle because they had no political compulsions but they found it difficult to openly oppose their chief ministers. Although the NEC had been put up for coordinated regional development and to act as a regional planning commission, the States had been trying to use the Council to extract maximum funds. An unwritten policy had been developed that the six States that were lagging behind in development should be brought at par with Assam, which was the best off among the seven States in resources and infrastructure. I got this approach gradually modified. This could not be done overnight. My stand was that the States got their development funds directly from the Centre and they should use that channel to achieve the desired parity with Assam. The fact was that most of the other States like Meghalaya, Mizoram, Nagaland and even Arunachal Pradesh were erstwhile districts of Assam, administered by the latter. They had now become separate States and naturally were far behind in terms of their level of development. Further, Assam's population was more than double the combined total population of the remaining States and geographically Assam was in the centre of the region with surface communication to each of the six States passing through Assam. Thus, infrastructure development in Assam, particularly in terms of surface communication benefited all the other States. Development of roads consumed a large portion of our budget. It took me some time but with much difficulty I managed to get the focus of the NEC planning changed to a regional more than a State oriented approach. A spin off from the new approach was that Assam which had been to an extent neglected by the NEC on the basis of the specious parity theory, began getting its due share. My Chief Minister, Prafulla Mohanta, with whom I had very cordial relations, was naturally very happy. At one time some chief ministers in the Council tried to pass a unanimous resolution recommending to the Government of India that the governors who had no executive responsibility should be dropped from the Council. My chief minister was opposed to this move and managed to get a couple of other chief ministers to dissociate themselves from the proposal. Thus this endeavour of a few chief ministers was foiled. Notwithstanding these differences, I managed to maintain cordial personal relations with all the chief ministers and ensured that all decisions taken by the Council were unanimous.

There were several major projects of the NEC, some completed and some in the pipeline. I decided to visit them all and see what could be done to make them function efficiently and those in the pipeline, completed soon. Among these was the Ranganali Hydroelectric Project in Arunachal Pradesh which had been approved in 1987 at an estimated cost of Rs. 312.78 crores. The cost was first revised to Rs. 774.12 crores in 1991 and a second revision was made in 2001 to Rs. 1455.45 crores. There were bureaucratic and technical hassles but ultimately this project was successfully completed. This was a typical example of how delay in execution leads to escalation in costs. Our major project in the Health sector was the Dr. Baruah Cancer Institute at Guwahati and Sri Shankar Netralaya also in Guwahati. The latter was set up in collaboration with the Shankar Netralaya at Chennai. I invited the then President, K R Narayanan, to inaugurate this hospital which has now emerged as a medical institute of excellence with state of the art equipment and a very modern building. Our other major institutions and projects were the North Eastern Electric Power Corporation (Shillong), the Regional Institute of Medical Sciences (Manipur), the Regional Institute of Medicine and Nursing (Mizoram), the LGB Mental Hospital (Assam), the Regional Nursing College (Assam), the Regional Dental College (Assam), the Regional Institute of Pharmaceutical Science and Technology (Tripura), the North Eastern Police Academy (Meghalaya), the North Eastern Institute of Science and Technology (Arunachal Pradesh), the North Eastern Institute of Water and Land Management (Meghalaya) and North Eastern Institute of Space (Meghalaya). I inaugurated the latter in 2001 registering the presence in the North East in Space Technology.

As Chairman NEC I found it very satisfying to have a wide exposure to development activities. It was a new experience for me and I was happy to be associated with such developmental activities of the region. After I left Assam in 2003, the NEC was restructured. A Central minister became its chairman and Sikkim was made the eighth member of the Council. The governors and the chief ministers continue to be members of the Council. Three members nominated by the President have also been included in the Council.

16

Rajiv Gandhi had signed the Assam Accord with the leaders of the student movement in Assam. This led to the latter joining mainstream politics in the State. A whole lot of concessions was given by the Centre to Assam. These included an IIT, Kalashetra and two Central universities. These institutions got completed during my tenure in Assam.

An IIT for Assam was a major project. As Chairman of the Board of Governors of IIT, with the help of an able Director, Professor Bargohain, we were able to complete the IIT project. All the other IITs in the country had come up with foreign collaboration. IIT Guwahati was set up with no foreign assistance and an outlay of 800 crores. When I took over as Chairman, the IIT had just started and was functioning from a hired building in the city. It was in an embryonic stage. We decided to develop an IIT campus, north of the Brahmaputra. I had the satisfaction of seeing this campus come up brick by brick. It became the prettiest IIT campus in the country. We also held the first convocation of the IIT during my tenure. The other two educational ventures were the Central universities at Tezpur and Silchar. The former got completed earlier and we held the first convocation with President Narayanan delivering the convocation address. We had Dr. Abdul Kalam, the then Scientific Advisor to the Government of India, to deliver the second convocation address. Work on the Central university at Silchar was slow and this university had not fully come up while I was Governor in Assam. A vice-chancellor was appointed and a large amount of construction of buildings and other infrastructure facilities were completed during my tenure. The university became fully functional not long after I left Assam.

The Shankardev Kalashetra is a unique complex for cultural activities with a big auditorium, open-air stage, galleries for exhibitions and so on. This was also inaugurated by President Narayanan during my tenure in Assam. At the inauguration I expressed a wish which touched the people of Assam. I stated that the USA had three capitals, political capital at Washington, commercial capital at New York, and intellectual capital at Boston.

Similarly, we in India have three capitals — political capital at New Delhi, commercial capital at Mumbai and now cultural capital at Guwahati. Bhupen Hazarika, one of the best singers of our country, known for his golden voice and an icon of Assam, wrote to me as follows:-

"Respected Shri Sinha

To me you are a great lover of Assam's heritage, today's positive efforts for peace and a pragmatic dreamer of a new future.

With my Bihu regards

Bhupen Hazarika"

Republic Day was being celebrated in Assam at a very low-key with a police parade at which the Governor took the salute. The army did not participate in the parade on the plea of its commitment in counter-insurgency operations. The DG Police was opposed to the army's participation because the limelight may shift to the army as command of the parade would devolve on the army. He also had problems working with the army due to ego hassles. Ultimately, we had to move him out from that appointment. No Republic Day At Home was held at Raj Bhavan because it was felt that guests coming to Raj Bhavan may find it unsafe going back home after sunset.

I decided to celebrate the Republic Day function with all fanfare as in the other States in the country. We not only started having a joint parade of the army, paramilitary and police but also added cultural items to the parade, as is done in Delhi. The air force also participated with helicopters showering rose petals. We made tight security arrangements in view of the militant threat. On the first occasion I got the spectators' stands filled to capacity with school children and soldiers in civilian clothes with their families. All this was done to give an appearance of normalcy. As the situation started improving this arrangement was not necessary as a large number of people on their own started coming for the parade. We also organized At Home at Raj Bhavan, despite an acute shortage of space. The Raj Bhavan is located on a hilltop with a small lawn which could barely accommodate 200 people. Very limited parking space at the top of the hill was available for about six vehicles only. I organized a shuttle transport service from the gate to the top of the hill. This was not a very satisfactory arrangement but we had no other option.

There was a ledge providing flat space some 20 feet below the road climbing up to the Raj Bhavan. My wife and I in our walks to the gate discussed the possibility of making use of that only available flat space on the way to Raj Bhavan. I made out an ambitious plan for having a three storey structure constructed to meet the essential requirements for a functioning Raj Bhavan. The ground floor could provide covered parking space for about 30 cars, the first floor could house the Raj Bhavan secretariat , the second floor at the level of the road could have the Durbar Hall, the third floor could have a suite of rooms for VIPs and the fourth floor could be a terrace connected with a footbridge to the Raj Bhavan lawn. This would ensure that there would be enough parking space for VIP cars during various functions, the other cars to continue to park below the hill in the open space outside the gate of the Raj Bhavan. The Governor's Secretariat used to be at Dispur along with the State Secretariat. This was about 12 kilometers away. It was not a good functional arrangement. The Governor's Secretariat could now be moved to Raj Bhavan. We had a temporary Durbar Hall in a tin-roof building which could accommodate about 200 people. We could now have a proper Durbar Hall with a seating capacity of 400 people. The VIP suites would meet our shortage of bedrooms. The terrace connected with a foot bridge to the lawn would double the space for holding At Homes during Republic Day and other occasions. The ledge on which I had proposed the new construction overlooked the Brahmaputra, commanding an excellent view of the river. I wanted every room in the proposed building to have windows with a view of the river. I spelt out my ideas to Bordoloi, the PWD Executive Engineer looking after Raj Bhavan. He was enthusiastic about the proposal but had reservations on three technical points. — whether the ground could bear the load of the proposed structure, whether a sufficiently strong retaining wall could be put up on the hillside and whether a cantilever bridge could be constructed from the road to the ground floor to be utilized for car parking. We had experts from IIT and the Geological Department to carry out soil tests and they cleared doubts about the ground bearing the weight of the proposed structure and the retaining wall. We had to be very careful about this requirement because Assam experiences heavy rains during the monsoons causing frequent landslides. The stumbling block for this project was the proposed cantilever bridge for which we took the help of railway engineers.

Getting funds from the State Government for this 15 crore project did not present much problem. My cordial relations with Mohanta, the Chief Minister, ensured that the finance department cleared this project very promptly. When Meghalaya separated from Assam, the capital of Assam had to be shifted from Shillong to Guwahati. Assam lacked the infrastructure of a State capital. The secretariat and legislature were housed in temporary buildings. Initially, a very modest Raj Bhavan was constructed, more like a temporary residence for a governor. For the first few years the two States had a common governor. During the first decade of Assam and Meghalaya having separate governors, militancy had erupted. Providing a proper Raj Bhavan had been a low priority. Moreover, there was some indecision regarding the site for the new capital of Assam. Indira Gandhi had laid the foundation stone for the new capital at Chandrapur, 30 kilometers from Guwahati. The Government of India provided 200 crores to the State Government for the construction of a new capital for Assam. There was resistance among the local people to the capital being constructed at Chandrapur. They preferred the capital remaining at Guwahati. After over 20 years, the State Government took a decision that the State capital would remain at Guwahati. The State legislature and the secretariat were in temporary accommodation. It was proposed to construct permanent buildings to house them and work on the State legislature building had started. The time was opportune for me to make a bid for the construction of a new wing for the Raj Bhavan and the State Government had no difficulty in sparing Rs. 15 crores for my project from the hitherto unutilized amount of Rs. 200 crores, given by the Centre for the construction of a new capital.

The remarkable thing about the new wing being constructed at Raj Bhavan was that we did not employ any professional architect or interior decorator. I spelt out my requirements to Bordoloi, the Executive Engineer, and he executed it in a brilliant manner. The PWD is often criticized for its stereotyped approach. Bordoloi showed that given an opportunity, the PWD could rise to the occasion and execute a project in an imaginative and creative manner. I was happy to find that he was not conventional in the office accommodation he created on the first floor for the Governor's Secretariat. He followed the pattern of a modern corporate sector office with cubicles and glass partitions. I suggested to him that we should pattern the architecture of the annexe on the lines of the Ahom capital at Sibsagar. The footbridge connecting the building to the Raj Bhavan lawn copied the design of the Rang Ghar at Sibsagar. This style had also been used for the gate of the newly constructed Kalashetra at Guwahati. The footbridge giving an arch effect looked like the inner gate of Raj Bhavan, with the road passing under it. We called it the Lachit Gate and the new wing, Lachit Wing. I had already given a facelift to the outer gate with Lachit's cannons and canon balls used in the battle of Saraighat. I left the furnishings of the VIP suites to my wife asking her to do them up in a five star manner. The furniture, carpets, decorations and fittings were all bought in Kolkata. They give a very luxurious look to the rooms along with a breathtaking view of the Brahmaputra. I concentrated on the furnishings for the Durbar Hall. The Ashoka Hall in Rashtrapati Bhavan has a statue of Gautam Buddha which provides the backdrop for important functions in the hall like oath taking ceremonies, awards conferred by the President and other such events. I chose to have a huge painting of Mahapurush Shrimant Shankardev as a backdrop on the stage of the Hall. The statues of Shankardev are forbidden but paintings are permitted. We found a local artist who executed this task for us very well. We got local artists to do all the other paintings for us. Flanking the painting of Shankardev on the two side walls were large paintings of the two icons of Assam, Lachit Borphukan and Lokpriya Gopi Nath Bordoloi. The two walls on either side from end to end had paintings of Assamese Bihu dance and tribal dances of various tribes of Assam. At the opposite end on the wall was a painting of a long stretch of the Brahmaputra showing the famous Kamakhya temple, the Sukreshwar Hill from which Lachit had set out to fight the battle of Saraighat, the Shiva temple on the island in the river and the Lachit Wing of Raj Bhavan on the bank of the river. With chandeliers, carpets and cushioned chairs, the new Durbar Hall had a gorgeous look.

All of us connected with the project felt very proud on its completion. I invited Mrs Surabala Bordoloi to come to see the Lachit Wing. She came in a wheelchair and was thrilled to see the new construction. She had tears in her eyes when she saw the large painting of her husband in the Durbar Hall. I had planned to invite Mr L P Singh from Delhi to see our new construction. When he was the combined Governor of Assam and Meghalaya, he had selected the excellent site on the top of a hill near the Brahmaputra for a temporary Raj Bhavan. He was a close friend of my father and was fond of me. I used to call him uncle. He had blessed me when I had gone to pay my respects to him in Delhi, before taking over as Governor of Assam. Unfortunately, he passed away by the time Lachit Wing was completed.

I invited the Press, school and college students and various dignitaries for a tour of Lachit Wing. They were all very impressed and were full of praise. I had a fear that I may be criticized for the extravaganza and the huge expenditure. There was no criticism whatever for what had been done. In fact, there was a sense of pride among the people because Assam now had a Raj Bhavan with a totally Assamese ambience and worthy of the leading State of the North East. The old wing of the Raj Bhavan was now named Chilarai Wing after the great warrior of the Coch Rajbansi tribe in Lower Assam. This wing had also been given a facelift with a beautiful glass room added to it.

Successive Presidents, Prime Ministers and other VIPs coming to Raj Bhavan were very appreciative of the décor of Lachit Wing and the gorgeous scenic beauty one saw from it. I received King Gyanendra of Nepal in our new wing of Raj Bhavan and he was also full of praise for it. It gave me great satisfaction and a sense of achievement to see the poorest Raj Bhavan in the country become one of the best Raj Bhavans.

17

Besides ULFA, there were also other terrorist outfits in Assam. The biggest amongst the latter were the Bodo terrorists. Bodos are the original inhabitants of the Brahmaputra Valley. Aryan migration from the mainland and Mongolian from the East, reduced them to a minority. Initially, the Bodo terrorists had made common cause with the ULFA but later they broke away because of their incompatible goals. Whereas the ULFA wanted a separate sovereign Assam State without any change of political boundaries, the Bodos wanted a separate Bodoland State for themselves carved out from the present State of Assam.

Bodos constitute four percent of the population of Assam. They were not in a majority in any of the 24 districts in Assam. On the basis of being the original inhabitants of the State who had been deprived of their land by subsequent immigrants, they claimed half of Assam. This was an obviously unacceptable demand. One could not undo what had happened through thousands of years of history. A little before I had taken over as Governor of Assam, large scale ethnic clashes had taken place between Bodos and Adivasis in which some 700 people were killed. On my arrival in Assam, I found some 2 lakh refugees, mostly Adivasis, living in various camps.

There were two terrorist groups among the Bodos. The larger group was Bodoland Liberation Tigers (BLT). These were mostly

Hindus who wanted a separate Bodoland within the Indian Constitution. The other group was National Democratic Front of Bodoland (NDFB) comprising mostly Christians, who wanted an independent Bodoland outside the Indian Constitution. Bodos inhabited Lower Assam and were active in blowing up railway tracks and road/rail culverts. They had been responsible for explosions which resulted in the derailment of the Brahmaputra Mail and North East Express in which several hundred passengers were killed.

A little after I had taken over, there were two instances of explosions on railway tracks with a few casualties. I decided to get the security forces to implement the strategy General Russell had devised in 1947 to protect refugee trains through Punjab. Suitable modifications to that plan were made to suit conditions in Assam. We had train movement restricted to daylight hours with pilot engines or goods trains preceding passenger trains. The railway track was divided into sectors and responsibility given to various elements of the security forces for the security of those sectors. They had to provide road patrols, railway trolley patrols, and static guards at important culverts. Village Home Guards were also mobilized. Besides, helicopter patrols were organized on as required basis. This arrangement worked well. In Lumding sector which was allotted to the CRP, I was informed that deployment had not taken place because they had sought clearance from the DG CRP. I immediately spoke to the Deputy Prime Minister and got orders issued for deployment of the CRP in Lumding sector. By the time this was done, one goods train suffered minor damage to the engine and one individual was injured due to an explosion. This incident only showed the tendency of paramilitary forces referring operational matters to their headquarters at Delhi, defeating the purpose of setting up a unified command. The headquarters of paramilitary forces at Delhi have no responsibility for operations. Operational command has to be exercised by the State Government and on its behalf by the Army in a unified command.

Assam had been repeatedly broken up. Its different districts or regions had become separate States. Meghalaya, Nagaland and Mizoram had been districts of Assam. They were now full-fledged States. Arunachal Pradesh used to be administered by the Governor of Assam. It first became a Union Territory and then a State. One of the examples of the Centre's discrimination against Assam quoted by the Assamese people was that whereas their State had been repeatedly broken up, large States like Uttar Pradesh, Bihar,

Madhya Pradesh and Andhra Pradesh with longstanding demands for separate States, had not been divided. Later, the first three States were bifurcated but Andhra Pradesh continues to keep its boundaries intact. Since my aim was to win over the Assamese people, I felt I must assure them that there would be no further division of Assam. The Chief Minister and the State Government fully supported this assertion.

Notwithstanding my opposition to further division of Assam being unpopular with Bodos, I tried to build bridges with them. The Assam Sahitya Sabha has been a strong literary movement in the State commanding much regard among the people. The like of such an institution does not exist in any other State of our country. The Bodos had also set up a Bodo Sahitya Sabha and I was happy to associate myself with it. They invited me to inaugurate two successive annual sessions of the Bodo Sahitya Sabha. I arranged for financial assistance from the Government of India for their function. I also requested the army to provide logistic and other assistance for these non-political and literary functions. I made it a point to speak the opening paragraph of my inaugural address in the Bodo language which was quite a tongue twister for me. All this helped me in forging friendly relations with moderate Bodos.

LK Advani, the then Deputy Prime Minister, wrote to me to start negotiations with the Bodos, as their efforts to do so from New Delhi had not been successful. I contacted various moderate Bodos, notably Bineshwar Brahmo. I tried to convince them that their demand for half of Assam when their population was only four per cent was not reasonable. I agreed with them that the Bodoland Autonomous Council set up under the Assam Accord did not fully meet their legitimate aspirations. The Council had not been delegated adequate authority and resources. Moreover, the Bodos were a minority within the Council territory. I assured them that suitable solutions could be found and a viable Bodoland Territorial Council could be established with a greater delegation of powers. The boundaries of districts could be readjusted creating new districts of predominantly Bodo areas. We made a good progress in our discussions. Unfortunately, Bineshwar Brahmo, one of the well-educated and liberal Bodos, was shot by NDFB terrorists, in the evening of the day we had had fruitful and encouraging discussions at Raj Bhavan. This was no doubt done to derail the talks he had been having with me. Another reason may be that he was for the Bodo language to adopt the Devanagri script while the

NDFB under Christian influence advocated Roman script. The assassination of Bineshwar Brahmo was a set back for the dialogue process started by me. However, after some time the Ministry of Home Affairs at Delhi took up the threads and an agreement was reached to establish four new Bodo districts under the Bodoland Territorial Council with greater devolution of power and financial resources. This helped in getting the Bodos back into the national mainstream.

There were also some minor tribal terrorist outfits like the UPDS and the DHD in the tribal districts of Karbi Anglong and North Cachar covered under the Sixth Schedule of the Constitution. These indulged in inter-tribal violence and had connections with terrorist outfits in neighbouring Nagaland and Manipur. Violence from these two States used to spill over to these two tribal districts of Assam.

18

Our three-prong strategy against militancy yielded good results. Intensified and coordinated military operations under a joint command had been inflicting heavy attrition on the militants and there were signs of demoralization amongst them. There was also growing isolation of militants from the people. The latter process had begun with the ULFA killing Sanjay Ghosh, a young Oxford graduate who had been doing commendable social work on Majuli island and had become very popular among the local people. In fact, the ULFA leadership had been issuing conflicting statements about Sanjay Ghosh which had only further damaged its image. The killing of Sanjay Ghosh had taken place at about the same time as I took over as Governor of Assam.

We had a succession of good Generals in command of the army deployed in Assam. They had known me earlier and extended full cooperation. This was of great help. Among these was Lt Gen Nirmal Vij. He had worked with me when I was commanding the Western Army some fifteen years earlier. I found him a great asset and there was complete synergy between us. I had the opportunity to again work closely with him when he was the Army Chief and I was Governor of Jammu and Kashmir. One day Vij informed me that he had received feelers from some militants living in camps in Bhutan that they wanted to surrender with weapons. I told him that I would get the Government of India to approve a rehabilitation package for them and they would be eligible for cash award for the weapons they bring. We wanted to keep the ongoing negotiations a secret till we were sure that it would work out. In 1991 when the Congress had come to power, Hiteshwar Saikia had arranged a mass surrender of 3000 militants. There were allegations that a large number of these were not militants but his own chosen men. They were each given 2 lakhs for rehabilitation out of which they had to refund 1.5 lakhs in easy instalments. Of course no one refunded any money. The genuine militants who had surrendered were allowed to keep their weapons with them. In some cases they had even been given a Personal Security Officer (PSO) by the Government. These individuals were called SULFA (Surrendered ULFA). They became very unpopular with the local people for their anti-social activities. They had been indulging in extortions and other such activities. No doubt some of them had been of help to security forces in tracking down militants. Given this background, fresh surrenders by the ULFA had to be handled very carefully.

Vij having done all the leg work, we decided to have the surrender ceremony at Thakurbari not far from the Bhutan border. I informed the Chief Minister. Despite some reservation he agreed to accompany me for the surrender function. On the night before the scheduled date he telephoned me saying that members of the Finance Commission were coming and he had to be in Guwahati for a meeting with them. Therefore, he would not be able to go for the surrender function. I told him his absence at Thakurbari may be misunderstood and the army may be criticized for organizing a repeat of the SULFA drama. I suggested that he should send a message which could be read out at the function by one of the cabinet ministers to be detailed to accompany me. He readily agreed to my suggestion. Yet in some of the newspapers his absence was misinterpreted saying that the army had organized the surrender on its own and it was probably a repeat of the SULFA misadventure. One hundred and fifty militants, with weapons, surrendered at the function in Thakurbari. Apart from a minister who accompanied me, we had old freedom fighters present at the surrender to give it a look of public participation. The rehabilitation package worked out for the surrenderees was different from what had been given to SULFA. We called these RULFA (Reformed ULFA). They were kept in training camps for one year with a stipend of Rs. 2000 per month in which they were given free training in a vocation of their choice along with free board and lodging. They had various options like agriculture, fishery, computers, cooking, vehicle driving, typing, and so on. At the end of their training, their accumulated allowance of Rs. 24000 minus 4800 given to them as pocket money at the rate of 400 per month was given to them along with seed money to start their business. We even got some of them to form cooperatives to work collectively under existing Government of India development programmes which provided financial sudsidy. Soon the people realized that the rehabilitation plans for RULFA were different from SULFA. The approach adopted by us was highly successful. It opened the floodgates for surrender. By the end of my term as governor, some 3000 militants with weapons had surrendered and 2500 militants had been killed in encounters. This broke the back of militancy in Assam. We also recovered one crore in cash from the militants, which they had extorted from the people.

The Kargil War of 1999 was a source of great anxiety to me. Having taken part in operations in that area in November 1948 and having served in that terrain during my subsequent tenures in the Army, I knew too well how difficult it was for the infantry to assault those forbidding heights. I marvelled at how our young officers led their troops magnificently from the front. The smiling picture of Captain Vikram Batra on the TV screen after he had successfully captured the highest feature, over 16,000 feet high made me feel proud of our young officers in the Army. A few days later this officer in another daredevil attack won yet another astounding victory, but he got killed in that operation. This brave officer was posthumously awarded the Param Vir Chakra. While our young officers and men were making the supreme sacrifice in the service of the Nation, some misguided politicians were trying to play petty party politics. The Congress Party at Delhi had put up an inflated balloon in the form of a bus turned upside down in front of their party office. It was to make fun of the failure of Vajpayee's bus journey to Lahore. I was surprised at how any responsible person could resort to such a low act, in an hour of national crisis. There was great resentment among the people and the Congress had to remove that balloon. Politics is a strange game in our country. I recalled that during the 1962 war, the Communists had painted Long Live Mao-Tse-tung on the walls in Kolkata.

The ULFA gave a call to boycott the war effort in Kargil. They declared their support for Pakistan's efforts to "liberate" Kashmir. They argued that the war in Kargil was for the right of self-determination for the people of Kashmir, just as the people of Assam were fighting for their self-determination. The ULFA had misjudged the mood of the people of Assam. Kargil was our first televised war. It had aroused great patriotic fervour in the entire country including Assam. The ULFA also unsuccessfully tried to derail one of the troop special trains moving from Assam to Kashmir. This aroused strong anti-ULFA sentiments amongst the people. As the bodies of Assamese soldiers killed in Kargil started arriving by air at Guwahati, I made it a point to receive every body bag that arrived at the airport and the army made all the arrangements to honour the martyrs. The body bags were sent to their homes where they were given military funeral. I got my staff to arrange publicity for this in the Press. Capt Jinto of Jorhat was posthumously awarded the Vir Chakra for gallantry in Kargil. I went to his house to condole with his parents. A few weeks later when the Prime Minister arrived to inaugurate the Numaligarh Oil Refinery in Jorhat, I requested him to visit the parents of Capt Jinto and offer his condolence. He agreed to do so. The Kargil War had a good effect on our fight against insurgency in Assam. The call for boycott of the war effort issued by the ULFA was resented by the people of Assam. The arrival of the bodies of Assamese soldiers killed in Kargil and all the publicity given to that had a big impact on the people. Many army officers told me that previously when army convoys passed through villages, the people gave the soldiers a sullen or an indifferent look. Now they had started waving to them. This gesture in the wake of the Kargil War reflected their changed mindset.

Taking advantage of the changed scenario, we organized peace marches in various parts of Assam. We approached close relatives of ULFA leaders and they agreed to participate in these marches. The peace march at Guwahati was very impressive. The mother of Paresh Barua, the ULFA commander-in-chief and the brother of Arbind Rajkhowa, the ULFA President, participated in this march. The marchers floated two thousand burning earthen lamps in leaf boats on the Brahmaputra. It was an impressive scene.

April 7 was the ULFA Raising Day. This was the day when this terrorist outfit was raised at Sibsagar in 1980. Normally, the ULFA used to step up violence on this day every year. We decided to have a surrender ceremony of ULFA militants at Sibsagar ground on their Raising Day. The Chief Minister also attended the function. This was watched by nearly 20,000 people. This was certainly a high watermark of our success in combating militancy in Assam.

The ULFA leadership got rattled by the way things had been working against them. They now thought of a new strategy. Their movement had started against the influx of illegal migrants from Bangladesh and the failure of the Government to stop it. After the top ULFA leadership had taken refuge in Bangladesh, they had dropped their old agenda. The new strategy evolved by them was to target Biharis living in rural areas of Assam and force them to go out of the State. Some people said that they were doing this also to hit out against a Bihari Governor. Over a hundred Biharis were killed in a short time. There was great panic among them. Thousands of these people started converging at railway stations to escape to Bihar. A serious situation had suddenly developed, which had to be tackled vigorously. There were several lakh Biharis, mostly labourers, living in different parts of Assam. If they quit, the space vacated by them would be occupied by illegal migrants from Bangladesh. Moreover, the refugees going back to their home would have to be accommodated in refugee camps in Bihar. This could become the cause for retaliatory violence by Biharis against Assamese travelling by train through Bihar. Biharis are known to be a volatile people and I feared a violent reaction from them. I had received reports that at a few meetings in Bihar effigies of Assamese people had been burnt and I was severely criticized saying that despite being a Bihari, I had failed to provide them protection. The situation was grim and I felt I must act vigorously to deal with this serious and alarming development.

I used my army contacts to get additional troops moved into Assam from neighbouring Meghalaya, without waiting for clearance from Delhi. I informed the Deputy Prime Minister and got his ex-post-facto approval. Apart from deploying the army, paramilitary and police in sensitive areas, I got the police to organize village volunteer guards of both Assamese and Biharis to protect the Bihari population. We did not have weapons to give them nor was there enough time to train them. These volunteers were called upon to defend themselves with sticks and even stones. Their important task was to pass information about militants to the nearest post of the security forces so that the latter could deal with them. Various ingenious methods for passing information like burning haystacks, raising alarms, sending runners and so on, were organized. I personally toured the affected areas extensively. The Chief Minister was in full agreement with all that we were doing to deal with the menace.

During my tours of the affected areas I addressed the Biharis telling them that if they fled from Assam to Bihar their conditions there would become worse. Having lived for generations in Assam, they had lost their roots in their State of origin. They would have to live in refugee camps. I told them of the miserable conditions under which in similar circumstances, Kashmiri Pandits had been living in refugee camps for the last many years. I also tried to invoke their pride by reminding them of the martial traditions of Bihar. They would not be true to those traditions, if they beat a cowardly retreat from Assam. They should stay back in their homes and in conjunction with their Assamese neighbours, give a fight to the militants even without weapons. I assured them of massive deployment of security forces who would be there to come to their help promptly. I also told them that the back of militants had been broken. They could not afford to move round in large numbers. They moved stealthily in small groups of two and three. With the support of security forces readily available even unarmed organized groups could deal with these few militants. To the Assamese people I appealed that it was their duty to protect the Biharis living with them for generations. I explained the game plan of the militants. They wanted to throw out the Biharis and bring Bangladeshis to replace them. The local people were much against Bangladeshi immigrants and this line had a telling effect. My exhortations had the desired impact on both the Bihari and Assamese people in the affected areas. With reinforcement and quick deployment of security forces, we got over the crisis situation and the ULFA gave up their heinous offensive against unarmed Biharis.

Although frustrated by their failure to succeed in their criminal designs, the ULFA opened a new front. This was of false propaganda and a personal tirade against me. They gave a vicious twist to what I had been doing to restore normalcy, saying that I had been going round urging the Biharis to attack the Assamese in retaliation for the attacks on them. I should be recalled from Assam because I was promoting disharmony amongst the two communities. There were very few takers of their blatantly false propaganda. The fund of goodwill that I had earned among the people of Assam stood me in good stead. The Assamese Press came out in full support of me. Bezbarua, the highly respected Editor of *Sentinel*, the leading English newspaper of Assam, wrote a strong editorial supporting me and a scathing attack on the ULFA. He is highly regarded among the Assamese intelligentsia and had been in the vanguard in opposing illegal migration from Bangladesh to Assam. Thus the canard against me sought to be raised by the ULFA was nipped in the bud. However, there were two connected instances, which need to be mentioned. Tarun Gogoi, the President of the Congress Party in Assam which was in the Opposition, appears to have got carried away by the ULFA propaganda. He issued a statement that on coming to power after the State elections which were due shortly, he would refuse to take oath administered by me. One of our leading national newspapers the *Hindustan Times*, conducted an opinion poll amongst its readers enquiring about my proactive role as a governor in deeling with this crisis. I was shocked to find that 70 percent people polled, voted against me and only 30 percent in my favour. Obviously, those who voted against me were ill-informed about the ground realities.

I was now completing four years as Governor of Assam and it had been a period of much stress and strain. I had also suffered some personal tragedies. Air India started a direct flight from Guwahati to Bangkok which I was invited to inaugurate. They offered a free ticket for my wife and I. Two of my very dear friends from our student days Bepin and Sachhoo (Sachitanand) were staying with us in Guwahati. They were both widowers. We decided to go on a few days' holiday to Bangkok. I had been to Bangkok from Burma soon after the Second World War in 1945. It was then a small city almost like a mofussil town. In the last four decades, thanks to a flourishing tourism industry, it had become a very modern metropolis. We also went to Pattaya Beach, where we relaxed for a couple of days. On return to Guwahati after a nice five days' break I was told that the ULFA was not aware that I had been to Bangkok otherwise they would have contacted me there. The ULFA were known to have contacts in Bangkok and their leaders used to frequently visit that place.

An underground ULFA source tried to contact me in Guwahati. Major General Gaganjeet Singh who had been working in Assam for some time and had developed sources among the underground, recommended that I meet the individuals. My Special Officer in Raj Bhavan, Debashish Sharma from the Assam Administrative Service also recommended that I meet the individual. I had complete confidence in Debashish. He had been working closely with me for the past four years. Along with Debashish I went to Kolkata to meet the underground ULFA leader said to be close to Paresh Barua, the ULFA Commander-in-Chief. Debashish recognized him. A secret meeting was arranged with him at which Debashish was present. It was agreed that Paresh Barua would meet me outside India. They wanted the meeting in Bangkok but I did not accept that because of known ULFA presence in Bangkok. Further, my going to Bangkok again would compromise secrecy. I preferred Singapore and this was agreed to. It was also decided that no security agency be involved at the meeting place because Paresh Barua feared that he may get caught in a trap. I assured the ULFA man that I would not allow that to happen. I would be happy to hear what Paresh Barua may have to say and exchange views with him. The meeting could be dangerous both for him and for me. We had to trust each other. It was agreed that there should be no weapons or guards at a neutral meeting place in Singapore and I be accompanied only by Debashish. They agreed to my ADC accompanying me to Singapore but not being present at the meeting.

This was a bit of a cloak and dagger operation and a governor is not supposed to get personally involved in such a venture. However in national interest I felt that the risk was worth taking. The whole thing had to be kept a closely guarded secret and the less the number of people knew about it the better. I contacted the Deputy Prime Minister who got the Prime Minister's approval for it. RAW, our external intelligence agency, was informed. My brother was then No. 2 in its hierarchy. RAW felt that the effort was worth making as it may provide an opening for talks and an eventual solution.

My wife insisted on accompanying me to Singapore. I appreciated her fears and I gave in. Four of us — my wife, Debashish, my ADC Anubhav Negi and I proceeded to Singapore. Anubhav insisted on carrying his pistol with him. He was very devoted to me. Apart from being from my battalion (3/5 Gorkha Rifles) his father Anand Negi had also served with me in the battalion when I was commanding it. The date for the meeting had been fixed and we were told that a preliminary meeting would take place at Singapore with the underground person I had met at Kolkata and then a meeting with Paresh Barua.

We reached Singapore on the appointed date. I was quite excited about my mission. I waited for three days at Singapore but no one contacted us. Obviously the ULFA leadership had changed its mind. Maj Gen. Gaganjeet Singh, through whom the ULFA underground had contacted us, told me that there could be two reasons for the failure of my mission. The intelligence agencies of Bangladesh and Pakistan who controlled Paresh Barua's movements may have got to know about it and prevented him from leaving Bangladesh. The other possibility was that Paresh Barua may have changed his mind fearing that he may be trapped by Indian intelligence agencies. Be that as it may, my mission to Singapore became fruitless. I was disappointed. However, I had the satisfaction of making an attempt towards resolving the Assam problem, despite the personal risk involved in it.

19

The State Assembly elections were due in 2001. Political parties began gearing up for the contest as the polling date approached. So far as the conduct of the election was concerned, I had no doubts about our ability to repeat our performance of 1999 when we had conducted two parliamentary elections in quick succession because the first Vajpayee Government had lost the 'No Confidence' motion in the Parliament. The level of violence in 1999 was much higher. There were many doubting Thomases at that time who felt that in view of militancy, it would be difficult to hold peaceful elections. We made elaborate security arrangements. The army was deployed to dominate the general area to provide security to polling operations. The air force flew helicopter patrols to give warnings of any emerging security threat. I issued an appeal to voters to exercise their franchise and vote without fear for the candidate of their choice. My printed appeal was widely distributed and even dropped from helicopters. I also addressed the people to that effect on the television. We managed violence free polls with a voter turnout of over 70 percent. With the security situation having improved considerably we were confident that we would again have violence free elections in 2001, with a good voter turnout.

The AGP, as the ruling party, had to contend with the anti-incumbency factor. A scandal surfaced involving the Chief Minister which had an adverse effect on the poll prospects of AGP. A lady by the name of Sanghamitra serving in a low grade appointment in the Legislative Assembly Secretariat had been recommended by the Chief Minister to be made a member of the State Public Service Commission. It was a statutory appointment and I had to approve of her appointment. I felt that she did not fulfill the requirements for that appointment. Normally, senior officials approaching retirement or eminent non-officials were appointed as chairman or member of the Public Service Commission. Apart from being a low grade employee, she was too young to be considered for the appointment. I, therefore, did not accept the recommendation of Mohanta. That was the only time in three years that I disagreed with him on any issue. He came to see me and stated that the lady was very talented in music and art. I explained to him that her artistic talent was no qualification for appointment as a member of the Public Service Commission. I suggested that he might consider appointing her in an Art Academy or in an appointment connected with fine arts. He saw my point of view and accepted my decision. I forgot about this case till I read of it in the newspaper a few months later, along with a public assertion by the lady that she had got married to Mohanta in a temple at Mumbai. The claim made by the lady caused a big stir and this worked against Mohanta and his party. Moreover, the last minute tie up between the AGP and BJP did not work out. The two parties had been opposing each other for some time. The Congress won the elections, securing an absolute majority.

Tarun Gogoi came to see me along with Kamal Nath, the central observer of the Congress Party. Gogoi wanted to be sworn-in as chief minister immediately. I told him that I had no problem administering the oath of office to him, but prior to doing so, I would need official intimation of the results of the election and of his being elected the leader of his party in the State Assembly. Both the requirements got fulfilled the following day and I promptly administered the oath of office of chief minister to him and to the ministers as recommended by him. That was the first such function held in our newly constructed Durbar Hall. After the swearing-in, the Press asked Tarun Gogoi how he had agreed to take the oath administered by me, when in the previous year he had issued a statement that he would refuse to be sworn-in by me. Tarun Gogoi told the Press that he had never said so and the Press had misquoted him. They did not ask him as to why he had not issued a contradiction when that statement allegedly made by him, had appeared in all the newspapers of Assam.

I held a farewell dinner at Raj Bhavan the following day for Mohanta, the outgoing Chief Minister and the previous Council of Ministers. There were adverse comments on this by some Congress leaders other than the new Chief Minister, saying that I was pro-AGP and anti-Congress. I was surprised that the common courtesy shown by me was being so misrepresented. I realized that the era of my close and cordial relations with the State Government was now over.

Tarun Gogoi called on me a few days later. Although a qualified lawyer, I was surprised that he raised certain legal issues which were misconceived. He said he wanted to reopen the LoC scam case in which Mohanta had been exonerated by me. He felt that I should have acted on the advice of the Council of Ministers and not taken a decision on my own. I told him that this case had to be treated differently. In this case the chief minister himself was the alleged accused and it would have been illogical for me to ask for the advice of the Council of Ministers, over which he presided. Moreover there were precedents in Bihar, Maharashtra and Tamilnadu where the governors had exercised their discretion in dealing with cases where the CBI had recommended the prosecution of the chief ministers. The only difference was that in the three instances, the governors had accepted the recommendation of the CBI, whereas I had not done so. A governor had to exercise his discretion where a serving chief minister was involved. Anyway, I told Tarun Gogoi that he could take any action in the matter as he liked. He could not succeed in getting the LoC scam case reopened.

The second point raised by the new Chief Minister was the affidavit filed by the previous government in the Supreme Court on the controversial IMDT Act. He wanted that affidavit withdrawn and a fresh affidavit filed incorporating the views of his government. I told him that it was a legal issue on which I was not in a position to comment. As a layman, I felt that an affidavit once filed could not be withdrawn. With his legal background, he felt otherwise. I later learnt that the Supreme Court did not agree to the affidavit filed by the previous government being withdrawn but allowed the new government to file a fresh affidavit. The Court would examine both affidavits.

The one lakh shallow tube wells installed in Assam during the tenure of the Mohanta Government, had been a success story turning Assam from a rice deficit to a rice surplus State. It had been hailed by the Planning Commission. As part of vendetta politics, the new government tried to corner officials involved in the project with procedural irregularities and even corruption charges. I am glad that nothing came out of this attempt.

The new State Assembly was summoned after the elections and I had to deliver the Governor's address as drafted by the State Government. The address stated that to protect the interests of the minorities, it was imperative that the IMDT Act should continue in Assam. This was diametrically opposite to my personal views, well known throughout Assam. My report to the President recommending its repeat had been widely published. I had, however, no option but to read the Governor's address as drafted by my Government. The following day when my address was published in Assam, it raised a storm. I was criticized for having betrayed my earlier stand, calling for the repeal of the Act. The respected leading journalist of Assam, Bezbarua, wrote a strong editorial castigating me for my volte-face and added that I was now trying to curry favour with the Congress Government. I felt it was necessary for me to correct the misconception. I had a Press statement issued from Raj Bhavan, clarifying that it is a universal practice in all parliamentary democracies that the address of a Head of State is drafted by his Government and is required to be read out by him without making any changes. This address did not reflect my personal views. Those were the views of my Government. My views on the IMDT Act were well known. This cleared the air and the criticism against me died down. Bezbarua, the Editor of the *Sentinel,* who had written a highly critical editorial, was apologetic. He told me that he was not aware of the nuance of parliamentary democracy as brought out in the Press release issued by Raj Bhavan. However, the Chief Minister Tarun Gogoi was up in arms regarding the Press release. He issued a statement that I had acted in an unconstitutional manner by issuing that Press release. He would be taking up the matter with the Centre. I ignored his outburst. He never raised the matter with me. Even if he took up the issue with the Centre, nothing came out of it. This was a ticklish constitutional issue and I leave it to constitutional pandits to opine whether in the circumstances, my action was correct.

There were two other occasions of a similar nature concerning the influx of illegal migrants from Bangladesh. The Border Security Force organized a national level seminar at Shillong on border management in the North East. I was invited to inaugurate the Conference. I highlighted the threat posed by the unabated influx of illegal migrants from Bangladesh. I also said that in my personal view, the IMDT Act encouraged this influx and should be repealed. Tarun Gogoi reacted sharply by issuing a statement that the Governor must be reined in. I felt that the language used by Tarun Gogoi for his Head of State was inappropriate. He could have expressed his disagreement with my views, more politely. There was yet another instance concerning this issue. On a tour to Silchar I visited some of the border posts of the BSF. I was asked by the media about the problem of infiltration from across the border. I told them that this was continuing and we had to have more effective measures. They asked if the IMDT Act should be scrapped. I replied in the affirmative adding that it was my personal view. On reading of this in the newspapers, Tarun Gogoi appeared to have lost his cool. He now announced that he would ask for the recall of the Governor. Perhaps he was doing all this as part of vote bank politics and was playing to his constituency. He never took up this issue with me. Whenever he met me he was always very correct and there was no tension between us. We got on well.

I did not hear anything from the Centre on this issue. The NDA Government was in power at Delhi. Both Vajpayee and Advani were in agreement with my views about the IMDT Act. It is interesting that the entire press in Assam was supporting me on this issue and was critical of Tarun Gogoi. Normally, a chief minister who is a popular leader and represents the majority of the people should command the support of the people rather than a governor nominated by the Centre, who is invariably from outside the State.

20

The situation in Assam had become normal. Yet the danger of militancy reviving was ever present. Militant camps in Bhutan were still intact and the top militant leadership was in a safe sanctuary in Bangladesh. As I have mentioned earlier, I felt impatient about the King of Bhutan procrastinating all the time. A few months after I left Assam he did strike against the militant camps and we provided stops on our side of the border. He handled the situation well. He was perhaps right in taking his own time in mounting the operation. As for the top militant leadership in Bangladesh, I am afraid we have remained a soft State and have not been able to take hard decisions. Even a very unfortunate incident that took place on the border with Bangladesh did not make us react and take strong action. In several areas on the Indo-Bangladesh border, there are small pockets of territory that are in adverse possession of the other side. At Dawki on the Shillong-Sylhet road there was one such pocket behind our BSF post. Taking advantage of this, the Bangladesh Rifles had taken up position behind our post cutting off communication to it and inflicting damage. I knew that area well. In 1958 East Pakistan forces had attacked our border post at Karimganj in South Assam. It was decided that we retaliate in the Dawki area. I was sent with one company supported by mountain guns to do the needful and we completed our task successfully. The message went home to the other side. There were no further such border incidents. Nearly half a century later a similar situation had arisen. Dawki was now on the Meghalaya/Bangladesh border. The local commanders of the BSF decided on retaliatory action against the Bangladesh Rifles in Mankachar on the Assam/Bangladesh border in Lower Assam. The Deputy Commandant of the BSF battalion launched a highly unprofessional attack on a Bangladesh Rifles post. The tactical plan was unsound and there was no back-up support for the offensive action. The attack failed. The Deputy Commandant got killed along with a few of his men. Some of our boys were taken prisoners. They were tortured and their dead bodies returned slung on poles like the body of dead animals. Pictures of their bodies slung on poles appeared in all our newspapers. There was a strong reaction all over the country. I visited the Manakachar post and I was horrified at the manner in which the BSF had conducted the operation. The army unit which was not very far from Mankachar had not even been informed or called up to support the operation. Of course India launched a strong protest with Bangladesh and that was all. I was given to understand that elections were to take place in Bangladesh shortly and any strong action by us would weaken the position of Sheikh Hasina who was reported to be friendly towards India. The same Hasina a little later had no compunction in seeking assistance of the Jamaet-e-Islami, a radical Islamist organization, for elections in her country. As for the BSF, I do not know if any action was taken against the commanders responsible for the fiasco. I conveyed my strong views in the whole matter to Vajpayee when he visited me a little later. To my regret even this was of no avail.

Notwithstanding the limitation of our being unable to attack the militant camps in Bhutan from where the militants carried out hit and run raids, our gains in counter-insurgency operation had been very substantial. We eliminated some 2500 militants in encounters, took the surrender of 3000 militants with weapons and recovered Rs. 1 crore in cash. However, our real success lay in bringing about a mind change among the people. There had been 81 separate incidents in rural areas, where villagers had apprehended militants. They lynched 37 of them and handed over the remainder to the security forces. I have already mentioned how the surrender of ULFA militants on the ULFA Raising Day at the site where the ULFA had been raised in Sibsagar, was watched appreciatively by a crowd of 20,000 local people. We had come a long way from the time when ULFA militants were the heroes of the people and they enjoyed widespread support.

In 2002, when I completed my tenure of five years as Governor of Assam, the Government of India decided to give me a second tenure in Assam for another five years. I was happy to accept this. I had the satisfaction of being sworn in again as Governor in the new Durbar Hall that I had got constructed. My swearing-in by the Chief Justice took place against the backdrop of the large portrait of Assam's patron saint, Mahapurush Shrimant Shankardev. I was overwhelmed by the welcome given to me by the people of Assam for my second tenure in their great State.

With normalcy returning to the State, we took some major steps to promote tourism. We organized the Brahmaputra festival on an island in the mighty river. Both the army and the air force cooperated in organizing the festival. The Kaziranga Game Sanctuary has always been a major tourist attraction. We got the army to create a few high grounds in the sanctuary to enable the animals to climb up to them during floods in the river. A beautiful viewpoint for tourists was also constructed. A tourist hotel under thatched roof with the look of a village but having modern amenities was set up near the sanctuary. This became quite popular with the tourists.

I wanted to develop two more sites in and around Guwahati. We had already developed Vashishta, the Ashram of Guru Vashishta of Ramayan, and the Lachit Park. One of the two additional sites I had in mind was the spot where Lord Northbrook, the then Governor-General of India, had landed in 1884, and announced the formation of the province of Assam. Before that announcement Assam had been part of the Bengal Presidency. The Governor-General had come up the river by steamer from Kolkata. An old structure on the river bank put up for the occasion was still extant but in a state of disrepair. Few people knew of its significance. In 1911 King George V had come by sea to India. The Gateway of India at Mumbai commemorates that event. I wanted a park with a gate developed in the vicinity of the landing site of Lord Northbrook and name it the Gateway of Assam. I also wanted a concrete platform made near the river bank which could be used for cultural functions. The battle of Saraighat in 1671 was fought on the river in close vicinity of this site. Lachit Borphukan had come down from the adjacent Sukreshwar Hill and boarded a boat to lead his men against the Mughal fleet. A *son et lumiere* depicting the battle of Saraighat with spectators seated on the platform on the river bank could become a good tourist attraction. I got a business house to sponsor the Gateway project and on its completion to get the Tourist Department to agree to organize a Sound and Light show. I had a dry run of this show. I felt this could be a major tourist attraction.

Another project was the site on the North Bank where there were three stone inscriptions in Sanskrit referring to the victory of King Prithu of Kamrup (modern Assam) in an ambush over the army of Bakhtiyar Khilji in early thirteenth century. The account given in these inscriptions is corroborated by the account given by Minhas, the chronicler of Bakhtiyar Khilji, in the "Tabakat-i-Nasri". He had accompanied Bakhtiyar Khilji on this fatal expedition. This site was lying in a state of neglect and was unknown to most people. Bakhtiyar Khilji had been the Governor of Jaunpur in UP from where he had set out and conquered Bihar and then Bengal. He had destroyed the Nalanda University and had burnt down its world famous library. His foray into Assam with 12,000 horsemen had resulted in a disaster when his army while crossing the Brahmaputra fell a prey to a carefully laid ambush by Prithu. The bulk of his army got decimated. Bakhtiyar Khilji lost his life. The importance of this invasion lay in the fact that it was the first invasion of Assam from the West. During the Sultanate and Mughal periods, Assam faced seventeen invasions which were all foiled by the Assamese people. The most well-known invasion was of Aurangzeb's forces comprising nearly one lakh soldiers in the seventeenth century. The invaders had been routed by Lachit Borphukan in the battle of Saraighat. Thus Assam was the only province of India which had not come under the Delhi Sultans or the Mughal Emperors, while the rest of India succumbed to them.

I felt Kanai Borso Sil should be developed into a tourist spot with a translation of the inscriptions and the account of Minhas recorded in golden letters on black granite slabs, in a well-developed garden. As Chairman of the NEC, I allotted funds for this project but bureaucratic hassles delayed the work being started. There was a conflict between the State Archaeological Department and the Archaeological Department of the Government of India regarding their jurisdiction over the site. This took a long time to resolve, leading to considerable delay in the execution of the project.

Soon after my marriage in 1949, I was posted in Jammu and Kashmir which was then a non-family station. My wife and I remained separated till I was posted in Mhow in 1956. After our wedding in 1949, I was posted to my battalion in Gurais across the 11000-foot Razdhan Pass. The Pass used to remain blocked with snow for nearly six months in a year. There was no telephone connection to Gurais in those days. Computers or helicopters were unknown at that time. Letters carried by Dak runners took a long time. During winter the runners would, in good weather, venture to cross the Pass, about once a month. Thus one was cut off in Gurais from the rest of the world during the winter months with letters taking months to reach Patna, where my wife was staying with my parents. In 2003, the Gorkha battalion that I had commanded was located in Gurais. They invited me to visit them. My wife was excited at the prospect of doing so. My youngest brother, Chakru, was then posted in Jammu and we also wanted to visit him. Akhnoor is an hour's drive from Jammu. In 1977, I had commanded the division at Akhnoor. The beautiful Flagstaff House in which we had lived was on the bank of the Chenab. My wife and

I decided to take a short trip to J&K. We stayed at Jammu for a couple of days with my brother and visited Akhnoor, with the army extending warm hospitality to us. Thereafter, we proceeded to Srinagar where we stayed at the Raj Bhavan with the then Governor, Girish Saxena. The Chief Minister of the State was Dr Farooq Abdullah, an old friend. He gave us the State helicopter in which we flew to Gurais and spent some time with the battalion. No one was now with the battalion from the time when I had commanded it over 30 years ago. However, there was Pranab Bora in the Battalion who had been my ADC in Assam. He had come down from his picket to meet us. As the wife of the commanding officer, my wife used to take keen interest in welfare activities. We met officers and soldiers serving in the battalion whose fathers had served with me in the battalion and whose mothers had interacted with my wife. I was visiting Gurais after a gap of fifty years. So much had changed during this period. A new generation was now serving in the battalion and the older generation had faded away. There were signs of several other changes. Roads had now come up and convoys of heavy vehicles crossed the Razdhan Pass. There were now a few helipads and helicopters which had not been heard of in my time were now flying to that location. Electricity had come to Gurais Valley and troops were now living much more comfortably with modern amenities. With television, internet, and helicopter, they were no longer cut off from the rest of the world in the winter. While wondering about all the changes that had taken place, I almost felt like a man from the Moon coming to a world in which he had lived a long time ago. Yet there was so much that had not changed. There was still plenty of trout in the Kishenganga. The snow clad mountains, including Harmukh, looked as formidable as before. The latter is a square top feature which looks alike from all the four sides. And of course the 25000 feet high Nanga Parbat was there in all its majesty. I got the helicopter pilot to fly us over the 13000 feet picket which I had held with my troops for a year. Seeing this picket from the air I found it so familiar. Nothing had changed. I could identify each track bend and each mountain slope near my old picket. The world had stood still on this hill for the last half a century. Old memories came gushing back to me.

While I was on my short trip to Jammu and Kashmir rumours spread that I had come on a preliminary visit to look round and see things before I took over as Governor of Jammu and Kashmir. There was no basis for this wild conjecture. I was at pains to deny the rumour. This thought may not have entered the minds of the decision makers at Delhi at that time. However a few months later what was then a baseless rumour turned out to be true.

On return to Assam, we decided to proceed abroad on a month's leave to meet all our four children. We planned to spend a week with each. Our son was in UAE and our eldest daughter in Spain. Towards the end of our stay in Spain I received a telephone call from the Prime Minister. He wanted me to take over as Governor of J&K. This came as a complete surprise to me and I felt bowled over. My wife and children were not at all happy at the prospect of my being uprooted from Assam and sent to Jammu and Kashmir. Things had settled down in Assam and I could now have a much more peaceful time there. The situation in Jammu and Kashmir was boiling. We had only recently been there and seen for ourselves the disturbed conditions. My wife said that my move was tantamount to moving from the frying pan to the fire. I told her that the frying pan had ccoled down and we would douse the fire. My children were concerned at my accepting such a challenging assignment when I was in my late seventies. I told them that as an old soldier I could not ignore the call of duty to the Nation. In case I found my health was not coping up with the requirements of my job, I would request to be allowed to hang up my boots. The Prime Minister wanted me to proceed to Kashmir forthwith but I requested to be allowed to complete the remaining two weeks of my leave. We were due to go to our other two daughters in the USA the following day. My request was agreed to but I was told that I had to proceed to Kashmir immediately on return from leave. I said I would do so within three days of my return to Guwahati.

While I was in the USA with my youngest daughter, Assamese NRIs in the neighbourhood, who were aware of my visit to my daughter, had planned a reception for me. Word had spread that I would soon be moving to Kashmir and they decided to make it a farewell reception.

There were quite a few Kashmiri Pandits also living in Masachusettes. They wanted to have a joint reception for us with the Assamese NRIs. The combined reception for us was a farewell by the Assamese and welcome by the Kashmiris. They held this reception in a hotel and also invited our daughter, son-in-law and our 5-year old grandson. I did not realize that there would be so many NRIs from Assam and Kashmir in Masachusettes. The local newspapers prominently covered this function describing it as unique. The farewell speeches of my Assamese hosts were touching and so were those of Kashmiri Pandits when they described how they had been made victims of ethnic cleansing. I told them that I was aware of their plight and assured them that I would do my best to mitigate their suffering.

I returned to Guwahati and as I had committed, we were ready to leave within three days. There was hardly any time for farewell functions. I declined all invitations saying that I desperately needed time to complete my packing. The Chief Minister was in Delhi and he returned only a day before we were due to leave. There were streams of visitors coming to see us at Raj Bhavan, which interfered with the limited time we had for packing. Their outpouring of affection was overwhelming. We took time off to go to Mrs. Bordoloi. The old lady treated me like a son and she had been a mother figure for me.

She blessed us and was quite moved. The farewell visit was also emotional for us. I realized that we would perhaps never meet her again. The following year she passed away. I wrote from Kashmir to her son, Robin, who was now a minister in Assam, that like him, I felt orphaned and indeed all Assam had been orphaned. Lokpriya Gopi Nath Bordoli was an icon of Assam. His widow who survived him for half a century, was regarded as the mother of Assam.

Tarun Gogoi had returned to Guwahati from Delhi to bid us farewell. Both he and his wife were very gracious. Along with a very large number of people, they were at the airport to see us off. There was a police guard of honour at the airport. Nearly six years earlier the then Chief Minister Mohanta and other dignitaries were there to receive us at the airport with all the protocol formalities of the guard of honour and formal introductions. The welcome given to me in 1997 was a very formal affair. I could even feel that the people at the time had apprehensions about the popular government being dismissed and 'military' rule imposed on Assam. In 2003 the feeling was entirely different. I could feel the warmth and affection of the people who had come to bid us farewell. Tarun Gogoi, who had maintained correct personal relations with me, showed marked cordiality. My father had landed with me at the airport when I had arrived to take over as Governor of Assam. Alas, he had passed away and he was not there to see the affectionate farewell that I was accorded.

The newspapers of Assam and the people of Assam showered unprecedented affection on me. I was overwhelmed by their kindness and also by a feeling of humility. The newspapers had referred to me as "Our man in Raj Bhavan," "More Assamese than any Assamese", "A true son of the soil of Assam". They were overgenerous. I quote what the leading newspaper in Assam, the *Sentinel,* wrote in its front page of 1 June:-

SINHA DID SO MUCH, YET WENT UNSUNG

Conscious citizens of Assam are aghast that no public organization of the State, particularly those who swear to fight for the cause of indigenous people of our composite milieu, had the time to organize a public function to bid farewell and say a big "thank you" to Lt Gen (Retd) S K Sinha who did so much for their cause in the past seven years (*sic*) of his stint as Governor of the State and that too with so much of personal effort, time and energy. Governors have come and gone from Assam or will continue to do so. But what this section of the citizens strongly feel that Lt Gen Sinha had created a niche for himself in the hearts of all Assamese by taking up their just causes at the right forums and levels.

His report to the President of India on the influx issue will continue to determine the course of the political events in Assam till the Government of India takes appropriate steps on it, even if political parties and organizations who have vested interest in encouraging the influx try to put the issue under wraps.

According to observers, it was Mr Sinha's report which sensitized not only the Centre but also the national political parties and organizations in other parts of the country about the issue. His great effort to propagate the bravado and heroism of the legendary Lachit Borphukan in the rest of India is another example of his deep commitment to the people of Assam. Even though Lachit Borphnkan's bravado was eulogised by the leaders of the Assam Movement during 1979 to 1983, the organizations appeared to forget that they had a duty to thank Mr Sinha for having instituted an honour for the best cadet of the NDA in the name of Lachit Borphukan. Himself, being a soldier, Mr Sinha spoke from the heart, whenever he used to speak on Lachit Borphukan's brilliance as a military strategist.

One might write off Mr Sinha's great work to sink the shallow tubewells in Assam to usher in "green revolution as part of his official duty, but the fact cannot be ignored that it had the stamp of his personal effort which was too deep for anyone not to recognize it.

Overall Mr Sinha would be remembered as the best Governor Assam ever had. Several senior citizens told the *Sentinel* that his departure would create a void in Assam's leadership which would be difficult to fill up while regretting that no organization felt it its duty to organize a public farewell for this great friend of Assam."

I received a very warm letter from Satish Kakat, a veteran Congressman and an associate of Lokpriya Gopinath Bordoloi. He wrote, "No one not even any Assamese in recent times has been so sincere in serving Assam and its people. You have been singularly successful in injecting a sense of self pride in the Assamese people projecting the heroes of Assam as the pride of the Nation."

As we departed from Guwahati after an affectionate farewell, with our plane climbing into the clouds, I felt sentimental. I recalled various incidents during my tenure in the State. Throughout my tenure of six years, I was greatly privileged to have the love and affection of the people of Assam, in an abundant measure. Nothing I had done or I may do, could repay my gratitude to them. I had started by trying to win their hearts and minds but in the process I found they had won my heart and mind. I decided that although I was going away from Assam, my association with that beautiful State and its great people should continue for ever. A feeling dawned on me that hereafter I could be a NRA (Non Resident Assamese). The ULFA leaders operating from Bangladesh are also NRAs but they are of a totally different kind. They are playing the role of Badan Borphukan, the traitor who had brought the Burmese to Assam in early nineteenth century. The Burmese carried out much slaughter and perpetrated untold atrocities on the people of Assam. The ULFA is now all out to destroy Assam promoting infiltration of illegal migrants from Bangladesh like what vote bank politicians have been doing for long. The irony is that the ULFA had been raised to fight against this illegal influx that threatens the State's demography and the Nation's security. As for me, I shall be a NRA of a very different mould, always striving for the welfare and prosperity of the State.

I have been great admirer of General Douglas MacArthur, the great American war hero and Pro Consul of the twentieth century. He was hailed as the American Ceaser. In my own humble way, I tried to live up to the ideal of service to one's country, as showed by him. When he was sacked from Japan by his Government, he had delivered his historic speech in which he had said that old soldiers never die, they fade away. When I was superseded by the Government for the appointment of Army Chief, I immediately resigned. I issued a statement that I do not question the decision of the Government, I accept it. I have decided to fade away from the army. As Ambassador in Nepal, I had done much to promote cordial Indo-Nepal relations and had contributed towards restoration of democracy in Nepal. I was instrumental in getting the Bank Road in Patna named after BP Koriala, the first elected Prime Minister of Nepal. I had come from Kathmandu to Patna with the Prime Minister of Nepal for the renaming function. I had also initiated a case for installing a statue of BP Koirala in Patna. After nearly two years, this statue was complete and the Prime Minister of Nepal was invited to unveil it. I was then living in retirement in Patna. The State Government invited hundreds of people to the function but omitted to invite me. MacArthur was the Conqueror of Japan and as Pro Consul, the creator of modern democratic Japan. When the Japanese Peace Treaty was signed in the USA, MacArthur was living in retirement. He was not invited for the function. There was yet another remote parallel. MacArthur's father had been the Governor General of the Phillipines. Douglas MacArthur had lived in the Phillipines for few years. Before the Second World War, he served as Military Adviser in the Phillipines. He helped to modernize the Phillipines Army. He fought valiantly for the defence of the Phillipines, when the Japanese attacked and conquered the Island. MacArthur was ordered to proceed to Australia. He was very popular in the Phillipines and had said that he would always be with the Phillipines Army in spirit. He returned and liberated the Phillipines. The Phillipines Army started a unique new tradition. At evening roll calls names of soldiers are called out and they respond saying 'Present". At this Parade they started the practice the first name to be called out would be of Douglas MacArthur and the senior person at the parade would say "Present". Without any such ceremonial, I felt that I shall always be present in spirit in Assam. I have mentioned these three near parallels to bring out the coincidence of events rather than to compare myself with a great all time war hero. Even a remote attempt at such comparison would be equating the sublime with the ridiculous.

Lt Gen Ajai Singh succeeded me as the Governor of Assam. He and I had been friends for long, having served together in the Army. His thinking on Assam was on the same lines as mine. He told me that he would continue with all the policies initiated by me. There were two works that I had started but they were not yet complete. These were the Gateway of Assam and the Konoi Borso Sil projects. I have already referred to them earlier. In a rare gesture of friendship, Ajai invited me to inaugurate the Gateway of

Assam project. Seldom is a former governor so invited. He was very hospitable and so was Tarun Gogi. A few months later, he invited me again to inaugurate the Konoi Borso Sil project, when it was completed. I was only too happy to avail of these opportunities to go from Kashmir to Assam and meet old friends.

There are two major pilgrimages in Jammu and Kashmir. These are Mata Vaishno Devi in Jammu and Shri Amarnath in Kashmir. I was the Chairman of both Shrine Boards. I was only too happy to help any pilgrims from Assam who contacted me. Several ministers, legislators and officials with whom I had known in Assam would contact me. Several official delegations from Assam visited Jammu and Kashmir. They would invariably come to meet me and I was delighted to extend hospitality to them. A cultural troupe came from Assam and they enthralled the audience with Bihu dance and other cultural items. I inaugurated their function and also called them over to the Raj Bhavan, for a function in their honour.

The Vivekanand Kendra of Guwahati, in co-operation with Sattradhikars (heads of monasteries) of Assam, organized a mega function in Delhi on the philosophy of Mahapurush Shrimant Shankar Dev in 2006. I was invited to inaugurate this meet. I readily accepted the invitation and came from Srinagar to Delhi for it. I was delighted to meet many old friends. A very large contingent had come from Assam for this conference. A whole lot of people from Assam living in Delhi also participated in this event. The large gathering made me feel that Assam had come to Delhi. Some Sattradhikars in their speeches said that they wanted me back as Governor in Assam. I told them that was not possible. However they extracted a promise from me to attend a conference of Sattradhikars in Guwahati. I had studied the life of Shrimant Shankardev who had flourished in the fifteenth century during the Bhakti era. He was the only Hindu saint of that era, who had tried to break the shackles of the caste system in Hindu society. I urged that the teachings of this great Saint should be propagated throughout the country. The meet in Delhi was a big success and a step in the right direction.

There was yet another conference in Delhi organized by the apolitical intelligentsia of Assam on security, political and economic problems of Assam. Some well known apolitical personalities of Delhi civil society participated in this conference. I was asked to inaugurate this conference. I came over from Srinagar, delighted at the prospect of interaction with old friends from Assam.

During my tenure in Assam, the back of the ULFA had been broken and they had been completely isolated from the people. Not long after I left, the Bhutan Army wiped out their camps in that country. The ULFA was in total disarray with their remnants surrounded by the Army in the jungles of Upper Assam. The people of Assam had no sympathy for the ULFA. At this stage, an ill advised decision was taken to suspend operations and start indirect peace talks, through a group of well meaning citizens acting as middlemen. The ULFA was obviously trying to extricate its surrounded elements and get breathing time to rest and regroup. The Government of India fell into their trap. This was not the first time that on the plea of talks, the ULFA had led the Government up the garden path. This had happened in early nineties after Operation Rhino. This time again, after getting the necessary breathing time and rescuing their surrounded elements, the ULFA followed their old tactics. They disowned the Peace Consultative Group. They now struck on Independence Day in 2006 attacking a school in Dhemaji, in which about 30 school children were killed. The people of Assam were horrified at this barbaric act and there was widespread protest in the State. Sporadic acts of violence started taking place in Assam. The Assamese people strongly condemned this senseless violence. The ULFA also got back to targeting the Hindi speaking population in the State, killing some one hundred innocent people. I started receiving messages from various people in Assam to do something in the matter. There was nothing that I could do, other than write to the Prime Minister giving my views. After some time, I got an opportunity to visit Assam to attend a meeting of Sattradhikars of Assam, organised at Guwahati. I had committed myself to attend this meeting during the conference in Delhi on the Philosophy of Mahapurush Shrimant Shankardev. The seminar at Guwahati was attended by Sattradhikars from all over the State, including distant and remote places. It was an impressive gathering. I urged them to organize peace marches in their respective areas. I later learnt that their peace marches had a good effect.

While in Guwahati, I was shocked to learn of rumours about how the State Congress had bought the support of the ULFA during the State election in 2005. National games were to be held shortly. I read in the newspapers that the Chief Minister had appealed to the ULFA to allow the National games to be held peacefully. This lowered the dignity of his office and showed his lack of confidence in the Security Forces to ensure that the National games were held peacefully. I was horrified to hear a rumour that the State Government had also paid the ULFA, a large sum of money under the table to buy peace for the National games. I heard this rumour from several sources, including a former minister from the Congress Party.

During the five years that had elapsed after I had left Assam, I remained in constant touch with the State though frequent visits to Guwahati and interaction with people from the State, both in Jammu and Kashmir, and in Delhi. I was happy to have lived up to my desire to be a NRA.

Notwithstanding the setbacks to the security situation in Assam, it is my ardent hope that the dreams of "Sonar Asom" (Golden Assam) will be realized one day with the people of the State enjoying peace and prosperity. No matter where I am, if I can in anyway contribute to achieve that goal, I will consider myself truly blessed. It will ensure realization of the objective that I was working for as Governor of Assam. My earnest desire has been that the people of Assam be proud of themselves and the rest of India be proud of Assam. I can do no better than close this chapter on Assam by the invocation that I used to make at the end of all my speeches in Assam, "Joi Ai Asom, Jai Hind" (Victory to Mother Assam, Victory to India).

3 PARADISE IN PERIL: Kashmir Imbroglio

1

After a warm and affectionate farewell at Guwahati airport, I arrived in Delhi for an overnight stay before proceeding to Srinagar. As I was familiar with the Kashmir problem and had visited Jammu and Srinagar only a few months earlier, the requirement for my being briefed at Delhi about the situation in the State was dispensed with. However, Rustum Nanavaty, who had retired as Army Commander from Jammu and Kashmir, three days earlier, was on his way to his home in Pune. He met me at the J&K House in Delhi and briefed me about the strategy of suppressive fire, which was being pursued on the Line of Control (LoC). As soon as Pakistan artillery opened fire from across the LoC, which they often did, to facilitate infiltration by terrorists, we would bring down heavy retaliatory fire silencing their guns. This had been working well and we were having the upper hand in these exchanges. He also told me about the new Chief Minister, Mufti Mohammad Sayeed, who had taken over a few months earlier. The previous Chief Minister, Dr Farooq Abdullah had been friendly and cooperative. He was popular among army officers. Mufti having been Union Home Minister earlier and being feted as a leader who had come to power in Kashmir as a result of what was acclaimed as the first free and fair election in the State, had perhaps a chip on his shoulder. Rustum briefed him at his headquarters in Udhampur. At that briefing he had suggested that army officers could be utilized in civil appointments at district level in sensitive areas to tone up the administration. This had been tried out during the Second World War in States like Bengal and Assam and after Independence, in the North East. Mufti blew up at this suggestion, saying that he had not become Chief Minister to hand over the State's administration to the army. He could have been more tactful in expressing is disagreement, particularly when quite a few junior officers of Rustam were present at that meeting. Rustam was upset over this incident.

A few years after I had quit the army, I had met Mufti when he had accompanied VP Singh to my house in Patna in the late eighties. VP Singh had resigned from Rajiv Gandhi's Cabinet over the Bofors issue and was trying to form a new party with a view to capturing power in Delhi. He had come to my house in Patna and asked me to join his party. I had declined saying that I did not want to join active politics, although I had unsuccessfully contested for Patna parliamentary seat as an Independent candidate. On the second occasion, when VP Singh came to my house, Mufti had accompanied him. We had lunch together. That was the first time I met Mufti who had earlier like VP Singh, been in the Congress Party. At that meeting I had a long discussion with Mufti about the Kashmir issue. I had been associated with Kashmir from day one, in October 1947, when the Indian army went to Kashmir to rescue the people from the barbaric invasion of tribal raiders led by Pakistan army. I have earlier mentioned how I had gone to Srinagar with the first lot of troops in October 1947, my close association with the first Indo-Pak War in Kashmir of 1947–48 and my assignment in 1949 as Secretary of the Indian delegation to the UN for delineating the Cease Fire Line in Kashmir. Besides, I had served for many years during my army career in all the three regions of the State.

After my long discussion with Mufti, he told VP Singh that he was much impressed with my knowledge of Kashmir. A couple of years or so later, VP Singh became Prime Minister and Mufti was made Union Home Minister. VP Singh initially asked me to take over as Governor of Jammu and Kashmir but two days later changed his mind and wanted me to go as Ambassador to Nepal. Thirteen years later, I was now on my way to take over as Governor of Jammu and Kashmir. Destiny had decreed that Mufti and I should work together, he as Chief Minister and I as Governor. I hoped that our previous association would help us in forging a good working relationship. A governor and a chief minister being on cordial terms, is good for the State. I appreciated Mufti's gesture of sending the State aircraft to Delhi to take me to Srinagar.

As my plane approached Srinagar airport, my thoughts went back to the momentous days of October 1947, when I had landed at the same airport. The situation was very critical at that time. The enemy was over 5000 strong and had captured Baramulla, a mere thirty miles from Srinagar. Baramulla was connected with a good tarmac road to Srinagar and there was no obstacle nor any defending force en route. On the first day, when we had landed at Srinagar we had only about 250 troops. It took us some ten days to build up sufficient strength to launch a counter-offensive. After initial contact with the enemy at Baramulla, we had to retreat to the outskirts of Srinagar, in the area of Shelatang. The decisive battle for Srinagar was fought at Shelatang on 7 November 1947. The grit, bravery and devotion of the Indian soldier and the enthusiastic support of the local people helped us to turn the tide. That was over half a century ago. In 2003, we were embroiled in an ongoing insurgency in Kashmir, which had claimed some 40,000 lives. Only a few weeks ago, 27 Kashmiri Pandits had been massacred in the village of Nandigram in the Valley, 35 Hindus were massacred at Kulhan in Doda and the famous Raghunath Temple in Jammu had been attacked by the militants. The overall security scenario was grim. Kashmir has been one of the hotpots of the world. In 1947, we had rescued the Valley from the depredations of tribal invaders who had caused havoc on the innocent people of Baramulla and other towns and villages in the Valley. In 2003 our task was to rid Kashmir of the scourge of Islamist terrorism, launched by Pakistan from across the border. Irrespective of the stupendous difficulties faced by us, I was determined to do my best to achieve this goal in our national interests and for the good of the people of the State.

Mufti Mohammad Sayeed and some senior officers were at the airport to receive me. There was also a police guard of honour for me. I was meeting Mufti after fifteen years. We had last met in my house at Patna. I had read his statement in the Press saying that no army officer should be appointed governor of Jammu and Kashmir. Either he had been overruled or he had been persuaded to accept my appointment.

I arrived in Srinagar on the morning of 4 June 2003 and the same afternoon I was sworn in as the seventh governor of Jammu and Kashmir on the grounds of the picturesque Raj Bhavan, which once used to be the palace of Maharaja Hari Singh's youngest wife, the mother of Dr Karan Singh. While I was being sworn in as governor, musketry fire could be heard in Srinagar city and guns from both sides boomed on the Line of Control.

Mufti had impeccable credentials. He had been a senior Congressman, who had been President of the State Congress for some years. He had been winning elections from the predominantly Hindu constituency of Ranbirsinghpura in Jammu. During the Janta regime, he had been Union Home Minister the second most important political appointment after that of the Prime Minister. Mufti has been the only Muslim appointed to that high political office. Even great freedom fighters like Maulana Abul Kalam Azad and Rafi Ahmed Kidwai had not held that office. Although Mufti had been changing political parties from Congress to Janta Party and now People Democratic Party (PDP) that he had founded, his secular image had remained intact. Yet I had heard some disturbing reports about him. I have already mentioned what Rustam Nanavaty had told me at Delhi of his brush with him, I had heard rumours about his dubious role, in the late eighties during the attack on Hindu temples in his home district and elsewhere in South Kashmir. Mohammad Shafi, General Secretary J&K Awami National Conference wrote, "Mufti Mohammad Sayeed in connivance with senior Central Congress leaders engineered communal riots in Islamabad (his home district) by burning temples". Hilal Ahmed War, a former militant, wrote in his book that the kidnapping of his elder daughter Rubaiya had been stage managed to secure the release of five extremists held in jail. This was part of a deal to help Mufti build a political base for himself in the Valley. I heard about the Rubaiya episode from many sources.

The five extremists on arrival in Pakistan played a stellar role in starting militancy in Kashmir. Apart from all this, I was not comfortable with his slogan of Healing Touch for militants and their families. I felt that it was more important for us to provide healing touch to the victims of terrorism than to the perpetrators of terrorism. His party was able to get the approval of the Government of India for pension being given to the families of militants killed in encounter with security forces. Nowhere in the world families of terrorists receive such bounty from the State. This largesse has not been extended to militants in the North East or to the families of Naxalites. Giving such benefits amounts to encouraging terrorism. Mufti also tried to show that he was equidistant between India and Pakistan. Two of his statements issued soon after I took over as Governor shocked me. Vajpayee had given a firm reply to Musharraf at the UN when the latter in violation of the Shimla Accord had raised the Kashmir issue at that forum. In a comment to the Press, Mufti termed the acrimony at the UN between India's Prime Minister and Pakistan's President as unfortunate adding that sooner they started a dialogue for peace, the better. This was at a time when our national stand was that we could not have any dialogue with Pakistan till she stopped cross border terrorism. In another statement, Mufti had stated that the best solution for the controversy over Baglihar Hydel project on the Chenab, was to place it under the joint control of India and Pakistan. I felt that if Baglihar was placed under joint control, there would be a demand for Kashmir being placed under joint control of the two countries. True enough when Musharraf later came out with his four point proposal for Kashmir which included joint control, Mufti welcomed it. I saw a BBC programme on the TV called Question Time India organized at Srinagar. There were three panelists, namely, Mufti Mohammad Sayeed, Omar Abdullah and Sajjad Lone, presenting their views before an indoor audience of a few hundred people. Each panelist first put across his views on the Kashmir issue. Sajjad and Omar were very articulate in presenting their views. At the end of the discussion the anchor asked the audience whether India or Pakistan was responsible for the Kashmir problem. Almost everyone in the audience raised his hand to convey that India was responsible. Sajjad smiled while Omar spiritedly said that the few people in the hall did not represent the views of the majority of the people of the Valley, much less of the State. Mufti chose to remain silent. That programme was a disastrous projection to the world, of India's stand on Kashmir. In October 2005 terrorists gunned down Ghulam Nabi Lone Minister of State for education in Mufti's Cabinet, inside his official residence in the high security zone of Ministers' bungalows in Srinagar. The following day Mufti at his Press Conference was talking about his policy of healing touch for the militants. No wonder Lone's son Shoaib Lone who later won the Assembly By-election from his, father's constituency, made serious allegations of involvement of Mufti and his party in his father's assassination.

Notwithstanding the above disturbing facts, I felt I must go all out to develop cordial relations with Mufti. Despite my efforts, cordiality in our relations became difficult to achieve. Some of this may have been my fault or the fault of circumstances but Mufti cannot escape his share of blame. In an effort to establish good relations, I sent Eid greetings card and later New Year greetings card to the separatist leaders like Syed Ali Shah Geelani and Mirwaiz Omar Farooq as a gesture of goodwill. There was of course no response from them.

2

The Raj Bhavan at Srinagar has an interesting history. I got to know of it also in an interesting manner, soon after I had quit the army in 1983. Little did I then realize that one day I would be living in it.

In 1946, I was serving at General Headquarters (now Army Headquarters) in Delhi. Colonel FHB Ingall, a flamboyant cavalry officer was my boss. He was a bachelor living in the Viceroy's house with his friend Douglas Currie, Military Secretary to the Viceroy. He was known to have high connections. Once or twice every month he used to go on a holiday to Kashmir. We heard that he was friendly with the Maharaja and he frequently visited Kashmir for fishing and bird shooting. The young officers in the Directorate in which we were serving, thought that he must be having a girl friend in Kashmir.

Ingall was very kind to me. He put me up for accelerated promotion and I became a Major out of turn, a couple of months before Partition. At the time of Partition, he recommended my name to Lt Gen Sir Dudley Russell, the Army Commander of the newly set up Delhi and East Punjab Command (now Western Command). Ingall had been Russell's principal staff officer when the latter was commanding a division at the battle of Alamein in North Africa and later commanded an armoured brigade under him in Italy. I was appointed General Staff Officer (Operations) in Russell's Headquarters. In August 1947, Ingall opted for Pakistan Army. He was promoted Brigadier and as Commandant raised the new Pakistan Military Academy at Kabul. In December 1947 during the first Indo-Pak War, I had to report two bits of information which had visibly upset Russell. First, the raiders had received logistic support at Kakul in which Ingall was said to be involved. Second, we had captured a prisoner from 6/13 Frontier Rifles. This was Russell's old battalion in which he had served for many years and which he had commanded.

After I quit the army in 1983, I received a letter from Ingall who had retired and settled at California in the USA. He sent me his autobiography, *The Last Bengal Lancer*, requesting me to write a review of his book for Indian readership. The book made a very interesting reading covering Ingall's life as a horsed cavalry officer serving on the North West Frontier and playing polo and pig-sticking in the pre Second World War days in peace stations. It also gave his experiences as a tank commander in that war followed by an account of his service in Pakistan. There was of course no reference to Pakistani tribal invasion of Kashmir in which he had been reported to have been involved.

I was much interested to read what Ingall had written about Kashmir. In 1930 he was a Captain serving as Adjutant of his regiment located at Sialkot. One day the Mess Havaldar came to see him and requested for release from the army because his daughter was getting married. Ingall advised him to take leave and after getting his daughter married, return to the regiment. The Havaldar told him that his daughter was getting married to Maharaja Hari Singh of Kashmir. The Maharaja had two wives but had no children. The astrologers had said that if the Maharaja got married to a girl born under a certain constellation of stars, he would be blessed with a son. It was very important for the Maharaja to have an heir. Search teams were sent out all over Dogra country to locate a girl who met the requirement. A girl was found in a village near Chamba and she happened to be the daughter of the Mess Havaldar. The wedding was performed with much pomp and splendor. A new palace was built for the new Maharani. Ingall attended the wedding and was treated as a VIP because of his association with the bride's father. The British Resident in Kashmir noted this and had Ingall posted on his staff. A year later the prediction came true. A son was born to the Maharaja in France. He is Dr. Karan Singh. The Maharaja and the Maharani with the newly born Prince returned to Kashmir. There was tumultuous welcome for them. The entire population of Srinagar was fed free for a few days as the guest of the Maharaja. Every house, houseboat and shikara in Srinagar was illuminated for a few days. The palace built for the new Maharani is the present Raj Bhavan at Srinagar where I had now come to live for the next five years. We certainly live in a small world.

When Dr. Karan Singh came to see me once at Raj Bhavan, I mentioned about Ingall's book. He told me that he had fond memories of the palace, now Raj Bhavan, where his mother lived. He wanted to read Ingall's book. I got him the book from the USI Library at Delhi.

3

My being sent to Jammu and Kashmir got undue publicity in the media. The impression conveyed was that due to the success achieved by me in Assam, I had been specially selected for Jammu and Kashmir. I received numerous letters of congratulations from friends and also from many people whom I did not know. They expressed the hope that I will succeed in resolving the Kashmir problem. An old friend who had served with me in the army, Brigadier OP Vohra, wrote, "Nehru faltered, Indira slipped, Sinha settled". He was counting the chickens before they were hatched and comparing the sublime to the ridiculous. I am mentioning this only to bring out the sort of reaction among some people to my being given the very challenging assignment in Jammu and Kashmir. While on my way from Guwahati to Srinagar, I had been interviewed by a popular TV channel, *Aj Tak*. I was asked questions pertaining to Assam and my plans for Jammu and Kashmir. I had emphasized in my interview that the best solution for militancy was to bring about a mind change among the people, misled by separatist ideology. I had succeeded in doing so in Assam. My endeavour would be to try and repeat that in Jammu and Kashmir.

Circumstances had thrust a high profile image on me. No chief minister likes to have a high profile governor who may steal his thunder. Matters can be worse if such a governor also happens to be proactive. I am mentioning this to provide a backdrop for the unfortunate course, our relations took as time moved on. My swearing-in-ceremony at Raj Bhavan was a simple affair. There were quite a few friends I recognized at the function. I was happy to find Dr Farooq Abdullah present at the function. I had known him for some time. I had had occasions to interact with his revered father, a legendary leader of Kashmir. The warm manner in which Farooq and I met, may not have pleased Mufti. They were bitter enemies. Much later, when I hosted an Iftar Party at Raj Bhavan, Mufti and Farooq were with me. Seeing them together, a Press correspondent asked them if they had made up and become friends. Farooq replied emphatically, "Good Heavens No. We are sworn enemies". His son, Omar was married to the daughter of a Sikh army officer who had been my student at Mhow. At the inauguration function of Shri Mata Vaishno Devi University, Mufti got into acrimony in public with Farooq Abdullah for not using Aukaf funds for higher education (Bala Ghulam Shah University came up a year later). Both the President and I felt uncomfortable over the controversy between them in front of a large audience in our presence.

I had shared the platform with Farooq at public meetings in Kolkata and Delhi. The former was at the annual function of *The Statesman* and the latter at a function organised by Hindustani Andolan, an NGO working for clean politics. After I had spoken on the subject, Farooq spoke. He had a good dig in Urdu with a pun on words *Saaf Sayasat achhi bat hai magar jo saaf karega uska safaya ho jaega* (clean politics is good but anyone practicing it will get wiped out). There were also a few senior army officers present at the swearing in function, who knew me well. In all my three post-

Army assignments in Nepal, Assam and Kashmir, there was a strong presence of the army. This proved to be a source of much strength to me.

After the swearing-in function, I was besieged by Press correspondents and TV channels. I was asked if I was going to take over control of the unified command in Kashmir as I had done in Assam. I tried to dispel their fears saying that I had done nothing of the sort in Assam. We wanted the Chief Minister to head the unified group of Assam but he had declined to do so. Therefore the Chief Secretary presided over that apex body in Assam. The terminology used in Assam, unified group was different but its function was the same as unified command in J&K. In the case of Jammu and Kashmir, the Chief Minister had been presiding over the meetings of unified command and that arrangement would continue. The Governor had only constitutional and no executive role. There was no question of my interfering with the functioning of the unified command. My interaction with the Press took a long time. I was keen to dispel any doubts about my functioning beyond the role prescribed for a governor under the Constitution. Despite my clarifying this unequivocally, the Valley Press conveyed that I would act like a new broom pursuing my own agenda. We were to go for tea after my interaction with the Press. I found Mufti impatiently waiting. I felt that I had perhaps not made a good beginning with him.

Mufti had acquired a bigger than life image as Chief Minister. Apart from his past record which included a tenure as Union Home Minister which appointment had never been held by anyone from Kashmir or for that matter by any Muslim in the country, the Assembly elections of 2002 had given him a big boost. For the first time the international media had been allowed to cover elections in Kashmir. The international Press acclaimed that election as free and fair. This was a feather in the cap of the NDA Government at New Delhi. Hitherto, India used to be accused in international circles of rigging elections in Kashmir. For the first time elections in Kashmir had been internationally acclaimed as free and fair. The NDA Government was naturally claiming credit for it. This had not happened earlier during Congress regime. I mentioned to Vajpayee that it was not in our national interest to propagate that for the first time free and fair elections had been held in Kashmir. Asserting that 2002 had been the first free and fair election implied that previous elections in the State had been rigged. This contradicted our long-standing national claim of democracy functioning in

Kashmir. I felt that our stand should be that the 2002 Assembly elections proved the credibility of the democratic process in the State. The ruling party both at the Centre and in the State had lost in that election. My viewpoint was ignored for partisan reasons. The NDA Government was more keen to score brownies over the Congress on this issue. Be that as it may, the fact remained that Mufti had emerged as the Chief Minister as a result of an internationally acclaimed free and fair election. This had given him a big image. He was being viewed as the mascot of democracy in Kashmir. It is true that some of the previous elections in Kashmir had been rigged. An important fact contributing to militancy in Kashmir had been that elections had been rigged in 1987. However, the 1977 elections to the State Assembly was universally recognised to be free and fair. This had endorsed the leadership of Sheikh Abdullah and the agreement he had reached with Indira Gandhi.

Mufti was gracious enough to host a dinner party in my honour the day after I was sworn as Governor. He had invited my entire family, including my brothers who had come to attend my swearing-in function. A large number of people including editors of newspapers were at the dinner. I was told that a journalist was heard saying at that party, that a high profile Governor and a high profile Chief Minister carried seeds of discord. This was a very perceptive remark.

In an effort to build bridges with Mufti, I invited him for a quiet dinner at Raj Bhavan. I learnt that he was fond of drinks and possibly a quiet dinner laced with drinks, could lay a good foundation for cordial relations. Mufti came with his wife, daughter Mehbooba and one granddaughter. Being a shrewd and well-informed politician, he was aware of my good personal relations with the top leaders of the NDA Government, then in power. He appeared very amenable while talking about various subjects but was averse to accepting any suggestion on Kashmir. His stock answer to any such suggestion was that Kashmir was different from Assam. I suggested that it would be better for the Unified Command to have one combined headquarters for both Jammu and Kashmir, instead of two separate ones for Jammu and for Kashmir. I also suggested that the Army Commander in J&K should be included in the unified command. He had been kept out of the counter-insurgency loop, although his two subordinates, the two Corps Commanders in Jammu and Srinagar, were included. Mufti maintained that there was no need for any change as things were working alright. He reiterated his pet theme of Kashmir being different from Assam. So far as his daughter Mehbooba, was concerned, she kept telling me of the atrocities being committed by the army. I tried to explain to her the difficulties faced by the army in such operations. There was a mechanism within the army of taking suitable action against anyone committing excesses. She was not convinced and harped on the grievances of the people. Mehbooba was the President of the People's Democratic Party (PDP). She appeared more uncompromising than her father who was the Patron of the Party. This was the first and the last occasion I had of interaction with her socially. When there was a bomb blast close to the gate of Mufti's house in Srinagar while Mufti had gone to Delhi, I telephoned to inquire about her welfare. She was a bit cold in her reply.

I realized that my dinner diplomacy had not borne fruit. Nevertheless, I felt I must continue my efforts to build bridges with Mufti. I am afraid I failed. So long as he was chief minister, I tried to keep our differences under wraps. I even repeatedly praised him in my public statements and denied that I had any differences with him. The Press tried to expose our differences and came out with some juicy cartoons. My relations with Mufti worsened with the change of Government at Delhi in May 2004. We were now on a collision course for the rest of my tenure as Governor of the State. This reached its climax in the last couple of weeks of my five year tenure as governor and thereafter Mufti making baseless and unbecoming allegation against me causing a national controversy. I shall recount various aspects of our unfortunate relationship as I proceed with the narrative of my tenure as Governor of Jammu and Kashmir.

4

Kashmir has been one of the most complex and complicated problems facing our Nation for the past over sixty years. It has lingered, defying solution. There are several dimensions to the Kashmir problem — religious, historical, political, military, economic and ethnic. We have always maintained that Kashmir is an integral part of India. Our Parliament has called for the liberation of the portion of the State in illegal occupation of Pakistan. Yet we have not evolved a proper road map to achieve our national goal. We have been reacting to situations, as they have been arising, in a knee-jerk manner, instead of having a long term plan. Of course efforts have been made sporadically through dialogue and confidence building measures to evolve a solution without any clarity in our mind of the contours of the desired solution and how it can be achieved.

The low intensity conflict in Kashmir has been a vicious mix of insurgency, terrorism and proxy war. The level of violence has been much higher in Kashmir than in Assam, and there is a deeper and direct involvement of Pakistan, through a proxy war. We were ill-advised to take this issue to the United Nations in January 1948. This only complicated matters for us and made Kashmir into an international issue.

Militancy in Kashmir has essentially been a product of religious fundamentalism and religious intolerance. Separatists have tried to give it respectability by projecting it as a nationalist movement and a freedom struggle. The separatists and terrorists are all from one religious community. They ensured the ethnic cleansing of the Valley by driving out over three lakh Kashmiri Pandits. These hapless people have been living as refugees in their own country, in various refugee camps for the last nearly two decades. However, the separatists blame the Kashmiri Pandits for running away from Kashmir. They also blame the then Governor Jagmohan for conspiring to send the Kashmiri Pandits out of the Valley, with a view to giving their "freedom movement" a bad name. The facts are entirely different. Several Kashmiri Pandits had been massacred, their women folk abducted, their temples vandalized and constant threats held out to them from loudspeakers in mosques. The slogan "Kashmir Banega Pakistan" was being constantly raised and a feeling generated that this will happen very soon. Jagmohan's firm handling of the situation prevented this happening. Mufti Mohammad Sayeed, the then Union Home Minister acknowledged Jagmohan's contribution in the Parliament on 25 April 1990 when he stated, "Jagmohan had to function in a vacuum in a situation when there was no respect for the law or the authority of the State Government. He braved terrorists, instilled courage in Government officials who had almost given up the situation as a lost cause." Mufti may have spoken so in Delhi but he never spoke in that strain in Kashmir. He dare not repeat this for fear of losing political support. Jagmohan has been vilified in Kashmir as a Hindu fundamentalist, an accusation the separatists were to levy against me later. Mufti is widely believed to be hand in glove with the separatists. Today, he is part of their bandwagon in Kashmir denouncing both Jagmohan and me.

To appease the separatists the official terminology used for Kashmiri Pandits who moved out of the Valley is migrants and not refugees. Migrant implies that a person has moved out of his own volition. Refugee on the other hand is a person who has been forced to seek shelter outside and is eligible for aid from the United Nations. These "migrants" housed in camps in Delhi, Jammu and Udhampur had been living in subhuman conditions for a decade and a half. Even the NDA Government which was in power at Delhi had done little for them.

On taking over as Governor of J&K, I decided to visit all Kashmiri Pandit "migrant camps". In Delhi they were staying in abominable conditions in halls at Lajpat Nagar and Harijan Colony. The ceiling of the hall in Lajpat Nagar used to leak during rains. Families were accommodated in cubicles in halls, partitioned with cloth curtains. No one from J&K Administration had ever visited these camps in Delhi in the past thirteen years on the plea that they were the responsibility of the Delhi Administration and not the J&K Government. They were citizens of Jammu and Kashmir and I felt it my moral responsibility as Head of that State to take interest in their welfare. The residents of these camps were in tears when they saw me amongst them. I tried to help them out with little things like water cooler, medical facilities, admission of children to schools and so on. I spoke to Vijay Kapoor who was then the Lieutenant-Governor of Delhi. I had good personal relations with him. He had earlier served as Chief Secretary of J&K. He was very responsive to my request. He allotted DDA flats to Kashmiri Pandits on very liberal terms. We made arrangements for redressal of their complaints. Resident Commissioner of J&K in Delhi and a Commissioner of Delhi Administration were asked to meet once a month to take care of their complaints. I was told that Mufti did not appreciate my taking interest in the welfare of Kashmiri Pandits.

The living conditions in the "migrant camps" at Jammu and Udhampur were even worse. They were living in shacks with tin roofs which used to become very hot in summer. Seven to ten people were crowded in one small room. After my visit to these camps, I spoke to Mufti. He felt that if he improved their living conditions, they would become too comfortable and would not return to the Valley. He was prepared to provide them comfortable living conditions in the Valley but not in Jammu. Of course there was no question of their return to the Valley till the security scenario improved radically. The terrorists were saying that Kashmiri Pandits would be allowed to return to the Valley provided they joined them in the "freedom struggle". I spoke to Vajpayee about these "migrants" and he sanctioned an increase in the monthly subsidy being given to each family in the camps.

When President Abdul Kalam came to J&K in July 2003, I requested him to visit the "migrant camps". Mufti and I accompanied the President to one of the Kashmiri Pandit camps in Jammu. The President was horrified to see their living conditions. He suggested to Mufti to improve their lot. Mufti gave him the same reply as he had given me that he would do so in the Valley but not in Jammu. Being a constitutional head like me, the President could not do anything in the matter.

The following year Manmohan Singh who had now become the Prime Minister came to J&K. I suggested that he visit a Kashmiri Pandit camp in Jammu. He agreed to do so. The night before he was to visit the camp, Mufti and I were present at dinner with him. Mufti mentioned to the Prime Minister during dinner, why he did not want to improve the living conditions in Kashmiri Pandit camps in Jammu and he would do everything for them in the Valley. I did not want to get into an argument with Mufti on this issue. I remained quiet. After dinner, when I was alone with Manmohan Singh, I gave him my point of view on this issue. I think he appreciated what I told him. The next day Mufti and I accompanied the Prime Minister to the camp at Muthi. He went inside one of the small rooms occupied by nine members of a family. I could see that he was moved. His eyes were moist. Perhaps, it reminded him of the time when he himself was a refugee on coming from West Pakistan in 1947. Soon after, he addressed the inmates of the camp with Mufti and me sitting on either side of him. The Prime Minister announced at that meeting that each Kashmiri Pandit family in Jammu and in Delhi will be provided a modern two bed room and a sitting room flat. The Government of India will provide the necessary funds for this. I could see Mufti looking uncomfortable. I felt very grateful to the Prime Minister for his prompt decision. His generous announcement was much applauded by the Kashmiri Pandits present at that meeting. True to his word on return to Delhi, Manmohan Singh released Rs 51 crores for 1024 two room flats at Muthi, Parkhov and Nagrota. The State Government, deliberately or otherwise, delayed identifying land and completing the construction of flats. With the change of chief minister, work on this project was speeded up and I had the satisfaction to see this project completed during my tenure in the State. The new Chief Minister Ghulam Nabi Azad, not only had the completion of the sanctioned flats expedited but also started a new mega project at

Yagti. A well-planned modern township with all amenities in the foothills close to Jammu was started for 4224 Kashmiri Pandit families at the cost of 294 crores. With improved security situation in the Valley, Kashmiri Pandits in large numbers started coming for their annual Kheer Bhiwani pilgrimage to Srinagar. Fifty thousand of them came in my first year as governor. It was heart-warming to see the warm welcome extended to them by the local Kashmiri Muslims. The political leaders and separatists may be having their own agenda but the common man in Kashmir still was guided by his age old pluralistic values. Many Kashmiri Muslims would often tell me that Kashmir was incomplete without Kashmiri Pandits. This greatly encouraged me to work for communal amity and brotherhood in Kashmir, through promoting *Kashmiriyat*.

5

The treatment meted out to Kashmiri Pandits and the activities of the separatists convinced me that religious fundamentalism was the root cause for militancy in Kashmir. We could achieve success over militancy in the State only through reviving the old pluralistic values which were still cherished by many people. In fact, Kashmir had a unique record of amity and brotherhood across religious divide in the past. Sheikh Noorudin, the patron saint of Kashmir was revered equally by the Hindus who called him Nund Rishi. The central message of this saint was "There is one God with hundred names. There is not a single blade of grass which does not worship him". It was the Sheikh's preaching that kept the Kashmiri ethos within the overall cultural mainstream of India. The followers of Rishi order abhorred killing. Like the Jains they were careful not to harm even insects. Sheikh Nooruddin went to the extent of refusing to walk on the grass, lest it be damaged. Laleshwari a Hindu poetess saint was also equally revered by both Hindus and Muslims. The latter called her Lal Ded. In the old days Kashmiri Pandits had taught Muslims the Holy Qoran. Sufi Islam of the Rishi cult with vegetarian Muslim clerics was prevalent in Kashmir. This was the antithesis of Wahabi Islam. The latter of late had been spreading in the State. A Muslim shepherd Buta Malik had rediscovered the Holy Amarnath cave. He and his descendants had looked after the cave for generations. Even today there is an old Shiva Temple in Pahalgam, where a Muslim functions as a priest and distributes *Prasad* to devotees. In Jhangar, a Ziarat (grave of a Muslim saint) is looked after and maintained by Hindus. Apart from having common surnames like Bhatt and Malik, Hindus and Muslims in Kashmir have normally exclusive surnames of the other community like Abdul Rahim Bhagwan, Mohammad Shafi Pandit, Amarnath Mulla and Kuldip Khoda.

I recall that when I arrived in Srinagar with the first lot of troops in October 1947, we had been given three tasks in order of priority. Drive the enemy out of the Valley, defend the airfield and restore order in the city of Srinagar. After the situation was stabilized on the front, I was asked to go into the city to assess the requirement for deploying troops there to restore order. In those days, the area astride the 20 kilometers stretch of road, from the airport to the city, was totally uninhabited without any buildings. I had apprehensions of violence raging in the city as the Maharaja and senior officials had fled to Jammu and the civil administration was reported to have collapsed. When I entered the city, I had a pleasant surprise awaiting me. There was no communal violence or tension. The city was reverberating to the slogan of "Hamlewar Khabardar, Ham Kashmiri Hindu Muslim Sikh Tayyar". As one who had witnessed the carnage in Delhi and Punjab during the Partition holocaust, what I saw in Srinagar was like a dream. It was what I like to call *Kashmiriyat* in action. No wonder Mahatma Gandhi had said that he saw a ray of light in Kashmir.

How different the Kashmir of 2003 was from the Kashmir of 1947. I realized that in this ever changing world, drastic changes are not unusual. Allama Iqbal, the greatest poet of Kashmir and hailed all over India as one of our great national poets had composed the inspiring lines of Taran-e-Hind, *Sare Jahan se Achcha Hindustan Hamara, Ham Bul Bulain Hain is ke Yih Gulistan Hamara, Mazhab nahin sikhata apas mein bair Rakhna, Hindi hain ham Hindustan Hamara"*. He later composed Taran-e-milli *"Chin Arab Hamara, Hindustan Hamara, Muslim Hain Ham, Sara Jahan Hamara"*. Jinnah who had once been hailed as the Ambassador of Hindu-Muslim unity changed radically. He joined the vanguard of communal politics with his two nation theory. He threatened that he would have India Divided or India Destroyed. After the creation of Pakistan, he got back to his secular moorings. His famous address to Pakistan Constituent Assembly in August 1947 confirmed this. Similarly Kashmiris who had strayed away from their unique heritage of *Kashmiriyat* could also have a change of mind. I felt that the revival of *Kashmiriyat,* which stands for amity and brotherhood across any religious divide, was the best antidote to religious fundamentalism, the basis for militancy in Kashmir. I decided that I must go all out to revive and promote *Kashmiriyat.*

Soon after taking over as Governor of Jammu and Kashmir, in one of my speeches as also while interacting with the Press, I stated that Jahangir was no doubt right when he described Kashmir as Paradise on Earth for its breathtaking scenic beauty. However, for me what was more important was the fact that *Kashmiriyat* was the message of Paradise. I had seen *Kashmiriyat* in action in Srinagar in October 1947 and reviving it would be my prime concern. Some separatists ridiculed me saying that they did not have to learn *Kashmiriyat* from a non-Kashmiri. They also were critical of my concept of *Kashmiriyat*. In fact, my efforts to promote *Kashmiriyat* became a major bone of contention by the end of my tenure in Kashmir. When the fundamentalists found that my efforts were having some impact, they developed a counter strategy of propagating that I was a Hindu fundamentalist. The last month of my five years tenure saw a non-issue being exploited by them, along with some unscrupulous politicians. This led to an unfortunate religious divide among the two religious communities of the State. I shall deal with this towards the end of this book.

6

On taking over as Governor, I paid obeisance at all the major religious shrines of different faiths in the State. I wanted to do this to underscore the pluralistic ethos of our Nation. I also decided to visit all the divisional level Headquarters of the army and paramilitary forces, besides the three Corps Headquarters and one Command headquarters of the Army. Concurrently, I also decided to visit all the then fourteen civil district headquarters in the State. During the dinner Mufti had hosted to welcome me, I had mentioned to him my intention of undertaking a wide ranging tour of the State for a better understanding of the situation. Mufti did not raise any objection nor express any reservation.

I placed "Chadars" at Charar-e-Sharif and at Hazratbal. I visited Mata Vaishno Devi in Jammu, Gompa in Leh, Pathar ka Gurudwara in Ladakh & Church in Srinagar and Jammu. At all these holy places I prayed and sought Divine blessing for peace and prosperity in the State. At Charar-e-Sharif, local people complained that their toilets were choked and non-functional. They also told me that they experienced difficulty in accommodating pilgrims during Urs. The deputy commissioner assured me that he would get the toilets cleaned within 15 days. I told him that I would come again after 15 days to see if the work had been done. I requested the minister in charge, Ghulam Hasan Mir, to accompany me to Charar-e-Sharif after 15 days. He agreed to do so. I was happy to see that the work on the toilets had been completed. The minister explained to me the development works planned at Charar-e-Sharif and showed me some under construction. As for accommodation for pilgrims during Urs, I asked the army to put up some sheds under Operation Sadbhavana. They readily agreed to do so and put up a long shelter with jute matting on the floor to accommodate about one thousand pilgrims. Mufti came to see me and appeared unhappy about my visit to Charar-e-Sharif. He said that a governor's visit required prior preparation and had political implications. He would have liked adequate notice about my visit to Charar-e-Sharif so that necessary preparations could be made and all concerned could receive me there. I assured him that I shall abide by his advice in the future. My visits to the army, the paramilitary and the civil districts were completed in about a month's time. I visited all army formations at divisional level and above, and was briefed by the formation commanders. The army was happy that I had gone to meet them. They felt I was part of them and showed much regard for me. Many of the senior officers knew me from my days in the army and many had served under me. I also visited sensitive areas on the LoC. This included a visit to Kargil, accompanied by my wife. She had her first experience of artillery fire during that visit. Seeing stepped up activity on account of my visit, the Pakistan observation post, across the LoC, brought down artillery fire. My wife was visiting a local school at that time. I also decided to visit the troops at Siachen at a height of 22,000 feet above sea level. This is the highest battlefield in the world. General Nirmal Vij, the Army Chief had been the Corps Commander in Assam, when I was the Governor of that State. Earlier, he was a Colonel General Staff when I was the Army Commander of the Western Theatre. We had been good friends. He telephoned to dissuade me from going to Siachen Glacier. He was concerned about my going to that height at my advance age. I thanked him for his concern and assured him that being an old soldier and having served at high altitudes, I would be alright. I managed to visit Siachen and was much impressed by the high morale of the soldiers in those difficult conditions. One of the battalions I visited was from my Regiment, the Fifth Gorkha Rifles (Frontier Force). They knew me well. I had been the Colonel of the Regiment and the President of the Gorkha Brigade. My interaction with Gorkha soldiers, speaking to them in their language went down very well. I was told that I was the first governor of the State to have visited Siachen.

To ensure that the paramilitary did not feel neglected, I made it a point to visit IG level headquarters of the BSF and CRP. I also visited BSF troops deployed on the border. Their response to my visit was very positive.

My visits to the army and the paramilitary gave me a good idea of ground realities and of the security scenario in the State. It was also good for the morale of these personnel to have the governor in their midst. Most of the areas visited by me were well known to me. I had served for several years in all the regions of the State, during my army career.

I also visited all the then fourteen civil districts where apart from interacting with the local civilian officials, I met some local leaders. These visits were a familiarization tour in which my intention was to meet the officials informally over a cup of tea. In a few districts, the deputy commissioners organized a formal meeting with district officials. I never gave any directions or instructions as that would have been interfering with the functioning of the State government. Of course, I meant to apprise the Chief Minister of any point that required action to be taken. It appears that my visits conveyed a wrong impression to Mufti. He sent the Chief Secretary to me to apprise me that my visits gave the impression that the State had been placed under Governor's rule. I told the Chief Secretary that my visits were only a familiarization tour. As mentioned earlier, I had spoken to the Chief Minister of my intention of touring the State and he had raised no objection nor expressed any reservation. A copy of my tour programme was invariably sent to the CM's secretariat. The State helicopter for these visits was made available to me after obtaining the CM's personal approval in each case. My tours were now complete. If I had been informed of the CM's reservation earlier, I could have cancelled my visits to the civil districts. The Deputy Chief Minister, Mangat Ram Sharma, and some other ministers who met me, welcomed my visits to the civil districts saying that it was good for the people to see the Governor in their midst. In retrospect I feel I was wrong and had got carried away by my enthusiasm. I should have discussed my visits to the civil districts with Mufti. I should also have taken into account his ego and his susceptibilities. I had no problem on this account in Assam but things there were different.

In view of the growing misunderstanding between Mufti and me, I was prepared to go the extra mile to develop good relations with him. Mufti sent the Law Minister Muzaffar Hussain Baig to me one evening. He came on a social call. My relations with Baig were good. He told me several times that he treated me as his father. During the course of our meeting, that evening, he told me that the Aukaf Board was being mismanaged by the Abdullah family, who treated it as their fiefdom. He also mentioned that there was much corruption in the organization and the government would be taking action to set things right. After a few days, the chief secretary came to me late one night with an ordinance, providing for the government to take over the Aukaf Board, the same night in a cloak and dagger operation. I hesitated to append my signature to the ordinance but realized that it would only worsen, my relations with Mufti. As a constitutional head, I had to go along with the recommendation of my council of ministers. I had an option and that was to say that I needed time to examine the ordinance. Had I done so, it would have caused quite a turmoil with the Opposition making much of the whole issue. That would have caused embarrassment to Mufti. In any case, the Abdullahs had the option to go to the court over the issue. I therefore, obliged and signed the ordinance reluctantly.

The second instance was the appointment of the Chairman, State Public Service Commission. This is a statutory appointment requiring the prior approval of the Governor. There is a specific provision in the constitution to that effect. Mufti sought my approval for the appointment of Muhammad Shafi Pandit, a senior IAS officer for this appointment, which I readily accorded. Not known to me Mohammad Shafi Pandit was directed to join the Aukaf Board and another person appointed Chairman of the State Public Service Commission, who did not have the requisite qualifications for the job. Some six months later, Mufti again sent me a proposal for the appointment of Mohd Shafi Pandit as Chairman of the State Public Service Commission and at the same time sought my *ex post facto* approval for the appointment of Akhtar Murtaza as Chairman who was now superannuating. Apart from the appointment having been made in an illegal manner, there was no provision in the Constitution, for *ex post facto* sanction being accorded. I realized that if I refused to approve his recommendation, the government would face a crisis. All the appointments made in the previous six months on the recommendation of the illegally appointed chairman, would become null and void. I had no intention to embarrass Mufti. I turned a Nelson's eye to the irregularity committed by him. I accordeed necessary *ex post facto* approval and also approved the appointment of Mohammad Shafi Pandit for the second time.

The other two instances of my going the extra mile were of a personal nature. When I took over as governor, I found that both in the Raj Bhavan at Srinagar and the Governor's suite in J&K House at Delhi, we had paintings of Mata Vaishno Devi but not of any other shrine, I decided to have paintings of Hazratbal and the Gompa in Leh put up in the Foyer of Raj Bhavan and in the Governor's suite at Delhi, to emphasize our secular tradition. I commissioned a young artist from Assam who had done several paintings for me at Guwahati Raj Bhavan, to do the paintings of Hazratbal and the Gompa. Her painting of Hazratbal was outstanding and everyone admired it. Dr Kalam on a visit to Srinagar appreciated it a lot. Mufti who was with him at that time also much praised the painting. I got the Assamese artist to make a duplicate of the Hazratbal painting. As a gesture of goodwill I sent it to Mufti, with a letter saying that as he had admired the painting so much, I had a duplicate made and was presenting it to him. For three months I received no acknowledgement from Mufti. I wondered whether Mufti had received my letter and the painting. I asked my secretary to write to Mufti's secretary to enquire if my letter and painting had been received by the Chief Minister. We got a reply from Mufti's secretary that the painting had been received and was much appreciated by Mufti. The painting adorned the wall of Mufti's sitting room. However, not once did Mufti thank me for the painting, nor did he ever mention it to me.

The second personal instance was equally strange. Mufti wanted to organize a Kashmir Food Festival at Dubai to promote tourism to Kashmir. The festival was being organized at short notice in Dubai during the festive season when it is very difficult to get hotel accommodation there. The Kashmir contingent was very large including Mufti, Tourism Minister Ghulam Hasan Mir and a whole lot of officials, many with their families wanting to have a foreign jaunt. I had met Omar Abdullah, President of the National Conference, in the plane a couple of days earlier. He had told me that since hotel accommodation was not available in Dubai, he was going on a holiday with his family to Bangkok. Anil Goswami the Tourism Secretary sought an appointment with me. I was surprised because I had been told that the State government officials had been forbidden to visit Raj Bhavan. Anyway I agreed to meet Goswami. He met me in my office and told me that the State Government was organizing a Kashmir food festival in Dubai shortly. He wanted to know the telephone number of my son, who was then India's Consul General in Dubai. I was amused why he had come to ask me that information which he could easily have obtained from my ADC or private secretary. It could also be obtained from ministry of external affairs or for that matter from the State Government's contact man in Dubai. Anyway, I gave him the telephone number but I realized why he had come to ask me for it. He obviously wanted me to get my son to help out. I immediately rang up my son who told me that he had received the request from Kashmir and was going to write to Delhi that Kashmir food festival could not be organised that season as all accommodation was fully booked. Already there was a big function of Karnatak Government being held in Dubai. I told my son that whatever his difficulties, he must go all out to have the Kashmir food festival organized properly. I also told him that in view of my strained relations with Mufti, my son's recommendation to have the festival next year will be misunderstood. Dubai has a large Indian population and many Indians there, are doing very well in business. The Indian Consul General wields considerable influence. My son managed to arrange accommodation for the large Kashmir contingent, helped in organizing the Food festival and organised a largely attended Press conference for Mufti. The latter was very appreciative and thanked him. It is the convention that when a Prime Minister or a Chief Minister goes abroad, on return home, he briefs the President or the Governor. Mufti never bothered to do so nor did he ever mention his visit to Dubai to me. A week later I accidentally met Ghulam Hasan Mir, the Tourism Minister and Mehbooba, Mufti's daughter in the VIP Lounge at Delhi airport. They told me how my son had helped them at Dubai and without his help they would not have been able to have such a successful function in Dubai. Perhaps Mufti thought that as his daughter had expressed their appreciation of my son's role in Dubai, there was no need for him to say anything to me.

I have mentioned these instances to show that despite my efforts, I failed to build cordial relations with Mufti. In fact, our relations started getting worse as time passed, particularly after the UPA Government came to power in Delhi.

7

The three prong strategy of coordinated operations, economic development and psychological initiatives had worked well in Assam. I felt that with suitable modifications this strategy could work equally well in Kashmir. Apart from the much higher level of violence and proxy war in Kashmir, we also faced a media war. To deal with this new dimension we had to ensure proper information management. This became an additional prong for our strategy in Kashmir. As in the case of the third prong, which I called psychological initiatives instead of psychological warfare, I proposed to call the fourth prong information management rather than media management. The latter terminology seems contrary to the concept of freedom of the Press, so important for a functioning democracy. However, the most powerful democracy of the world appeared to have a different view. They had what they called embedded journalists in Iraq.

8

A unified headquarters had been functioning in Kashmir under the Chief Minister, but there were certain organisational infirmities in it. There were two unified command, one each for Kashmir and Jammu. This was because insurgency first erupted in Kashmir and later spread to Jammu. When that happened a separate unified command was set up for Jammu region, instead of expanding the existing one. I felt that we should have a one combined unified command. However, two core groups chaired by the two Corps Commanders and working under the unified command, could continue.

The two Corps Commanders were also security advisers to the State government. Although this arrangement allowed the army to coordinate and control the operations of paramilitary officers, there was a tendency on the part of BSF and CRP to refer operational matters to their Directors General in Delhi before implementing directions from the army. Directors General of paramilitary forces had no operational responsibility and as such any reference of operational matters to them militated against unified functioning of the army and paramilitary. I had faced this problem in Assam. I tried to impress upon all the security forces, the army, the paramilitary and the police to develop cordial personal relations at all levels to facilitate smooth functioning. Apart from frequently inviting their commanders to social functions at Raj Bhavan, I also held joint at-homes to felicitate winners of gallantry and distinguished service awards for all the forces, twice a year after Independence and Republic Days.

It was strange that the Army Commander who was overall commander of the army in the State was kept out of the counter-insurgency loop. His two subordinates, the two Corps Commanders were included in the unified set up. Normally, the Chief Minister presided at the meetings of the unified command but there were occasions when the Prime Minister or the Home/Defence Minister attended the meeting of the unified command and presided over it. On these occasions the Army Chief, the two Corps Commanders, Home/Defence Secretary, Director General of paramilitary forces, Chiefs of Intelligence agencies attended these meetings besides the Chief Minister, Chief Secretary, DG Police and other officials of the State Government. It was undermining the position of the Army Commander to exclude him from such meetings. My suggestion encountered strong opposition from the State Government and surprisingly also from the Home Ministry. The Union Home Secretary told me that if the Army Commander was included at these meetings, the Corps Commanders would be inhibited from giving their views. I told him that if the Corps Commanders did not get inhibited when the Army Chief attended the meeting, why should that happen when the Army Commander was present. I also told him that the Corps Commanders operated under the directions of the Army Commander, irrespective of whether the latter was present or not at these meetings. Having served both as an Army Commander and as a Corps Commander, I saw no logic in the argument advanced by the Union Home Secretary. Moreover it made little sense to exclude the Army Commander who had operational responsibility for all military operations in the State and include Directors General of paramilitary forces, who had no operational responsibility. I took up the matter with the Union Home Minister and I got this lacuna rectified. The Army Commander was ultimately included in the Unified Command.

Within a week of taking over as Governor, I came across a voluminous report prepared by Bhandari Committee on conduct of counter-insurgency operations in J&K. Bhandari was Special Secretary in Ministry of Home. He was due to retire on 31 May 2003 and he submitted his report on his last day in office. Army Headquarters was represented in this committee by Director General Military Operations and Director General Military Intelligence. Director Generals of paramilitary forces and Director Intelligence Bureau were also included in this Committee. I went through the Bhandari Committee report very carefully. I had strong reservations about two of its major recommendations. It recommended compartmentalization of areas of responsibility between the army, the paramilitary and the police with each reporting directly to the Unified Command. The implementation of this recommendation would have vitiated the coordination of all security operations by the army and sidelined the army's role, defeating the concept of unified functioning. The second totally unacceptable recommendation was to transfer the newly raised Rashtriya Rifles for counter-insurgency operation in J&K from ministry of defence to ministry of home. This force had been raised some ten years ago and had been doing very good work in combating militancy. The personnel of Rashtriya Rifles, both officers and personnel below officer rank were on deputation from the army. The expenditure on this force was met from the defence budget. It made little sense to transfer control of this force to ministry of home. I checked up with the Army Chief as to how the two army representatives in this Committee were a party to these recommendations. I was told that they had opposed these two proposals. They had not been shown the final report. Normally, a report of a committee has to be signed by all its members and any member having contrary views is allowed to attach his note of dissent. I found the report did not bear the signature of its members and was signed only by its chairman. I was told that the State Government had conveyed its concurrence of the report to the home ministry and the report was likely to be approved by the latter shortly. I wrote my detailed comments on this report running into several pages. I also took up the matter with the Union Home Minister and succeeded in having this report shelved. Acceptance of this report would have weakened the concept of combined and coordinated functioning, so vital for success in the conduct of counter-insurgency operations.

In my interactions with the army, I stressed a few points. Cordon and search operations cause much inconvenience to the people and often do not yield much results. Surgical operations based on good intelligence targeting militants and with minimum collateral damage were a better option. I stressed on the need to build cordial relations with the local people. The Corps Commander Lt Gen Nirbhay Sharma had a good idea. He directed soldiers at check points, interacting with civilians calling them "Jee Hazoor". As for human right violations, I urged that we must make every effort to avoid them and when such instances come to light, no attempt should be made to shield the guilty. I also from time to time offered advice on tactical matters as and when necessary. Besides, I advised that the army must be tactful in dealing with the paramilitary and the police. The latter have complexes and often indulge in one-upmanship. The Army was the major player in counter-insurgency and with their greater resources, professionalism and discipline had been inflicting much greater attrition on militants but it need not indulge in one-upmanship by publicizing these facts. No attempt should be made to show off its better performance as that would ruffle feathers. I was happy that the army was responsive to my suggestions. They were particularly appreciative of my praising the achievements of the army on different occasions and defending it publicly against the vilification campaign launched against it. Throughout my five years tenure, at all times I received maximum cooperation from the army at all levels.

The results achieved by our security forces during my time were commendable. The average daily rate of killing of civilians, terrorists and security forces came down from 10 a day in 2003 to about 1 a day in 2008. More terrorists were getting killed in encounters than the combined total of civilians and security forces.

9

Conventional wisdom stipulates economic development and reduction of unemployment for success in combating militancy. Government of India had been pouring more funds for development in Jammu and Kashmir than in any other State of the country, both per capita of the population and in absolute terms. In this regard certain statistics are revealing. In the Tenth Five Year Plan the allocation to J&K was Rs 14,399 crores as against Rs 2,536 crores to Bihar which has a population eight times more than that of J&K. People below poverty line in J&K is 3.7 percent against the national average of 26 percent. There are 3.5 lakh government jobs in J&K which works out to 34.5 per thousand population of the State. Eighty percent of the salary of State employees is met from funds provided by the Centre. It is also true that because of rampant corruption, funds get siphoned off to a large extent. Despite all the Centre's largesse, the level of animosity towards India had remained high among a large section of the people in the Valley. Compared to economic development in Indian administered Kashmir, Pakistan Occupied Kashmir stood nowhere, yet by and large there is not much animosity in POK against Pakistan. Of course in Northern Areas comprising Gilgit and Baltistan, which are treated as a colony by Pakistan, things are different. The point that stands out is that ideological or religious considerations matter more in influencing the mindset of the people. Notwithstanding this, economic development is of great importance. Along with economic development it is imperative that psychological initiatives be undertaken vigorously and in an imaginative manner to bring about a mind change among the people. In 2004, Prime Minister Manmohan Singh on his first visit to Kashmir on assuming his high office, announced a development package of 24,000 crores for the State. Chief Minister Ghulam Nabi Azad on coming to power launched a crusade for development.

The tribes living on the mountains, Gujjars and Bakerwals, require special consideration. They are economically backward and they feel neglected. They have not much sympathy for the separatists nor are they religious fundamentalists. On a visit to Dehradun, I had seen the potential of microhydel project based on watermills in hilly terrain. Dr Anil Joshi had pioneered this technique in Uttarakhand. I invited Dr Joshi to Jammu. We planned to put up 1000 microhydel projects in J&K primarily for the benefit of the people living on the mountains. They had never seen an electric bulb in their villages. A microhydel project could generate about 5 kilowat of electricity providing 30 to 40 light points in a village. By day the available power could be used for grinding corn and operating loom. The State Government was not too enthusiastic about this scheme. I recall that during the visit of President Kalam in 2003 I had advocated mini hydel projects based on their success in Bhutan but Mufti preferred mega hydel projects. The army responded enthusiastically to my proposal for microhydel projects. During the visit of Prime Minister Manmohan Singh, I got his approval for this scheme with funds to be provided by the Government of India. I wanted this scheme to be executed by the army rather than the State Government. I had several reasons for this. First, the army had a better reach in remote areas than the civil administration. It was therefore in a better position to execute and maintain the project as also to train the local people to operate it. Second, the projects would be executed much faster by the army. Third, there would be no siphoning of the funds nor any political considerations in selecting sites. Fourth, if the project was executed by the army, the credit for it would go to India as the army was perceived as an instrument of the Centre. It will also help in promoting cordial army-public relations, so important for counter-insurgency operations.

Although my recommendation was accepted by the Prime Minister, the bureaucracy created unnecessary hassles which delayed execution of the scheme. Like the one lakh shallow tube well project in Assam I wanted the one thousand micro hydel project in Jammu and Kashmir executed in one year. Instead of ministry of defence providing all the funds to the army under Operation Sadbhavana, it was decided to involve three ministries in Delhi for providing funds to the army through the State Government. One third was to be provided by Ministry of Home under Border Area Development Scheme for border areas, one-third by Ministry of Non-Conventional Energy for interior areas and one third by Ministry of Defence under Operation Sadbhavana.

I had inaugurated the first microhydel project at Poonch and I went to inaugurate the thousandth such project in Baramulla District. I was accompanied by the Army Commander, Lt Gen Hari Prasad and the local Army formation commanders. From the helipad at Baramulla we drove by car to the site of the project about 20 kilometers in the hills. I was delighted to see the Indian national flag fluttering in every village enroute. The villagers holding paper national flags had lined the road near their villages to greet us. And there was tremendous enthusiasm at the project site where a large gathering of the local people had assembled for the function. It reminded me of Assam when on completion of the one lakh shallow tube well project, I used to tour the villages with lush green crops in the field and the villagers enthusiastically telling me, that thanks to shallow tube wells they had a crop growing in winter for the first time, on land which used to remain fallow on account of lack of water.

It gave me great personal satisfaction that the microhydel project scheme had successfully been completed by the army and it was so popular and beneficial for the, local people. Having served in border areas of Jammu and Kashmir for several years, I had long association with Gujjars and Bakerwals. I was determined to do whatever I could for their welfare. Earlier, I was doing all this through the Army which was always very receptive to my suggestions. With the change of chief ministers, the State Government also started cooperating. This was of great help. We lowered the minimum educational standard for these tribes by two years for recruitment to Central paramilitary Force and State police on the lines of relaxed educational standard for Gorkha soldiers in the army. We also developed a number of boys and girls hostels for their children. Medical and veterinary cover was arranged for these people and their animals when they went up in the mountains to graze their animals. A cut imposed in reservation quota by the previous regime was restored. We got Government of India to award Padma Bhushan to the senior Gujjar leader of the State, Mian Bashir.

10

The third prong of my counter-insurgency strategy was psychological initiatives. These had been highly successful in Assam, particularly the novel approach of striking the emotional chord of the people. I wanted to work on similar lines also in Jammu and Kashmir, but here the big hurdle was deep-rooted religious fundamentalism. The old tradition of amity and brotherhood cutting across religious divide embodied in *Kashmiriyat* had got greatly eroded. Matters were compounded by the constant anti-India propaganda in the print media of the Valley. The Government turned a Nelson's eye to seditious writing appearing in the Press everyday. Sedition is a crime punishable under the law in all countries. Pakistan was financing such writings in Kashmir. Margaret Thatcher had rightly said that media is the oxygen of the terrorists. In Kashmir they were getting this in more than abundant measures. I found that both the Central and State Government were indifferent to the media war being waged in the Valley. Delhi was more concerned with projecting our point of view internationally. My priority was to do so in the Valley. The Press in Jammu with one exception was different. It had no anti-India bias but nurtured a grievance on account of neglect and discrimination by the State Government. Although closely linked to psychological initiatives I decided to make information management, the fourth prong of our strategy.

The army was carrying out a commendable civic action programme under Operation Sadbhavana to win the hearts and minds of the people. It organised medical camps, ran schools in remote areas, provided vocational training, arranged veterinary cover for animals, constructed roads and bridges and so on. Besides, it came to the rescue of the people in a commendable manner during natural disasters like earthquake, floods and snow tsunami. In 2005, we had both a snow tsunami and an earthquake of great magnitude. I shall later elaborate the praiseworthy work done by the army and the air force during these calamities.

I took personal interest in the various activities of the army under Operation Sadbhavana. We had the budget for Sadbhavana increased from 16 crores in 2003 and to 92 crores in 2006. One of our major programmes was "Sair-e-watan" (Bharat Darshan). School children, both boys and girls in batches of approximately 50 would be taken on a tour for a couple of weeks to various places in India like Delhi, Agra, Jaipur, Bangalore, Hyderabad and Mumbai under the care of an army officer and his wife. Local army units at various locations in the country would extend them hospitality, helping them out with transport and accommodation. Many of these children from remote areas had not even seen Srinagar city. During this tour we wanted to show them the secular ethos of our nation and the material progress the country had been making. On some occasions, the President received them in Rashtrapati Bhavan and Governors in their Raj Bhavans. The children were taken to various religious places like Jama Masjid in Delhi, and the Dargah at Ajmer Shareef. They were thrilled to travel in a railway train for the first time. The Delhi metro was a great hit with them. They were also occasionally given a glimpse of Bollywood. On return to Kashmir each batch was brought to Raj Bhavan for an hour's interaction with me followed by tea. They were also given token presents. Besides school children, we also organized similar tour programmes for some senior citizens from rural areas and even Imams from different places. During my tenure as governor in five years I interacted with about 4000 children and also a few hundred senior citizens and Imams. During interaction I would tell them about the history and other details of places they had visited. I also invited questions from them on any issue they wanted to raise with me. I exhorted them to share their experience of the tours with their friends and relatives in their villages. This was an excellent programme for bringing about a mind change among the people. Many told me that they were proud to be citizens of such a great country.

Twenty-seventh October 1947 was the day on which the first lot of Indian troops had landed in Srinagar to rescue the people of Kashmir. I was an eyewitness to the events of October/November 1947. For many years the separatists had launched a totally false propaganda turning facts on their head. They had spread the canard that the Indian Army came on that date and like an army of occupation unleashed atrocities on the people. The raiders came to rescue the people but could not succeed. To vilify India, it was also touted that the Indian Army's illegal arrival in Srinagar was an act of aggression on Kashmir soil as troops had come before the Maharaja had signed the Instrument of Accession. In fact India had made out plans for annexing Kashmir even before Independence. Muslim majority Batala area of Gurdaspur district in Punjab had been made inclusive to India to provide road communication from India to Jammu and Kashmir. Work on Pathankot-Jammu road had commenced immediately after Independence. We had at the international level, been projecting the facts concerning those days rebutting Pakistan's false propaganda. However, we did not sufficiently stress that the United Nations had accepted the legality of India's position on Kashmir, when it had directed all Pakistani forces to withdraw from Kashmir and allowed Indian forces to remain in the State till plebiscite, India was to take over responsibility for maintaining order in Pakistan Occupied Kashmir, after the withdrawal of Pakistani Forces, till plebiscite was held within Kashmir. We had done little to contradict the false propaganda being unleashed by the separatists through a highly biased local Press. The local people were being misled. Ever since the start of militancy, 27 October was observed as a Black Day with Black flags displayed all over the Valley and a 'hartal' (strike) in Srinagar. I decided to counter this by holding a function at Baramulla to pay tribute to the memory of the martyrs who laid down their lives defending Kashmir. In Jammu a function was being held on that date at the statute of Brigadier Rajendra Singh of the Kashmir Army, who had laid down his life at Uri fighting against the Pakistan invaders. He delayed the enemy for two precious days in his advance to Baramulla. On the same lines, I decided to hold a function at the memorial of Lt Col Dewan Ranjit Rai at Baramulla. He had led the first lot of troops of the Indian Army that landed in Srinagar on 27 October 1947 and had got killed at Baramulla. I was told that there may be adverse reaction in the Valley over our holding the function at Baramulla and the Srinagar Press which was anti-India, would black out news of the proposed function at Baramulla. I decided to test the waters and have a low-key function. I asked the Corps Commander, Lt Gen Nirbhay Sharma to make necessary arrangements. On 27 October 2003, I laid a wreath at Colonel Rai's memorial. We also held a small meeting within the Army campus attended mostly by soldiers with a sprinkling of some civilians. We located a 98 year old Italian nun Sister Emile, who was an eyewitness to the vandalizing of the convent and the hospital in Baramulla and the atrocities committed by the tribal raiders in October 1947. She came in a wheel chair and spoke a few sentences at the meeting. We also located Ghulam Rasool Kar, a veteran political leader who had worked in National Conference with Sheikh Abdullah. He is the oldest political leader in the State and he had personal knowledge of the happenings at Baramulla of October 1947. He spoke at the meeting recalling the horrendous events of that time. There were also two or three other old timers of that period who spoke at the meeting. At the end I wound up the meeting giving my account of what I had seen of ravaged Baramulla when we liberated the town on 8 November 1947. There was no adverse reaction to this meeting. I was pleasantly surprised that the Srinagar Press had not blacked out this event. I was encouraged to organize the function on October 2004, a little more elaborately. This time we had a much bigger gathering at the meeting mostly of local civilians. In October 1947, a young man of Baramulla, Maqbool Sherwani, had tried to save the lives of Sikhs and Hindus from the tribal raiders and had even misled them to delay their advance to Srinagar. The raiders had crucified him in 1947 and we had recovered his body nailed to the wall, when Baramulla was liberated. The army constructed Maqbool Sherwani Auditorium at Baramulla to be used as community hall by the local people. Our function in 2004 was held in this hall with a large attendance of local civilians. I had a documentary film prepared on the happenings of October 1947 in Baramulla. This was shown at the function and was much appreciated. In 2005 in the wake of the big earthquake in Kashmir in that month there was still greater public participation. In 2006 we had a peace march of 5000 people in Baramulla and this time we added the relief work done by the army in the 2005 earthquake to the documentary film. I made the function at Baramulla an annual event which I as the Governor of the State would inaugurate every year. I invited Muzaffar Hussain Beg from PDP. I was on friendly terms with him he spoke at the function. Taj Mohiuddin another minister who was from the Congress was also invited to speak at the function. I had known his father Brigadier Khuda Baksh of the Maharaja's Army in 1947. The presence of these ministers at this function had the desired effect.

I also decided to showcase the army's role in Jammu and Kashmir during war and peace. For this purpose I got the Corps Commander, Lt Gen Nirbhay Sharma to establish a museum with pictures and artifacts. For security reasons that museum had to be inside the Army campus in Badami Bagh Cantonment. The museum was completed in a year, utilizing one of the existing buildings. At the entrance we had two large pictures of our two great war heroes and martyrs — Brigadier Rajendra Singh who delayed the enemy at Uri for two crucial days in October 1947 and Brigadier Mohammad Usman who was the victor of the biggest battle of the J&K war of 1947–48 at Naushera. Apart from war pictures in the museum, we also had pictures of various Sadbhavana projects and assistance rendered by the army during natural calamities. A small auditorium was added to the museum where documentary films could be screened. There was also a small restaurant for visitors. I invited the President of India to inaugurate the museum. Dr Abdul Kalam was much impressed by it. The army organised regular visits to the museum, particularly of school children.

There was a nice old museum in Srinagar from the days of the Maharaja. I wanted this museum expanded and renovated with a hall developed with artifacts of *Kashmiriyat*. This hall could display in golden letters the words of Mahatma Gandhi during Partition, "I see a ray of light in Kashmir". At that time the whole subcontinent was engulfed in communal violence of an unprecedented scale, during the Partition holocaust. Kashmir Valley was then the only place where there was no communal violence or communal tension. Besides the Mahatma's quotation, this hall could also have artifacts pertaining to various Kashmir saints, notably Sheikh Nooruddin also known as Nund Rishi and Laleshwar also known as Lal Ded. They are equally revered by both Hindus and Muslims. The pictures of important Ziarats (graves of saint) with their history could be displayed in this hall. Despite all my efforts this project could not take off and remained on the drawing board. This had to be executed by the State Government and many hassles came in the way.

I decided to have a statue of Major Som Nath Sharma put up at the airfield. Som was an old friend of mine. I often met him before Independence in Delhi where we were both serving as majors. He was a year or so senior to me in service and during the war in Burma had served in the same battalion as my uncle who was years senior to both of us. The battalion was then commanded by General Thimayya. Som and I had come together to Kashmir in October 1947. He had met with an accident and his one hand was in plaster. He was commanding a company and had insisted that he should not be left behind because of his temporary disability and be allowed to go to war with his troops. On arrival at Srinagar, he with his company was assigned the task of defence of the airfield. He was very upset about this because he wanted a more active role in fighting the enemy advancing towards Srinagar. I tried to assuage his feelings saying that the task assigned to him was very important. The airfield, was our lifeline for bringing troops to Kashmir. If we lost the airfield we would lose Kashmir. With winter approaching when the grass airfield would be out of commission due to snow, it was imperative that we completed our troop build up within the next few days. It so happened that Som's date with destiny came after a few days, on 3 November, 1947. The enemy outflanking our defence on Srinagar-Baramulla road had approached within 2 kilometers of the airfield at Badgam. Som was dispatched with his company to stop the advance of the enemy. He was outnumbered 7 to 1 but he fought a brilliant action holding the enemy till reinforcements arrived. His forward platoons were overrun but he continued the fight inspiring the remaining platoon. In the process he got killed by a burst of automatic fire. This battle gave us our first victory in battle in the first war that we fought on attaining Independence. Som was posthumously awarded the

Nation's highest award for gallantry, Param Vir Chakra. He was the first recipient of this award. On taking over as governor, I decided to put up a memorial to him. A new terminal building was being constructed at Srinagar airport. I persuaded ministry of civil aviation to make a small plot available to the army to put up a statue for Som. They accepted my request and the army had a suitable bronze statue of Som installed. My intention was that this should be a permanent reminder to the people visiting the airport that Som had saved the airfield in November 1947. This would also convey a message to the people that Som had not only saved the airfield but had also saved Srinagar city from suffering the fate of Baramulla at the hands of the rapacious and barbaric raiders. I unveiled Som's statue on 3 November 2004, the anniversary of his martyrdom. The army organized an appropriate function for the occasion. I invited Som's two brothers and one sister with their spouses for the function as my guests to stay with me at Raj Bhavan. They all have been my friends. His one brother had retired as Army Chief and the other as Engineer-in-Chief. His brother-in-law had retired as Major General in the Corps of Signals. Som's father had been a Major General and the head of the Medical Corps in the Army. The family had a unique record of service in the army. The function to unveil the statue of Som was attended by the deputy chief minister, cabinet ministers and several senior civil and military officers. Mufti kept away from this function.

I visited the site at Badgam where Som had got martyred. This is some 25 yards from a Ziarat at that place. I asked the army to put up a suitable memorial for Som at that site. A nice design was made out for this on a granite background. A sketch of the battle and the Som's heroic action were displayed in golden letters. While I was at Badgam, the local people requested me to have repairs done to the Ziarat. I asked the army to renovate the Ziarat. The following year in 2006, I was happy to see that the army had renovated the ground outside the Ziarat with boundary wall, footpath and water taps providing ablution facilities. The local people now requested that the inside of the Ziarat be also renovated, which again the army did at my request. The army spent some 20 lakhs on this project and made an excellent job of it. When the renovation was complete, I went there to inaugurate it. After the inauguration, a largely attended meeting of civilians was held at the site. The local people thanked me and the army for what had been done for the Ziarat. This received a fair amount of publicity. Separatists and some religious fundamentalists did not like the

Army gaining popularity among the local people. A meeting was convened of Islamic clerics and a Fatwa issued against the army for working on a Muslim religious shrine. Non-Muslims are forbidden to do so. The Fatwa stated that it was sinful for a Muslim to receive any assistance from a non-Muslim for construction/improvement of a mosque or Ziarat. It also asked the local people to return the money spent on the renovation of the Ziarat. It asked the government to forbid the army from interfering in religious matters. Of course no one returned any money. We decided not to have any confrontation with the clerics on a religious issue as that could be counter-productive. However, I got a statement issued by the army saying that the renovation of Badgam Ziarat had been undertaken at the request of the local cleric and the local people as indeed several other such ziarats over the past few years. This was the first time objection had been raised to this goodwill gesture. The army had people of all faiths including Muslims serving in it. Further, the army was an instrument of the Government of India and it used funds made available to it by that Government. Funds of Government of India are used to subsidize Haj Pilgrimage and this was not considered sinful. How can Government funds utilised for renovation of Ziarat be something wrong ? Nevertheless, the army would hereafter not undertake such work in the future.

Ghulam Nabi Azad came up with a very good idea of holding an essay competition for school children on Mahatma Gandhi. The separatists issued a boycott call for this as they said that it would subvert the minds of school children. The fundamentalists also joined in giving the boycott call as they felt this was not in line with Islamic ideology. Despite their boycott calls, 50,000 school children from all over the State participated in the competition. The Chief Cleric of the Valley issued a Fatwa against Ghulam Nabi Azad.

On 3 November 2007, when I went to place a wreath at Som's memorial at Badgam, I was invited as a chief guest at a public meeting in a newly constructed Shaif-ul-Alam Hall named after the parton saint of Kashmir. He was an embodiment of interreligious amity and brotherhood, equally revered by both Hindus and Muslims. It did my heart a lot of good to hear several prominent civilians including Professors of Kashmir University, Imams and leading citizens paying tribute to Som and to the Indian Army for saving and serving the people of Kashmir. This was for the first time since the start of militancy in Kashmir that such a meeting had been held and people had spoken so openly, undeterred by any fear of the terrorists. I was concerned about the safety of the citizens who had spoken at the meeting as they could be targeted by the terrorists. I asked the police to take special measures to ensure their security. Fortunately, they did not suffer any attack. This was a good indication of changing times in Kashmir.

As part of psychological initiatives to combat religious fundamentalism, the root cause of militancy in the State, I had been working on propagating *Kashmiriyat*. I set up a centre for Kashmir Studies in Kashmir University. I chose Professor Meem Hai Zaffar, an eminent scholar as director of this centre. He is an outstanding scholar of history and philosophy, known for his secular outlook. He has also studied Sanskrit. He organised an international seminar on *Kashmiriyat*. Scholars from Pakistan, Central Asian Republics besides Indian scholars from different universities in the country, participated in this seminar. In my inaugural address I stressed on the values of *Kashmiriyat* and how it can show the way to the rest of the world. The seminar was a great success. We also organized another international seminar on Kashmir and Central Asia. The separatists maintain that Kashmir has more in common with Central Asia than the rest of India. I got scholars and diplomats from Central Asian Republics to come for this seminar. The Central Asian Republics have a majority Muslim population and they are secular. They are opposed to terrorism and are friendly with India. I felt that interaction with them would have a beneficial effect in Kashmir. We signed memorandum of understanding between Kashmir University and Central Asian universities. I wanted students and teachers from these universities to come to Kashmir University and vice versa. Towards the end of my tenure as governor I expanded the activities of the Centre for Kashmir studies redesignating it as an Institute and getting it registered as an autonomous society within the University. I shall be discussing this later in this look.

The city of Srinagar was founded by Emperor Ashoka in the 3rd century BC. Kalhan in his book *Raj Tarangini* has mentioned this. There is a site in Badami Bag cantonment which is supposed to be the place where the city was founded. It has a small pond with a temple in the middle and a small bridge to the temple. The Temple has pronounced Greecian architecture and is made of slate. It was originally a Buddhist temple which was changed into a Shiva Temple. I had a painting of this Temple made and put up prominently in the Foyer of the Raj Bhavan at Srinagar. To highlight Srinagar's association with Ashok, I started a Samrat Ashok Golf tournament at Srinagar. We invited a team of golfers from Patna, the ancient city of Pataliputra which was the capital of

Ashok. Patna also happens to be my home town. These annual tournaments were a great success. A team of 40 to 50 golfers from Patna with their families would come to Srinagar for three to four days. We extended hospitality to them which was much appreciated. Chief Minister Azad and I would participate in the tournament playing for Kashmir. The Chief Minister and I also hosted dinners in honour of the Patna team. Similarly, when we went on a return visit to play at Patna, the Patna Golf Club of which at one time, I was the President was very hospitable and made excellent arrangements for forty golfers and their families from Kashmir. Ghulam Nabi Azad was supposed to accompany us to Patna but dropped out at the last moment because of the death of his father-in-law. Dr Faroq Abdullah went with us to Patna and took part in the tournament. The Governor and the Chief Minister of Bihar hosted meals in our honour. This tournament was good fun for all participants but my main purpose was to underscore the historical link between Srinagar and Patna. It countered the propaganda of the separatists that Kashimir had more in common with Central Asia than India..

11

The fourth prong of my counter-insurgency strategy was information management. As I have quoted earlier Margaret Thatcher had rightly said that the media is the oxygen for the militants. In Kashmir, the media had been providing a great amount of oxygen to the militants, much more than anywhere else. The Valley Press was constantly churning out rabid anti-India views. Even Pakistan Press was not as venomous as the Valley Press. There was a panel of a large number of writers who were writing vitriolic articles against the Indian stand on Kashmir, all the time. Their articles appeared to be well-written and well-researched but they took liberty with facts, twisting them out of context and even indulging in total falsehoods. We learnt that they were being heavily financed from across the border. There was a marked difference between the Srinagar and Jammu Press. Whereas, the former was communal and anti-national, the Jammu Press did not carry such baggage. However, one newspaper in Jammu, for reasons not difficult to guess, was an exception.

The line being constantly projected by the Valley Press was that India had obtained Kashmir's accession in a fraudulent manner. Various versions kept coming out periodically. Some would say that no instrument of accession was ever signed by the Maharaja.

Another version would be that he was made to sign under duress, after Indian troops had landed in Srinagar. India was accused of planning aggression against Kashmir from Day one. Mountbatten had persuaded Radcliff to make the Muslim majority Batala subdivision of Gurdaspur district in Punjab, inclusive to India. This was done to provide India a land link with the State of Jammu and Kashmir. The bridge on Ravi at Pathankot started being constructed and work began on Pathankot-Jammu road well before the crisis in Kashmir. This was being done to buttress the accusation of India's evil designs in Kashmir. The tribal raiders from Pakistan had come to rescue the people of Kashmir suffering atrocities at the hands of the Maharaja's army. The Indian army came to Kashmir to suppress the freedom struggle of the Kashmiris and stayed on as an Army of occupation. Jawaharlal Nehru had publicly promised self-determination to the people of Kashmir but later went back on his word. India had failed to honour UN Resolutions on Kashmir. She had prevented plebiscite being held in Kashmir. It would also constantly be put across on the basis of half-baked facts that Kashmiris were a separate nation. They had more in common with Central Asia than India. Pre-Islamic history of India was ignored and dubbed as myths and legends. The history of Kashmir began with the arrival of Sufi saints led by Sheikh Hamadan in the fourteenth century. This was in line with some rabidly communal historians who imply that the history of India commenced with the invasion of Sindh by Mohammad-bin-Qasim in 712. I recalled that in my earlier tenures in Kashmir, before militancy had erupted there, I interacted with many Kashmiri Muslims who were proud of the pre-Islamic history of Kashmir. Sheikh Mohammad Abdullah's family had no inhibition in accepting their Kashmiri Pandit ancestry. Things had changed a lot from my early days in Kashmir. The other argument often touted was that the country had been partitioned on the basis of religion. Kashmir was a Muslim majority State and should legitimately have been a part of Pakistan but a big fraud was committed on the people of Kashmir by making Kashmir a part of India. Indian secularism was a farce. Events at Ayodhya and in Gujarat fully established this fact. Jagmohan as Governor of Kashmir had organized the evacuation of Kashmiri Pandits to give a bad name to the freedom struggle of the people of Kashmir. Massacres of Kashmiri Pandits at several places and of Kashmiri Sikhs at Chhatisinghpoora were carried out by Indian intelligence agencies to malign Kashmir's freedom struggle. The Chhatrsinghpoora incident had taken place at the time of the visit of President Clinton to India and Pakistan had been quick to assert that it was the handiwork of the Indian Army. Similarly, for the same reason, Indian intelligence agencies were accused to have vandalized Hindu temples in South Kashmir. Alleged human rights violations were used to build a sense of hysteria against the Indian Army and for generating anti-India sentiments. There is no shortage of human rights activists and people with bleeding hearts in our country. They would join the chorus for the sake of cheap publicity. Of course, there was complete silence over gruesome human rights violations by the terrorists like slitting throats of people including small children, public hangings, rapes and so on. All this was only a sample of the type of hostile propaganda being carried out by the Valley Press. Freedom of Press is an essential prerequisite of a functioning democracy and must be zealously safeguarded but does this imply license to violate the law of the land on sedition or promoting disharmony amongst citizens? Not only was nothing being done to curb such tendency but in a way newspapers indulging in such activities were encouraged by providing them facilities in terms of government advertisements, accommodation for journalists and so on.

At the international level the anti-India propaganda on Kashmir spearheaded by Pakistan was being countered by the Ministry of External Affairs. During the cold war period, the West tilted towards Pakistan but things had changed after the dismemberment of the Soviet Union. During the Kargil war, Pakistan, for a change, had found herself totally isolated, internationally. The external publicity cell of Ministry of External Affairs was doing well. However, within Kashmir we had hardly been doing anything on this front. It appeared that the government both at the Centre and in the State to parody a line from an English poem believed in "Let my silence speak for me more than their loudest notes". The Army on its own had been doing some work to counter false propaganda, but it required a more subtle and professional approach. The Central Intelligence Agencies did not show much interest in this. I wanted a "media war" to be fought in a coordinated manner by all agencies of the State. I stressed the need for this to the Prime Minister and the Home Minister. I suggested that we have an informal information management group in Raj Bhavan, under my chairmanship to work out coordinated plans. No publicity should be given to the functioning of this group. They approved of my plan. For the first one year I was handicapped in commencing work. I had no Public Relations Officer. It took me nearly a year to get one posted on my staff. I was fortunate in having the services of Madan Mantoo, an experienced PR man with good contacts, posted on my staff.

We got representatives from Ministries of Home, External Affairs, and Information and Broadcasting plus Army Headquarters, Northern Command, the two Corps and the central intelligence agencies to attend meetings of this group, held every six months. Initially, we did not have any representatives from the State Government but after I discussed my plans with the new Chief Minister, Ghulam Nabi Azad, we included the State CID and the State Information Department in this Group. Azad himself attended meetings of this group, a couple of times.

I made out a paper giving thrust lines for our media campaign. Documentary films were prepared. A number of articles were written based on those thrust lines, I wrote quite a few articles myself. We got them published under pseudonyms. We took up various issues like Kashmir's accession, Plebiscite, Kashmiri nationhood, our human rights records compared to those of Pakistan Army in Baluchistan and NWFP or American Army in Iraq and Afghanistan. We projected the Indian viewpoint on these and other issues as also contradicted the hostile propaganda on various points. We emphasised that the future of the Princely States was to be decided in 1947 neither on the base of religion nor the wishes of the people. It was for the ruler of the State to do so. This was clearly stipulated in the Indian Independence Act of 1947, passed by the British Parliament. Jinnah, the founder of Pakistan had been making that demand because he was wanting Hyderabad, the largest and richest Princely State of the size of France, to accede to Pakistan. One of his ministers, Sardar Abduls Rab Nishtar had said what has Kashmir to offer except mountains. Hyderabad, would be a much bigger prize. As for Kashmir's accession being secured in a fraudulent manner how come that Maharaja Hari Singh and Sheikh Abdullah who lived for many years after Kashmir's accession, never mentioned this. Both had legitimate reasons to nurse grievance against the Indian regime. The Maharaja from the very beginning and the Sheikh after the initial few years. The United Nations Resolution calling for the withdrawal of Pakistan's forces from Kashmir while Indian forces were to remain in Kashmir, was a recognition of India's legal position in Kashmir. So was the UN agreeing to the 200 square miles of Tilel Valley, which had been No Man's Land, being made inclusive to India, while delineating the Ceasefire Line. We also highlighted how Pakistan had secured the accession of Baluchistan. We located a document signed by

Mountbatten, Jinnah and the Khan of Kalat on 4 August, 1947. It said that on Pakistan coming into being, Baluchistan will revert to its status in 1876, before it was annexed by the British. In January 1948 the Khan of Kalat was summoned to Karachi and forced to sign the Instrument of Accession which was exactly the same as the one signed by the Maharaja of Kashmir or any other ruler of a Princely State in either India or Pakistan. The Baluchistan Assembly refused to ratify the Instrument of Accession signed by the Khan of Kalat and that was the beginning of insurgency in Baluchistan. We brought out the difference between the treatment meted out by Pakistan to Akbar Khan Bugti, the separatist leader in Baluchistan and by India to Syed Ali Shah Geelani the hard core separatist leader in Kashmir. Musharraf had organized an air attack on Bugtis hideout killing him. This had led to widespread hostile reaction not only in Baluchistan but also in other parts of Pakistan. In the case of Syed Ali Shah Geelani when he was ill in Ranchi Jail, Mufti had him released and sent the State plane to Ranchi to take him to Mumbai for treatment. A Kashmiri Pandit doctor took good care of him. On recovering, Geelani returned to Kashmir to continue his anti-India tirade. In 2007, he was more seriously ill, requiring major surgery for a terminal disease from which he was suffering. He wanted to go to the USA for treatment. The US Government refused to give him a Visa because of his terrorist links. Though a great votary of Pakistan, he did not want to go there for treatment. Instead he went to Mumbai where Indian doctors treated him with great care and compassion. The complicated surgery on him was miraculously successful. He returned to Srinagar in good health and at his welcome reception he thundered against India. He wanted the international community to impose sanctions on India for illegal occupation of Kashmir. Similarly, Yaseen Mallik a known terrorist involved in killing of air force children and Kashmiri Pandits went to Mumbai for treatment of a serious disease. He too was treated with great care and compassion by a Kashmiri Pandit doctor. This had an impact on Yaseen Mallik. He chose to give up the gun but continued with his separatist activity in a non-violent manner. On the holding of plebiscite, we brought out that it was Pakistan which had failed to comply with the provision of 13 August 1948 UN resolution which it had accepted. Obviously, Pakistan realised that memories of atrocities in Baramulla and the Valley by the tribal raiders were fresh in the memory of Kashmiris, and with Sheikh Abdullah around, Pakistan ran the risk of losing the plebiscite. On Kashmiri nationhood we argued that the facts of history proved that Kashmiris were not a separate Nation. Even for the sake of argument, if one were to accept that Kashmiris were a separate nation, then by no stretch could the people of Jammu or Ladakh be included in that category. Gujjars, Bakarwals and the Muslims of Jammu and Kargil could not also be part of the Kashmiri nation. Claiming separate nationhood for Kashmir would only lead to the dismemberment of the State of Jammu and Kashmir, which was not acceptable event to the separatists. We tried to work out a mechanism for prompt contradiction of false and exaggerated allegations against the army. Instead of the contradiction being sent after the allegation had appeared in the Press and that being blacked out or printed so inconspicously as to escape attention, I felt that the army's version even if an interim one should come out along with the allegation in the Press. This was difficult to achieve but we endeavoured to do so. There were two instances of rape which occurred about the same time, one in Kashmir and the other in Baluchistan. Major Rahman of the Indian Army was alleged to have raped a mother-daughter duo in Handwara. For one month newspapers in the Valley were writing about this allegation criticizing the Indian Army. First, they said that the officer concerned was a Hindu and the army had mentioned a Muslim name. Later, when they found that the person was actually Rahman, they dropped that tirade. Preliminary inquiry revealed that the officer had visited the house of the alleged victim alone during the night. The army immediately suspended the officer and legal proceedings were started against him. On the basis of forensic and other evidence during the court martial, rape could not be proved. However, the fact that the officer had gone to the house of the lady alone that night was proved. He was dismissed from the service, for conduct unbecoming of an officer. The other case was reported from Quetta in Pakistan. A lady doctor was alleged to have been raped by a Pakistan Army Major. No FIR was allowed to be lodged with the police nor was any inquiry held. There were widespread protests and violent disturbances. The lady doctor was fortunate that her husband did not hold anything against her and accepted her, though her father-in-law being more orthodox, refused to accept her, saying that she had become impure. She stayed in Karachi for some time and then migrated to Canada with her husband. President Musharraff on tour in the USA was asked about this incident at a Press Conference. He replied that it is simple get raped: get money and get a visa to Canada. His answer came in for much criticism both in the international Press and in Pakistan Press. We used these two incidents to highlight how the approach of the Indian Army to such incidents was different from that of the Pakistan Army. We also wrote articles from Buddhist point of view on the destruction of Buddha's statues in Swat Valley of Pakistan and earlier of the Banyan statues in Afghanistan. The article expressed fear about the destruction of the next largest Buddha statue in the world near Kargil. We brought out that Pakistan had been liberally using heavy artillery in Baluchistan and North West Frontier. So had America been doing in Iraq and Afghanistan. These weapons cause area damage, killing many innocent people. India had never used such heavy firepower during two decades of militancy in Kashmir. A series of articles were written about the plight of the people in Northern Areas of Kashmir under Pakistan occupation. Many of our articles could not get published in newspapers with wide circulation. Those that were published caused quite a flutter.

I repeatedly requested Shiv Raj Patil, the Home Minister, for special allocation of a few crores to Raj Bhavan for our media offensive. He said he would consider the matter but took no decision. Lack of funds was a major handicap for us and so was a lack of proper staff infrastructure. We were not able to get our articles translated into Urdu and published in Urdu newspapers which have a wider reach. I tried to persuade one of our national newspapers to bring out a Srinagar edition. This would have ensured availability of a national newspaper in the morning in the Valley with a few pages devoted exclusively to news on Kashmir and projecting our national viewpoint. National newspapers were no doubt available in the Valley but only in the afternoon and without much Kashmir-centric news and views. People like to read newspapers with their morning cup of tea. Moreover, most of the local correspondents of national newspapers were writing biased reports and articles. With lack of funds and proper support from Delhi, we were not able to be more proactive in fighting the media war.

The editor of one national newspaper agreed to bring out a Srinagar edition. I met him and his staff over lunch in Delhi. There were of course difficulties as it required heavy investment and was not likely to be a viable economic proposition. There was also the question of security and difficulty of finding local correspondents without any anti-India bias. The editor ultimately decided to call off his earlier decision. My plans for a Srinagar edition of a national newspaper remained stillborn.

I met Priya Ranjan Das Munshi, the Information and Broadcasting Minister. I requested that the Song and Drama Division of his ministry should put up a show for us in Kashmir. I had seen a programme by them in Assam and also one on Women Empowerment in Jammu. Their shows were a combination of sound and light and episodes presented on four or five stages like a theatre. Sound and light was interspersed with episodes presented on different stages with proper costumes and properties. These stages would remain hidden in darkness and come to life when lights were focused on them. I wanted to project a show on Kashmir Through The Ages. My idea was to showcase Kashmir's historical connection with the rest of India including the founding of the city of Srinagar by Ashoka the Great, the achievements of rulers like Lalitaditya in the ancient period and the great liberal ruler Zainul Abedeen, popularly known as Bud Shah in the medieval period. The philosophy and poetry of Sheik Noorudin and Laleshwari epitomizing *Kashmiriyat* were also to be projected. Priya Ranjan Das Munshi accepted my proposal and we started working on the script which they wanted us to provide. I roped in a few historians to work this out for us. Dr Fida Mohammad Hussain the most eminent and senior historian of Kashmir agreed to assist us. I had been meeting him and was much impressed by his vast knowledge and liberal views. It took us some time to complete the text which had to be developed into a script for presentation keeping various technical considerations in view. NN Singh, Director of Song and Drama Division was from the North East. I had interacted with him when I was in Assam. He was very cooperative. Such projects require mobilisation of some 2000 artists and technicians. The expenditure for putting up the show runs into crores. I am afraid the whole process got delayed for one reason or the other. We were getting ready to put up the show towards the end of my tenure in Kashmir. By then the controversy over diversion of land for Amarnath Yatra erupted and this project had to be given up.

It will always be one of my regrets that due to various constraints, we were not able to do enough on information management. Had we been able to do more, which was possible, if New Delhi had given us the required resources, I am sure, it would have had great impact and helped in our endeavour to win the hearts and minds of the people, as also bring about a mind change.

12

I am a family man much attached to my children and grandchildren. When I was a young officer in the army, I spent long years in the field either in Jammu and Kashmir or in the North East. Army families were not allowed in those areas. My wife and children would stay with my parents at Patna while I would be serving in non-family stations. I would visit them during my annual leave every year. My wife would say that as I used to be away from the children for most of the time, when they were growing up, I was unduly indulgent towards them. She would even accuse me of spoiling them. Our children knew of my weakness for them and they had coined a special word for me. They would say that our Daddy is chickpeck a derivative from henpeck!! All our four children did exceptionally well in their studies, putting at rest the forebodings of my wife that I was spoiling them. The three girls earned merit scholarships to go to the USA to do their PhD. Our eldest daughter had topped in Delhi University. Our middle daughter had stood first in the country in her school leaving examination. The youngest got a national merit scholarship during her college education in India. My son also had a good academic record. After doing his postgraduation from Delhi University, he took the All India Civil Service Examination along with over a hundred thousand candidates and competed for the IAS in his first attempt. He decided to join the Indian Foreign Service. As parents, my wife and I were very happy about the academic achievements of our children. Our children had a much better academic record than us. My wife could not complete her final examination for a BA degree from Benares Hindu University because her last paper got postponed and the priests would not accept postponement of our chosen date of marriage. I had done my BA (Honours) from Patna University and was a postgraduate student when I joined the army. Our children became better qualified than us academically. Like all parents we were only too happy to find that our children had done much better than us.

When children grow up and get settled in life, they have to go out to live their own lives. Old parents have to come to terms with this reality. In our case our three daughters were settled abroad and our son being in the Foreign Service remained abroad most of the time. This made life a little lonely for both my wife and me. However, we made up for it, by taking trips abroad to our children once every two to three years and similarly our children and grandchildren came on a holiday to us in India, every two years or so. Thus we could meet each other after every one to two years. However, it was difficult for all of us to be together at one time because of our different commitments. After the grand children grew up, they had to adhere to their school schedules. I remember an amusing incident when I was Governor of Assam. My son was posted in our High Commission in Pakistan. He sent our two grandsons, one aged 10 and the other 7 at that time, for their holiday to us in Guwahati. The boys were escorted from Islamabad to Delhi by a friend of my son and at Delhi the air hostess took charge of them for the flight to Guwahati. An intelligence officer was travelling in the same plane sitting next to these boys. He heard them talking about Pakistan. He had been working on a case in which we had apprehended militants in Assam with Pakistan connection. His curiosity was aroused to find out about these two small boys travelling on their own from Pakistan to Assam. He asked the boys where they were going. The boys told him that they were going to their grandparents. The officer felt that he had perhaps found a lead which could help him in getting some clues. Initially, the boys were vague in giving him answers. They told him that their parents lived in Pakistan and their grandparents in Assam. On further questioning these boys told him that their grandfather was the Governor of Assam. The Intelligence Officer knew me and he related this incident to me, when he met me. He told me that when he learnt the boys were my grandsons, he realized that he was barking up the wrong tree to find an intelligence lead.

We as a family had not got together for nearly 25 years. In 1999 we had planned a family meet at New York for our Golden Wedding anniversary. This did not materialize because at the last minute I was asked to take additional charge of Arunachal Pradesh and my leave got postponed. When I took over as Governor of Jammu and Kashmir, it was the earnest desire of my wife and I to organize a two weeks family get together. For the New Year of 2004 and my birthday on 7th January, we organized a family meet at Jammu. The Raj Bhavan being an old palace was large enough to accommodate all our four children with their spouses and our five grandchildren. The sixth and youngest grandchild arrived two years later. It was a wonderful holiday for all of us. We had a family group photograph taken. This was the first time in 25 years that all the family had got together.

We much enjoyed our collective holiday in Jammu. They organized a big birthday party for me on 7th January in which all my Raj Bhavan family consisting of officers on my staff also participated. This was the most gala birthday party, which I have ever had. My children and grandchildren gave me a surprise birthday present. This was a huge birthday card painted by them with each writing very affectionate greetings for me. I was much moved. I have preserved that card. It is my treasured possession along with a treasured memory.

The two weeks family meet was most enjoyable for all of us. I took time off to go out on picnics and sightseeing with all my family. I played billiards with my children and grandchildren. The billiard table in Raj Bhavan was put to use after a long time. I even went to see a movie screened specially for us and for army officers and their families. It was a good film on the Kargil war, titled LoC. It depicted very graphically how our young officers and men overcoming all hazards won a great victory under most difficult conditions. The Nation has every reason to be proud of its army.

Our two weeks family meet was like a dream which finished much too soon. Our children and grandchildren departed leaving the two of us. The children kept visiting us during my five years in Jammu and Kashmir periodically in ones and twos but not all together. I do not know if at all we will have another family meet with all of us together. Our youngest grandchild, Shiv, was born in 2006. He missed that family meet.

My son was posted as Consul General in Dubai. We had taken a week's holiday to visit him. A number of people from India kept visiting Dubai, including Jammu and Kashmir. They would mention to us about him. He had become very popular with the very large Indian community in Dubai. The Prime Minister came on a visit to Srinagar. He was accompanied by the Foreign Minister, Natwar Singh. Along with the Chief Minister and other dignitaries I was at the tarmac to receive them. I had known Manmohan Singh for some time. I had not met Natwar Singh before. He came up to me in the presence of the Prime Minister and told me that he had met my son at Dubai recently and he was doing very good work there. The Prime Minister gave me a smile. As a father I felt both very happy and beholden.

In January 2007, my son was posted as Ambassador to Venezuela. His appointment was reported in the national Press in a routine manner. The Press in Jammu and Kashmir gave prominence to his appointment under the heading "Governor's son appointed Ambassador". I received congratulations from several people. Both my wife and I were keen to go to far away Venezuela to see him installed as the country's Ambassador there. It was daunting to undertake such a long trip, particularly for my wife, who had breathing problems when she exerted herself. She had been to Ladakh the previous year, when she developed high altitude sickness from which she had not fully recovered. My son's silver wedding anniversary was on 31 August. We felt that we must take a trip to Venezuela for the occasion.

We flew to Caracas, the capital of Venezuela via New York. After a long flight to New York, one had to catch another flight to Caracas which took six hours. Both of us took the journey well. On our onward and return journeys, we took a couple of days off in the USA to be with our two daughters there. This was our first trip to a Latin American country. Venezuela being an oil-rich country, its capital Caracas, has all modern facilities. We spent a very pleasant holiday of ten days with our son and daughter-in-law. The Indian Ambassador has a big mansion and he lives adjacent to a beautiful golf course. My son threw a big party for his silver wedding anniversary. Over 200 guests came for the party comprising the local elite and the diplomatic corps including several ambassadors from different countries. Many guests complimented us for taking such a long journey to Venezuela at our age. Both my wife and I were now in our eighties. One of the guests remarked that it was unique to have both father and son concurrently being addressed as "Excellency". I was reminded of how my father had tears of joy when he had accompanied me to Assam, when I was sworn in as Governor of that State. My eyes became moist. I realized that there must be quite a few instances of father and son being so addressed, but it must be very rare indeed to have a father-son duo to have this privilege concurrently. It was God's mercy.

We returned to India after a very satisfying holiday in Venezuela. It gives supreme happiness to parents to see their children flourishing. The German philosopher Schopenhauer was right when he wrote that a father's ambition is to see his son do better in life than him.

13

Jammu and Kashmir is a popular tourist destination. It is also of much political and diplomatic importance. We had a spate of VVIP visitors coming to the State like the President, the Prime Minister, Union ministers, ambassadors of major countries and so on. The President, the Prime Minister and senior Union ministers normally stayed at Raj Bhavan. During my tenure in Jammu and Kashmir, the President visited us four times and the Prime Minister six times.

Within a few weeks of my taking over as Governor, President Kalam came on his first visit as President. I had had the privilege of hosting him at Guwahati on three occasions, twice when he was Scientific Adviser and once when he was President. He wanted to visit shrines of different faiths and we planned to take him to Mata Vaishno Devi in Jammu, Hazratbal in Srinagar, Pathar Ka Gurudwara near Leh and a Buddhist Gompa in Leh. Normally, the Governor and the Chief Minister of the State accompany the President on his tour. We were told that Mufti would not be going to Mata Vaishno Devi but at the last minute we received information that he would also be accompanying us to that Shrine. Kalam and I sat on the platform inside the Holy Cave of the Shrine. He went through the complete ritual of the "Aarti" while Mufti chose not to be on the platform and kept standing close to it. He did not want the red "Tika" to be put on his forehead nor the red thread tied on his wrist. We ensured that his sentiments were duly respected. So far as Kalam was concerned he had no inhibition on this score nor did Sheikh Abdullah and Farooq Abdullah have when they used to visit that Shrine. Farooq Abdullah used to often sing Bhajans with great gusto. After visiting Shri Mata Vaishno Devi Shrine the President proceeded to Srinagar. Mufti and I joined him in offering prayers at Hazratbal. We paid our obeisance to the holy relic (the Prophet's hair) which was shown to us. The President's visit to the Shrines in Ladakh, the Gurudwara and the Gompa also went off well.

Kalam was fond of interacting with school children. We organized an interaction session for him with about 400 children on the grounds of Raj Bhavan. I was impressed by the way this interaction session was conducted. It showed the President's great empathy with the children. He explained intricate scientific matters in a simple manner like a good teacher. He invited questions from the children. One of them stated that he wanted to become President of India and asked him, how he could achieve his desire. Kalam gave an interesting reply. He said that all that the boy had to do was to follow the routine that he observed when he was of his age. He then went on to give his daily routine at that age. He came from a poor family living near Rameshwaram in the South. His father would wake him up at the crack of dawn to offer morning Nemaz with him. Thereafter he would study for three hours before going to school. In the morning he took time off to distribute the newspaper in the town to earn a little money. During that time he would visit Rameshwaram Temple and take "Prasad".

He would go to school at 10 and would be very attentive in his class. On return from school he was allowed one hour to play by his mother and thereafter he studied till almost midnight with a short break for dinner. On holidays he put in additional hours of work at home in lieu of study at school. Another boy asked him why he was a vegetarian. He replied that when he went to college in the city he had to live in a hostel. There were two hostels, one vegetarian and the other non-vegetarian. The vegetarian hostel was cheaper charging only Rs 30 per month while the non-vegetarian hostel charged Rs 40 per month. His father could not afford a non-vegetarian hostel for him. Thus, he lived in a vegetarian hostel throughout the years he was at college and this made him turn a vegetarian.

Invariably, when a VIP visited the Valley, a "hartal" (strike) used to be called by the separatists in Srinagar. I was happy that this did not happen during the visit of President Kalam. Perhaps, it was because of the high regard everyone had for his intellectual attainments and his sincerity. A programme had been made for him to attend a function at Women's College in Srinagar. Normally, on the arrival and departure of a Head of State, whether the President or the Governor, the band if available, plays the National Anthem or the Anthem is sung. This was avoided in Kashmir University because the students were opposed to this practice as part of the anti-India sentiments that had developed during the years of militancy. There was an army school in the Badami Bag Cantonment primarily for army children in which we had allowed admission of some civilian children. There were also a few local teachers at the school. The Corps Commander told me that the civilian teachers and students had raised objection to singing the National Anthem during the morning Assembly. They wanted to be allowed to absent themselves from that daily ritual. I told the Corps Commander that teachers and students not wanting to do so, should be asked to quit. The school was for army children only and as a concession we had admitted some civilian children. The threat worked and they dropped their objection to the singing of the National Anthem at the school assembly. They began taking part in it. This had worked in an army school where staff and students were mostly from outside the State. Women's College in the town was a different proposition. I was apprehensive of the reaction of the students of Women's College to the singing of the National Anthem. The Principal of the college was confident that there would be no problem and she would be able to manage things. It was decided that we would not have a band at the college. On the arrival of the

President, a few girls will come to the stage and sing the National Anthem. To my pleasant surprise, not only the girls on the dais but the entire lot of students in the hall joined in the singing of the National Anthem. This was the first time that such a thing had happened in a college in the Valley since the start of militancy. I have a feeling that the students readily participated as a tribute to the President who commanded great respect among them.

While addressing school children in Leh Dr Kalam told them that Kashmir was embedded in the soul of India. This was a good riposte to Musharraf's assertion that Kashmir was in Pakistan's jugular vein. Nowadays vein can be repaired and blood changed through transfusion but soul is irreplaceable and unchangeable. I liked the simile used by the President and I often used it in my talks. During his first visit to the State, the President chose to address the members of the State legislature on good governance. He made an interesting power point presentation like a good teacher. This has been his life long profession. I was surprised that Mufti was not present for his presentation to the legislators nor was his daughter who was then an MLA. In his subsequent visits also the President would like to play the role of a teacher. I invited him to inaugurate Shri Mata Vaishno Devi University which he readily accepted. After the formal inauguration, he decided to take a class for the first batch of students. The Chief Minister, the Vice-Chancellor and I along with others sat in an adjacent room while the President was taking a class for one period of 40 minutes. Even when he came after the earthquake in 2005, he lectured to the students about earthquakes. He told them that till fairly recently it was believed that earthquakes could not be predicted. During his visit to Iceland he found scientists working on a project to give advance warning of earthquake. He also explained some of the aspects of this project and how it is possible for scientific knowledge to develop in the future when like the weather one may predict earthquakes. When that happened one would be able to save much loss of lives.

Kalam's visits used to have a good impact. The people were much impressed with his vast knowledge and sincerity. He showed much concern for the young generation. Every visit of his raised his popularity index with the people. He rightly started being called the People's President. We felt sorry that our political masters played petty politics and in the process, the popular desire of the people for his continuing as President for a second term, got overlooked.

I found the visits of the Prime Ministers to the State very helpful. Vajpayee had given a grant to Kashmir University during his first visit before I had taken over as governor. I was told that during that visit he had stayed in a room on the ground floor of the Raj Bhavan at Srinagar. The rooms on the first floor had an excellent view of the Dal Lake and the surrounding mountains. Putting up a lift in a building of wooden structure was a difficult proposition. However, we managed to have a concrete well for the elevator, adjacent to the Raj Bhavan. An opening on the wall of the well allowed it to be connected through a small wooden bridge to the first floor. The whole operation was completed in record time; it was ready by the time Vajpayee came for his next visit. He was thrilled to see the breathtaking scenic beauty around Raj Bhavan. I briefed Vajpayee about the counter-insurgency strategy I was working on. He had not been to Jammu in his earlier visit and was not scheduled to go there during that visit. I requested him to break journey at Jammu for a few hours. He told me that his party was also wanting him to do that and he would get his programme rescheduled. I also suggested to him that he should give a grant to Jammu University as he had done for Kashmir University. I mentioned that the people of Jammu felt neglected by the Government, both at the Centre and in the State. He saw the point and next day we went to Jammu for a few hours. He addressed a public meeting at which he was at his usual best drawing much applause. He announced a grant of Rs 30 crores from the Prime Minister's fund for Jammu University. We were delighted at his generous decision. We put this grant to good use by putting up a state of the art modern auditorium in the university. We called it the General Zorawar Singh auditorium. This became the pride of not only the University but of Jammu.

Manmohan Singh came to Srinagar in 2004 soon after taking over as Prime Minister. I had known him in Assam and had interacted with him only a few months earlier when he had accompanied Sonia Gandhi campaigning for the parliamentary election. I was much impressed by his humility and simplicity. I made two requests to him, both of which be readily accepted. The first was suitable accommodation for Kashmiri Pandits who had been living under subhuman conditions for 15 years and the second was funds for the one thousand microhydel projects. During his first visit to Kashmir as Prime Minister he announced a 24,000 crore aid package for the State which had a good impact. He had a unique and brilliant academic record as an economist. I remember that when he was Governor of Reserve Bank, his Professor at Cambridge was still teaching at that University. My cousin was then at Cambridge and that Professor was also his teacher. He told him that Manmohan Singh had been his best student during over four decades of teaching at that University. He had received Honorary Doctorates from various foreign universities. I wrote to him requesting him to accept D Litt honoris causa from Jammu University. He did us the honour of accepting my request. Jammu University became the first University in India to confer this degree on him. Later, I also invited him to deliver the first Convocation Address at Shri Mata Vaishno Devi University which I had started a few years earlier. As an example of his humility I quote an incident. After his first visit as Prime Minister to Srinagar and Jammu, at the end of his long tour, he was departing from Jammu. At the time of leaving Raj Bhavan, he told me that I need not bother to go to see him off at the airport. I insisted on doing so. It would have been a serious breach of protocol if I was not at the airport to see him off.

I cannot keep count of the number of ambassadors from different countries who visited the State during my tenure as Governor. Many came more than once. Every ambassador would make a formal call on me. They knew of my long association with Kashmir and were keen to hear my views on the Kashmir problem. I would give them the Indian point of view of the problem and brief them of the ground situation. I considered this as part of my counter-insurgency strategy to project our national viewpoint. The most fruitful such interaction I had was with Baroness Emma Nicholson. She was a member of the European Union Parliament. I struck a personal chord with her when I told her that her name had an Indian Army association. Her first name was the same as that of the wife of Field Marshal Lord Slim one of the great Generals of the Indian Army. Slim was from the Gorkhas and I was from a sister Gorkha Regiment. I served in Burma when he was the Army Commander. I had the privilege of meeting him and his wife in England on the Gorkha net. The surname of the Baroness being Nicholson reminded me of General Nicholson a well-known military leader of the 1857 war who got killed during the siege of Delhi. She told me that General Nicholson was one of her ancestors. This made a good beginning for our over two hour long discussion on Kashmir. I found her well informed on Kashmir and very receptive to what I told her. I also hosted a dinner for her in Raj Bhavan observing all protocol formalities. She was very appreciative of some of the tunes played by the army band. She remarked that she had heard that the Indian Army maintained all the old British traditions. I told her that her information was correct and that I could vouch for it having served in the British Indian Army before Independence. I also told her that during my visits to England I found that after the Second World War one could see American influence had crept in British Army Officers Mess. Today, the Indian Army was continuing with old British traditions more than the British Army. She had a big laugh. Her report to the European Parliament on Kashmir that came out a month or so later was very favourable to India and highly critical of Pakistan. It caused a flutter in the international world. Pakistan went all out to get her report scuttled or drastically amended by the European Parliament. Their efforts were in vain. The European Union Parliament endorsed her report by over 400 votes in favour and only 9 against.

14

Cross border terrorism has been at the root of terrorist violence in Jammu and Kashmir. In Assam along with terrorism we have been facing unabated influx of illegal migrants, changing the demographic contour of the State. Half-hearted attempts had been made to fence the border for several years in Assam and the fencing to this day after nearly a quarter of a century is not yet fully complete. No doubt the riverine terrain there is a handicap but that is no justification for not completing the fencing of the land border. The problem there was lack of political will and the crores spent on fencing for years getting mired in corruption and inefficiency. It has been deplorable that the 267 kilometers of fencing on Assam/Bangladesh border has not been completed for so long. In Punjab fencing on the border had been completed in record time of about two years and it has been a good deterrent for smuggling and for cross border terrorism during the period of terrorism in Punjab. Of course ultimate success over terrorism was achieved by the people of Punjab rejecting terrorism and the separatist philosophy.

In Jammu and Kashmir we had a 750 kilometer long Line of Control from near Chhamb to NJ 9480, near Kargil. Having been part of the Indian delegation to the UN in 1949 when this line (then called Ceasefire Line) was delineated and later also seen it demarcated on the ground, I was fully aware of the difficulties of terrain. Both infiltration and exfiltration across the LoC had been taking place for many years, the former for ingress of trained terrorists and the latter for sending misguided young men for terrorist training. Army and paramilitary were no doubt deployed on the border but it was not possible to completely seal the border due to the very difficult mountainous terrain along this long border.

General NC Vij, the Army Chief in 2003 sponsored the idea of fencing the border. I fully supported him but there were many doubting Thomas. There was divided opinion even within the army. Some felt that the obstacle may not serve the purpose. No obstacle in history had prevented penetration by a determined enemy. The Long Wall in China, the Maginot Line in France, the Siegfried Line in Germany, Bar Lev Line in Sinai had all been broken through by the attack. The Himalayas the most difficult natural obstacle in the world, had been crossed by the Chinese Army in 1962. Supporting Vij's proposal, I maintained that in the past determined attackers had overcome obstacles because the defender had failed to defend them adequately. The lesson from history was that an obstacle by itself could not stop the enemy. It had to be supplemented by adequate deployment of troops. The army worked out an imaginative pattern of deployment of troops in three tiers. The first tier was ahead of the obstacle to give warning and channelise infiltrators; the second was on the line of obstacle and the third in depth to act as both reserve and to block infiltration routes. There was of course opposition from separatists and some politicians. Vij also had to persuade the decision-makers in New Delhi to go along with his project which required on outlay of 292 crores.

Although I was fully supportive of Vij's obstacle plan I had doubts about our ability to execute the plan in a short time-frame. Initially, when the work was started, we had to take advantage of folds in the ground to prevent interference by Pakistan using direct firing weapons. The work was also being done only by night. A few months after the work started, ceasefire was declared by both sides on the LoC. This enabled the Army to complete the stupendous task in a little over one year. It was a Herculean effort to move and erect such a large quantity of barbed wire, iron pickets and other stores in the forbidding mountainous terrain covering a length of 750 kilometers. I had known Nirmal Vij for a long time and had high regard for his professionalism. As Army Chief, he displayed great dynamism in executing such a difficult project. He was constantly visiting the State to personally monitor the progress of construction of the fencing. The fact that the fencing was completed in record time was largely due to his personal effort. The fencing was fitted with various electronic gadgets and warning system. I often visited the forward areas and personally saw the tremendous obstacle that had been put up. Fencing of the LOC had the desired result in the first year bringing down infiltration to almost zero level.

I was much impressed by the contribution Vij had made in combating militancy in Kashmir. He is a native of the State of Jammu and Kashmir and the first person from the State to have become the Chief of the Indian Army. On his retirement in January 2005, I had a road in Jammu city named after him. I am glad Mufti cooperated in this. The road on which Vij had his home, and where his father was then living was named after him. A public function was organized for renaming the road. Mufti participated in this function. I made it a point to bring Vij's outstanding achievement in Jammu and Kashmir to the notice of both the Prime Minister and the Defence Minister, urging them to suitably recognize the same. I am glad that soon after his retirement the Government appointed him Deputy Chairman of Disaster Management Board of which the Prime Minister is the Chairman. He was also given cabinet rank. This was for the first time in India that any army officer was given this rank.

Two natural disasters took place in the Valley in 2005 which caused extensive damage to the barbed wire fencing along the LOC. The damage due to the "snow tsunami" of February-March was repaired during the summer months when the snow melted. Not long after the repairs to the fencing, the big earthquake of 8 October, 2005 took place. The extensive damage caused by the earthquake could be set right only in the summer months of the following year. Work on the fencing could not be carried in the snow bound areas during the winter months. Infiltration picked up in 2005 and 2006 due to large gaps in the fence for long periods. There was also another factor. The infiltrators developed new techniques for breaching the fence. Damage to the fence in winter was an annual feature and the fence had to be repaired when the summer set in. This problem did not affect the fencing in Jammu province where most of the area does not have any snowfall. Despite these difficulties the fencing of the LoC has been of great help in countering infiltration and keeping it at a low level.

15

I received total cooperation from the army at all levels. My cordial personal relations with senior army officers were of great help in our functioning. The army always responded positively to any suggestions or requirements projected by me. I felt overwhelmed by some of the letters received by me from senior army officers at different levels of command on retirement or on transfer. I take the liberty of quoting below one each from different levels of command. These reflect their generous sentiments towards me :-

1. General NC Vij, Chief of the Army Staff (on retirement).

At the close of my innings, I write to convey my most humble gratitude to you, for all the sage advice, I received from you on various issues from time to time. I have been more than fortunate to have your guidance in 4 Corps (in Assam) and now in J&K, which has been of the greatest value. I must also state unequivocally that you are by far the wisest senior officer of the army, perhaps of all times. The kind of vision and knowledge that you possess is not possible to emulate for anyone as it is God's gift to you backed by 62 years of highly professional exposure in various fields. What is more gratifying is your continued love for the army with such intensity. Army is that much richer for your indulgence.

2. Lt Gen SS Dhillon — Corps Commander in Kashmir Valley (on transfer).

"I would like to take the opportunity to state emphatically that you have been a pillar of strength during the triumphs and tribulations as well as vicissitudes and jubilations during any tenure as GOC of this valiant Corps. I have truly valued your guidance and support especially during the tragic earthquake that struck in October last year. The relief and rehabilitation efforts got a tremendous impetus primarily due to your personal unflinching indulgence.

As a renowned soldier and as impeccable statesman with first hand ground knowledge of the Kashmir problem, you have played a stellar role in the unfolding events of Jammu and Kashmir. Your role at the helm of affairs at this crucial juncture will undoubtedly be greatly recognized in the annals of history of the State. Your boundless energy and lucid memory of epic, historic moments have been immensely stimulating and enlightening to one and all. You shall always remain a father for all of us in uniform".

3. Major General RS Mehta — Divisional Commander In Kashmir (on transfer).

"In my eyes and many in uniform like me as also within the

'Awaam' of our vast country, you are the country's outstanding soldier-statesman. Today, when you speak passionately and most eloquently about your dream of Naya Kashmir you find believers in the State and in the country. Intoxicating change is in the air and His Excellency has reason to be happy in his quiet and dignified manner because he has driven the change at the apex level. We are indeed proud of you, Sir".

16

General elections to the Parliament were announced in early 2004, well before they were due. Media reports and the popular view was that the results were a foregone conclusion. It was widely believed that the NDA Government under Vajpayee would come back to power. Campaigning for the election had started. The Deputy Chief Minister, Pandit Managat Ram Sharma, with whom I had very cordial relations told me that Sonia Gandhi accompanied by Manmohan Singh and Ghulam Nabi Azad were coming and enquired if I could put them up at Raj Bhavan. I told him that I would have no problem in putting up Sonia Gandhi I had done so in Assam because I felt that as the widow of a former Prime Minister she was entitled to that courtesy. She now also had an official position, being the Leader of the Opposition. My staff told me that during her previous visit to the State she had not stayed at Raj Bhavan and my putting her up when she was coming to campaign for election may be misunderstood by the leadership in Delhi. I ignored their advice. I told Mangat Ram Sharma that she alone was welcome to stay in Raj Bhavan as had happened in Assam, even when she held no official position. However, there should be no political meeting or activity at Raj Bhavan and the other leaders accompanying her could stay elsewhere. I had known both Manmohan Singh and Ghulam Nabi Azad from before and I would have been happy to put them up at Raj Bhavan but this would send a wrong message of my aligning myself with the Congress Party, particularly when these leaders were campaigning in an election. I had first met Ghulam Nabi Azad in Srinagar soon after I had taken over as Governor. He was a well-known national leader who had a meteoric career in national politics, starting as a Youth Congress leader in the Sanjay Gandhi era of Congress politics. There was a generation gap between us. He had come on a social call to me at Srinagar and I found him very affable. We talked generally about Kashmir and I told him of my old association with the State, starting from October 1947, when he was not born. He showed a lot of interest in what I mentioned of the old days. I presented him a copy of my first book, *Operation Rescue* giving, my personal account of the 1947/1948 war in Kashmir. I made a general point which he appeared to appreciate a lot. I said that Kashmir was a national issue in which political parties at the Centre should adopt a common policy. The Congress and the BJP may have many conflicting policies for the rest of India but over Kashmir they should take a common stand. He agreed with my views. I took to him at our very first meeting. I felt he reciprocated my feelings. Despite the generation gap between us, we appeared to have a common outlook. I had met Manmohan Singh a couple of times when I was in Assam. He had been an MP from that State. I had been much impressed by his scholarship, sincerity and humility. Although I did not put up Manmohan Singh and Ghulam Nabi Azad in Raj Bhavan, I extended hospitality to them by inviting them to meal while Sonia Gandhi was staying with us. Little could I then think that I would soon be working with them when the former would be Prime Minister and the latter Chief Minister.

17

Most unexpectedly and to the surprise of most people, the NDA Government fell and the UPA Government came to power. It was widely known that although I took to public life after resigning from the army, I had not joined any political party. I was, however, close to BJP's top leadership and known to be opposed to the Congress and to Nehru-Gandhi dynasty. This had come out in the numerous articles that I had been writing in edit pages of national dailies when I was not holding any official position. I confess I was deeply shocked by the election results. Given my warm personal relations with Vajpayee and other top leaders of the BJP this was natural. I had nothing personal against Sonia Gandhi. However, the thought of her becoming Prime Minister was abhorrent to me. I had suffered White Man's rule in my youth and I did not want to be ruled by a White person in the closing years of my life. I seriously contemplated resigning but with Manmohan Singh becoming Prime Minister, I felt I must continue, and do my bit for the Nation in Kashmir. After the UPA Government came to power, it started appearing frequently in the Press that BJP appointed Governors will be changed. This had happened in 1977. Morarji Desai Government carried out a wholesale change of Congress appointed governors. This was repeated by Indira Gandhi when she returned to power in 1980. Although the NDA Government on coming to power in 1998 had not done so, there were precedents that the UPA Government could follow. The names of governors to be removed were appearing in the national Press with my name high in the list. I was fully prepared to quit when asked to do so. Locally within Jammu and Kashmir there were frequent reports appearing about me and a few names as my likely successor. It was being repeatedly alleged that I belonged to the RSS cadre and I was a BJP appointee, I was very close to Vajpayee and Advani, I was anti-Muslim because as Governor of Assam I had submitted a special report to the President on illegal migration from Bangladesh, I was communal because I had been taking undue interest in Mata Vaishno Devi and Shri Amarnathji pilgrimages, and so on. I was also told that Mufti who had good links with the Congress high command at Delhi was lobbying desperately for me to be removed. He was making an all out effort for a person close to him, to succeed me. His name was frequently appearing in the Press. As far as the allegations against me were concerned, almost all of them except one were totally false. I was never in the RSS. I had spent forty years of my life in the army and there was no question of anyone in the army being from the RSS cadre. I was not a BJP appointee as governor. I had been appointed Governor of Assam by the Gujral Government. However, I had been transferred from Assam to Kashmir by the Vajpayee Government. The charge of my being anti-Muslim because of my report to the President was absolutely false. That report was based entirely on security and demographic considerations. It was in the interest of the people of Assam, irrespective of their religion and also in the interest of national security. There were some senior and respected Assamees Muslims who had agreed with my views. It was a matter of great satisfaction to me that the Supreme Court gave a landmark verdict upholding my recommendation on repealing the controversial IMDT Act 1983 and quoting extensively from my report on the subject to the President. As for my being communal because of my taking keen interest in the Shri Amarnath and Shri Mata Vaishno Devi pilgrimage, the allegation was equally baseless. J&K Assembly had passed the Shrine Board Acts with the Governor as the Chairman of these Boards. I would have been failing in my duty if I had not taken keen interest in the functioning of these Boards. The allegation that I had been close to Vajpayee and Advani was no doubt true but, this was more of a personal than a political relationship. I chose to ignore the allegations and made no attempt to contradict them or have them contradicted. The UPA Government changed some NDA appointed Governors for their past links with the RSS. I was surprised that I was not included in that list. I have a feeling this was because of the controversy that arose at that time in connection with the Amarnath Yatra. Possibly, in view of the coming Maharashtra elections, the UPA Government decided not to remove me from Kashmir, lest this be viewed as an anti-Hindu act.

My relations with Mufti had started on a wrong note. My efforts to go the extra mile and remove misunderstandings had not worked. I tried to keep our differences under wraps. I felt that the dignity of the office of both the Governor and the Chief Minister had to be maintained. This was particularly necessary in a sensitive State like Jammu and Kashmir. I always went out of my way to show my regard for him. Whenever I was asked about differences between us, I would say that I had great regard for the Chief Minister. We may have different points of view but we had no differences between us. I must also give credit to Mufti. He himself never criticized me in public, even though some of his party functionaries would not only do so but often do this in an unbecoming language. The Press over which he was known to exercise influence would often be critical. I saw a telling cartoon in one of the local newspaper showing Mufti and I hugging each other and each trying to stab the other in the back!

My relations with the NDA Government at Delhi had been very cordial. It was widely known that my relations with the Congress leadership at Delhi were not too good even though at the State level, I enjoyed very good relations with the local Congress leaders. With the change of government in Delhi my relations with Mufti started nosediving. I heard from many sources how Mufti was desperately trying to get rid of me and have a governor of his choice in the State. A senior army officer from Delhi came to Srinagar at that time. He had been to call on Mufti where he was told by the latter's staff that I would soon be leaving and the State would have a new governor. This officer met me later and enquired when I was leaving. I told him that I had no information and added that what he had heard at the Chief Minister's residence may well be true.

18

The Constitution provides the Governor, with the right to information but there was often an attempt on the part of the State Government to deny me information that I sought. Similarly, there were attempts to deny me legitimate facilities. I decided not to make an issue of these and deal with them in my own way. However, controversy regarding the duration of Amarnath Yatra attracted nationwide attention. I shall discuss that separately.

I wanted to be briefed by the DG Police regarding security arrangements for 15 August 2003 functions. The DG police was not made available. Perhaps Mufti felt that it was not right for me to show undue concern. Anyway, I asked the Corps Commander to brief me, which he readily did. As the security adviser of the State government he was responsible for overall coordination of security in the Valley. He briefed me about the arrangements made by the army. Security in the city was being organized by the police but he was in broad picture of what had been arranged. I asked for a monthly briefing by the head of the state CID, about militant activities. This was the normal practice in Assam. This was also being done for my predecessor in Jammu and Kashmir. However, I was told that any information required by me will be personally provided by the Chief Minister. It made little sense for me to ask Mufti to give me a monthly intelligence briefing. I decided to do without CID briefing. I had the other Intelligence agencies available to me. The heads of the two Central Intelligence agencies, RAW and IB in the State, had no problem in briefing me regularly. Of course, military intelligence had no problem in doing so either. Thus my being denied briefing by the CID did not matter. After quite a few months, the head of the CID also started coming to brief me. Omar Abdullah, the President of the National Conference narrowly escaped a grenade attack at the entrance of a grave yard in Anantnag. He had gone to pay his respect to one of his party workers who had been killed in a terrorist attack. A National Conference delegation had met me complaining about lack of adequate security for its President. The Government had ordered an inquiry. I asked for information about the results of the inquiry. Despite repeated reminders, this was never made available to me. There was yet another serious incident. Terrorists had forcibly taken over a civilian car in Kathua and driven through 17 police Nakas till they were finally intercepted by the army at Akhnoor Bridge. En-route they had fired upon some civilians inflicting casualties. I wanted to know how they got through 17 police Nakas without being checked. There was obviously something wrong in the functioning of these Nakas and suitable corrective action was required to be taken. I was told that an inquiry had been ordered and the required information would be sent to me on its completion. I waited for that information for over six months. In the meanwhile another incident took place. Some terrorists forcibly took over a scooter rickshaw on Akhnoor-Jammu road. Despite information of them being given to the police, the terrorists in the scooter rickshaw managed to cross the police Naka without being checked. They saw a car on the outskirts of the city with a red light and opened fire. A senior IAS officer travelling in that car was injured. Thereafter the terrorists escaped to a nearby jungle. The army was called out and the terrorists were killed in the ensuing encounter. After repeated reminders the police sent me some eighty page inquiry report. I was amazed to see how these serious lapses were sought to be covered. The report started with analysing a statement issued by the US President and the dialogue commencing between India and Pakistan. I failed to see any relationship between all this and the functioning of the police Naka. It was also stated that any action against policemen found lax would demoralize the force. As for failure to intercept the scooter rickshaw, it was mentioned that the police havaldar at the Naka was engaged in doing some other work and the police sentry being an ex-serviceman was not up to the mark. I was amazed to read all this. The DG Police, Gopal Sharma had perhaps not read the inquiry report and had forwarded it to me thinking that I would not read the long report. I sent for him and pointed out several lapses in the report. He agreed that the inquiry officer was blameworthy in producing such a report after over six long months. He promised to take suitable action. I told him that I was not for any witch-hunting or fault finding. I only wanted that such lapses should not recur. I advised him that Nakas must have suitable wireless communication, lighting arrangement by night, obstacles on the road to slow down vehicles, double sentry so that while one sentry checked the vehicle the other covered him, sentries should be in a bunker for protection and so on. Next day, I was surprised to read in the newspapers that I was interfering with the functioning of the State Government.

Apart from denial of information there was a deliberate attempt to deny me facilities. Most of the time when I asked for the use of the State aircraft or a helicopter, it was not available and even when made available, at the last minute some more important commitment would come up or the excuse of some technical problem would be given. Governors of Assam and J&K were permitted use of air force plane and helicopter but the demand had to go through the State Government and the State Government had to foot the bill for their use. This raised hassles if the State government was not cooperative. There was an old Government of India letter which provided for Governor of J&K using air force helicopter without any charge being levied by the Ministry of Defence. This went back to the time when the State Government had not acquired helicopters. This letter had lapsed. I tried to get the order revived with the help of the Defence Secretary and the Air Force on the personal level, but Finance was raising objections. I took up the matter with Pranab Mukherjee who had taken over as Defence Minister. He saw my point of view and a special Government order was issued allowing me use of air force aircraft and helicopter without any payment for the same by the State Government. My request for them were required to be made directly to the Air Force and the State Government was kept out of it. This solved my problem. However, after the change of chief minister, there was no difficulty in my having the use of State aircraft or helicopter, whenever I required them. There were other minor instances in which I found the State government not cooperative. Government of India had sanctioned a new bullet proof car for the Governor and made funds available for it. The car had to be obtained by the State Government. It took nearly two years to arrange one for me. On one occasion when my staff asked for a bullet proof car for me, a junior functionary of the State Government wrote back that one was not available and Raj Bhavan should make alternative arrangements. I brought the impropriety of such reply to the notice of Mufti but he ignored it saying that there was shortage of bullet proof cars. Although the State Government had enough Jammer vehicles to detect explosives on the road, no such vehicle was made available for my carcade. Whenever I travelled by road in the State, my staff would borrow such vehicle from the army which was always readily made available.

Another instance of the State government and Raj Bhavan being on different wavelengths was the case of the appointment of Justice Jha as Chief Justice of J&K High Court. He was a Judge in Patna High Court and had been selected for promotion and posting to our High Court by the Chief Justice of India and the collegium of Supreme Court Judges. As per the prescribed procedure, the concurrence of the State Government had to be obtained before the President's Secretariat issued the necessary notification. The Law Minister had sent the recommendation to me and the State Government. The State Government's reply had to go to the Law Minister through me. For over six months the State Government would not send a reply. Possibly, Mufti did not relish the idea of having a Chief Justice from Bihar knowing that I was from that State or may be he was interested in the acting Chief Justice continuing indefinitely. Whatever may have been his reason, Mufti would not send me the State Government's recommendation despite three reminders to both me and him from the Law Minister. When I wrote to Mufti to expedite his recommendation, his bland reply was that the matter was under the consideration of the State Government while the Law Minister kept sending me reminders. I got fed up with the inordinate and deliberate delay by the State Government. I wrote to the Law Minister drawing his attention to a provision in the guidelines issued by Government of India for appointment of Judges. It stated that if the views of the State Government was not received within six weeks, Government of India could proceed on the assumption that the State Government concurred with it. A notification from Government of India was issued appointing Justice Jha as Chief Justice of our High Court. I had not known Jha from before. I met him for the first time when I administered the oath of office to him. Mufti did not take too kindly to Jha and the relations between the Chief Minister and the Chief Justice remained strained. I invited the Chief Justice and his wife for dinner at Raj Bhavan. While we were having dinner, a powerful explosion took place not far from the gate of Raj Bhavan, which shook because of the blast. I told the Chief Justice that it was his initiation to militancy in Kashmir.

There was another instance in which Mufti's men tried to raise hassles over the appointment of Sunil Hali as High Court Judge. There had been no Kashmiri Pandit on the bench of Jammu and Kashmir High Court for a long time. Despite the fact that two successive Chief Justices of the State and the collegium of Judges had recommended his case and it had also been approved by the Chief Justice of India, Mufti and his law minister were blocking his appointment. I threatened that I would have to write to the Prime Minister bringing to his notice the State Government's prejudice against a Kashmiri Pandit and attempt to undermine the independence of the judiciary. This worked and the State Government communicated its concurrence to me and I forwarded the same to the Centre. Sunil Hali was appointed a judge of the High Court after his case had been under consideration for over two years which must be a lone case of such inordinate delay.

Shivraj Patil the Home Minister came to Srinagar one morning in 2005 and went to the holy shrine of Amarnath. After lunch, he was to attend the meeting of the Unified Command in the afternoon before returning to Delhi the same day. Between his visit to the shrine and the meeting of Unified Command, he and his party had a working lunch with me at Raj Bhavan. No other person was invited for this lunch. Mufti was in town but chose to boycott the meeting of the Unified Command. This led to controversy in the Press with Mufti's staff claiming that intimation about the meeting of Unified Command had not been given to Mufti. Ministry of Home issued a statement clarifying the position and stating that intimation was sent to Mufti and also acknowledged. This was the first time that a chief minister had boycotted the meeting of the Unified Command attended by the Union Home Minister. Three years later after I had left Kashmir and when controversy was raging over diversion of land at Baltal to Amarnath Shrine Board, I read in the papers that Mufti had boycotted that meeting to register his protest against my interfering in the functioning of the State Government. If I was in any way doing so, he could have written to me or taken up the matter with the Government of India instead of boycotting the meeting of the Unified Command. Perhaps, he had been irked by the Union Home Minister going to Amarnath Cave and having lunch with me, showing proximity to me ! There was an instance in which Mufti interfered with the functioning of Kashmir University undermining my position as Chancellor. I wrote to him in the matter. I shall mention details when discussing higher education in the State, later in this book.

19

In April 2003 Vajpayee at a public meeting in Srinagar extended his hand of friendship to Pakistan. This was welcomed by Pakistan. It set in motion various CBMs (Confidence Building Measures), with Pakistan. Government of India sent twelve point proposal to Pakistan. These included the opening of Srinagar-Muzaffrabad Road, free medical treatment to seriously ill patients from Pakistan in Indian hospitals and seats for students from Pakistan in technical institutions of higher education. Pakistan accepted these proposals in principle but wanted Srinagar-Muzaffrabad Road to be opened under UN supervision. It also extended medical and educational facilities in Pakistan but for people from Kashmir only. Pakistan Government added that they would also provide assistance to victims of atrocities by Indian Security Forces in Kashmir. Mufti welcomed Pakistan's "positive reaction" when involving the UN with Srinagar-Muzaffrabad Road was against India's declared national policy. Moreover, no Indian Government could possibly accept aid from Pakistan for victims of so called atrocities by Indian Security Forces. I was surprised that such a conditional acceptance of our proposals by Pakistan was welcomed by Mufti. It only showed how our thinking was out of tune with each other. Ultimately, after discussions between India and Pakistan, agreement on various CBMs was reached with UN not to be involved in the opening of Srinagar-Muzaffrabad Road and no mention of assistance for so called victims of atrocities by Indian Security Forces. Understandably, Mufti wanted to claim credit for the opening of Srinagar-Muzaffrabad Road. National Conference maintained that this was an old proposal which had been mooted by Sheikh Abdullah. Anyway months ahead of the scheduled date of the opening of this road, there was much hype about it. Hoardings were put up on roads indicating distance to Muzaffrabad. There were PDP's green flags all over. A day before the opening of this road, the tourist centre building in the city was attacked and put on fire by militants. Luckily, the first batch of people going to Muzaffrabad by bus were in an adjacent building and were not hurt. I visited the site and I found that it was a serious security lapse on the part of the police. I mentioned this to Mufti but no action was taken in the matter. The Prime Minister and Sonia Gandhi arrived at the airport in the morning. Mufti and I alongwith senior dignitaries and officials received them. We were to travel by Air Force VVIP MI-17 helicopter to Badamibagh near the site where a public meeting was to be held and then the first bus was to be flagged off by the Prime Minister and Sonia Gandhi. The helicopter had cushioned seats in rows of two. Sonia Gandhi entered the helicopter first followed by the Prime Minister, me and Mufti in that order. I found her sitting in the front row and the other seat was occupied by the Prime Minister. On seeing me Sonia Gandhi stood up saying that I should sit in the front row with the Prime Minister and she would move to the second row. I told her that it was perfectly alright and I could sit in the second row. She insisted and vacated her seat for me. She insisted on doing this again on our return trip. I was much impressed by her courtesy and regard for protocol. At the public meeting, it appeared that Mufti wanted to hog all the credit for himself and his party for the opening of the road to Muzaffrabad. On the dais there were seats only for the Prime Minister, Sonia Gandhi, Mufti and his daughter in her capacity as the President of PDP. The Deputy Chief Minister and I were seated near a tent some distance from the dais. This tent was earmarked for clerks of Prime Minister's office. Central ministers who had come from Delhi and some other dignitaries were accommodated in chairs immediately below the dais. It had never happened before that a Governor was treated in such a manner at a public function in his State. The regard shown by Sonia Gandhi in the helicopter for me was in sharp contrast to the lack of regard shown by Mufti at the public meeting. I decided to ignore the slight meted out to me. I considered it too trivial and in any case Mufti's term was to expire soon. It so happened that a few weeks later, the Prime Minister came to flag off the first train from Udhampur to Jammu. The Prime Minister, the Railway Minister, the Chief Minister, myself and some others sat on the dais. Travelling in the car from the helipad to the meeting ground, talking about the seating arrangement at the meeting in Srinagar, for flagging off the bus to Muzaffrabad, the Prime Minister told me that it should not have happened. I do not know whether my being slighted during the opening of the Srinagar-Muzaffrabad Road was deliberate under Mufti's direction or it was something done without his knowledge. Whatever may have been the case, Mufti should have apologised for what happened. I found such niceties beyond him.

Despite our strained relations I was at pains to ensure that I should not do anything in my relations with Mufti which could be termed unbecoming. However on certain issues which were matters of principle I could not compromise. There were two such instances.

The Vice-Chancellor of Agriculture University at Jammu had completed his term and a search committee had been appointed to select his replacement. The search committee sent me three names including that of the retiring Vice Chancellor. I found that the initial appointment of the Vice Chancellor was irregular. The University Act required that the Vice-Chancellor should be an eminent academician with teaching experience but this gentleman did not meet that requirement. He had no Ph.D or postgraduate degree nor any teaching experience. He had been a bureaucrat. The new university had not made much progress under him. Moreover, there was a case of alleged molestation filed against him by a lady teacher which was pending in the Supreme Court. Mufti wanted me to give him a second term. He came to see me and said that he had announced his selection and it would embarrass him if he was not given a second term. I told him that he should not have made such an announcement without my approval. I also told him that I had no personal interest in the matter. My conscience did not permit me to approve of a second term for his nominee. I knew Mufti was very upset with my decision but I could not help it.

The second instance was of the Panchayat Bill passed by the State Legislature. There were four thousand Panchayats in the State. In two thousand Panchayats elections had been held but in the remaining two thousand, elections could not be held due to security reasons. The State Assembly had passed a bill

presence in Srinagar at that time was good for the morale of the people and helped to coordinate the relief efforts being made jointly by the civil administration, the Army and the Air Force. I may add that the army voluntarily gave up their one day's ration which came to about 200 tons, for the civil population. This was a very noble gesture. Two days later the State assembly's budget session started at Jammu. I had to read the Governor's address prepared for me by the State Government. I was surprised to find no mention in the address of what we had come to call "snow tsunami". As I started reading the address, the Opposition members stood up. The Leader of the Opposition, Abdul Rahim Rather, spoke loudly, "During the snow crisis in the Valley we had our 80-year old Governor rushing to Srinagar in a freighter aircraft while the Chief Minister was opening a photo exhibition in Delhi". Someone added it was like Rome burning and Nero fiddling. Mufti was present in the assembly. It must have cut him to the quick, further worsening our relations. Something similar happened during the big earthquake in October that year. I had gone to Baramulla for the annual function of the Baramulla Convent. As the wheels of my helicopter touched the ground the earthquake started. The helicopter started wobbling badly and we feared it might topple over. I thought that the helicopter had developed some technical problem. We did not realize that it was an earthquake till we saw a portion of a building falling. The General who had come to receive me at the helipad rushed off to Uri after the frequent sharp tremors for about half an hour. I followed him to Uri and Tangdhar, the two worst affected areas in the State. On return to Srinagar, I sent for the Secretary Red Cross and briefed him about what had happened. I directed him to move all our disaster relief stores to Uri and Tangdhar and organise relief work. I made the prefabricated shelter stores at Baltal with Amarnath Shrine Board available for earthquake victims. There was a meeting of Congress Chief Ministers being held at Chandigarh. Ghulam Nabi Azad then a Union cabinet minister was attending that meeting. He was immediately dispatched to Srinagar in a special Air Force plane to coordinate relief on behalf of the Centre. He did a yeoman's work in mobilizing assistance from all over the country. I met him frequently during that period and I was very impressed by his drive and energy. He, however, told me that the local officials were not too cooperative. Mufti was in Delhi when the earthquake took place. He returned to Srinagar but could visit Uri only the following day, where some people showed him black flags.

The army rose to the occasion splendidly. We organized operations in there phases of rescue, relief and rehabilitation. The army and the air force were the major players in the rescue and relief phases. Rehabilitation which came up later had to be carried out largely by the civil administration. Within 72 hours we were able to contact all villages many of whom were in very remote areas. As the mountain tracks had got damaged the villages were not easily approachable. One army patrol trying to reach a marooned village became a casualty. On account of a tremor, a huge loose boulder came hurtling down and hit the four men of the patrol. They died there and then. Despite suffering casualties due to earthquake and its own accommodation also getting badly damaged the army was carrying out, rescue and relief operation in high gear. The civil administration also joined in but their presence in remote areas was nowhere near the army's. We had to rely primarily on the army. The army promptly set up relief camps in tents and ran kitchens for the people. People from remote areas were brought to relief camps where they were provided food and shelter. Army cooks worked round-the-clock. It was the month of Ramzan and "seri" had to be provided for those observing Ramzan and by day food had to be cooked for the children and those who were not fasting. Casualty evacuation was carried out mostly by air. Small army and air force helicopters were used to bring casualties to improvised army hospital at Uri in tents and to the civil hospital at Tangdhar. The army hospital at Tangdhar had got destroyed due to the earthquake but the civil hospital building had remained intact. Serious cases were flown in bigger Air Force MI-17 helicopters from Uri and Tangdhar to Srinagar. All the hospitals in Srinagar, both civil and military were receiving casualties round-the-clock. Very serious cases were evacuated by transport aircraft from Srinagar to Delhi. Though over 1000 people were killed due to the earthquake and many more injured, no one died due to lack of medical care or lack up food and shelter. I was constantly touring the earthquake affected areas and wherever I went, I found the people full of praise for the army. They wanted all relief given to them though army channels. Of course no statement was issued by anyone praising the commendable work done by the army. The Press chose to be silent about this. In fact within a few months the separatists and the PDP a partner in the ruling coalition stepped up their demand for the withdrawal of the army from Kashmir. While these politicians were making this demand, I found during my tours to border areas, the local people would tell me that they would not be able to survive without help from the army.

Rehabilitation was a later and long drawn out phase in which the civil administration was primarily involved. However, the army undertook to rehabilitate three completely destroyed villages, one each in Poonch, Uri and Tithwal. It took them about a year to reconstruct these villages making them truly model villages. I visited each of these villages and was surprised to find that they had been provided all the facilities of modern living like street lighting, sports auditorium, community centre, health clubs, vocational training centres, schools, dispensary and so on. Perhaps, these had become the most modern villages of our country.

Muzaffrabad had been the epicentre of the earthquake. The people in POK had suffered the ravages of earthquake much more than on our side Govt of India offered helicopter for relief work but Pakistan would not accept them unless they had their own pilots to fly the helicopters. We could not agree to this. Thus our friendly gesture did not materialize. There was much criticism on the other side of the Pakistan Army not responding promptly to assist the earthquake victims. They were too busy repairing their defences as they anticipated that Indian forces may attack taking advantage of the situation. The terrorists living in various camps went all out to help the people and earned much goodwill.

21

The Coalition Government of the Congress and the PDP had come to power on 2 November, 2002. It had been agreed by the two parties that for the first three years the Chief Minister will be from the PDP and for the latter three years from the Congress. The tenure of the J&K Assembly unlike other States in India, is six years. Thus Mufti Mohammad Sayeed had to vacate the office of chief minister in November 2005 and be succeeded by a Congress chief minister. As the date for the change approached, there was much speculation whether Mufti would continue for another three years or as per the agreement, relinquish the office of chief minister. No doubt there had been marked improvement in the internal situation in Kashmir and the peace process with Pakistan had been progressing, the most dramatic being the opening of Srinagar-Muzaffrabad road. Not unnaturally Mufti tried to hog the credit for all this. Congress Party did not have a leader in J&K, of the required stature to succeed Mufti. The only person who could be considered as a successor was Ghulam Nabi Azad who was then a Central Minister. He had earned his spurs in politics primarily at the Centre. In 2002, he had played a major role in the Congress emerging as the second largest party in the assembly after the National Conference and ahead of the PDP. At that time, he had shown a disinclination to take over political office in the State preferring to remain in politics at the Centre. In 2005, it was circulated by the media that Azad was indispensable for the Congress Party at the Centre, and could not be spared for Jammu and Kashmir. There was another point being made, Azad not being a Kashmiri Muslim, he would not be acceptable to the people of the Valley.

As the time for change in November 2005 approached, Mufti started inaugurating projects or laying foundation stones at high speed. He began doing this at the rate of about two a day. At times it would even be three a day. The aim appeared to claim credit but more importantly to convey the message of his indispensability. Simultaneously, a media blitz was launched in the national Press that Mufti should not be disturbed. In national interest the Congress should forego its claim for chief ministership. Even *Pioneer*, a national daily, with pronounced BJP leaning, came out with an editorial in support of Mufti. The theme song in the national Press was that changing horses in midstream would be detrimental to resolving the Kashmir imbroglio. I knew that Mufti had a strong lobby among journalists in Delhi but I was not aware he had such a wide reach. The Congress high command was sought to be influenced through the national media. The latter had been cultivated by Mufti over a long period. It was being propagated that after all Mufti had been an old Congressman. He was the best bet for the Nation in Kashmir.

Congressmen in Jammu and Kashmir were opposed to Mufti continuing as chief minister. There was a feeling amongst them that the Congress Party had got marginalized in J&K during his chief ministership and if he were to continue for another three years, the Congress Party would get wiped out in the State. Despite the strong feeling of local Congress leaders, I was getting reports that the Congress high command had taken a decision allowing Mufti to continue. So far as I was concerned, I knew that my views in the matter did not matter but I made no secret of my views to the Central Government, that the continuance of Mufti as CM was not in national interest. Arjun Singh, a senior Cabinet Minister at the Centre came to Srinagar and was staying with me at the Raj Bhavan. The speculation about the change of chief minister was at its peak at that time. He asked me what would be the impact in the

State and on the peace process if the Chief Minister was changed. I gave him my frank views. The improved internal security scenario had come about primarily on account of the operations of the security forces, specially the army. This improvement was not due to any political steps taken by the State Government. As for the peace process with Pakistan it was being orchestrated from Delhi The State Government and Mufti had hardly any role in it. I added that I felt a change will be for the good in resolving the Kashmir imbroglio. I had put across similar views to both the Prime Minister and the Home Minister. However, I knew that the decision on this would be taken by the Congress high command and not by them.

Ghulam Nabi Azad's name was doing the rounds as a possible successor to Mufti. It was surprising that three senior Congress leaders from the Valley came to see me separately to tell me that the appointment of a non-Kashmiri Muslim as chief minister of the State will not be taken well in the Valley. I failed to appreciate the logic of their argument. Azad's ancestors had been from the Valley but they had migrated to Doda district of Jammu province. He spoke Kashmiri fluently and was married to a very eminent Kashmiri Muslim lady who was known as the nightingale of Kashmir and was a recipient of the Padma Shri award. He was a son of Jammu and a son-in-law of Kashmir. This was a formidable combination for a chief minister of Jammu and Kashmir. Moreover, Azad was the leading political figure of the State at the national level with wide experience of governance as a Central Cabinet minister for decades. The objection to his being made chief minister was perhaps due to the personal ambition of the Congress leaders in the Valley who had come to convey their views to me. In any case, they should have known that I would not be having any role to play in the selection of a new chief minister and that the matter would be decided by the Party high command.

By 27 October, 2005 it appeared almost certain that Mufti would continue despite some important Congress MLAs lobbying in Delhi, for a change. I got reports that Mufti was holding a Press Conference at 4 P.M. on that date to announce his continuance in office. The journalists were disappointed as Mufti talked to them only about earthquake relief measures. When some journalists asked him about the change of chief minister, his reply was that there may be surprises. When asked about the Congress MLAs camping at Delhi, his reply was that it is normal for MLAs to visit the national capital. I was given to understand that Mufti's body language indicated that he was continuing.

It came as a big surprise to me and to almost everyone in the State when the evening news on the television announced that the Congress high command had decided that Ghulam Nabi Azad would be taking over as Chief Minister. I was delighted to hear this news. I had occasion to interact with Azad during earthquake relief operations. I was much impressed by his dynamism and sincerity. I had asked him if it was true that he did not want to give up his berth in Delhi and come to his home State. He told me that it was not so and he would not mind coming to the State. He added that he would gladly do whatever his Party high command directed. I was told that at the last minute decision to induct Azad in the State was taken due to the Congress MLAs threatening to resign, if Mufti was allowed to continue.

I expected that after the announcement on the TV about Azad to be the next chief minister on 27th evening, Mufti would come to see me with his letter of resignation on the 28th. Surprisingly, there was no word from him on the 28th. Some people told me that the decision of the Congress high command had greatly shocked Mufti who had been given to understand from authoritative sources that he would be continuing. On 28th, he had remained incomunicate. However, on the 29th, Mufti sought a meeting with me. I immediately guessed the purpose and promptly gave him time to come and meet me. Mufti came at the appointed time. He took out his letter of resignation from his pocket and handed it over to me. I offered him tea but he declined. He soon got up to leave. The meeting was a very chilly affair despite my trying to be as courteous as possible. Of course Mufti could not know that if he had been allowed to continue for another three years, I would have sent my letter of resignation to the President. I felt that continued strained relations between the Governor and the Chief Minister in a sensitive State like Jammu and Kashmir was not in national interest. Anyway, Destiny had willed it otherwise. Instead of my resigning, Mufti resigned. I escorted Mufti out to the verandah where a whole lot of journalists and TV cameras were waiting for him. I was asked if I had accepted Mufti's resignation. I confirmed I had done so and had asked him to continue till alternative arrangements were made. They now started asking him questions and I came away. Some of the newspapers commented that in view of the strained relations between us our meeting had lasted for less than five minutes.

An hour later, Ghulam Nabi Azad came to see me. The atmosphere was so drastically different. There was much bonhomie.

We discussed matters very amiably over tea. He staked a claim to from the Government and gave me papers with the signatures of the MLAs supporting him. I told him that I would verify his claim and soon give my decision about calling him to form the State Government. As we came out of the room to the verandah, there were a number of journalists and TV cameramen waiting for us. They asked me if I had accepted Azad's claim to form the government. I replied that he had handed over a list of his supporters in the State Assembly with their signatures. I will complete the process of verifying his claim within the shortest possible time. I hoped to announce my decision within twenty four hours. It was now the turn of Azad to answer questions from the media. He handled them with his usual tact and aplomb. I was bowled over by his remarks pertaining to me. He said that the State was fortunate to have a Governor with vast experience and maturity who was both a statesman and a soldier. He looked forward to serving the State under his guidance. I doubt if any Chief Minister, on the eve of taking over the reins as the Head of the Government, has ever expressed such warm and generous sentiments towards his Governor. This held out hope for a complete U-turn in relations between the Raj Bhavan and the State Government. I realized that I had now entered a new era of my tenure as Governor of the State. We developed the most cordial relationship between us which came as a breath of fresh air and was in the best interest of the State and the Nation.

22

Ghulam Nabi Azad taking over as Chief Minister brought about a sea change in the functioning of the administration. I was very impressed by his transparent nationalist and secular outlook. Having been in the administration for a long time at the Centre in key positions, he had a wide vision. He had a whole lot of new ideas and he showed tremendous zeal and drive. I was convinced that the State would thrive under his leadership. So far we had done well with conflict management. Time had now come for us to proceed towards conflict resolution.

I shared with Azad my thinking on Kashmir and the road map I had for the future. He also gave me his views and with his long political background gave me useful inputs. There was complete identity of. views between us and the whole atmosphere of functioning had changed overnight. I told Azad that I would concentrate on various psychological initiatives to keep all demographic groups in the State happy and isolate the separatists. My aim was that despite the inevitable boycott calls given by separatists we should have a large voter turnout in the assembly election due in 2008. In 2002 we had the international media observing our elections and they acclaimed it as free and fair. This time we should also have diplomats from important countries and international bodies like ASEAN, OIC, European Parliament and so on. Azad wanted to work on development projects and on good governance eradicating corruption. He wanted to go all out to achieve his objectives and usher a "Naya and Khushal Kashmir" (New and Prosperous Kashmir). He had close personal relations with various ministers at the Centre. He could obtain tremendous amount of funds from the Centre for the State. Never before had such a lot of funds come to the State and never before had a chief minister driven himself so hard, working for the people. Azad had a most gruelling schedule, working 16 to 18 hours a day, even at the cost of his health, when he would be indisposed. I often had to caution him to go slow. Our regard for reach other increased as time passed, like the lengthening shadow of the afternoon Sun. I felt Providence had been very kind to have him and me working together because that was in the best interests of the State and the Nation. During the nearly three years that we worked together as governor and chief minister, there was not a single instance in which there was any difference of opinion between us. We met frequently and shared our thinking on all issues with each other. Visitors from Delhi remarked about this. I recall AK Antony, the Defence Minister, who had been a chief minister, saying that he had not known of a governor and a chief minister having such close relations.

I was also much impressed by Azad's appreciation of the army carrying out its onerous duties in Kashmir under such difficult circumstances. He would often praise the army in his public address and stand by it. No political leader had been so favourable towards the army without any fear of losing votes on that account.

Notwithstanding all the favorable turn of events with Ghulam Nabi Azad taking over as chief minister, there was a fly in the ointment which caused me worry. Initially, it was a speck of dark cloud on the horizon and remained so for nearly three years. In the last fortnight of our working together that speck like a galloping cancer spread across the horizon and the sky became overcast. Soon after I left Kashmir, there was a cloudburst wrecking what Azad and I were trying to achieve. Mufti was not reconciled to losing power. He and his daughter had links in the power coterie of the Congress high command which they utilised to undermine the position of Azad. Some members of the coterie were jealous of Azad. They were happy at his moving out of the inner circle in Delhi to take over his assignment in Kashmir. They did not want him to make a success of the challenge that he had accepted and return triumphant to Delhi. It suited them to oblige Mufti.

23

Whereas Congress, the major coalition partner in the State Government had loyally cooperated with the PDP when Mufti was the Chief Minister for three years, the PDP was using every possible tactic to frustrate Azad. It was often said that the NC, the party in Opposition, was co-operating more with Azad than the PDP, his coalition partner. The key portfolio of finance was with Tariq Hamid Qarra. The functioning of government hinges round its finance department, which controls allocation and release of funds. I felt that the situation now in Kashmir was the same as I had seen in Delhi in late 1946 and early 1947. Liaqat Ali Khan as Finance Member in the Interim Coalition Government had brought the Government to a grinding halt. Like the Muslim League in the interim Government at Delhi in 1946/47, the PDP was trying to make things as difficult as possible for the Coalition Government in the State. Azad was getting all the support and more from the Prime Minister and the Union ministers with whom he enjoyed good personal relations. He could get generous allocation of funds from the Centre, the like of which had never happened before. Yet full use could not be made of those allocations due to the non-cooperation of the Finance Department in the State administration. Azad expressed his frustration publicly on this score. At a public meeting in my presence he once said that he had obtained 5000 crores from the Centre but the State had not been able to utilise the money.

The first shots were fired by the coalition partner in the first few weeks of Azad coming to power. Muzaffar Hussian Baig from the PDP was the Deputy Chief Minister. A lawyer by profession who had done well at the Bar, Muzaffar Baig is perhaps the ablest political Leader of Kashmir. He suffers from migraine which is a bit of a handicap and because of it or otherwise, he is given to fits of temper. I got on well with him and he would tell me that he looked up to me as his father. He also got on well with Ghulam Nabi Azad. They addressed public meetings in Doda together at which Muzaffar praised Azad sky high. This was not appreciated by Mufti. The latter decided to withdraw him from the Cabinet. Azad wanted to retain Muzaffar but he could not do so, because Mufti was adamant. Azad wanted to give the finance portfolio held by Muzaffar to someone from the Congress. As Chief Minister it was his right to allocate portfolios to ministers in his Cabinet. Mufti insisted that the finance portfolio remained with the PDP and nominated his henchman, Tareeq Hamid Qarra. The Congress high command forced Azad to accept this arrangement. The day after his resignation, Muzaffar Baig held a Press conference at which he publicly criticized Mufti. Three or four days later he made up with Mufti by going to his house and telling the Press that he treated Mufti like his father. Politics is a strange game. Political leaders can do somersaults at the drop of a hat. The whole episode sent a message that Mufti continued to be powerful and could call the shots.

Mufti took up the issue of demilitarisation of Kashmir in right earnest. While he was chief minister, he had not raised this issue but now both he and his daughter became vociferous on this point. After an alleged incident of human rights violation, Mehbooba thundered that the army must pack up its bags and quit Kashmir immediately. Mufti was also fire and brimstone saying that nothing short of demilitarisation would satisfy him. He went to Delhi vowing to get Delhi to agree to his demand. Azad issued a statement contradicting Mufti that given the situation in the State, demilitarisation was not possible. He also taunted those who were asking for demilitarisation to first surrender their security guards before making such an impractical demand. At one of the army functions that I was attending, the Press on the sidelines asked me my views on demilitarisation. I tried to clarify what demilitarisation meant. It would mean that the Indian Army will have to move out of the State, lock stock and barrel. President Musharraf on different occasions had asked for certain areas in Kashmir demilitarized. His aim was to allow a free run for the militants in those areas. He had, also added that he would get militants to stop their violent activity in those areas. This implied his admission of the fact that Pakistan was controlling militancy in the State, which it had always been denying. Of course Pakistan was too well known for its duplicity and going back on its words. It had been repeatedly violating written agreements. She had been constantly doing so starting from Standstill Agreement, to Ceasefire Agreement, to Shimla Accord, and to Lahore Declaration. Without naming Mufti or his party I said that demilitarisation was not possible at any time in a border State. Jammu and Kashmir had been invaded by Pakistan four times and is facing an ongoing proxy war from Pakistan. China had also invaded the State once. How can Government of India ever agree to demilitarise this border State. Even after militancy was over and normalcy restored, the army would still be required to defend the border against external aggression. I quoted the example of Punjab where after the militancy phase was over deployment of the army continued for defending the border. I added that once the internal situation improves and there is no need for assistance from the army, troops will be returned to barracks. That was not demilitarisation. My views were reported prominently in the Press. Some people criticised me for being proactive. As a governor I had taken an oath to defend the integrity of India and uphold the Constitution. What was wrong in my expressing my views on this issue ?

While Mufti was in Delhi doing his best to get the Centre to agree to demilitarisation, the Cabinet ministers of his party decided to boycott cabinet meetings saying that their boycott would continue till the Government accepted the demand for demilitarisation. Many people thought that PDP's game plan was to quit the government on this issue, pampering to separatist sentiments. Their withdrawal would lead to the fall of the Government and the PDP would be hailed for sacrificing power for the sake of the people. They could cash in on that in the election that would follow. Others including me thought otherwise. We felt that the PDP would continue in office till as late as possible enjoying the fruits of office. There was a risk of the party disintegrating if in spite of its withdrawal of support, the Congress managed to continue in office. Azad assured me that he could muster the required numbers even if the PDP withdrew support. Many like me felt that the PDP will not ditch the coalition then, but would do so, close to the time of the Assembly election, choosing a populist cause to quit. This is exactly what happened two years later in 2008 a little before the election.

Two serious cases came to light soon after Ghulam Nabi Azad became Chief Minister. The first was a sex scandal case in which cabinet ministers, senior bureaucrats, senior government counsel, the Assistant Advocate General and senior police officers were involved. Ministers of both the Congress and the PDP were involved. Among the bureaucrats was the principal secretary of Mufti, a senior IAS officer. There were reports that Mufti had known about the case but had not taken any action. It is possible that his principal secretary who was himself involved influenced him. Anyway Azad took the right decision to hand over the case to the CBI. The individuals involved including the ministers, the principal secretary and the assistant advocate general went to jail and were in prison for some months. They filed an appeal and came out on bail. The case was still to be finally disposed off when I left the State. My big relief was that no army officer was involved in this case. Had any been involved, the separatists would have raised much hue and cry to whip up anti-Army and anti-India sentiments.

The other case was of a very serious human rights violations in which a totally innocent person was picked up and killed by the police for the sake of claiming credit in anti-militancy operations. A senior SP and some other officers and men of the police were involved. Azad ordered immediate legal action. For the first time an officer of the rank of senior SP was put behind bars in the State on this account. There were also a few cases of excesses involving the army. Those found guilty were severely dealt with. Some seventy army personnel over a number of years were found guilty of excesses in different cases. They were dismissed from the service and given terms of imprisonment varying from 2 years to 14 years. Every effort was being made to prevent human rights violations but in such operations involving so many personnel it is difficult to totally prevent such cases. Their numbers were much less than what one learns of foreign armies in such operations elsewhere in the world.

24

I had nothing against the Congress Party although their party had tried to portray me as a Hindu communalist, when I had sent my report on influx of Bangladeshi immigrants to the President from Assam. My mother's family including my mother had been Congress workers. My grandfather on the mother's side had been a prominent Congress leader of Bihar. The year 1962 had been a watershed in my thinking, as a nationalist and as a soldier, I started feeling disillusioned with the leadership of Jawaharlal Nehru. No doubt he had been one of our great leaders who had made tremendous sacrifice for the country and who laid the foundation of democracy in our country. He nourished and promoted the sapling of democracy. The tendency to be carried away by adulation for Nehru and ignore the stupendous contribution of Sardar Vallabhbhai Patel and Subhas Chandra Bose had become the weakness of many in the country. I confess I as an individual was equally blameworthy on this account. Nehru had been my icon in my young days. The Sino-Indian war was a traumatic experience for all of us. There was now a growing realisation among many of us of the failures of Nehru's Kashmir, Tibet and China policies. Much as I had in my youth, disliked Churchill and admired Nehru, as a student of military history, I now compared these great historical figures as war leaders. The comparison between Churchill of 1940 and Nehru of 1962 was too glaring. Both faced the gravest crisis of their lives. Britain's field army had virtually been completely destroyed, in events leading to evacuation from Dunkirk. She was isolated internationally, Her major ally France, had fallen. The USA and the USSR were still to become allies, the former by choice and the latter by compulsion. Hitler and the Axis had overwhelmed the whole of Europe. Britain stood in imminent danger of invasion. Taking over as Prime Minister in such circumstances, Churchill thundered. We will fight on the beaches, we will fight on the streets, we will fight in our houses, but we will never surrender to the scourge of Nazism. He mobilised his Nation and kept up the spirit of his people, ultimately leading his Nation to a resounding victory in the Second World War. He became one of the greatest war leaders of all times. Things were so different in India in 1962. The Indian Army had suffered a humiliating defeat in the Himalayas but only a small fraction of the army had been involved. The bulk of the Indian Army was intact. India was not isolated internationally. The West was fully supportive. China had hardly any international support. Apart from Sino-Russian differences the Soviet Union had been talking in terms of friends and brothers. The weather and terrain were favourable to India. The Himalayan Passes were getting closed. Chinese forces were on the wrong side of the Passes from their point of view. They were without heavy artillery, armour and air support. They were in no position to face the Indian forces on the plains. With all these advantages, Nehru gave up and lost the will to lead the Nation at war. He could only talk in terms of his heart going out to the people of Assam. He accepted a humiliating ceasefire.

Initially, I may have had reservations about what appeared dynastic succession of Indira Gandhi, but in 1971 I became her admirer when she emerged as an Iron Lady. This was followed by disillusionment in 1975 when she imposed the Emergency. Apart from Jayaprakash Narayan being a family friend, I admired him for the sacrifices he had made for the Nation—his selflessness and his championing the cause of democracy. I was overlooked by Indira Gandhi for appointment as Army Chief largely because of my connections with Jayaprakash Narayan, even though by that time, he was no more.

As Governor in Assam, I was up against the Congress both at the Centre and in the State, The Congress has been patronising illegal migration from Bangladesh, ignoring national security interests for the sake of votes. During the latter part of my gubernatorial tenure in Assam, I had to contend with a Congress chief minister. He publicly criticised me on the issue of illegal migration of Bangladeshis in unbecoming language, but he never raised that issue with me. He maintained a correct and cordial relations with me at the personal level.

In Jammu and Kashmir, my relations with Chief Minister Mufti Mohammad Sayeed had soured despite my best efforts. We had reached a state of cold war between us, even though we both observed a correct posture towards each other in public. The facade of civility was punctured by Mufti and his party, after Mufti ceased to be chief minister. When Mufti was Chief Minister, my relations with the Congress Ministers in his Cabinet particularly the Deputy Chief Minister, Mangat Ram Sharma were very friendly. After the arrival of Azad as Chief Minister, my cordial relations with the State Congress were further strengthened. Thus as Governor of Kashmir, I found myself on very friendly terms with the State Congress but on no terms with the party high command in Delhi. In fact due to the connections of Mufti and his daughter in the high command, I was possibly in the doghouse with the central leaders of that party. This did not matter to me as I have always been apolitical but I was surprised that the Congress high command could be a party to weakening the hands of its own party chief minister.

25

On taking over as chief minister, Azad announced a three prong strategy for ushering "Naya Khushal Kashmir", (prosperous and peaceful Kashmir.) The three prongs of his strategy were eradication of corruption, promotion of economic development and introduction of a new work culture. He launched a crusade to achieve these goals. If he could not achieve complete success, it was not due to lack of any effort on his part. In my own way, I tried to support him in his endeavours to the maximum extent.

The first prong of Azad's strategy in Kashmir was eradication of corruption. This disease has been spreading like a galloping cancer in the public life of our country. Indira Gandhi referring to corruption as a global phenomenon, had given a sort of permissiveness to this malady. Transparency International had given a very poor rating to India for corruption. Within India, it had declared that Bihar was the most corrupt State in the country with Jammu and Kashmir as number two. This happened towards the closing months of Mufti's chief ministership.

The top leaders of the Opposition Party led by Omar Abdullah came in a delegation to see me over the Transparency International declaring the State as the second most corrupt in India. As any Opposition in a democracy would do, they were trying to point their finger at Mufti, holding him responsible for the ignominy brought to the State. I gave the delegation a patient hearing. At the end, when it came to my turn to speak, I said that I felt greatly relieved that they were not accusing me. As Bihar was given the top position among corrupt States, I feared that they might have come to say that a Bihari Governor had brought the contagion to Kashmir. They had a big laugh.

Azad made serious efforts to reduce corruption. Hitherto, the law enacted by the Parliament about legislators defecting from their party being disqualified from membership of the legislature did not apply to Jammu and Kashmir. This Act had not been ratified by the State Legislature as stipulated under Article 370 of the Constitution. Similarly, the enactment about restricting the size of the State Cabinet to 10 percent of the strength of the State Legislature was not applicable in Jammu and Kashmir. Mufti had a jumbo cabinet of over 20 percent. By introducing both these laws, Azad tried to curb corruption and promote political probity. He also enacted a law whereby the property of individuals accused of disproportionate assets could be attached. Jammu and Kashmir is the only State where such a law exists. The property of 12 individuals running into several crores was attached. There was criticism that this was being done only in the case of petty officials and not against any political big wigs. Reports of scam in forest department running into hundreds of crores came to light. Azad promptly set up a high powered inquiry committee to examine the matter. One of the senior most bureaucrats of the State, BR Kundal, who soon after took over as chief secretary, was given this task. He completed his inquiry in record time. It showed the indisputable grave culpability of Tareeq Hameed Qarra, former forest minister and now finance minister, as also of Mohammad Afzal the current forest minister. Qarra had appointed an individual said to be related to him, as managing director of State Forest Corporation, superseding seventeen senior officers. This gentleman had been absent from duty for 13 years. And what was more culpable, he held two passports, one American and one Indian. As managing director, he was responsbile for various fraudulent transactions which were sanctioned by Qarra. This led to the State getting defrauded of hundreds of crores. There were similar other findings of the Kundal Committee against Qarra's successor Mohd Afzal. The contents of Kundal Committee report appeared in the Press. It created quite a storm. The Opposition took up the matter in the budget session of the assembly in a big way. They demanded the resignation of both Qarra and Afzal. The PDP argued that the Kundal Committee had not found any specific fraudulent act committed by its two ministers. It targeted the Opposition (National Conference) accusing them of scam in the forest department when the leader of the Opposition, A R Rather was the forest minister. Azad had been forthright in dealing with Peerzada Mohd Sayeed, a Cabinet minister of his own Party who was also the President of the State Congress. Peerzada was dropped from the Cabinet. I thought he will act similarly in the case of their two PDP ministers. One MLA had accused Peerzada's wife of corruption. She is reported to have taken bribe from him and had threatened him. No inquiry had been conducted against Peerzada but there may have been prima facie evidence against him. Azad asked for Peerzada's resignation from the Cabinet. Thus, I was expecting him to drop these two PDP ministers from the Cabinet. He took the stand in the Assembly that Kundal Committee report had not nailed the two PDP ministers for any specific corrupt act on their part. The report was being sent to the Vigilance and Crime Departments of the State for necessary action. The law will take its course. The Assembly was adjourned sine die and the budget passed in one day without any discussion. That was the shortest budget session in the history of the State. I had a feeling that Azad was forced to act in this manner on account of pressure from his Party high command, to ensure that the Government did not fall. The same thing had happened earlier when the PDP had raised a ruckus over demilitarisation and the PDP ministers were boycotting Cabinet meetings. At that time Azad was confident that his Government would not fall, even if the PDP withdrew support. Apparently the high command thought otherwise and wanted the coalition government to continue at all costs. Along with many people, I was convinced that the PDP will not withdraw support from the government till a little before elections in October 2008. Till then it would continue in government at all costs as it did not want to be deprived of the fruits of office. Party funds were required to be bolstered for the coming elections. The PDP had also to guard against the party disintegrating, if it came out of the government. It would therefore continue in government till the last and walk out just before election, choosing a populist cause from which it could get maximum political mileage. This is exactly what happened when the PDP stabbed the Congress in the back in June 2008, leading to the unceremonious fall of the Azad led Congress government. However, the best laid plans do not work out, as ardently desired. Despite all its machinations the PDP failed to come to power after the 2008 Assembly elections.

The second prong of Azad's strategy was development. In a span of less than three years he was able to achieve a tremendous lot. Never before had Government of India released so much funds and never before such a lot of development had taken place in all sectors. The much delayed Baglihar and Dul Hasti Hydro projects were completed and a major hydel project started at Nimmo-Bazga in Ladakh. Rupees 850 crores were spent on construction of hospitals. Government Medical College at Jammu was being upgraded to the level of AIIMS. Work on 200-bed hospitals in each of the 22 districts of the State was started and was making good progress. A network of roads and bridges was being completed including the longest cantilever bridge at Akhnoor and the longest bridge in the Valley at Benami. Two kilometers of road was being blacktopped everyday and some 10,000 kilometers had been blacktopped. Construction of Mughal Road from both ends, Poonch and Shupiyan, progressed fast and the road was nearing completion. Buildings were being constructed for 2000 primary and middle schools. Eighteen new degree colleges were started. Great emphasis was given to higher education. I shall be discussing that separately later. Agriculture sector registered a growth of 3.62 percent which is nearly double the national average of 2 percent. There was nearly 50 percent growth in production of fruits from 10 lakh tonnes to 14 lakh tonnes. Encroachments on land near Hazratbal were removed and the ground levelled to accommodate one lakh people for Eid prayers. The area around Hazratbal was beautified and electrification carried out on a large scale to add to the beauty of the area. A unique Haj House, the best in India was completed in record time providing all facilities to Haj pilgrims under one roof. A modern Amanath Yatri Nivas was also completed at Jammu in record time. A tulip garden, the largest in Asia with lakhs of flower bulbs, came up in Srinagar. The much awaited State Legislature building was also completed in record time. Progress on the development front may have been still more spectacular if finance department had fully cooperated. I have already mentioned earlier that the PDP minister in charge of finance in the coalition government was acting like the Muslim League finance minister in the Interim Government at Delhi before Partition.

As for work culture, special arrangements were made to ensure that all employees were punctual in coming to work at the Secretariat. Double shifts were introduced for fast completion of projects. However, it was difficult to bring about a radical change and get the bureaucracy to deliver. One particularly bad case came to my notice. In 2004, I found that the State Table of Precedence had many flaws with many absurd equations. Government of India had drawn up the Table for senior officers of the rank of commissioners/ IG police/major generals and above. For lower ranks, it was left to the State governments to work out their protocol status. I discovered that the State Table of Precedence had altered equations laid down by Government of India which had not happened in any other State. For example a Chief Justice of a High Court was placed higher than a Judge of Supreme Court. The former on promotion is raised to the Supreme Court bench. Ambassadors of Foreign countries were accorded much lower status than given to them in the Central Table of Precedence. There were numerous other such anomalies. As for officers below the rank of commissioner/IG police/major general, where the discretion was left to the State Government, equations formulated in the State Table of Precedence were equally bizarre. I pointed out the major anomalies. A Cabinet subcommittee of three ministers under the deputy chief minister was set up in 2004 to revise the State Table of Precedence. The revised Draft State Table of Precedence continued to have many anomalies. I myself drafted a State Table of Precedence and sent it to the government. The Cabinet Subcommittee approved of the draft sent by me and recommended its acceptance. This case made no further progress in four years, and was still awaiting Cabinet approval, when I left Kashmir. This case reflects, very poorly on the work culture of the bureaucracy.

26

There are eight universities in Kashmir. These include four government and four private universities. I was the Chancellor of the four government universities and one private university, the Shri Mata Vaishno Devi University. The Chief Minister was the Chancellor of the remaining three private universities set up by the Aukaf Board. There were Baba Ghulam Shah University at Rajouri and the two Islamic universities at Anantnag and Badgam in the Valley.

I took very active interest in the functioning of the universities as their Chancellor. I was fortunate in having very good Vice Chancellors in these universities and I encouraged them to interact with me directly. I had excellent working relations with each of them.

Kashmir University at Srinagar had been the hotbed of separatist politics. Its Vice Chancellor Professor Nashir-ul-Hasan had been assassinated by the terrorists in 1990. No governor had visited the University since then. I decided to visit the university on taking over as governor. I felt that a Chancellor must keep in close touch with the university. Sooner I visited the university, the better. My security staff was not very comfortable with my going to the university campus. However, necessary security arrangements were made for my visit to the university. I rang up the Vice Chancellor and told him that I would be visiting him and I wanted my visit to be kept a low key affair. I would meet him and some senior members of the faculty in his office. When I arrived at the university I could see sullen faces of the students. I decided to cultivate them gradually. In my following visit I went round the campus. I was surprised to find that work on the university auditorium had been held up for nearly 20 years, for one reason or the other. The foundation stone of the building had been laid by Sheikh Abdullah and the building was yet to be completed. Funds were arranged and work started in earnest. In a little over a year we managed to complete the auditorium with a seating capacity for 2500. The Vice Chancellor, Professor Tareen had been doing good work but due to a controversy surrounding his daughter, doing work for the university, he had to relinquish his appointment. Professor Tareen was from Hyderabad and they wanted a local person as Vice Chancellor. Mufti felt that having a Vice Chancellor from outside may even create law and order problem. I accepted his recommendation and we appointed Professor Wahid as Vice Chancellor. I had been attending seminars at the university to establish an intellectual rapport with the students. I could feel that gradually I was becoming more acceptable and there was no hostility towards me. In one of the international seminars a foreign delegate referred to me as Professor Sinha which caused much laughter. In 2005 I learnt that Mufti had directed funds for the North Campus to the South Campus and had arranged to have the latter inaugurated by Sonia Gandhi. I had no information of this till

I read about it in the newspaper. I did not want to make an issue of this but at the same time I felt that as the Chancellor I should not have been kept out of this decision. I wrote a strong letter to Mufti in this regard and he sent me an unconvincing reply. I am glad that the visit of Sonia Gandhi got cancelled for security reasons and so was the foundation stone laying function. I was opposed to the President of a party inaugurating a function in a Government institution. Unfortunately, the distinction between the Party and the Government in a parliamentary democracy is not being maintained by the Congress in our country. There was an All India inter-university football tournament which I was asked to inaugurate. When I arrived, as per normal practice the band played the National Anthem. Both the students and the faculty ignored the playing of the anthem. They did not stand up. I told the Vice Chancellor that conditions were not at that time conducive to playing the national anthem. We should move gradually in the matter. After a year an All India meet of economists took place in Srinagar and we held the function in the new auditorium of the university. The audience had a large number of delegates from outside the State. This time when the National Anthem was played everyone including students and faculty of the university, stood up. Thereafter, we had no problem on this score. However, an undercurrent of anti-India feelings persisted among some elements in the university. They were not too happy about the setting up of the Centre for Kashmir Studies. I have already mentioned earlier the international seminar on *Kashmiriyat* organised by the Centre. On Professor Wahid completing his tenure, we selected Professor Reyaz Punjabi from Jawaharlal Nehru University, as his successor. He is a local with a wide vision who is keen to bring about improvements and enrich the educational atmosphere in the university. A few months after his arival, my term in Kashmir expired. Jammu University had come up much later than Kashmir University. It had not suffered on account of militancy like the Kashmir University. It had a very young Vice Chancellor, perhaps the youngest in the country, Professor Amitabh Mattoo. A Cambridge graduate, he had done a stint as a teacher in Jawaharlal Nehru University. He was in position when I arrived as Governor in the State. An academician of repute, he was much in demand for seminars and conferences all over the world. He showed tremendous drive, zeal and determination. He is gifted with a wide vision. The university was humming with intellectual activities under his leadership. A seminar or a conference often at national or international level was held almost every week. I was invited to inaugurate several seminars and to deliver memorial lectures. I delivered three or four memorial lectures at the university. Another priority area for Mattoo was the building of modern infrastructures. I have already mentioned the General Zorawar Singh Stadium that we got constructed in the university and which has become a showpiece and a pride of the people of Jammu. A state of the art infrastructure for the school of Biotechnology in the university was also put up. The university established campuses at Doda, Udhampur, Poonch and Kathua to bring higher education close to the people in remote areas. Jammu University was the first University in the country to receive 1S0-2002 certification. I recommended the Vice-Chancellor for the award of Padma Shri, which he richly deserved. That was duly conferred on him.

There are two Agriculture universities in the State, one in Srinagar and the other in Jammu. The latter had been established a year or so earlier and was still in an embryonic stage. Professor Alam was the Vice Chancellor of the Agriculture University at Srinagar. I often visited his university and was happy with all the work he was doing. I attended a few seminars and inaugurated some new buildings. The university established Krishi Kalyan Kendras in remote areas of the Valley to impart training and give an impetus to agriculture production. On completion of Professor Alam's term I gave him a second term to continue as Vice Chancellor after discussing his case with Azad. Zargar, the Agriculture Minister was not involved with the functioning of the university. He wanted his nominee from the State, appointed Vice Chancellor; Professor Alam, being from U.P, was considered an outsider. Zargar was unhappy with my decision and had a case filed by one of his people in the High Court questioning my authority to grant a second term to Professor Alam. This case was duly dismissed.

The newly established Agriculture University at Jammu was having teething problems. We needed a Vice Chancellor with drive and vision. I selected Professor Nagendra Sharma an Agriculture Scientist who had experience of running deemed agriculture universities. He put life in the university both in terms of academic activity and the building of infrastructure. He managed to get funds from the Indian Council of Agriculture Research. The State was facing a financial crunch and was not able to help him much. Yet in a short time, with the funds that he had been able to mobilise, he put up excellent infrastructure with modern utilitarian buildings. The Agriculture University campus came up very well and has become, one of the best in the country.

I considered Shri Mata Vaishno Devi University as the flagship of Shri Mata Vaishno Devi Board. It was a gigantic task to build a new modern university entirely on our own without any assistance from the Government. We bought 400 acres of land for 13 crores in a rural area near Katra, which is the base for the pilgrimage to Mata Vaishno Devi. Many people had doubts about the success of our venture. It was felt that it would be difficult to attract faculty and staff to such a remote area. I saw the university come up brick by brick. In a short time it came to be recognised as an institution of excellence, with students passing out, getting hundred percent placements in corporate sector. We built it as a residential university teaching various technical subjects like Management, Computer Science, Biotechnology and so on. I picked on Professor Bansal from IIT Delhi to be the Vice Chancellor of the University. An academician of repute, he proved to be a person with tremendous drive, dedication and vision. In a remarkably short period of four years, he made my dream come true. I kept visiting the campus ever so often and I always found him confident and reassuring to accomplish the very difficult task I had given him. And of course he always welcomed me. There was no question of his feeling that I was breathing down his neck. The inauguration of the university had been done in August 2004 by President Kalam and its first convocation was addressed by Prime Minister Manmohan Singh in May 2008. I was keen that the first convocation be held before June 2008, when my term as Governor was expiring. A beautiful air-conditioned auditorium with a capacity for 1000 was ready in time for the convocation. Infrastructure for administrative, instructional and residential accommodation for twelve hundred students was completed, with more accommodation under construction to accommodate up to 2000 students. Nearby the construction of the 250 bed, state of the art cancer hospital, was nearing completion with some faculty in position and equipment on its way. We were hoping to commission this hospital by the end of the year. We had plans to eventually develop the 250-bed cancer hospital to a 750-bed multidisciplinary hospital and then a medical college as part of the Shri Mata Vaishno Devi University. Manmohan Singh was most appreciative of our efforts to put up such a modern University in a rural area in just four years. L K Advani the leader of the Opposition, on a pilgrimage to Mata Vaishno Devi, was invited to address the students at the university. He was full of praise for what he saw at the university. Many of the people of Jammu who came to the university for the first time for the convocation said that seeing was believing. They could not imagine that such a complex could come up in a rural area some 40 kilometers away from a city. The university auditorium was smaller in size than the General Zorawar Singh Auditorium or the Auditorium of Kashmir University but it was the cynosure of all eyes for its artistic beauty. I was told that someone who had come for the convocation remarked that like Shah Jahan, the great builder who gave the country splendid monuments, General Sinha would be remembered for the three beautiful university auditoriums and the stunning Mata Vaishno Devi University and Jammu Agriculture University campuses. This of course was a hyperbole. I am mentioning this only to bring out how some people coming for the first time got carried away when they saw such a modern university complex, in a rural setting. As Governor of Assam and Chairman of the Board of Governors for IIT Guwahati, I had been associated with putting up the first indigenous IIT of India. The other five IITs in the country had been put up in collaboration with foreign countries like USA, USSR, UK and Germany. The IIT at Guwahati was put up by Government of India using its own resources and without any foreign collaboration. I had the privilege to see IIT Guwahati, come up, brick by brick and become one of the prettiest IIT for its scenic beauty. It is located on the bank of the Brahmaputra in a cluster of low hills. I had also had the satisfaction of holding the first convocation of the IIT. In the case of Shri Mata Vaishno Devi University, I had the added satisfaction of being able to do all that without any financial support or any assistance from the Government. The credit for translating my dream into reality must of course primarily go to Professor Bansal the Vice Chancellor and also to Dr Arun Kumar my Principal Secretary and the Chief Executive Officer of Shri Mata Vaishno Devi Shrine Board. We had the blessings of the Mata in our endeavour to set up this University.

I had no role to play in the three other private universities, two of them set up by Aukaf Board and one by Jamait Ahal-e-Hadees. For all these universities, the State government under Mufti provided land free and gave other assistance. This of course was not done for Shri Mata Vaishno Devi University. I got the army to also give some assistance to the Islamic University at Avantipur in the Valley. I will mention more about it later in this book.

I was influenced by President Kalam's effort to revive the ancient Nalanda University in Bihar. Shardapeeth was a renowned ancient university like the Taxila University, now in Pakistan. The ruins of Shardapeeth are near Muzaffrabad in Pakistan Occupied Kashmir. The Kashmiri Pandits have a sentimental attachment for Shardapeeth. Professor Aryaz Zazgi had been to POK and he had taken a number of pictures of the ruins of Shardapeeth. He organised a photo exhibition of those pictures. He invited me to inaugurate the exhibition. He was very enthusiastic about Shardapeeth. This showed that not only Kashmiri Pandits but also other Kashmiris were attached to Shardapeeth. I conceived the idea of putting up a Shardapeeth University at Srinagar, on the lines of Shri Mata Vaishno Devi University in Jammu province. As this University would be a minority institution in Kashmir, we could have 50 percent reservation for students. We proposed 40 percent reservation for Kashmiri Pandits and 10 percent for Kashmiri Muslims with the remainder open to all in the country on the basis of merit and eligibility. I wanted reservation for Kashmiri Pandits as a first step for their return to the Valley and eventual rehabilitation there. I also wanted reservation for Kashmiri Muslims at this university to promote our pluralistic ethos. I nominated Professor Amitabh Matto as the Pro Chancellor of the university. He is a Kashmiri Pandit who had achieved tremendous success as Vice Chancellor of Jammu University. We identified temple land near Srinagar which we could buy. Funds for the university were to be provided by Shri Amarnath Shrine Board assisted by refundable loan from Shri Vaishno Devi Shrine Board. I discussed this project with the Chief Minister. Being a nationalist to the core, Azad was thrilled to learn of this project and was enthusiastic in its support. Unfortunately, in June 2008. when a communal tsunami swept the Valley, this project had to be given up and it became a non-starter.

27

Besides being Chancellor of universities in the State I had other ex-officio responsibilities. I was Chairman of Ex-servicemen's Board and of the State Red Cross, I was also Chairman of the two Shrine Boards. My wife also held an ex-officio appointment. She was the President of Association for Social Health in India (ASHI), J&K Branch and Nehaghar. These were NGOs, the former for rehabilitation of widows and the latter for looking after orphans. Initially, these were active only in Jammu but later they opened centres in Srinagar. They also adopted a village named Jagti, near Jammu.

Being an ex-serviceman myself, it was natural for me to take keen interest in the welfare of ex-servicemen. I found the facilities offered to ex-servicemen were much less in J&K than in the neighbouring States of Himachal, Punjab and Haryana. The bulk of the ex-servicemen in the State were from Jammu region and much less from the Valley. There was an inbuilt reluctance on the part of the Kashmir dominated State Government to provide support for ex-servicemen, who were viewed as essentially a Jammu problem.

As Ambassador in Nepal, I had put up a self-supporting sainik rest house at Kathmandu to provide suitable accommodation for our Gorkha ex-servicemen, both officers and personnel below officer rank. Apart from providing excellent living accommodation at very cheap rates, we also had a highly subsidised canteen for them. We could do all this because we had let out one floor in that building complex for commercial purpose. Initial investment on capital expenditure for putting up the building had been met with funds from both ministry of defence and ministry of external affairs in Delhi. The Government of Nepal had no role in this project. It was meant for Gorkha personnel who had served in the Indian Armed Forces. The British Army Chief on a tour to Nepal, visited the Bhartiya Gorkha Sainik Nivas at Kathmandu and was much impressed. He told me that it was the best such rest house for ex-servicemen he had seen anywhere. I wanted to have a similar sainik rest house in Srinagar and in Jammu. Expenditure for setting up such rest houses had to be shared by the Centre and the State Government but land had to be provided by the latter. Mufti cooperated with me in setting up a sainik rest house in Srinagar. I laid the foundation stone for it and I had the satisfaction to see it completed during my tenure. On Azad coming to power, we were able to get a prime plot of land in Jammu and work on a sainik rest house was to start after getting over the usual formalities. Azad was sympathetic towards the requirements of ex-servicemen. He set up a Cabinet sub-committee to go into their problems. Monetary grants for gallantry award winners which was abysmally low in the State was jacked up. Annuity was raised for Param Vir Chakra from Rs 2000 to Rs 1.25 lakhs, for Maha Vir Chakra from Rs.8000 to Rs 1 lakh and for Vir Chakra from Rs 500 to Rs 50,000. They were still not comparable with such grants in the neighbouring States. We launched a special drive for raising collections for Armed Forces Flag Day. This increased from 7 lakhs in 2003 to Rs 14.5 lakhs in 2008.

We tried to beef up Red Cross activities in the State. I selected Nehvi, a retired civil servant, to be Secretary of the State Red Cross. He showed ingenuity and drive in improving the functioning of Red Cross. During the natural disasters like earthquake, floods and snow tsunami, the Red Cross rose to the occasion. He raised funds for the Red Cross through a novel scheme for training in Jammu and Kashmir Universities. We also introduced annual contributory dinners, a practice common in the USA. Nehvi wanted to try it out in Kashmir. Although I was skeptical about it, he was enthusiastic and I gave him the green signal for it. He made a success of the scheme. It proved to be a good fund raiser. The other routine Red Cross activity of providing succour to destitute, running Red Cross Centres for treatment and medicine, providing ambulance service were all stepped up.

I was concerned about deaths due to road accidents in the State. In a mountainous State, bus accidents, caused large casualties with vehicles going down hillsides. With militancy getting contained and casualties brought down to a much reduced level, we found that more people were now dying due to road accidents in the State than due to militancy. Although it was strictly not within the charter of duties of the Red Cross, I felt it could become the nodal agency for organizing a conference on the subject. The idea was to launch a coordinated drive by different agencies of the State in cooperation with the private sector and the civil society. We tried to involve various Government departments like PWD, Police, Health and Transport as also transport operators, NGOs and leaders of civil society. My idea was to bring all the various government departments, private companies and concerned citizens together on one platform and evolve a policy both for prevention of accidents and for reducing casualties through prompt and proper medical care. Accident prone areas had to be identified and corrective action taken, Road worthiness of vehicles had to be checked and competence of drivers of vehicles had to be tested. There had been instances of untrained drivers in their teens, without a driving license, driving vehicles including buses and meeting with accidents in which a large number of people had got killed. Speeding and overloading of vehicles were a menace. Police alone could not enforce all the regulations. People's participation with volunteers acting as traffic warden to ensure that rules were not broken, could be considered. We could make a start by having First Aid centres at intervals of say 20 to 30 kilometers on highways. These to have communication facilities, ambulance vehicles, first aid staff of trained Red Cross volunteers. Trauma centres were required to be established in hospitals along the road to which casualties could be evacuated. I discussed my ideas with Azad. He was fully supportive. I gave the task to Nehvi to carry out research and prepare a concept paper. I also asked him to get the national Red Cross associated with our venture. Nehvi collected a lot of statistics and produced a draft concept paper. He also obtained approval in principle from National Red Cross for our effort. They agreed to participate in our venture. I contacted Ministry of Surface Transport and the Planning Commission and got a favourable response from them. I am afraid the whole process took a long time to take shape. We were hoping to hold a conference to be inaugurated by me and presided over by the Chief Minister. Before we could finalise the date for the conference, controversy broke out over Amarnath Yatra. My term expired and I came away from Kashmir. This project remained stillborn.

I was also ex-officio Chairman of the two Shrine Boards set up by Acts of the State Legislature — the Shri Mata Vaishno Devi Shrine Board in Jammu and Shri Amarnath Shrine Board in Kashmir. These boards had been set up before I took over as Governor. On taking over as Chairman of these boards from my predecessor, I tried to further improve the functioning of these boards. These were two major commitments. I shall be discussing them separately.

28

With ceasefire holding on the LoC since November 2003 and the level of violence in the State decreasing, near normalcy was returning in the State. The overall situation had much improved. A bonhomie in Indo-Pak relations started developing with exchange of cricket teams and increase in people to people contacts. The start of composite dialogue between India and Pakistan and various confidence building measures raised hopes of our moving towards resolving the long festering Kashmir problem.

Tourist arrivals in the Valley had begun to rise rapidly. 28,000 tourists came to the Valley in 2002 and this number started growing rapidly every year reaching up to six lakhs. In 2008 we were hoping that the figure may go up to seven lakh but the Amarnath land agitation caused a big setback. Even so, the figure was about four lakhs in 2008. Tourism is the main industry of the Valley and increase in tourism is of immense economic benefit to the local people.

Another welcome development was visits of various delegations from Pakistan to Kashmir, from time to time. One of the earliest delegations to come from Pakistan was of journalists. They first arrived in Jammu and were overwhelmed by the warm welcome they received there. They visited a Kashmiri "migrant" camp near Jammu and they were horrified to see their terrible living conditions. They were not aware of the problem of Kashmiri Pandits and expressed their sympathy for them. After a successful visit to Jammu, the Pakistan delegation arrived in Srinagar. Having been feted so well in Jammu, they were naturally expecting a better welcome in Srinagar. Surprisingly, this did not happen. Their visit to Kashmir University got soured by sloganeering for Azadi (independence). They were expecting the people of the Valley will express desire to merge with Pakistan. The meeting of these journalists with Yaseen Mallik of JK Liberation Front was reported to have been a bit of a disaster.

A theatre troupe from Pakistan came to stage a play on Bulle Shah, the legendary Sufi mystic from Firozpur of the medieval period. The play staged by the troupe was excellent and very gripping. It conveyed the message of Sufi philosophy in a powerful manner. The leader of the troupe called on me at Raj Bhavan. I discovered that she was the daughter of a Colonel who like me had served in the undivided Indian Army during the British era. I found much in common with her thinking. There was no reason for hatred and enmity that had erupted between our two countries since 1947, should persist. She felt strongly about this. I used to invite Sufi musicians from Pakistan for the inauguration of Amarnath Yatra every year and found interacting with them rewarding.

There was a delegation of 30 vice-presidents and CEOs of corporate sector from Pakistan. Some came with their spouse. I invited them for lunch on the lawns of Raj Bhawan at Srinagar. I was impressed by these bright young business executives. Some of them were women. They were no different from their counterparts in India. They spoke well and were a knowledgeable lot of young people. They showed no communal or fundamentalist inhibitions. I reminisced with them about pre-partition days and of the Lahore I knew of that time. As a young army officer I was taken by the elegance and beauty of Lahore. We used to call it the Paris of the East. The Mall was attractively modern and Anarkali had the old world charm. I also talked to them of my old friends with whom I had served in the undivided Indian Army before 1947. Two of them gained eminence in Pakistan. One was Yahya Khan with whom I had served in Delhi when he was a Major and I a Captain. I had also served with Tiger Niazi when we were captains together in Indonesia. We met again after 27 years in 1972 at Jabalpur Prisoner of War camp when we were both General officers, he a step ahead of me as Lt Gen and I a Maj Gen. We were happy to meet each other. We had a drink together and talked of the old days. I had deliberately worn my Frontier Force tie for the lunch with the Pakistan delegation. I told the Pakistan business executives that the Frontier Force was formed by the British in mid nineteenth century. It comprised the Frontier Force Regiment, the Frontier

Force Rifles, the 5th Gorkha Rifles and the Hazara Mountain Battery. The former two are now in Pakistan Army and the latter two are serving in the Indian Army. The Frontier Force tie is worn by all the four. I belonged to 5th Gorkha Rifles (FF) and we are the only one of the four who used the suffix of Frontier Force. After lunch I gave a short address in which I mentioned that I belonged to a generation which had sweet memories of the pre-1947 days. We have so much in common in our ancestry, culture, heritage and history. It was my earnest desire that before I pass away the new generations in both countries restore the old amity that existed between our people without disturbing the separate political identity of the two countries. I told my audience that it was up to their generation to restore old values. They had come to Paradise on Earth and they should go back to their country with the message of Paradise. That message was the message of *Kashmiriyat*, promoting amity and brotherhood across any religious or other divide. I also told them how we in India were upholding secular values. As a case in point I mentioned that though our religious minorities were less than 20 % of our population all the top key appointments in Delhi were held by individuals from different minority communities. The President was a Muslim, the Prime Minister a Sikh, the all powerful President of the ruling party a Christian, the Army Chief a Sikh and the Head of Intelligence a Christian. This was something unique which has not happened in any democracy of the world. The audience stood up and gave me a standing ovation. The leader of the Pakistan team expressed very warm sentiments. He said they had spent a most pleasant afternoon in excellent weather and in the breathtaking scenic beauty in a most friendly atmosphere. They will always fondly cherish the happy memory of the afternoon spent in the Raj Bhavan at Srinagar. He even added that I should be treated as a father figure for both India and Pakistan.

A delegation of political leaders, academicians and businessmen from POK under a former Chief Justice came to Kashmir. Unlike most other such tours, a call on the Governor was not included in its itinerary. I was surprised when my staff told me that four of the delegates from Northern Areas wanted to meet me. I had it conveyed to them that I would be delighted to receive them.

Their leader was the former deputy chief executive officer the highest elected post in the Northern Areas Council, whose members are elected from a limited constituency. The Council had very little powers delegated to it. The chief executive officer is a nominee of the Central Government and he presides over the Council. The other three individuals were a journalist, a teacher and a businessman. They were all from Gilgit.

This was for the first time that delegates from Northern Areas had been allowed to visit Kashmir. This was part of the thawing process in Indo-Pak relations and Musharraf's attempt to acquire the image of a liberal. Be that as it may, I was intrigued why these delegates wanted to meet me. The reason soon became clear. They started off by saying that they had read my Republic Day address of 2004 in which I had asked for the opening of the Kargil-Skardu road. That was of great importance for them. The people in Northern Areas had more in common with the people of Kargil and Ladakh than with the people of the Kashmir Valley. And now the real reason for their coming to see me came out. They had come to see me on Saturday, when their visa was expiring on Monday. They were to return to Pakistan via Wagah. They wanted me to get their visa extended by two days. I told them that they had made a difficult request. Offices in Delhi were closed for the week end and will open only on Monday. Had they approached me earlier, there would not have been much difficulty in getting their visa extended. Anyway, I assured them that I would do my best to get their visa extended.

I decided to take advantage of their visit to know from them about conditions in Northern Areas. I asked them about the constant influx of Pathans and Punjabis into Northern Areas. Three of them said that it was a very serious problem for them. Not only was the Pakistan Government not stopping them but it was facilitating their influx with a view to changing the demography of the region. The leader of the group tried to play down the problem by saying that this affected only the towns and not the rural areas, where the vast majority of people lived. I explained to them how we had under the provisions of Article 370 been preventing demographic change in Indian Administered Kashmir. They told me they had heard of it and they much appreciated the functioning of democracy in India.

I then enquired about the textbook controversy in Northern Areas. There had been violent agitation on this score. Anti-Shia views had been incorporated in textbooks prepared by Pakistan Government. The bulk of the people of Northern Areas are Shias. They said that the matter was being looked into by Pakistan Government. The latter had taken note of the strong views of the Shia people of the region.

I also asked about the provisions of the Crime Control Act enacted in the British days. Anyone from a community declared criminal, going out of the jurisdiction of a police station had to obtain the approval of the police. They said that this law was not being seriously implemented.

I had not been to Gilgit but had heard about the scenic beauty of the region. They were very happy to talk about this I mentioned that I knew the son of the Mehtar (ruler) of Chitral. I had met him in Dehra Dun. He had passed out from the Indian Military Academy. He had joined the Chitral Scouts. They told me that he had risen to the rank of Coloned and had commanded Chitral Scouts. He had died and his son was now commanding Chitral Scouts. Chitral had lost its separate political identity and was now merged with Northern Areas. In the old days, Mehtar, the ruler of the State recognised the Maharaja of Kashmir as his overlord.

After an hour's interaction over tea, I presented them with token gifts. They told me that they were happy to see that I knew of their problems and I was so friendly towards them. They complained that when they met senior leaders in Pakistan they found they were not aware of their problems. I obtained their full address from them for getting their visas extended. They readily gave these details including their telephone numbers.

Although Saturday was not a working day in Delhi, I managed to contact senior officials of ministry of external affairs, ministry of home and RAW. Two of them were my close relations, a brother and a cousin. I got their verbal clearance and assurance that their visa would be extended. They kept their word and necessary extension was given on Monday. In the meanwhile in anticipation of formal approval, I arranged for the army to take them to Kargil for a day. They were most grateful and conveyed their thanks to me. I prepared a report of my meeting with them and sent it to the intelligence agencies in Delhi. I also informed the State Government. I am afraid no one appeared interested in cultivating them. Over a year later I contacted the intelligence agencies and I was surprised that they had not used the lead I had given them!

Pranab Mukherjee took over as External Affairs Minister. I had met him a couple of times, when I was Governor of Assam. I was impressed by his realistic reaction to Musharraf's peace proposal, which he presented to the Parliament. I congratulated him for it. We discussed the Kashmir issue and I gave him my views. He was due to go to Pakistan shortly on his first visit to that country as

External Affairs Minister. I told him that Hurriyat and other separatist leaders were constantly visiting Pakistan High Commission in Delhi and also meeting Pakistani leaders when they came to Delhi. I suggested that he should meet dissident leaders of Northern Areas when he visited Islamabad. In fact our High Commission in Pakistan should keep in touch with them. After all, the whole of Kashmir including POK and Northern Areas was legally a part of India. That has been our stand since 1947. I also briefed Pranab Mukherjee of my meeting with the four leaders of Northern Areas in Srinagar. He appreciated my suggestion and said that he would act on it. I had earlier discussed this matter with Azad and he too had agreed with me. Later, I learnt that our High Commission advised Pranab Mukherjee that it would ruffle feathers in Pakistan if he met leaders from Northern Areas. The matter was thus not pursued. I felt that we were being unnecessarily too defensive in pursuing our national interests.

29

Kashmir has been one of the most complex and intricate problems facing the world. There can be no easy or quick solution to this problem. Pakistan tried to settle the problem on her terms through military action. First, it was a tribal invasion backed by her army, then a mix of massive infiltration and conventional military offensive and then again through a full-fledged conventional war in which Pakistan suffered a disastrous military defeat. Two military dictators, Ayub and Yahya having faired badly, their two successors, Zia-ul-Haq and Pervez Musharraf tried different tactics. Zia-ul-Haq, the "Mulla in Khaki", evolved the strategy of thousand cuts to bleed India to death in Kashmir. It was a low cost and a long term option. A vicious mix of insurgency, terrorism and proxy war had been raging for a decade and half in Kashmir but not much headway was achieved beyond mounting casualties on all sides. In this ongoing low intensity conflict the terrorists who tried to don the mantle of freedom fighters suffered more casualties than the combined total of innocent civilians and our security forces. Nearly all the innocent civilians were killed due to terrorist attacks but hostile propaganda was constantly trying to portray them as martyrs felled down by Indian Security Forces . There may have been a small percentage killed due to cross-fire but 99 percent were victims at the hands of terrorists, whether deliberately or inadvertently. The propaganda machine supporting the militants constantly harped on one lakh Kashmiris getting martyred, when the combined casualties of security forces, civilians and terrorists was about 40,000. Pervez Musharraf with his commando background tried military infiltration in Kargil across the LoC to force India to come to terms. The misadventure failed and for the first time Pakistan found herself totally isolated internationally. After the Kargil fiasco, Pervez Musharraf seized political power through a military coup. He now tried his hand through other means, political and diplomatic, to secure Kashmir. His policy of enlightened moderation alarmed the fundamentalists in his country. There was perhaps poetic jusitce on Pakistan which has been the promoter of Jehadi terrorism against both its eastern and western neighbours now herself becoming a victim of Jehadi terrorism. Not only the fringe areas on the border but also in its mainland, major terrorist attacks had started taking place. With his ill-advised dismissal and arrest of the Chief Justice, Musharraf, dug his own grave and his descent from power followed rapidly, leading to his eventual political eclipse. The new democratic regime with all its internal problems and its problems on the country's western border is hardly in a position to take major initiative to resolve the Kashmir problem. Today in the wake of its surrender to extremists in Swat, Pakistan's survival is threatened. The future is unpredictable. We should be on high alert.

India has justifiably always maintained that Jammu and Kashmir has been an integral part of India. There is a unanimous resolution passed by our Parliament requiring the portion of the State of Jammu and Kashmir (POK and Northern Areas) in illegal occupation of Pakistan to be liberated. We have, however, done precious little to redeem this pledge. The only Prime Minister to publicly voice this claim emphatically, was Narsimha Rao. In his address to the Nation from the Red Fort, he rubbished Pakistan's claim that Kashmir was the unfinished agenda of Partition. He asserted that liberation of Kashmir territory in illegal occupation of Kashmir was the only unfinished agenda of Partition. I have always felt that we as a Nation have been unduly defensive and even apologetic about Kashmir. Had we aggressively been asserting our right to POK and Northern Areas, our acceptance of LoC being made an international border could be a good fall back position and part of give and take in an agreement with Pakistan. Shimla Accord may have been based on a secret and unwritten understanding of converting LoC into an international border but it failed to achieve this objective beyond redesignting the ceasefire Line as Line of Control. The former has a temporary connotation but the latter implies acceptance of ground reality on a more permanent basis. Manmohan Singh's assertion that borders cannot be changed in Kashmir is very apt and correct. There is, however, certain vagueness about it. Do borders mean the pre-October 1947 borders of the State or the present LoC. The latter is a more realistic interpretation. After Kargil, it has received due international recognition.

Whereas we have always successfully foiled Pakistan's military adventurist action in Kashmir, we always acted defensively except in 1965 when we advanced to the outskirts of Lahore. We have not only refrained from any military offensive but also any political offensive to settle the Kashmir issue on India's terms, as categorically articulated by our Parliament. Successful defensive action can prevent defeat. Victory can be achieved only through offensive action. We have given no indication of any military or political plan to liberate POK or Northern Areas. India has been a peace loving country. Given today's international scenario it is not very realistic to undertake the task of liberating areas in illegal occupation of Pakistan or China. However this should not rule out diplomatic offensive nor for that matter covert action

Although we have refrained from any military or political offensive, we have been taking initiatives to settle the Kashmir issue peacefully. This was undertaken by Nehru just before his death when he had sent Sheikh Abdullah to Pakistan as his emissary. And again by Vajpayee when he travelled by bus to Lahore. This process got derailed when Pakistan stabbed us in the back at Kargil. Vajpayee persisted in his initiatives despite the fiasco at Agra. In April 2003 he sprang a pleasant surprise when he boldly extended a hand of friendship in his address from Srinagar. This set in motion a peace process leading to ceasefire on the LoC from November 2003 and commencement of composite dialogue. On coming to power in May 2004, Manmohan Singh continued that process. Various confidence building measures have been taken, notably the opening of Srinagar-Muzaffrabad Road and Poonch-Rawalkot Road. The recent commencement of cross-LoC trade is another manifestation of that process. However, despite all my efforts no progress was made in the opening of Kargil-Skardu Road, of much importance to us.

The thinking in Delhi has been that in the long term through economic development and some political sops we can win over the separatists in Kashmir. We should try to get them to join the electoral process. This had worked in 1975 when Indira-Sheikh accord was signed. The Congress Chief Minister Syed Mr. Qasim, stepped down and Sheikh Abdullah was installed as Chief Minister. Subsequently, the Sheikh won a resounding victory in the 1977 Assembly elections, widely accepted as the first free and fair election in Kashmir. This approach had also worked in Mizoram. The Congress Chief Minister stepped down and the leader of the militants, Laldenga was installed as Chief Minister. In 2002 Assembly elections of Kashmir, People's Conference a separatist party led by Sajjad Lone had participated by proxy in the elections even though the separatists had given a boycott call. It was not unreasonable for Delhi to seek a solution of the Kashmir problem through the electoral process in the State and through Track II diplomacy with Pakistan. However, unlike Sheikh Abdullah or Laldenga, there was no towering political leader available in Kashmir. There are too many separatist leaders, all with almost equal standing—Syed Ali Shah Geelani, Mirwaiz Omar Farooq, Yaseen Malik, Sajjad Lone and Shabir Shah. Apart from Vajpayee extending his hand of friendship to Pakistan in April 2003, the NDA Government took two other initiatives. First, it appointed one of our very distinguished civil servants NN Vohra, as interlocutor for Kashmir. He had a very good track record, having served as home secretary, defence secretary and principal secretary to the Prime Minister. I had met him a few times and I thought he was a good choice. The other initiative was to start dialogue with the separatists. LK Advani, the Deputy Prime Minister held two meetings with Mirwaiz Omar Farooq, a cleric and a leader of the so called moderate group of Hurriyat. On coming to power the UPA continued with these initiatives. Manmohan Singh had a couple of meetings with Mirwaiz.

Vohra's role as interlocutor got circumscribed because the Hurriyat leaders refused to hold talks with a civil servant. They wanted to deal only with political leaders. However, I am sure he must have been doing good spade work for talks with separatist leaders. During my visits to Delhi, I met Vohra a few times and discussed the Kashmir problem with him and apprised him of my views. Vohra was also our interlocutor with the European Union. I remember he came to Srinagar with a large delegation of members of the European Union Parliament. He brought them to the Raj Bhavan for briefing by me. I had nearly two hours interaction with them. After they went back to Europe they issued a statement hyphenating India and Pakistan. However, a year later Baroness Ema Nicholson came to Kashmir. She had been commissioned by the Europen Union Parliament to prepare a report on Kashmir. Vohra did not come to Kashmir with her but I am sure he must have interacted with her at Delhi. I had a long session with the Baroness. I have already written about her report on Kashmir which was favourable for India and critical of Pakistan.

As regards Mirwaiz having talks with the Deputy Prime Minister of the NDA Government and the Prime Minister in UPA Government, I had reservations. I wrote to the Prime Minister saying that by his having talks with only Mirwaiz and not other separatist leaders we were giving him undue importance. We were inadvertently building his image and he was getting projected as the sole spokesman of the people of Kashmir. I compared this to the course of events in India during the early forties of the previous century. Jinnah had returned to India and in 1940 he did not enjoy much following. As part of their policy the British built up his image. Churchill and Linlithgow, the then Viceroy did so, to suit British interests. The fact that the Congress leaders were in jail and incommunicado helped matters for Jinnah. In 1940 he may not have been a leader of great importance but by 1946 he had become the sole spokesman of the Muslims of India. It was not in our interest to build the image of Mirwaiz and make him appear as the sole spokesman of Muslims of Kashmir. I urged that other separatist leaders should also be invited for talks. I think the Prime Minister did hold talks with one other separatist leader but the focus was still on Mirwaiz. I also suggested that like the British in early thirties we may consider holding a Round Table Conference. Mahatma Gandhi was undisputedly the tallest political leader with unmatched mass base throughout the country in the thirties. Jinnah at that time had left India taking a break from politics and practicing law in London. Yet the British invited several political leaders of various insignificant groups and a whole lot of rulers of Princely States. The idea was to show to the world the complexity of the Indian problem and also that Mahatma Gandhi was one of the many leaders in India. Similarly we could convene a Round Table Conference on Kashmir. It would show to the world our earnestness to find a political solution of the Kashmir problem through consensus. At the same time it will underscore the complexity of the problem focusing on so many stakeholders with different agendas cutting Mirwaiz to size. It would also show that there was no one political leader who could speak for all the people of the State.

I am afraid the First Round Table Conference was held at Delhi in haste and not enough spade work had been done for it. The separatist leaders boycotted the meet and in their absence the whole purpose of holding the Round Table Conference was lost. On the eve of this conference there was an unfortunate incident. Four young schoolboys got killed in Handwara in crossfire during an encounter between the security forces and the terrorists. There was agitation in the Valley against the security forces for this and of course nothing was said against the terrorists. It was a good gesture that the Prime Minister and all participants at the conference observed two minutes silence in memory of these four schoolboys.

A Second Round Table Conference was held at Srinagar after a lot of preparatory work. Mirwaiz wanted to have another meeting with the Prime Minister. The PMO rightly kept him waiting for quite some time. I was told that Mirwaiz was getting desperate to get an invitation for a meeting with the Prime Minister. He held out the bait that if invited for a meeting with the Prime Minister, he would attend the Second Round Table Conference. He had no intention of doing so. He wanted to show his importance and being a notch above others, through his being repeatedly invited for talks with the Prime Minister. He had his desired meeting with the Prime Minister and gave the impression that he would attend the Second Table Conference. After his meeting with the PM, he issued a statement that he had been invited by the Prime Minister in connection with the Second Round Table Conference when the initiative for the meeting had come from him. He also said that he would not attend the Second Round Table Conference with so many Tom, Dick and Harry. Strange are the ways of politics.

The Second Round Table Conference was held at Srinagar with the Prime Minister in the chair. The location chosen was unfortunate. Tight security causing much inconvenience to the people and increased violence took away the shine from the conference. Delhi would have been a better place to hold this conference. The separatists again boycotted this meeting. A couple of weeks before this conference, terrorists had massacred some 30 Hindus in Doda. It was perhaps an inadvertent omission that unlike the First Round Table Conference when two minutes silence was observed for the four schoolboys, a similar gesture was not made for the large number of Hindus, who had been massacred in Doda. Such omissions only give credence to the charge of double standards and appeasement.

Being a Constitutional head, I did not attend the Round Table Conference. Azad briefed me about the proceedings of the conference. A lot of preparatory work had been done for the conference so that even with the boycott by the separatists, the deliberations of the conference could be fruitful. I could see that Ghulam Nabi Azad was the driving force behind it. Five working groups under the chairmanship of eminent personalities were set up to examine different aspects. These were as follows:-

1. Confidence Building Measures – Shri MH Ansari
2. Cross LoC movement – Shri M K Rasgotra
3. Economic Development – Shri C Rangachari
4. Governance – Shri N C Saxena
5. Centre-State relations – First Justice Ahmadi and then Justice Sagar Ahmad

These groups except the one on Centre-State relations, submitted useful recommendations, most of which were accepted by the Government. The group dealing with Centre-State relations was to deal with the all important political aspects of the problem. This group ran into trouble and it could not meet for a long time as its first Chairman resigned. A substitute was found. This group met a couple of times. It did not submit any recommendations. It was overtaken by subsequent events and became irrelevant.

Apart from the four point strategy of co-ordinated operations, economic development, psychological initiative and information management, I worked on a road map which was in no way contrary to what was being done by Delhi. I discussed this road map with Azad who was in agreement with me. I also briefed both the Prime Minister and the Home minister who endorsed it. I urged that the solution of the Kashmir problem should be Jammu and Kashmir centric and not only Kashmir centric. The demographic contour of the State is very diverse. No doubt Kashmiris are the largest group constituting some 45 percent of the population. There are 20 percent Gujjars, Bakarwals and Pahans who are also Muslims but they have a different identity and different aspirations. They are not Kashmiri speaking people. The 35 percent non-Muslims comprising Hindus, Buddhists, Sikhs and Christians are the third group. Hitherto, the focus had been only on Kashmiris. Terrorism and separatism were confined to Kashmiris. There was hardly any non-Kashmiri in the Hurriyat or other separatist groups. We should cater for all these three major groups and win their hearts and minds through various measures that I have already discussed. My second recommendation was that we should make careful preparation for the coming Assembly election in 2008. For the first time in 2002, we had allowed international media to observe elections in Kashmir. They had acclaimed that election as free and fair. In 2008 we should have the diplomats from important countries and organisations like the USA, Russia, China, the UK, France, Germany, European Union, ASEAN come and observe the elections. Depending upon our developing relations with Pakistan, we could even have diplomats from Pakistan come for this purpose. International community sending observers to watch elections in trouble spots had become common. This happened recently in Pakistan and in Nepal. And if inspite of the boycott call of terrorists, we had a high voter turnout of say 70 percent or more, that would be the most fitting vindication of India's stand on Kashmir. No doubt the separatists would argue that the Assembly elections were fought on local issues and could not be the basis for determining the future of the people of Kashmir. Our convincing counter to that would be that the high voter turn out would reflect the lack of support for the separatists and their cause among the people of Kashmir. As a case in point, in Assam when the separatists called for a boycott of elections in 1983, the voter turn out had been a mere 3 percent. Our argument would have carried much credibility both internationally and within Kashmir. In the event, inspite of the communal frenzy generated over Amarnath Yatra and mass protests and delayed elections in extreme cold in November and December the voter turnout in the 2008 Assembly elections, was over 60 percent. This only proved that had things been allowed to remain normal my plan would have worked and the bogey of plebiscite and self-determination, given a burial, once for all. Irrespective of which political party won the election, India would have been the real winner in a free and fair poll with a high voter turnout.

Plebiscite as a solution for the Kashmir problem had long been given up by many. Two successive Secretary Generals of the UN had said that it had now become irrelevant. Pakistan had been changing the demography of Kashmir in regions under her occupation. Musharraf must be given credit that with his rapid fire, out of box solutions, even he had given up talking about UN resolutions and plebiscite. However, plebiscite and self-determination continued to be the swan song of the separatists in Kashmir.

Musharraf first came out with his seven regional formula dividing Jammu and Kashmir into seven regions, the Valley, Jammu, Poonch-Rajouri, Kargil, Ladakh, POK and Northern Areas. This formula drew much flak because it meant revival of the pernicious two nation theory. A division of the State on communal lines would revive the ghost of the Partition holocaust. Musharraf revised this to a five regional formula with Jammu to include Poonch-Rajouri and Kargil to be included in Ladakh. Finally, Musharraf came out with his four point formula of LoC being made irrelevant, self-rule, demilitarisation and joint control. The PDP and the separatists went gaga over Musharraf's proposals. The PDP lapped up demilitarisation and self-rule in a big way. Mirwaiz an ardent Musharraf supporter gave the proposal a full throated support. This was not surprising, Musharraf managed to get elected President for a second term in a questionable manner. He imposed emergency in Pakistan. The people of Pakistan and the international community were unanimous in condemning these acts. However, Mirwaiz had burst crackers in support of Musharraf! In the international Press Musharraf was being praised for his flexibility and constructive proposals for resolving the Kashmir issue. There was no official reaction from India for some months to Musharraf's four point formula. Our bureaucrats argued that there was no need for us to react to every idea thrown up by Musharraf and given to the Press. Musharraf's four point formula had not been officially communicated to the Government of India, and there was no need to react. Our silence on Musharraf's four point proposal came in for criticism as an example of our inflexibility and rigidity.

A month or so after Musharraf's much touted four point formula had been floated, Jammu University organised a national seminar on Kashmir. Many prominent personalities including several retired top diplomats and individuals active in Track II diplomacy, attended this seminar. I was asked to inaugurate the seminar. In my inaugural address I mentioned that our Prime Minister had categorically asserted that borders cannot be altered. Any solution to the Kashmir problem ensuring that stipulation is not disturbed can certainly be examined. I then went on to give my personal views on Musharraf's four point proposal.

The LoC could be made irrelevant by converting it to a line of peace and prosperity with free movement of men and goods. However, this was possible only when Pakistan stopped cross border terrorism and dismantled the terrorist camps in its territory. If this prerequisite was not met then opening up the LoC will only facilitate infiltration of terrorists.

The second point of Musharraf's formula namely self-rule did not apply to Indian administered Kashmir, where self-rule exists in more than ample measure. Self-rule and democracy are synonymous. India is the most vibrant democracy of the Third World and within India Jammu and Kashmir enjoyed more self-rule than any other State in the country. No Act of Parliament applies to the State till it is ratified by the State Legislature. Even in economic matters Jammu and Kashmir has more autonomy than any other State in the country. It collects toll tax on goods and vehicles coming into the

State and this yields a revenue of 1000 crores a year. No other State in India collects toll tax at inter-state border. Self-rule needs to be introduced in POK where democracy stands derailed and in Northern Areas, where basic democratic rights are denied to the people like the right to vote for the Parliament. The latter is the only surviving colony in the world. Introduction of self-rule in POK and Northern Areas, will be most welcome. Pakistan should heed the recommendation in Baroness Ema Nicholson's report on harmonising the level of autonomy/self governance on both sides of the LoC.

The third point of demilitarization was impracticable in a border State which has been attacked repeatedly by its neighbouring countries. Pakistan has invaded Kashmir four times and China once. Even when total normalcy returns to Kashmir, the Indian army will remain deployed in Jammu and Kashmir to defend its borders. However, when normalcy returns the army can go back to barracks but that is not demilitarization as such. I also tried to rebut the oft repeated criticism of heavy concentration of Indian troops in Jammu and Kashmir. Troops to population ratio in neighbouring countries is higher as compared to what obtains in Jammu and Kashmir. This figure in Jammu and Kashmir is 1 per 40 population as against 1 per 37 in Waziristan and 1 per 28 in Tibet. These statistics evoked an angry outburst from Mehbooba Mufti saying that we do not have to be guided by what obtains in other countries.

The last point of joint control of Kashmir impinged upon India's national sovereignty. Pakistan cannot be allowed to get a foothold in Kashmir through a backdoor, having failed to secure Kashmir by other means. Durand Line between Afghanistan and Pakistan imposed by the British is not recognized by Afghanistan. This line divides Pashtuns. Would joint control by Afghanistan and Pakistan of Pashtun area on both sides of the Durand Line, be acceptable to Pakistan ? Whereas joint control is unacceptable in Kashmir, we can certainly consider a joint mechanism for promoting trade, tourism and cultural exchanges besides environment control, disaster management and so on.

A few weeks later I was happy to find that Ghulam Nabi Azad in one of his public speeches rejected Musharraf's four point formula. So did Pranab Mukherjee in the Parliament soon after he took over as External Affairs Minister.

Some months later, J&K Police organized another seminar at Srinagar on the Kashmir problem. I was invited to inaugurate this seminar. Dr Farooq Abdullah, and two former foreign secretaries Lalit Man Singh and Salman Haider attended the inaugural session. They were invited to speak after my inaugural address. In my address I gave a comprehensive projection of the Kashmir issue from day one that is 27 October, 1947 when I had come to the State as a young major with the first lot of Indian troops. I discussed Musharraf's proposals on the same lines as I had done at the seminar in Jammu. Farooq Abdullah and the two foreign secretaries spoke after me and none of them criticised my views.

The following day I was amused to read in the newspapers of the vice-president of PDP criticising me. He stated that the "Governor should shut up". I treated his outburst with the contempt it deserved. Later, I found that this was only the beginning of uncivilised tirade against me. During the last month of my stay in Kashmir, the PDP crossed all limits of civility in vilifying me and levelling fictitious and false accusations. It became even worse after I left Kashmir.

30

J&K Academy of Art, Culture and languages is a vibrant organisation it used to frequently hold various cultural functions. As Governor I was the patron of the academy and the Chief Minister was its president. I was frequently invited to inaugurate functions of the academy. My wife being fond of art and music with an impressive record in dancing from her student days at Benaras Hindu University, was only too happy to accompany me to these functions. Rafeeq Masoodi from Information and Broadcasting Service was appointed its secretary in 2006. I had known him when he was posted in Shillong and I was Governor of Assam. He has been a student of both Hindi and Urdu. His proficiency in both these languages is of a high order. During the Golden Jubilee Year of the Academy he was holding functions almost every fortnight inviting artists from all over the country. He also got foreign artists to perform for the academy, a number of times.

The people of Jammu and Kashmir have great artistic talent. Basoli paintings are famous all over the country. The great masters of vocal music, K L Saigal and Malika Pokhraj were from Jammu. Santoor is a well-known musical instrument of Kashmir. Pandit Shambhu Nath Sopori from the Valley is a highly respected and renowned musician. His son and student Bhajan Sopori has earned fame both nationally and internationally, as a great Santoor player. Bhajan's son Rustum has proved to be a very worthy son and grandson. He has been able to acquire international fame as a Santoor player at a very young age. Pandit Shiv Kumar Sharma from the State is another internationally acclaimed Santoor player. The Soporis have put up an institution called Sa Ma Pa in Delhi to promote music. These artists often performed at the J&K Academy of Art, Culture and Languages.

Shameem Azad, the wife of Ghulam Nabi Azad is the most talented singer of the State. Pandit Shambhu Nath Sopori had been her teacher. She reveres her Guru in the traditional Indian manner. She maintains family like relationship with the Soporis treating Bhajan as her brother and Rustum as her nephew. Shameem Azad is often referred to as the nightingale or Lata Mangeshkar of Kashmir. She has a golden and well-trained voice. She can sing equally well in different languages. Her songs in Telugu were a great hit and she got a special award from Government of Andhra Pradesh for her performance. She was awarded Padma Shri by the Government of India.

Shameem Azad is a lady of great charm and grace. She is the same age as our eldest daughter. My wife and I became fond of her and she reciprocated our feelings showing much regard for us. This was another link strengthening my very cordial relations with Ghulam Nabi Azad. Shameem had a serious ailment in her tongue, requiring major surgery at Mumbai. We were greatly relieved that she pulled through and recovered.

31

Nirmala Deshpande was a much respected old Gandhian. She was the President of the Gandhi Peace Foundation at Delhi. I had interacted with her during her visits to Assam. She used to visit Kashmir more fequently and often used to meet me. She was devoted to promoting peace between India and Pakistan and looked after various NGOs being run by the Gandhi Peace Foundation. She was happy with the improvement in the Kashmir situation. She also told me that on her visits to Pakistan she felt Musharraf was sincere about improving relations with India. She was appreciative of my efforts to restore peace and the work done by me during the snow tsunami in early 2005. She organized a peace march of school children and we made necessary security arrangements. A few thousand school children participated in the procession which terminated at the Police Golf Course in Srinagar. I was invited as Chief Guest to address the students. It was very encouraging that at the end of the function all the students enthusiastically sang the

National Anthem. Considering past inhibitions on this score, this was certainly a great achievement.

I was surprised that the Gandhi Peace Foundation nominated me for the award of 2005 Gandhi Peace Medal. This was given to me at a function on 2 October. The following year this was given to the Army and the Air Force as institutions for their highly commendable work in connection with the 8 October 2005 earthquake. In 2007, this award was given to Ghualm Nabi Azad for promoting amity and Gandhian ideals.

32

It is believed that before the era of Ramayan, the three manifestations of the Goddess, Maha Kali, Maha Lakshmi and Maha Saraswati pooled their collective spiritual strength to create a beautiful girl to live on earth and uphold righteousness. This girl was born in the house of Ratnakar in South India and was named Vaishnavi. She was endowed with both great beauty and intellectual ability. As she grew up, she wanted to go to the forest to meditate. Her parents reluctantly allowed her to go. She set up her Ashram near Rameshwaram. Through her spiritual attainment, she knew that Lord Vishnu will incarnate himself in human form as Ram to rid the world of evil symbolized by Ravan. Before setting out for the war against Ravan, Ram prayed to the Gods at Rameshwaram. He heard about a Sadhavi living in an Ashram nearby and went to seek her blessing. This Sadhavi was Vaishnavi. On seeing Ram she at once recognized him and said she had been praying to seek salvation by merging herself with the Creator. Ram told her that on return from the war on which he was embarking, he would again visit her. And this time if she recognized him, he would grant her wish. On the victorious conclusion of the war, Ram visited her in the guise of an old man. She was not able to recognize him this time. Ram told her that she had not till then acquired the level of spirituality to merge with the Supreme. He advised her to go to Trikuta Hills in the North and meditate. He also told her that as she advanced spiritually, people will hear of her and come to seek her blessings. He asked her to be kind to them, bless them and grant their wishes. Viashnavi came to Katra. A person by the name of Gorakh Nath was a tantrik. He got to know about Vaishnavi. He sent one of his disciples, Bhairo Nath to locate Vaishnavi. He managed to find her and started disturbing her in her meditation. He even started making advances to her. To escape from him, Vaishnavi went further up the Trikuta Hills and entered a Cave through which water flowed from a spring. Bhairo Nath managed to find her there and again started disturbing her. Vaishnavi transformed herself into her divine form with eight arms, each holding a weapon of war. She beheaded Bhairo Nath with such force that his head flew and landed on top of a neighbouring peak, while his torso fell at the mouth of the cave. Bhairo Nath begged her forgiveness. Vaishnavi took pity on him. She forgave him and asked him, if he wanted his life revived. Bhairo Nath said that he did not want to be born again. He could not have attained a more glorious death as had happened to him at Her divine hands. He wanted to be freed from the cycle of birth and death. He sought her blessing that he should not have notoriety attached to him and be remembered by posterity for his misdeeds. She assured him that he too would be looked upon with respect by pilgrims visiting her shrine. Their pilgrimage to her shrine would be deemed to be incomplete, if pilgrims after paying obeisance to Her, did not also go to the neighbouring peak where his head had landed. Thereafter Vaishnavi converted herself into three Pindies, five and a half feet tall rock, the top of which is only visible in the sanctum sanctorum, inside the Holy Cave. These Pindies represent Mata Maha Kali, Mata Maha Lakshmi and Mata Maha Saraswati.

About a thousand years ago, one Shridhar, discovered the Holy Cave. He was a pious man and received Vaishnavi's blessings to fulfill his pious wish to organize a Bhandara (free kitchen) when he did not have the required resources. His wish was fulfilled. Ever since then the Holy Cave in the Trikuta Hills became a very important pilgrimage, with increasing number of pilgrims offering prayers at the shrine.

Although I had served tenures in all the three regions of Jammu and Kashmir in the forties, fifties and sixties, including a tenure near Jammu, I had not heard of Mata Vaishno Devi pilgrimage. This was due to various reasons. First, I was too preoccupied with my military duties and did not have much opportunity of interacting with the civil society. Second, the information age had not dawned and people were not so well informed in those days. Third, the pilgrimage had not become so popular in those days. Even in 1977 when I was commanding a Division at Akhnoor, the number of pilgrims who had gone to the shrine that year was eight lakhs. I could see from my bedroom the lights on the hill along the track leading to the Holy Cave. The Bulawa (call) had not come and I had not felt the urge to go to the shrine. Army families were allowed in Jammu and Kashmir in those days, only for one month in a year. My wife came on a visit to me at Akhnoor and was surprised that I had not been to the Mata, even though for nearly a year, I had been living so close to the Shrine. At her instance, the two of us set out for this pilgrimage. We decided to go up from Katra and come down the same day. Katra was about an hour's drive by car from my house in Akhnoor. The shrine was being looked after by Dharmarth Trust and the family of Baridars used to be given the offerings at the shrine. A retired Captain from my Regiment was employed by Dharmarth Trust to manage the Yatra at the Bhavan. Between him and the army, we received VIP treatment but the facilities along the 12 kilometer track in the mountain were primitive. I was young enough to walk the round trip of 24 kilometer track but I felt my wife would not be able to do so. She went up and came down on a pony. Not used to riding a pony, she found the going tough and for a couple of days after the ride, her body was very stiff. She blamed me for my insisting on her taking the pony ride.

In 1986, Jagmohan, the then Governor of J&K decided that the Government should take over the management of the pilgrimage from Dharmarth Trust. That was the time when the State was under Governor's rule. Overnight, he had an ordinance issued constituting Shri Mata Vaishno Devi Shrine Board with the Governor as its Chairman. This was a very wise and bold decision. The ordinance was challenged in court and matters went up to the Supreme Court, which upheld the Governor's decision. The Baridars were given due compensation.

The Shrine Board had nine members. No active politician was to be made a member of the Board. Eminent individuals were nominated as members. A suitable infrastructure was put in place to manage the Yatra. The secretary to the governor was made the chief executive officer and an IAS officer in the senior scale was appointed additional chief executive officer. The latter functioned from Katra, the base for the Yatra. The Shrine Board had a staff of about 2000 comprising managers, priests, engineers, catering staff, computer scientists, medical staff, sweepers and so on. Begging was forbidden at the Shrine or along the mountain track. All cash offerings were required to be placed in donation boxes. Residential accommodation was constructed for pilgrims at Jammu, Katra and at Bhavan. The 12 kilometer mountain track was greatly improved with overhead covers for large stretches. These provided shelter from scorching Sun and from rain. It also protected Yatris from shooting stones. Toilets were provided at suitable intervals on the track. Medical dispensaries were also established along the route. The entire route had street lighting and arrangements were made to pump up water from tube wells to the Bhavan at a height of 6000 feet. Helipads were also constructed and helicopter service introduced for pilgrims, besides ponies, palkies and pithoos. Jagmohan showed much vision and dynamism in developing a massive infrastructure for the management of this Yatra. Though I had inherited a well-organized infrastructure functioning smoothly, I felt we should not rest on our oars. There should be constant effort to carry out further improvements and develop a dynamic approach to the management of the Yatra. Accordingly, we undertook various measures to improve the functioning of the Board and provide improved facilities for the pilgrims.

I took over as Chairman of the Shrine Board in June 2003 on assuming the appointment of Governor. I found the Board functioning very well. My secretary Dr. Arun Kumar, who later became a principal secretary was the chief executive officer. He was managing the Yatra affairs most commendably and was of great help to me. With the Yatra becoming more popular and with improved facilities, the number of pilgrims going to the shrine kept increasing every year. It was 54 lakhs in 2003 and rose to 75 lakhs in 2007. Our annual income from offerings and donations had risen from 66 crores to over 120 crores. Expenses incurred by us on development and establishment charges were also fairly high. A cap of 20 percent of income had been placed on expenditure over the establishment. This did not include capital investment on infrastructure.

Given the militancy situation in the State, we had to have proper security arrangements for the pilgrims. Raghunath Temple had been attacked by the militants in which a few devotees had been killed. Soon after I took over as Governor, a grenade was thrown on the pilgrims in Gulshan Kumar Langar near the start point of the track to the Shrine. Six pilgrims were killed and 28 injured. This required stringent security measures involving the army, the CRP and the State police. I carried out a review of security arrangements and ensured that they were fully coordinated and made foolproof. There was no terrorist attack on the pilgrims during the remaining five years of my tenure.

I found that pilgrims had to wait in a queue at the Shrine for an inordinately long time. On rush days when we had up to 44,000 pilgrims going to the Shrine, the waiting period in the queue would be up to three hours. I found this most unsatisfactory. I gave the staff a target which I knew was not easy to achieve. I wanted that no pilgrim should be made to wait in queue for more than 20 minutes. We organized waiting bays on the route near the Bhavan, where pilgrims could wait instead of standing for a long time in a queue. Sitting arrangements were provided in these bays along with plasma TV on which the Pooja being conducted at the sanctum sanctorum could be seen. Devotional music was also broadcast for the pilgrims along the route. The numbers allotted to the pilgrims were called out and also shown on the TV ticker, for the pilgrims to come out from the waiting bays and queue up for the Darshan. 1500 steel lockers were provided for the pilgrims to reduce complaints of loss of luggage. A steel flyover was provided for access to lockers without intersecting with the queue for Darshan. Separate routes were provided for pilgrims going for Darshan and those returning from Darshan. An escape route was also provided for use in the event of any natural/man-made calamity. These measures improved queue management, considerably reducing waiting time for pilgrims to about 20 minutes but on rush days it was still over 30 minutes. This was a great improvement over what the pilgrims had to go through earlier.

We constructed Trikuta Bhavan at Katra providing dormitory accommodation in a five storey modern building with modern facilities. The architecture of the building with a glass cupola above the courtyard is very attractive. A cafeteria has also been provided. We ensured that the building was kept spotlessly clean. Trikuta Bhavan has become a show piece. We spent Rs 6 crores over this building. It caters for pilgrims with a low budget, the charge per day being Rs. 50/-. Many people who have seen Trikuta Bhavan have told me that this is the best Dharamshala in the country. Besides, dormitory accommodation, the board also put up accommodation at Niharika complex in Katra. There were rooms of different size, both air-conditioned and non-air conditioned, with a total bed capacity of 272. We did not try to increase this number because of opposition from the hotel industry at Katra. However additional living accommodation was provided at Bhavan and en route at the half way house at Ardhkumari. By the simple arrangement of providing double steel bunks as in railway trains or in Army barracks, we doubled dormitory accommodation for pilgrims. We were lucky to find a suitable water source at the foot of the hill near Siar Dabri. We installed a tube-well and arranged for lifting 2 lakh gallons of water per day to the Bhavan. This project cost us 2.25 crores. A sewage treatment plant was installed at Bhavan at a cost of Rs 2.7 crores. A new dispensary was opened at Himkoti.

Free distribution of Halwa Prasad was introduced at Bhavan. Similarly, in association with donors, a free 'Langer' providing tea and 'Khichdi' was started. Besides, an alternate track was developed from Ardhkumari to Bhavan. A range of products including Amul (plain and flavoured milk as also sweet and salted lassi) and Verka products (flavoured milk and fruit based drinks) were provided. Nescafe vending machines, automatic Dosa making machine and chapatti making machines were introduced at Bhojanalays.

The new alternative track was further improved and a battery operated car service was started for old and infirm pilgrims. We started with 3 such cars in October 2003 and in 2007, 15 battery operated cars started round the clock operations between Ardhkumari and Bhavan. We also acquired an ambulance car for patients.

A tunnel and approach path were constructed at Ardhkumari at a cost of 2 crores to facilitate pilgrim traffic along the alternate track. The ambulance car could now operate not only between Ardhkumari and Bhavan but in an emergency, also from Ardhkumari to Katra. Ponies were not allowed to use the alternate track reserved for battery cars and pilgrims on foot. Ponies moved on the old track. A new communication system with 200 points was established on the tracks with a number of STD/PCO booths to provide connectivity.

A prestigious beautification project of a decorative marble arch gate called Darshan Deorhi along with a building for frisking, was put up at the starting point of the track from Katra to Bhavan at a cost of nearly 1 crore. Renovation/extension of Atka area at the Bhavan with an outlay of 3 crores has been started. It will provide accommodation for 500 pilgrims for Atka Aarti instead of only 80 at present. A new bathing ghat at Ban Ganga with toilets and beautification of the area was planned. A four-storey accommodation with two levels of underground parking has been planned at Jammu at an outlay of Rs 25 crores.

Helipad at Katra was expanded and a large helipad with hangar was constructed. The number of helicopters operating was increased and contracts worked out with helicopters operating companies. This led to reduction of helicopter fares from Rs 2000 to 1200.

My staff particularly Dr Arun Kumar the chief executive officer was of tremendous help in executing these projects. He was ably assisted by three successive additional chief executive officers at Katra—Rohit Kansal, Puneet Kumar and Manoj Dwivedi. I would also like to make a special mention of a highly devoted engineer, Shri Maini. He retired from Government service and for the last 20 years has been looking after various engineering projects of the Board in an honorary capacity. He has been an asset to the Board.

Along with all these improvements, measures were also taken to improve efficiency in functioning. Internet facilities were introduced including reservations for pilgrims through the computer. The welfare of the staff of the Shrine Board was also given due attention. Accommodation for them was constructed. At Nonman, 2 kilometers from Katra, a residential complex for Shrine Board staff was constructed.

We also decided to have projects to serve the civil society. Our two major projects are Shri Mata Vaishno Devi University and Shri Mata Vaishno Devi Institute of Medical Excellence. The former has become a very successful institution of higher learning. The first phase of the latter, a 250-bed state of the art modern cancer hospital was nearing completion. It was likely to commence functioning by the end of 2008, but due to agitation in the wake of Amarnath land controversy, the completion of this project got delayed.

A decision to set up a university at Katra by Mata Vaishno Devi Shrine Board was taken in 2001 and the State Legislature passed the Mata Vaishno Devi University Act. Over 400 acres of land was acquired in Kakriyal village for the purpose and the Board spent Rs 13 crores in purchasing this land from private parties. A little later Baba Ghulam Shah University was set up at Rajouri, an Islamic University at Anantnag and Trans-World Islamic University by Jamait Ahal-e-Hadees at Badgam. For these three universities, the State Government gave land free. Professor Chattoo from Baroda University had been appointed Vice-Chancellor of Mata Vaishno Devi University. He was on lien and was frequently visiting Baroda. He used to stay in Jammu and the University was to come up at Kakriyal. We were having problems with the villagers from whom land had been acquired. They had not been paid their compensation in full & they wanted further compensation. Plans for buildings had been made but except for a guest house, no other work had commenced. I recall that in July 2003 when I visited the site, there was only a dirt track which had become slushy due to heavy rains in the previous day. I could not reach the Guest House in a car. I had to travel in an army jonga. I gave the Vice Chancellor what appeared at that time almost an impossible task, that the university should start functioning from August 2004, if necessary, from temporary buildings. I had done something similar in Assam when I was the Chairman of a new IIT which had just started functioning from rented accommodation in the city, South of the Brahmaputra. Vacant land had been allotted for the IIT, North of the Brahmaputra. I had given the Director one year's time to shift the IIT to the site North of the river in temporary accommodation initially, while infrastructure and permanent buildings were being simultaneously built. This had worked and after a year we had managed to hold our first Convocation. After a couple of years the IIT campus came up very well, becoming one of the prettiest in the country.

I tried to drive the Vice Chancellor and his staff hard in pursuit of the one year target that I had given them. I visited the site several times and monitored progress. At University Council meetings, doubts were expressed about finding faculty and getting students to pay the high fee structure required for technical courses like Management, Information Technology, Biotechnology and so on. I sought an audience with the President, Dr Abdul Kalam at Delhi and invited him to inaugurate the University in August 2004. He accepted to do so. This put further pressure on everyone to speed up progress of work. A building for holding classes was got ready and we held the inaugural function in a big waterproof Pandal. Forty students had been enrolled and in a rare gesture, as mentioned earlier the President himself took the first class of the university for 40 minutes.

Although the Vice Chancellor had done well in the last year of his three year's tenure in organizing the inauguration of the university, we needed a more dynamic and dedicated Vice Chancellor who would stay at the campus and speed up work in establishing the university. I selected Professor N K Bansal from IIT Delhi to be the next Vice Chancellor. This turned out to be very fortunate. He put new life into the university, organizing the syllabus on the lines of IIT. He roughed out, living at the site. He also moved the students from Jammu to live in the campus. Hitherto, they used to commute in a bus wasting over one hour each way. We had completed construction of some hostel buildings for students. To attract faculty and staff, we got a branch of Delhi Public School opened in the campus to cater for schooling of their children. We provided land for the school which was also thrown open for the children in the neighborhood. The university made remarkable progress and within three years it was humming with activity with 850 students living on the campus. All visitors to the university were impressed by its layout and functioning. The first two batches which passed out from the university got 100 percent placement in corporate sector with good pay packets. A modern air-conditioned auditorium with capacity for 1000 was completed in time for the University's first convocation in May 2008. This required an outlay of 20 crores and it turned out to be one of the prettiest auditoriums of any university. Prime Minister Manmohan Singh delivered the convocation address and I conferred degrees on over 100 students who had graduated from the university in two batches. They were all well employed. This was the first university in the country which had the distinction of being inaugurated by the Head of the State and its first convocation addressed by the Head of the Government. All our guests at the convocation were most impressed by the function. The University had arrived on the national scene as an institution of excellence for higher technical education. All of us associated with the university were proud of the fact that we had been able to set up the university without any assistance from the government. I maintained that the university was the flagship project of the Board and lack of funds should not be allowed to come in the way of its development. We spent about 200 crores from the Shrine Board in setting up this university. Hopefully in another three to four years the university will become fully self-supporting.

My father as President of Mahabir Trust in Patna, a religious NGO, had started a Public School and a Cancer Hospital. Both these institutions were doing well. In 1999, when I was Governor of Assam I had accompanied him for the inauguration of the Cancer Hospital at Patna by the Dalai Lama. Despite limited funds with Mahabir Temple Trust, the Cancer Hospital at Patna over the years has come up well with the help of loans, donations and government assistance. It has become the leading cancer hospital in Eastern India. Mata Vaishno Devi Shrine Board had adequate funds and could set up a cancer hospital on its own. However, I did not want to take up this project till our University got fully established. By 2006 Mata Vaishno Devi University had got over its teething problems. I now decided to work on the cancer hospital project. I got the Shrine Board to approve of the project in principle.

I along with my principal secretary, Arun Kumar, went to various cancer hospitals at different places to see their functioning. We interacted with Tata Memorial Cancer Hospital at Mumbai, Rajiv Gandhi Cancer Hospital at Delhi and Mahabir Cancer Hospital at Patna. The staff at these hospitals were very cooperative and we found our visits fruitful. We also came across two experts in hospital construction and administration at Delhi — Shri Sunil Sachdeva and Dr YP Bhatia. The former is connected with the Medi-City project in Gurgaon which will have 1000-bed hospital of international standard. The latter has an NGO which advises on hospital construction and equipment. Both these experts volunteered their services and became our honorary advisers.

I also roped in Lt Gen LP Sadhotra who had just retired as the Head of the Medical Services of the Army. He had commanded the Army's most prestigious hospital, the 700-bed Research and Referral Hospital at Delhi. His home is in Jammu where he settled down after retirement. I had known him in the army when he was a young officer in my Division. I appointed him as the Director of our Cancer Hospital. He readily accepted my offer. He wholeheartedly devoted himself to developing the hospital.

I laid the foundation stone for the Cancer Hospital in 2007. Our plan was to develop Mata Vaishno Devi Institute of Medical Excellence in three phases. Phase I was a 250-bed state of the art modern cancer hospital with an outlay of 100 crores. In Phase II, this hospital was to be expanded into a multidiscipline hospital of 500 additional beds and in Phase III to a research centre and a full-fledged medical college, which would be a part of Shri Mata Vaishno Devi University. The Shrine Board allotted 45 acres of land adjacent to the University for this purpose.

By May 2008, the building for the Cancer Hospital was complete and we were in the process of installing equipment and appointing faculty. The whole process was nearing completion in a remarkably short time.

Yet another project was conceived. This was of a multimedia laser show. The idea was to have a musical fountain in which using latest laser technology, we could project figures of different shapes and colours on a water curtain combined with music and audio commentary. This project was estimated to cost 30 crores. This amount could be recovered in three to four years from gate money. We called the show Matri Darshan. The legend of Mata Vaishno Devi through music and commentary was to be presented on the water fountain with the help of laser. Similarly, during festivals like Ramnavmi, Janamashtami, Shivratri or Vijay Dashmi, legends connected with those festivals could be projected. It would provide entertainment for pilgrims staying overnight at Katra. The proceeds from this show would be available to meet the expenses of our

Cancer Hospital after the investment by the Board on this project had been refunded. This arrangement would enable free treatment being provided to the poor at the Cancer Hospital.

The laser project faced technical difficulties. We had to arrive at an agreement with a foreign firm in the UK to execute this project. No firm in India had the requisite expertise and equipment for this project. Much groundwork was completed but we could not get it started during my tenure. Hopefully, my successor would do so.

Yet another project conceived by us was an old age home with both dormitory accommodation and cottage. Old people with religious inclination could spend the last days of their lives here living under the benign shadow of the Mata.

While undertaking various new projects we also concentrated on improving facilities and infrastructure for pilgrims. I have already mentioned some of them. With only two tunnels at the cave we would not have more than 50,000 pilgrims visiting the cave in a day, with each pilgrim getting only a couple of seconds at the sanctum sanctorum. With number of pilgrims going to the Holy Cave having gone up to 75 lakhs and their numbers increasing every year, we had to find a way to increase the capacity at the cave for pilgrims. This could be done by boring a fairly wide third tunnel to accommodate two queues. Thus with the proposed tunnel we could double the capacity and cater for up to 1.5 crore pilgrims a year. Corresponding increase in infrastructure also had to be made. We had already located water source to bore another tube well and pump water up to the Bhavan. Himalayas are young mountains and one has to be careful while boring tunnels. We already had two tunnels to the Holy Cave and having a third tunnel had an element of risk. We consulted various experts. They considered a third tunnel feasible but were not prepared to stand guarantee for nothing going wrong. Konkan Railways who were considered an authority on tunneling in the mountains also were not willing to give guarantee that no harm would be caused to the Holy Cave by the proposed third tunnel. Jaypee Group had been doing a lot of tunneling in the Himalayas. They had tunneled in the Pir Panjal Hills for Baglihar Hydel project. They were willing to undertake the work for us at our responsibility. Both Arun and Mani felt that not much risk was involved. Mani had worked on the second tunnel and had practical experience. Being an engineer, his advice carried much weight. However, the decision to have the third tunnel had to be mine. I realized how lonely a person at the top can be while taking a crucial decision. If things work out alright, he may not be given much credit for it but in case things go wrong he has to be held responsible. My fear was that suppose in the process of tunneling the Holy Cave, collapsed, it would be a national disaster of great magnitude and my neck would be on the block for it. The thought of it gave me nightmares. A decision had to be taken by me to let things be as they were or go in for the new tunnel. I took the plunge keeping my fingers crossed. Thank God things worked alright and the third tunnel was nearing completion when I left.

Although the functioning of Mata Vaishno Devi Board was much appreciated by the people of Jammu and the pilgrims to the Holy Cave, our two flagships the University and the Cancer Hospital were a cause of envy among some people. I was surprised to find that Muzaffar Hussain Beg, the Deputy Chief Minister, saying in the Assembly that there should be no Vatican in Jammu and Kashmir. I found that some people were envious of the achievement of the Board. Some local political leaders of Jammu wanted to be included in the management of the Board for their vested interests. We were keen to retain the totally apolitical character of the Board. This would occasionally cause irritants and difficulties. The local people of Katra had a feeling that they were not getting any benefits from this pilgrimage. I commissioned a scholar from IIT Delhi to carry out a research on the economic benefits to the people of Katra accruing from this pilgrimage. He studied the matter in great detail and produced a scholarly report. It showed that as a result of the Yatra, 470 crores were being pumped into Katra's economy every year. This allayed the feelings of the people of Katra.

33

Amarnath Yatra to the 13,000 feet high Holy Cave in Kashmir is the most arduous pilgrimage in our country. Apart from the Yatra involving a long and difficult trek, weather conditions pose a serious problem. During heavy snowfall avalanches occur on the route and landslides take place during rains. Shooting stones are another problem. These have been leading to fatalties. There is also the problem of lack of oxygen at these heights as a result of which one has breathing difficulties. Every year some deaths occur among the pilgrims, due to cardiac arrest. Management of the Yatra, when the number of pilgrims had started running into lakhs became a major exercise, requiring a large infrastructure. With the onset of militancy, conducting the Yatra became difficult as militants began targeting the pilgrims on the Yatra route. In spite of the deployment of security forces, every year the militants attacked pilgrims on the Yatra route inflicting casualties. Notwithstanding the difficulties and dangers, pilgrims continued to go to the Shrine in large numbers. In 2002, 1.10 lakh pilgrims had gone to the Holy Cave for Darshan, when in 1980 their number was less than 20,000. This number increased to over 4 lakhs during my tenure, largely because of the improved facilities and better security arranged by us.

Legend has it that Lord Shiva and His consort, Mata Parvati had gone along the Pahalgam route to the Holy Cave. He released his Moon at Chandanwari and parted with his Nandi (Bull) at Pahalgam, earlier called Bail-Gaon. He shed the snakes at Sheshnag Lake and left his son Ganesh at Mahaganesh (Mahagunus Hill). At Panchtarni, he took leave of the five elements (Earth, Water, Air, Fire and Sky). He then proceeded to the Holy Cave with Mata Parvati. There he narrated to the Mata, the secret of life. Two pigeons in the Cave heard the narration and they became immortal. Every year some pilgrims see the pigeons in the Cave. They are not visible all the time. So when they are seen, it is considered a good omen. I saw the pigeons several times. However, there were a few occasions when I did not see any pigeon. The strange thing is that at that height, no birds are seen but these pigeons manage to survive there. Moreover, these pigeons do not multiply and their droppings are not to be seen anywhere. Whatever may be the reason for this, the presence of the pigeons at a height of 13,000 feet at the Holy Cave is a strange phenomenon, shrouded in legend.

There are two tracks from the Valley to the Amarnath Holy Cave. The Northern route is 12 km long from Baltal but is more arduous, involving a steep climb. The climb on the 34 km long southern route is more gentle, with two camps en route at Sheshnag and Panchtarni. In the previous centuries few pilgrims, mostly Sadhus, used to go to the Holy Cave. The southern route from Pahalgam was the traditional route. The northern route had not been developed till recently. There was once a tradition that pilgrims on reaching Amarnath felt that they had reached near Heaven and some would commit suicide by jumping from the top of the Cave. In the nineteenth century, Maharaja Pratap Singh passed a law prohibiting anyone from jumping from the top of the Cave. Even today human skeletons can be found on the ground below the Cave.

The Shri Amarnath Shrine Board Act was passed by the State Legislature and the Governor was made the ex-officio Chairman of the Board in November 2000. The Board got constituted in 2001 and started functioning from 2002. The provisions of the Shri Amarnath Shrine Board Act were exactly the same as that of Mata Vaishno Devi Shrine Board Act. However, there were two major points of difference. The land for the Mata Vaishno Devi pilgrimage had been transferred/acquired by that Board. In the case of the Amarnath pilgrimage the land had not been transferred to the Board, although the then Chief Minister, Dr Farooq Abdullah had promised in 2002 that this would be done. By convention, going back to centuries, the track going up to the Holy Cave along the two routes and the camping sites were made available for the Yatra. The second point of difference lay in the fact that the duration of the Amarnath Yatra used to be for one month only while the Mata Vaishno Devi pilgrimage was for all the year round. There was a large permanent staff of over 2000 working for the Shri Mata Vaishno Devi Shrine Board. In the case of Shri Amarnath Shrine Board, there was only an adhoc staff.

I took over as Governor in early June 2003 and the Yatra was to commence in July that year. The duration of the Yatra was for one month concluding on Shravan Purnima (Raksha Bandhan) which normally falls in August, the actual date varying every year as per the Hindu calender. I flew over the Yatra track a week before the scheduled date for the commencement of the Yatra. I found large number of pilgrims trekking up to the Holy Cave, on the Baltal route. I was told that this had become the normal practice ever since the Baltal track had been improved. The snow on the Baltal route melted earlier and many pilgrims did not want to wait for the commencement of the Yatra. On the Pahalgam route, there is normally a lot more snow and very few pilgrims go on that route before the commencement of the Yatra. I was concerned that pilgrims on the Baltal route going before the commencement of the Yatra, were exposing themselves to attack by militants as troops providing security did not got deployed before the official commencement of the Yatra.

A meeting of officials connected with the Yatra was held at Pahalgam in early July 2003. These included army, paramilitary and police officers besides civilian officials from various departments of the State government like Health, Supplies, Public Health Engineering, PWD and so on. Parvez Dewan, the Divisional Commissioner of Srinagar was the ex-officio Chief Executive Officer of the Shrine Board. The Deputy Commissioners of Srinagar and Anantnag were joint chief executive officers. The Shrine Board comprised nine nominated members with the Governor as the Chairman. The meeting at Pahalgam in early July 2003 was also attended by Chief Minister, Mufti Mohammad Sayeed and his daughter Mehbooba Mufti. The latter was not only the President of the ruling party (PDP—People's Democratic Party) but also the local MLA. I presided over this meeting. Mufti stated at the meeting that as the security situation was improving, he wanted minimum presence of uniformed personnel for the Yatra. I found this very strange. Every year including the previous year in 2002, pilgrims were being targeted by the militants and had been suffering casualties. I did not want to directly contradict the Chief Minister. However, while winding up the meeting, I made it clear that security of the pilgrims must be our top priority. Our objective must be to sanitise the Pahalgam-Holy Cave-Baltal track effectively by our security forces so that the militants could not attack the pilgrims. As for providing better facilities and infrastructure to the pilgrims, I said that I would like to concentrate on them from the following year. We could do little in that regard in 2003 as the Yatra was to commence very shortly. The meeting ended on a cordial note, even though I was a little disturbed about the different perception of the Chief Minister and I, with regard to security arrangements for the Yatra.

I sent for the Corps Commander who was also the security adviser to the State Government and expressed my concern regarding security for the Yatra. I suggested that the functioning of various elements of the security forces should be clearly defined and fully coordinated. He fully agreed with my views. We decided to have the army to dominate the entire 46 kilometer track from Pahalgam to Baltal by occupying tactical features and patrolling to prevent any ingress by the militants into the sanitised area. The BSF was required to ensure close protection of the track and provide escort for pilgrims on the track. The CRP was to guard the pilgrim camps at Pahalgam, Sheshnag, Panchtarni and Baltal, as also the Holy Cave. The State police was made responsible for checking identity of pilgrims and ensuring law and order in pilgrim camps. Security checks of pilgrims was necessary to ensure that no militant in the guise of a pilgrim, managed to enter a pilgrim camp. Prior to the commencement of the Yatra, I took a couple of trips on the Yatra route to ensure that the deployment on the above lines was complete. I stressed on cooperation and coordination at all levels to ensure that everyone worked as a team. It was very satisfying for me that 2003 was the first year, since the start of militancy, in which we managed a completely violence free Yatra. After the 2003 Yatra, we captured a militant who had been wounded in an encounter with the security forces in Anantnag. In his dying statement, he stated that he had been tasked to reconnoitre a safe route to attack Amarnath pilgrims, but the security was so tight that he could not manage to do so. We were fortunate that not only in 2003 but during the four subsequent years, from 2004 to 2007, during my tenure, we could manage a violence free Yatra along the sanitized track Pahalgam-Holy Cave-Baltal. In 2006 and 2007 militants had, however, managed to attack pilgrims outside the sanitized area. I left Kashmir a week after the 2008 Yatra had commenced. I am glad that violence free record was maintained also in 2008.

I felt that Shri Amarnath Shrine Board (SASB) should function on the same lines as Shri Mata Vaishno Devi Shrine Board (SMVDSB). As I have stated, the Acts passed by the State Legislature constituting these Boards were exactly the same. Earlier, the duration of this pilgrimage used to be a couple of weeks or so. The duration of the Yatra was now one month. However, to cater for increasing number of pilgrims, there was need to further increase this duration. We could not construct permanent structures as for Mata Vaishno Devi pilgrimage, because the land did not belong to us. Tented camps were put up on the route. The required organizational structure and staff of the Board was lacking and ad hoc arrangements were made every year. The Divisional Commissioner of Srinagar acted as the Chief Executive Officer of the Board for the duration of the Yatra in addition to his duties. Parvez Dewan, holding this appointment had shown a commitment to his additional responsibility and had done commendable work in getting the Baltal-Holy Cave track improved and widened. He was posted out to Delhi. I decided to appoint my Secretary, Dr Arun Kumar, as the chief executive officer. Arun had been functioning admirably as Chief Executive Officer of SMVDSB and was well-equipped to take on this additional responsibility which he readily agreed to do. This arrangement gave me a better control over the functioning of the Board. I also felt that there was a need for a permanent nucleus staff for SASB which could function in the Raj Bhavan. I appointed a retired Chief Engineer, I C Jandial, as Development Commissioner in November 2004 along with a skeleton staff. To provide funds for the functioning of SASB, I gave an interest free loan of Rs 2 crores from SMVDSB to SASB. Dr Farooq Abdullah as Chief Minister had given seed money of Rs 2 crores when SASB was set up with a promise of Rs 2 crores every year for the Yatra. After the change of government, the new Chief Minister, Mufti Mohammad Sayeed did not give any financial assistance to the Board. Anyway, I planned to make the SASB financially independent and not rely on assistance from the State Government.

After the successful completion of the 2003 Yatra, I organized a special function at which I invited representatives of all security forces and others who had assisted us in conducting the Yatra. The idea was to acknowledge the work done by them and to convey my appreciation for the same. Apart from entertaining them to tea, we gave them mementos. I made this a standard practice for subsequent Yatras.

We started planning for the 2004 Yatra soon after the completion of the 2003 Yatra. We planned elaborate facilities. We got funds from the Central Government for a Yatri Niwas at Jammu, but unknown to the Board, the State government had some accommodation constructed at Qazi Gund, which of course was of no use for Amarnath pilgrims. Later when Ghulam Nabi Azad took over as chief minister, the State government constructed Amarnath Yatri Niwas at Jammu. A modern building with all facilities for 1500 pilgrims was constructed at a cost of 5 crores in time for the 2008 Amarnath Yatra.

We made an ambitions plan of providing facilities for Amarnath pilgrims. The main feature of this plan was prefabricated shelters with wooden floors and insulated side panels, for accommodation of pilgrims. Both dormitory and room accommodation were planned. Open deep trench latrines were to be replaced by prefabricated toilets connected to leach pits. We proposed to construct 2000 such toilets. Prefabricated bath shelters with hot water facilities were also planned. A detailed project report was prepared which required an outlay of 20 crores. This amount was to be raised by the Amarnath Shrine Board without seeking any assistance from the government. I sent a letter to Mufti on 20 October, 2003 outlining the improvements that I had planned for the Yatra commencing in June 2004. On 27 March 2004 I sent a complete project report to him but there was no response from him. In my letter of October 2003 I had also made some other suggestions like the duration of the Yatra to be extended from one month to two months, ceiling of 3500 pilgrims going to the Shrine each day to be removed and the Shrine Board be allowed to operate a helicopter service from Baltal to the Holy Cave on the lines of what was being done by the Shri Mata Vaishno Devi Shrine Board from Katra. There were also other issues like control of registration of pilgrims to be given to the Amarnath Shrine Board as was being done in the case of pilgrims to Mata Vaishno Devi. Hitherto, their registration was being done by J&K Bank on payment of a nominal charge.

It was surprising that there was no reaction whatsoever from Mufti. Mangat Ram Sharma, the then Deputy Chief Minister, reacted very favourably. He came and saw the experimental prefabricated shelters for accommodation and toilet that had been put up at Raj Bhavan. He much appreciated these. He also made a mention of these at public meetings and announced that the Yatra would now be extended from one month to two months. I have a feeling that Mufti was not quite sure how to react to my proposals regarding Amarnath Yatra. The NDA Government was in power at Delhi and he may not have thought it prudent to take an anti-Yatra stance. He knew of my close relationship with the top NDA leaders. In May 2004 the NDA Government fell and Mufti got emboldened to take a tough stand. He was also now confident that he could have me removed.

Mufti dropped a bomb shell at a Press Conference, barely a fortnight before the commencement of the Yatra. He stated that there would be no change in either the duration of the Yatra or in the arrangements for it. Not having bothered to acknowledge my letter sent six months earlier and another three months earlier, he chose to take a unilateral decision and announced his decision to the Press, without discussing the matter with me. I was taken aback when I read his statement in the Press. Mufti banked heavily on the new UPA Government at Delhi to support him. The situation was embarrassing for me. We had announced the date for the commencement of the Yatra and some pilgrims had even done their booking. We had advanced money to firms for procuring prefabricated shelters. Some of the stores had reached Srinagar, on their way to Baltal. The State police was given orders to prevent the movement of prefabricated stores from Srinagar to Baltal. My letters to Mufti of October 2003 and March 2004 got leaked to the Press. This created a furore in Jammu. It was a piquant situation with the Governor and the Chief Minister getting involved in an open controversy. I had to keep the dignity of the office of the Governor and at the same time not make nay compromise with my obligations as the Chairman of Amarnath Shrine Board. To prevent the controversy taking a communal turn, I issued a statement that I had great regard for the Chief Minister who was very secular in his outlook. However, there were some differences with regard to the conduct of Amarnath Yatra, which we will soon resolve through discussion.

I asked Mufti to meet me. He came to see me. He appeared to have a closed mind and was not prepared to budge from his stand. As a shrewd politician, he had an answer for every point I raised with him. When I mentioned that he had not replied to my letters, he said that he had not seen them nor was he aware that the Deputy Chief Minister had made any announcements about the Yatra being extended and the improved facilities for pilgrims being planned. He also said that instead of writing letters to him, I should have discussed the matters with him. I did not want our meeting to be acrimonious. I did not ask that how come two letters from a Governor to a Chief Minister had not been seen by the latter. Further, I also did not point out that before announcing his decision about the Yatra, he should have discussed the matter with me. We then took up the all important issue of the duration of the Yatra. I explained to him the reasons for my wanting an extended Yatra. The year 2004 was the 'Malmas' year as per Hindu calendar with two Shravan months. This happens once in twelve years. From the religious point of view, there was a requirement for two months Yatra. There were, besides, other reasons. The Yatra had become popular and the number of pilgrims had been increasing every year. If the duration was not extended, the management of the Yatra would become more difficult as there would be greater rush during the limited period of the Yatra. The track along the northern route had been improved considerably and the snow normally melted on this route a few weeks earlier than the Pahalgam route. In view of this, pilgrims started going to the Shrine along the Baltal route, a few weeks earlier than the official date for the commencement of the Yatra. They got exposed to danger as Security Forces were not deployed during that period. No doubt a two months Yatra will impose a strain on the security forces but I had discussed the matter with both the army and the paramilitary. They could manage security for the extended duration. None of my arguments cut any ice with Mufti. He remained adamant that he could not agree to the duration of the Yatra being extended.

Mufti's reaction to the use of prefabricated shelters was strange. He argued that these would lead to environmental degradation and putting up permanent structures on forest land was not permissible. I pointed out that the prefabricated toilets with leach pits were eco-friendly and a great improvement over open deep trench latrines. Prefabricated shelters could be constructed before the Yatra and dismantled thereafter. They were not permanent structures, like the ones in few places like Chandanwari, Sheshnag and Pachtarni put up by the State Government. There was not much difference between pitching tents and putting up prefabricated shelters both were temporary accommodations, and could be dismantled. Prefabricated shelters would be more comfortable for the pilgrims and give them greater protection in adverse weather. I even showed him a prefabricated shelter and toilet installed at Raj Bhavan. Mufti was not convinced and he said that any prefabricated construction was not acceptable to him.

On operation of helicopter service under the control of Amarnath Shrine Board, he had an equally negative attitude. He said that the State had a Civil Aviation Department that could handle that operation. I pointed out that the Act passed by the State Legislature constituting the two Shrine Boards were identical and SMVDSB was controlling the helicopter operation from Katra. There was no reason why SASB could not do the same from Baltal, where helipads had been constructed for the purpose. Mufti's answer shocked me. He said that Kashmir was different from Jammu. How could a chief minister of the State make such differentiation between two regions of his State ? This only showed his mental make-up and was in line with his daughter Mehbooba's assertion that only a Kashmiri Muslim should be chief minister of the State. She ignored the fact that Bihar, Maharashtra Andhra Pradesh and Rajasthan with minority population of 10 percent or less had chief ministers from minority community. In secular India why couldn't a non-Kashmiri. Muslim who constituted 55 per cent of the population of the state be a Chief Minister?

As for relaxing the ceiling of 3500 per day and registration of pilgrims, Mufti's approach was again very negative. The ceiling of 3500 per day had been recommended by the Sen Gupta Committee in the wake of the snowstorm of 1996 in which over 200 pilgrims had died and many more injured. I pointed out that the report had also recommended that when the security situation improved and better infrastructure was available, that ceiling could be relaxed. Both these conditions had been met and there was now no reason why this ceiling should not be relaxed. On peak days 10,000–12,000 were already going to the Shrine, making a mockery of the ceiling. Divisional Commissioner Parvez Dewan who had functioned as CEO of SASB, had told me that the ceiling was a source of corruption. Anyone paying bribe at the police check post was allowed to go up. Registration slips and ceiling had no meaning. All efforts to prevent this blatant corruption had failed. J&K Bank did registration of pilgrims charging Rs 10 per pilgrim. I wanted the registration of pilgrims to be done by SASB without any charges, as was being done in the case of pilgrims going to Mata Vaishno Devi. Mufti's constant refrain was that Kashmir was different from Jammu.

My meeting with Mufti was completely futile. He was determined to oppose any suggestion that I made. I realized that it was no use continuing further a dialogue of the deaf with him. At the same time, I felt that as governor I should not make any public statement even remotely criticising the Chief Minister. In fact, I continued with my stand in public that I had great regard for him and we would resolve all differences. The media soon got to know of the acute differences between us on all matters pertaining to Amarnath Yatra. This became a raging national controversy. The fact that the police had detained the Baord's Development Commissioner, a retired Chief Engineer, for taking some prefabricated stores to Baltal was reported in the Press. I now realised that I could not stop the controversy flaring up.

The controversy over the duration of Amarnath Yatra got wide publicity in the media. Shiv Sena leader, Bal Thackeray announced that he would send a Jatha of 20,000 to Kashmir to protest against the State Government's decision. It was also stated that the Government of Jammu and Kashmir was levying Jizya tax on Hindus going to Amarnath, reminiscent of what Aurangzeb had done. In Jammu, there were protest demonstrations and the effigies of Mufti were being burnt. A Shankarcharya was supposed to be coming to Jammu to join the protest demonstrations. Four Hindu ministers of the Congress Party in the coalition government tendered their resignation on this issue. For the first time in the history of parliamentary democracy, ministers had come out openly in support of the Head of the State and taken a stand against the Head of the Government. In Jammu, the controversy had taken a communal turn. In Srinagar there was not much controversy and the common man remained unconcerned. Dr Farooq Abdullah stated that there was no harm in making the duration of the Yatra, even six months. There were however a few articles in the Press about the Yatra causing environmental degradation. Those who argued on these lines turned a Nelson's eye to the greater degradation of the environment by the normal tourist traffic. The pollution of Dal Lake was increasing manifold. The State Government was trying to promote normal tourism to the State but was placing hurdles in the way of pilgrim tourism to Amarnath. In one newspaper there was a reference to Amarnath Yatra promoting Hindu cultural domination of the Valley.

The situation had become volatile. I felt relieved when I got a telephone call from Ghulam Nabi Azad, then Minister for Parliamentary Affairs in Delhi. He told me that he supported my proposal for a two month's Yatra and he would see what he could do to resolve the crisis that had arisen. I had met Azad twice before. Once when he called on me soon after I took over as Governor and the second occasion was when he had come with Sonia Gandhi, a few months earlier, campaigning for the parliamentary election. I had found him amiable and friendly. I was pleasantly surprised when he rang me up on his own to convey his support for my stand in the Amarnath controversy. Late that night I got a telephone call from the Home Minister, Shivraj Patil. He told me that he was concerned about the controversy. Jammu and Kashmir was a sensitive State and I should dowse the controversy and not allow it to linger. He also told me that he had spoken to Mufti about it and in national interest the two of us should meet and resolve our differences. I felt that the Congress Party did not want to be seen to be acting against the interests of the Hindus. It did not want me to quit, which was on the cards for some time. Had this happened, when this controversy was raging, it would have been seen as an anti-Hindu act. In view of the forthcoming Assembly elections in Maharashtra, the Congress chose not to oblige Mufti and be seen as anti-Hindu. Thus, I was allowed to continue as Governor and perhaps accepted as a necessary evil. Mufti must have been very disappointed.

I asked Mufti to come over to see me. I told him that the controversy had taken an ugly turn which was not good for our State. He agreed with me and I now found him more accommodating. I was given to understand that he was wanting some face-saving formula. I was only too willing to help in finding one. I suggested that between his decision to have a 30 days Yatra and my proposal to have 60 days Yatra, we could settle for a 45 days Yatra. However, I wanted the formal Pooja to be performed by me on the auspicious date, 60 days before the end of the Yatra on the day of Guru Purnima. This would indicate the token commencement of the Yatra. This was agreed to by Mufti. I also wanted Service Yatra, the name given to Yatra performed by personnel posted for security and other duties to commence a fortnight earlier as per the normal practice. This was also agreed to by Mufti. When I went to the Holy Cave for the Pratham Poojan (First Prayer), there were thousands of Yatris already there. The Yatra started in full swing with thousands going every day. It became a full-fledged two months Yatra. Mufti also agreed to prefabricated toilets being put up but it was now too late for us to execute our plan for these toilets for the Yatra that year. However, a few such toilets could be put up towards the end of the Yatra. Unfortunately, a very unsavoury incident took place during the Yatra of 2004. Two ministers of Mufti Government, Yogesh Sawhney and Ghasu Ram, with their wives went by State helicopter to the Holy Cave. Helicopters do not switch off their engines at those heights. After dropping passengers, helicopters return to lower heights and go to pick up passengers when required. Secretary of Mufti did not send the helicopter to pick up the ministers, advancing technical reasons. The ministers and their families kept waiting. I was contacted late in the afternoon but it was now too late to get them down along the track before dark. I asked the army to look after the ministers and make them comfortable. It was a harrowing experience for them to spend a night at that height, without proper accommodation. On return, they issued a statement that the Chief Minister deliberately did not send the State helicopter to bring them back and left them and their families to die in the cold at that height.

I was happy that the controversy was at last resolved in 2004 and hoped that from next year, we would be able to conduct the Yatra as planned. I was mistaken. Mufti had not taken kindly to his efforts to restrict the Yatra to one month having been foiled. He felt that it was a loss of face for him. A public interest litigation had been filed by a private party from Punjab in the High Court against undue interference by the State government in the conduct of the Amarnath Yatra. Both the State government and the Shrine Board had been made respondents. We had to file our affidavit and so had the State government. Inevitably the stands taken by the State Government and the Board clashed. The case dragged on for some time. The Judge gave his verdict. It vindicated on all points the stand of the Shrine Board. This upset Mufti more. The State Government appealed against the verdict of the Single Bench. It engaged a leading lawyer from the Supreme Court to plead its case. Mufti told me that he could not allow the sovereignty of the State Government undermined. One of his ministers reiterated again that the State Government will not allow a Vatican to come up.

The following year's Yatra was approaching while the appeal of the State Government was still being heard in the High Court. The Division Bench gave an interim direction that the duration of the Yatra should be decided by the Shrine Board but the Board had to give two months written notice to the State Government about the date of the commencement of the Yatra, so that the latter could make adequate security arrangements. We were able to conduct a two months Yatra in 2005 but on the southern route from Pahalgam it could be only for six weeks, as there had been heavy snowfall and the clearance of the track got delayed by two weeks. The Court also allowed the Shrine Board to put up temporary prefabricated shelters for the Yatris and to operate a helicopter service for the pilgrims. I personally went up on foot and pony on the track to the Holy Cave to monitor the clearance of the track and the arrangements for the Yatra that were being made. I had made this my normal practice every year. I had also started the tradition as Chairman of the Shrine Board to offer obeisance at the Holy Shrine both on the first and last day of the Yatra every year.

I was happy that we managed four successive Yatras of two months duration in spite of all the difficulties created by Mufti. To promote secular values I started the practice of placing a "chadar" (cloth cover) at the holiest Ziarat (Shrine) in the Valley at Chrar-e-Shareef on the first day of Amarnath Yatra, soon after the Pratham Poojan. I also gct Amarnath Shriune Board to organise a Sufi music festival of 3 – 5 days at Srinagar and at times also at Baramulla and Pahalgam. We not only got renowned Indian singers for this festival but also foreign artists from Pakistan and Egypt. This was much appreciated.

In 2005, Mufti had to quit as chief minister and Azad now took over the reins of the Government. I was now confident that we would get all the cooperation from the State Government and we would not have to face any more controversies. This was not to be. For different reasons the Yatra of 2006 and 2007 got mired in controversies of different types. And in 2008 a communal storm erupted in the Valley over Amarnath Yatra.

Mahant Deependra Giri of Dashmi Akhara at Srinagar had been the custodian of Chhari Mubarak which is taken to the Amarnath Shrine for the Yatra. He used to be responsible for conducting the pilgrimage to Amarnath and used to collect the offerings at the Shrine. After the Amarnath Shrine Board was constituted, he was relieved of this function which was taken over by the Board. A Judge was appointed as arbitrator to determine the compensation to be given to him and other stakeholders of this pilgrimage, namely the Pandits of Mattan who performed the Pooja at the Shrine and the descendants of Buta Malik who had looked after the Shrine. The arbitrator fixed the amounts to be paid as compensation. As per this award, Deependra Giri was to be given Rs 1.02 crores. I paid him this amount and we also kept him as a member of the

Shrine Board. He was not fully satisfied with the amount. He wanted us to give him concessions and facilities for the large number of Sadhus who accompanied him with Chhari Mubarak. We maintained that the amount we had given him was all inclusive and we could not accept any further liability. He continued to be a member of the Shrine Board and attended all its meetings. He was fully supportive of our demand for two months Yatra in 2004 and in fact addressed a Press Conference as a representative of the Board to put across our point of view, which had not been accepted by Mufti. After we successfully managed a two months Yatra in 2004, we made a bid for two months Yatra in 2005. Deependra Giri was a party to this decision at the Board meeting and raised no objection on that account. However, he started issuing statements to the Press that from the religious point of view, the duration of the Yatra should be for one month only. Despite opposition of Mufti and his two key officials, the then Chief Secretary and the then DG Police, we had managed a two month's Yatra also in 2005.

Our experience of previous years had been that the Holy Ice Lingam melted after about two weeks of the commencement of the Yatra. This could be due to the body heat of the increasing number of pilgrims running into lakhs, offering obeisance at the shirne. Pilgrims undertaking the very arduous trek felt greatly disappointed in not being able to see the Lingam. The Board had been considering various measures to ensure that the Lingam be preserved throughout the duration of the Yatra. I insisted that nothing should be done to tamper with the Holy Lingam as such and any measure taken to prevent its melting should be as unobtrusive as possible. We carried out various experiments for doing so, like skating rink technique, brine trays, radiant cooking panels, refrigeration and air curtain. After experiment with each of these, we settled for the air curtain technique. These measures were discussed at various meetings of the Shrine Board at which Deependra Giri was present and he had never raised any objection. The air curtain technique was least obtrusive and its requirement of power was minimal. We settled for this option but could not proceed with it for legal reasons. As per the verdict of the Single Bench of the High Court, there was nothing to prevent us from going ahead with our plans but on the appeal field by the State government the Division Bench had issued interim instructions. These allowed us to have a two months Yatra, operate helicopter service and put up prefabricated shelters. Other issues connected with the Yatra remained sub judice.

In 2006 we were faced with a new problem. The Ice Lingam had not formed at all. This could be due to a host of factors. It could be as a result of global warming and the shifting of the glaciers. The other possibility was that the earthquake of 2005 may have affected the rock formation in the area. The water from the glaciers travelled along the gap between rock layers to the top of the cave and dropped at the site of the Lingam, leading to the formation of the stalagmite. We got experts from Snow And Avalanche Study Establishment (SASE) Chandigarh and Geological Survey of India Dehra Dun to examine the cause for the Lingam not forming that year. We summoned an emergency meeting of the Board at which Deependra Giri was present. He told us that this rare phenomenon had happened once before in the eighties. This was also confirmed by some other sources. We were relieved to receive information that the ceiling of the Holy Cave which had been dry had become moist as also drops of water had begun falling at the holy site. Small stalagmites representing Parvati and Ganesh had formed a few feet away from the site of the Lingam We were now hopeful that the Lingam would get formed for the 2006 Yatra.

A Lingam smaller in size than in previous years got formed at the Holy site. To ensure that this Lingam did not melt quickly we got some packed dry ice from Delhi and had it placed near the mouth of the Cave to keep the temperature down and delay the process of the melting of the Lingam. We were surprised that Deependra Giri issued a statement to the Press that the Shrine Board had put up an artificial Lingam which was an act of sacrilege. May be he was misled by reports about packed ice. In any case, the Chief Executive Officer and I were both in Srinagar at that time and he could easily have spoken to us before issuing such an inflammatory statement against the Board. It was unethical of him to level such an allegation against the Board without seeking clarification and when he had been a party to all the decisions taken by the Board. Some disgruntled Langar walas also decided to join in the controversy supporting the Mahant. The print and electronic media blew up the matter and the whole thing became a raging national controversy. I was told that some political elements were interested in getting the Board discredited and they had encouraged the Mahant to make this allegation. May be they had held out hopes to him that the Board could be dissolved, paving the way for the control of the Yatra to revert to him. Be that as it may, I decided in consultation with the Chief Minister to have a judicial inquiry to investigate the allegation. Justice Gupta, a former acting Chief Justice of J&K High Court, long associated with different Hindu religious bodies, was requested to conduct the inquiry. He agreed to do so. He visited the site and examined various documents, heard evidence of various individuals as also sought the advice of experts. His repeated requests to Mahant Deependra Giri to give evidence before him, was of no avail. The Mahant refused to appear before him. The Gupta Inquiry report totally exonerated the Board of the allegations and confirmed that the allegation of artificial Ice Lingam was baseless. The matter did not end there. The hostile elements filed a case in the High Court. After hearing their plea, the Court rejected their case. Despite all the controversy, it was a matter of satisfaction for me that we could conduct this Yatra, providing improved facilities like over 2000 prefabricated toilets and hot water for bath costing over Rs 2 crores. We also had some prefabricated and insulated living accommodation for pilgrims at various camps. The tentwalas were resentful of this because it affected their business. We worked out an arrangement whereby they could manage the prefabricated shelters on behalf of the Board and earn a percentage of the rent paid by pilgrims. This more than compensated them for the loss of income from the tents that they put up. We also allowed tents to be put up along with prefabricated shelters, leaving the choice of accommodation to the pilgrims. The rates for prefabricated shelters were higher. Yet, some politicians tried to raise the bogey that the Board was depriving the poor people of the area, their means of livelihood. Despite all the controversies and difficulties, 3.5 lakh pilgrims paid obeisance at the Holy Cave that year.

In 2007, we faced another problem. An Ice Lingam, thinner than the normal had formed. The date for the commencement of the Yatra was later than normal in that year. It commenced from 30 June to conform to the Hindu calendar. Many pilgrims had managed to have Darshan before the commencement of the Yatra as the snow had melted early and the Holy Cave had become approachable from Baltal. As per normal practice, security forces to be deployed for duties for the the Yatra and their families had been allowed to pay their obeisance before the start of the Yatra. An enterprising journalist took a picture of some overzealous security force personnel entering the sanctum sanctorum and putting vermilion mark on the Holy Lingam. It so happened that due to the abnormal heat in June, the Lingam melted early and on the day, the Yatra commenced, there was no Lingam. It was primarily a natural phenomenon. The Lingam normally melts two to three weeks after the commencement of the Yatra but that year it had melted earlier as the Yatra's commencement date was much later. However, some people tried to raise controversy by accusing the Board of neglect and not ensuring that no personnel of security forces entered the sanctum sanctorum. This controversy soon petered out and was not so serious as the one in the pervious year, regarding the allegation about an artificial lingam. Despite the pilgrims being aware of the fact that the Lingam had melted, they were not deterred and 3 lakh pilgrims visited the Shrine. This proved their reverence and attachment for the holy site. The Board now decided to have a door with locks, put up at the entrance of the Cave, for the future.

Conducting the Shri Amarnath Yatra had become a great strain on me and my staff, particularly when some people were creating unnecessary controversies. However, undeterred, we tried to do our best every year. The chief executive officer and other members of the staff carried out their onerous duties most diligently and we could meet all the challenges successfully. Some people told us that all those who tried to create obstacles in the conduct of the Yatra had suffered. Chief Minister Mufti Sayeed failed to get a second term in 2005. His secretary, a senior IAS officer and the overzealous additional advocate general who argued the case against the Shrine Board, in the High Court got involved in a sex scandal and both had to spend some time in jail. Qarra the PDP Forest Minister impounded the dozer, stopped black-topping the road to the Yatra camp at Baltal, for which funds had been made available by Government of India. His colleague, Gulchain Charan Singh Charak, the Congress PWD minister had got this work started. The PDP minister later got involved in a forest scam and his prima facie guilt was fully established by the Kundal Committee. He may have brazened out and stuck to his chair but this did much damage to his credibility. He lost his seat in the Assembly election. All this was a coincidence, but some thought it was Divine wrath !

I must not fail to record my appreciation of the local people of the Yatra area who are all Muslims. They gave us full support for the conduct of the Yatra. Besides their secular outlook, it was also a fact that the Yatra provided economic benefits to these poor people. This stood them in good stead also during the non-Yatra period. The common man in the Valley showed no communal bias and there was no opposition to the Yatra from them. A few hyperactive politicians tried to raise the pollution issue, turning a Nelson eye to pollution of Dal Lake or damage to the ecology due to the construction of Mughal Road. Canards were spread of Shrine Board levying tax on Ponywalas, Pithoos and Tentwalas. This was totally false. Rates for Ponywalas and Pithoos were fixed by the State Labour Department and the Board had nothing to do with that. Tentwalas were asked to pay a nominal amount for use of prefabricated toilets put up by the Board. Some politicians and communal elements were allergic to Amarnath Yatra but this was not the case with the common man of Kashmir. As mentioned earlier, one of them even wrote in the media that Amarnath Yatra was a symbol of Hindu cultural invasion and a measure for integrating Kashmir with the rest of India. This remained a lone voice, even though a few people may have been thinking on those lines.

I held a meeting of the Shrine Board in March 2008 to take stock of preparations for the 2008 Yatra. Besides the usual criticism of ecological damage, environment pollution, depriving locals of income and so on a new issue had been raised. The Government of Uttarakhand on account of global warming and melting of glaciers had restricted the number of pilgrims going to "Gomukh", the glacier where from the Holy Ganga originates, to 150 a day and had imposed a small levy on pilgrims going there. It was demanded that a similar daily ceiling and levy be imposed for Amarnath pilgrims. Those making this demand did not realize that the pilgrimage to Amarnath was not like that to Gomukh. There was no glacier at the Amarnath Holy cave. Amarnath pilgrimage was like the pilgrimage to Badrinath and Kedarnath at Uttarakhand at similar height in the Himalayas. There was no restriction on pilgrims going to Badrinath and Kedarnath. These pilgrimages were open for six months in a year and closed for remaining six months due to snow. I told the Board that this is a controversy which we will have to put up with. The opening shots for the 2008 Yatra had already been fired. However, none of us at that meeting could anticipate the tidal wave of antipathy towards the Shrine Board and Amarnath Yatra that would engulf the Valley a couple of months later. I shall narrate its details later.

34

Dr Kalam's term as President was getting over. He had endeared himself to the people of India, particularly the youth. He was rightly hailed as the People's President. There was a general expectation that he may get another tenure but this was not to be. The ruling party had its own agenda. The election of his successor to the Nation's highest office got mired in controversy, the like of which had never happened before.

All Governors were invited to Delhi for the swearing of the new President. On previous such occasions only Governors who happened to be in Delhi used to be invited. Having served as Adjutant General of the Army in charge of ceremonials and organizing several Republic Day Parade, Beating Retreat and other ceremonial functions at the national level, I was amazed to find tradition and protocol flouted at the new President's swearing in function.

A new President was always sworn in at Rashtrapati Bhavan but this time the venue was changed to the Parliament House. This was possibly done to cater for a larger audience. The out-going President never attended the swearing in of his successor. On this occasion the outgoing President was present and he changed chairs with the incoming President after the latter was administered the oath. As for protocol this was breached for petty political considerations. Selected dignitaries on whose party's support the ruling party was dependent, were seated ignoring protocol as laid down in the Table of Precedence. The three CPM-CPI leaders, Yachuri, Karat and Raja were seated in the front row. Two Chief Ministers, Mayawati and Karunanidhi were also in the front row and other Chief Ministers three or four rows behind. These two Chief Ministers sat in row ahead of their Governors. Seating arrangements may be a trivial issue and violating laid down protocol, may not be of much consequence but the violations betrayed an unfortunate mindset. Values were being given a go by for political expediency detracting from the solemnity of the occasion. Our democracy has not only got vitiated by dynasticism but also the line dividing the Party and the Govenment in a parliamentary democracy has been erased. Government funds are utilised for putting out advertisement extolling the achievements of not only Prime Minister, Ministers but also the Party President. The latter presides at Government functions and inaugurates Government projects. I felt sad reflecting on how values have changed in our democratic polity from the Nehruvian era.

35

A few months before my five year tenure as Governor was to expire, speculation started in the Press about my continuance. There were also reports about my likely successor. I heard rumours of Mufti trying for Wajahat Habibulla to succeed me. Being a retired IAS officer from J&K cadre he knew the State well. I had known his father Maj Gen Habibulla who was many years my senior in the

Army. It appears that the motive behind Mufti pitching for Wajahat was to have someone other than the Governor to take over as Chairman of Shri Mata Vaishno Devi Board and of Shri Amarnath Shrine Board. According to the provisions of the Acts under which these Boards were constituted, in case a non-Hindu was governor, an eminent Hindu would be appointed as Chairman of these Boards. Perhaps he felt that delinking these Boards from the Governor would weaken them. Mufti and the communal elements were not well disposed towards the Boards. Besides Wajahat, there were also some other names being floated as my successor. So far as I was concerned, I was looking forward to retirement after eleven continuous years as governor in two most sensitive States of the country. I had my house in Delhi dehired in January for renovation so that it would be ready for us to live when I retired in June. A senior Press correspondent of Jammu sought an interview with me. He inquired if I was wanting to continue in office. I was very categorical in my reply. I told him that I neither wanted to continue after my term nor would I accept another term, even if that was offered to me. I was well past eighty and I looked forward to a retired life, free of any official responsibility. I would like to spend the remaining years of my life reading, writing and playing golf. This was widely reported in the Press. This put at rest, for the time being, speculations about my continuing after my term expired.

In April 2008 Ghulam Nabi Azad spoke to me about my continuing in office. He told me that he would be happy if I stayed on for another term. I expressed the same views as I had done earlier, replying to the Press correspondent in Jammu. Azad then said that I should at least agree to continue for about four months to see through the Assembly elections in the State due in October 2008. I told him that I would have no objection in doing so for that short period. Professor Saifuddin Soz, the newly appointed President of the State Congress Party also came to see me. I had known him for some time and I had good personal relations with him. He told me that his party would be happy if I agreed to continue in my office at least till the forthcoming Assembly elections. I gave him the same reply as I had given to Azad.

As June approached when my term was to expire there was again much speculation in the Press about me and my possible successor. It was reported that whereas Azad wanted me to continue, Mufti and his party were very keen that I should depart soon. My relations with Mufti had not been too good but I must say to his credit that he had never said anything in public against me nor did I ever do so about him. His henchmen were of course always critical of me, often in an unbecoming manner. Functions in Raj Bhavan would be boycotted by PDP ministers except for Muzaffar Hussain Beg who would occasionally turn up. PDP ministers would boycott functions at Raj Bhavan even when they were held during the visit of the President and the Prime Minister.

My last month as Governor of J&K was full of high hope followed by much despair. The period between 25 May and 25 June saw the high tide and also an all time low tide. In fact, in the first fortnight up to 11 June, the date on which, the name of Vohra as my successor, was announced, happened to be the high watermark of my efforts to promote *Kashmiriyat* followed by the last fortnight of rapid descent to gloom trying to undo all the efforts of my past five years.

I have already mentioned that as part of my drive for promoting *Kashmiriyat* I had put up a Centre of Kashmir Studies in Kashmir University. We had organized successful international seminars on *Kashmiriyat* and Kashmir and Central Asia at the University. Scholars from Pakistan and Central Asian countries had participated in these seminars.

I met Madanjeet Singh, the UN Goodwill Ambassador based in France. He hailed from near Muzaffrabad, now in Pakistan Occupied Kashmir. In October 1947, he was in Srinagar when Pakistan had launched its first invasion of Kashmir and had captured Baramulla. I mentioned to him my experience of those days when I had seen *Kashmiriyat* in action at Srinagar though the then popular slogan of *Hamlewar Khubardar, Ham Kashmiri Hindu Muslim Sikh Tayar*. He narrated his experience of those days. He recalled that there was a labourer named Aasi. He sang songs in the streets and that had maintained the morale of the people. That was another aspect of *Kashmiriyat* in action which he had seen. A well read and scholarly person, Madanjeet caught the eye of Jawahalal Nehru soon after. He was taken into the Foreign Service. After a long career as a diplomat he became a UN Goodwill Ambassador. He settled in France and founded the South Asia Foundation. He had been very active in promoting social causes like women's education and empowerment, legal and Human Rights Institute and so on, in different countries of South Asia. He had given financial assistance for women's education to Kashmir University. He was appreciative of our efforts to promote *Kashmiriyat* through the Centre of Kashmir Studies. He suggested that this Centre should expand its field of activity to cover all South Asian countries and promised to give a grant of 4 crores to us from his South Asia Foundation. The offer was tempting and I readily agreed to his suggestion. We signed a memorandum of understanding between Kashmir University and South Asian Fondation. Our centre was redesignated as an institute and registered as an autonomous society within Kashmir University.

The Institute was set up to promote regional cooperation based on Bhakti-Sufi-Rishi-Culture embodied in *Kashmiriyat* in a broader historical and worldwide context. It was meant to provide a platform for scholars in the field of Kashmir studies and give an impetus to pluralistic culture and tolerant societies. Scholars from all the eight South Asia Countries were to be provided facilities for studies at the Institute.

I invited the President to inaugurate the Institute. She graciously accepted my invitation. The inaugural function was held in the auditorium of Kashmir University which has a capacity of 2500. The auditorium was filled to capacity with the audience overflowing to the verandahs on the sides. I was very encouraged by the response of the youth. We had delegates from all the eight South Asian countries. Sri Lanka was represented by Chandrika Kumartunga Bandarnaike, former President and Prime Minster, Afghanistan by Dr Ghaznaffar a senior Cabinet Minister, Pakistan by Begum Salima Hashmi, daughter of the legendary Urdu poet Faiz Ahmed Faiz, Mani Shankar Aiyar Union Cabinet Minister led the Indian delegation. Nepal, Bhutan, Bangladesh and Maldives also sent delegations led by eminent people of their countries. Never before had such a high level international gathering been held in the Valley. Messages of goodwill were read from the Prime Minister and Director General UNESCO. The Prime Minister stated "The initiative to resuscitate the age old traditions of Kashmir and to establish an institution which would serve as a melting pot of ideas and learning involving young people and others not only from the State and other parts of the country but also from the neighbouring countries of the Indian subcontinent is timely. I hope the Institute contributes to strengthening the composite culture of the State". Director General UNESCO in his message said, "This institute will undoubtedly make a unique contribution to the promotion of research and education in the region. UNESCO looks forward to cooperating with the institute in the framework of its various activities devoted to heritage based development in Kashmir, particularly in the wake of the devastating earthquake of October 2005. I hope that the new institute of Kashmir studies will help to reinforce the role of culture and education in ensuring a sustainable future for all peoples of the region".

In her inaugural address the President said, "The message of love, tolerance and compassion has left a deep impact on the lives of the people of Jammu and Kashmir. Their legacy over a period of time has etched itself so much into the collective consciousness of the region, that it cannot be eroded. *Kashmiriyat* is a living legacy which has withstood the test of time and it is now for us to continue it so that it is preserved for future generations". She added, "the institute will provide a platform for scholars in the field of Kashmir studies on pluralistic cultures and tolerant societies".

In my address at the function I reiterated that *Kashmiriyat* stood for amity and brotherhood among mankind cutting across religious divide. The teachings of Sheikh Noorudin also known as Nund Rishi and Laleshwar revered as Lal Ded, gave us the message of love and tolerance. I emphasized that it is in the fitness of things that our Institute will endeavour to spread that message to all countries of South Asia. The city of Srinagar was founded by Emperor Ashoka, the Prince of Peace in 3rd century BC and it was from this city that Bud Shah the great popular and liberal King had ruled Kashmir in the medieval period. I recalled how I had seen *Kashmiriyat* in action in Srinagar in October 1947 at the time of the Partition holocaust. Mahatma Gandhi had said then that he saw a ray of light in Kashmir.

That evening I hosted a banquet in honour of the President and other dignitaries who had come for the inaugural function. I invited the leaders and ministers of PDP and as was their wont, they boycotted both the function and the banquet. Perhaps promoting *Kashmiriyat* was opposed to their agenda.

The separatists had been wanting UN intervention to settle the Kashmir issue. In my own way and through the support of UNESCO, I had tried to bring UN into Kashmir, to promote peace through culture. This must have been very irksome to them. They tried to criticise the inaugural function by saying that people had been coerced to attend it to provide a large audience. Of course they couldn't say that about the VVIP, who had come from foreign countries. They picked on one sentence in the Institute's Vision document, Kashmir is an integral part of the cultural mosaic of Indian civilisation. This made their hackles, rise. They said that it sounded like Indian claim that Kashmir is an integral part of India. We ignored their outbursts which we felt were a result of frustration at the success of the Institute's inaugural function.

The following day we had a Sufi pop music show performed by the Junoon Band from Pakistan. The United Jihad Council in

Pakistan asked the Pakistan Government not to allow the band to go to Kashmir. The terrorists held out death threats to the members of the Band and the separatists called for a boycott of the musical function organized by us. They accused us of subverting the Islamic culture of Kashmir. Yet a crowd of several thousands assembled at Dal Lake to hear the Sufi pop music. Salman Ali the leader of Junoon Band in his opening remarks said that he had come to Srinagar to launch a musical Jihad for peace. Pakistan's leading English daily, *Dawn*, in its 28 May issue wrote a very positive editorial under the heading 'Breaking Barriers'. It wrote "music knew no boundaries... the people of Kashmir expressed their anger against religious militants and their violence".

The inaugural function of Institute of Kashmir Studies and the Sufi pop music show enthralling thousands of youth, rattled the separatists and fundamentalists. This time they did not issue Fatwa as they had done against the army when I inaugurated the renovated Ziarat at Badgam or against Azad, when he had organized an essay competition for school children on Mahatma Gandhi. They felt that they were losing credibility and following among the people as a result of our efforts to promote *Kashmiriyat*. They chose a non-issue of diversion of land at Baltal to Amarnath Shrine Board. Government orders sanctioning this diversion was issued at the same time as the inaugural function of the Institute of Kashmir Studies and the Junoon Band show. They tried to whip up communal passions on total falsehood. It took some time for their movement to gain momentum. Unfortunately, for want of a Director, the State Information Department was non-functional. While the communal and separatist propoganda was blowing full blast, no attempt was made by the State to expose their chicanery.

Another positive development in the fortnight ending 11 June was the progress made by us in setting up Shardapeeth University. We had identified land in Srinagar, which we were to buy from a Temple Trust. We had managed 20 crores to start the University. An ordinance was drafted and sent to the Chief Minister on the same lines as Shri Mata Vaishno Devi University, Baba Ghulam Shah University and Islamic University. The State had given land free to the latter two Universities. I had tried to help in the setting up of the Islamic University at Anantnag. I got the army to level its grounds, do landscaping and construct a prefabricated building as a gesture of goodwill. I had visited this University and had a good interaction session with the students. I found that very satisfying. I also gave a handsome amount from my discretionary grant for the

University library. The Government had also given land at Badgam free, for the TransWorld Islamic University. Not only Azad was supportive of the Shardapeeth University project but also Farooq Abdullah, with whom I had discussed the proposal. He appreciated the sentimental attachment of Kashmiri Pandits to Shardapeeth. He agreed that setting up of the university could be a first step towards their return to the Valley and their eventual rehabilitation. He added that their Kashmir Muslim neighbours would love to have them back. He was happy that we had catered for reserving 40 percent seats for Kashmiri Pandits and 10 percent for Kashmiri Muslims at Shardapeeth University. He was so enthusiastic about the project that he offered to get us land on the low mountains overlooking Dal Lake in Ganderbal for the University. I was much encouraged by his response. I had the draft ordinance for Shardapeeth University sent to the Chief Minister. This was reported in the Press. Some people wrote that Shardapeeth University Act should be brought through a Bill in the Assembly rather them an ordinance. They did not know that both Baba Ghulam Shah University at Rajouri and Islamic University at Anantnag had been established on the basis of ordinance. They criticised my sending a draft ordinance to the Chief Minister as unconstitutional as I was the approving authority for an ordinance. They failed to realize that I had sent the draft ordinance in my capacity as Chairman of Shri Amarnath Shrine Board and not as Governor of the State. I did not attach much importance to these quibbling objections of people with a communal bias.

Yet another positive development of early June 2008 was the successful holding of Samrat Ashok Golf Tournament at Srinagar. This was the third such tournament that I had started a couple of years earlier. Fifty golfers with their families had come from Patna, the ancient city of Pataliputra, which was Ashoka's capital, to underscore Srinagar's connection with Patna. We held a banquet cum prize distribution function at Raj Bhavan on 7 June. Both Ghulam Nabi Azad and Farooq Abdullah spoke at the prize distribution. They were overgenerous in their praise for me and what I had been able to achieve in Kashmir. Farooq Abdullah among other things also made a special appreciative reference of my work for the Amarnath Yatra. One of the local newspapers reported that the speeches of Azad and Farooq Abdullah were not as appropriate for a prize distribution function as it would have been at a farewell function in my honour. The veteran Congress leader and former Speaker of Lok Sabha, currently Governor of Gujrat, Balram Jakhar was on a visit to Srinagar. I invited him for the function. In his address he said that he had never in his long political career seen such cordial relations and bonhomie between a Chief Minister, the top leader of the Opposition and a Governor.

I now come to the last fortnight of my tenure in Kashmir from 11 June to 25 June when things started changing rapidly and going steeply downhill. I was reminded of a saying of a British Prime Minister, Harold Macmillan that a week is too long in politics. I found that a fortnight was much much longer.

The name of Vohra was announced in Delhi as my successor on 11 June. It took Azad by surprise. The newspapers had been reporting that Azad was trying to have my stay in Kashmir extended while Mufti was wanting an immediate replacement for me, after my five year tenure expired on 3 June. On 12 June all the newspapers carried the announcement of Vohra's appointment on their front page. The banner headlines in some newspapers said it all. The headline in one paper was Mufti wins Azad loses. Another paper's headline was PDP inflated Congress deflated.

I got to know about the appointment of my successor on the 11th evening. I was not bothered because I was looking forward to my retirement. I only wanted a fortnight to pack up and leave. I was happy that such a distinguished civil servant having long association with Kashmir would be succeeding me. However, I was sorry that the Congress high command had again undermined the position of its own party chief minister. The following day I proceeded to Riasi where the army had organized a big function for me to inaugurate the Pirpanjal Hostel put up by them for Gujjar and Bakkarwal children. I was very happy to see that in a remote area like Riasi, the Army had put up such an excellent hostel with all modern facilities. I addressed a large audience which included many senior Gujjar and Bakkarwal citizens. I said that I wished I had been seventy years younger. I would have preferred to join the Pirpanjal Hostel to any other hostel in the world. We live in an age of instant communication. Everyone present at the function knew that I would be leaving Kashmir very shortly and the name of my successor had been announced. I told the gathering that I had special feelings for the brave and patriotic Gujjar and Bakkarwal communities amongst whom I had lived on the mountains for many years, during my young days as an army officer. As Governor I had kept their welfare and development on my top agenda. I was glad that one of my last functions as governor of the State was with them. Some Gujjars and Bakkarwals who spoke at the function expressed very warm sentiments towards me. They said that with my departure they had a feeling of being orphaned. The inaugural function of the hostel had virtually become a farewell function for me.

I tried to speak to Vohra from Riasi to congratulate him on being appointed Governor. I could not get through to him from Riasi. I proceeded to Jammu for an overnight stay as scheduled, before returning to Srinagar. I managed to get through on the telephone to Vohra from Jammu that evening. He seemed to be in a hurry to come and take over. Possibly he was under pressure to do so. It was not difficult to guess from where the pressure could have come. He had been a Secretary when Mufti was Union Home Minister in 1990. I told Vohra that I would take a minimum of one week to pack all my things and leave. He did not appear too happy but reluctantly agreed. It appeared that he wanted me to leave even earlier. On return to Srinagar on 13 morning I told my wife that we would be leaving in a week's time. Amarnath Yatra was commencing on 18 June. That will allow me to inaugurate the Yatra before we left on 19 or 20 June. My wife threw up her hands saying that it was not possible for her to complete all the packing of our household goods spread at two places in Jammu and Srinagar. We had collected a whole lot of stuff over the last many years which had to be sorted out. We had decided to settle down in a small flat at Vasant Kunj in Delhi, where it would be difficult to accommodate all our things. Our second daughter, Minnie, living in the United States had rung up to say that she would come in a day or two to help us pack our things. I appreciated my wife's difficulties and decided to stay a week longer. Accordingly, I wrote to both Vohra and the Union Home Minister as also informed the Chief Minister on 13 June to say that I shall be relinquishing my appointment on 25 June. This was nothing unusual. Normally, ten to fifteen days is allowed to outgoing governors to pack up and depart. I took nearly three weeks to come to Kashmir and take over as Governor after my appointment had been announced. My predecessor had taken ten days to do so. Other governors in different States had taken longer. Yet Mufti and his party with the Press under their influence tried to make much of the so called inordinate delay in my departure and Vohra taking over. Their motive was quite clear to me. They wanted to withdraw support from the government and realized that if that happened, Governor's rule would have to be imposed. For obvious reasons, they did not want me in office when Governor's rule was imposed.

For the next week to ten days all sorts of rumours and

allegations were appearing in the Press. It was being said that I was trying to stay on till the end of Amarnath Yatra in the latter half of August and had intentions of staying on longer till the Assembly elections. It was also being said that I was desperately trying to get orders reversed and get another term for myself. I got my staff to issue a statement that I was departing on 25 June after my packing was completed. What took the cake was a statement of Qarra, the Finance Minister that his department would not pay for two governors and he would stop grants to Raj Bhavan. This not only showed the PDP's animosity towards me but Qarra's ignorance and lack of decency. There was no question of there being two governors. A governor assumes office only after he has been administered the oath. So Vohra could take over as governor only after being sworn in. I treated Qarra's statement with the contempt it deserved, and we did not even bother to contradict it.

It was normal for the PDP to make baseless allegations against Amarnath Shrine Board every year on the eve of the Yatra and during the Yatra. They were at their usual game again in 2008. This time, they also took up the issue of land diversion order at Baltal to Amarnath Shrine Board which had been approved at the instance of their Ministers. The PDP game plan was to arouse communal passions by totally misleading the people. Possibly, they chose to do so because of their fear of losing their credibility and following due to the mounting popular opposition to land diversion at Baltal. It gave them the populist cause that they were looking for to quit the government on the eve of elections. The separatists had been badly shaken by the overwhelming response to Junoon Band function despite their boycott call. They not only opposed the diversion of land to Amarnath Shrine Baord but also spread a baseless and ridiculous canard that the Shrine Board was putting up a Hindu township called Amarnath Nagar at Baltal, with a view to changing the demography of Kashmir. Can there be anything more absurd? The Baltal land is unapproachable and uninhabitable for nearly eight months in a year. Kashmiri Pandits have not been able to go back to their homes in the Valley. How can any pilgrim ever think of settling in a Amarnath Nagar at Baltal ? Thirty thousand Hindu and Sikh refugees came from West Pakistan in 1947 and settled in Jammu. Their number has now gone up to over 1 lakh. Whereas other such refugees who came from Pakistan in 1947 to other States in India, got full citizenship rights, two of them becoming Prime Minister and one Deputy Prime Minister, the refugees who came to Jammu have not yet been given full citizenship rights. They cannot vote in elections, they cannot get State Govt jobs, they cannot acquire land and their children cannot get admission in technical institutions of higher learning in the State. Given these facts there was no possibility whatsoever of any State government allowing a Hindu township to come up in the Valley, changing its demographic contour. The only time the State Government had made an exception was in 1950 when a few hundred Tibetan Muslim refugees had come to the Valley in the wake of Chinese Communist occupation of their homeland. Today, the descendents of these erstwhile refugees are enjoying full citizenship rights in the Valley — 570 of them are in the voters list in Zadribal and 160 in Idgah constituencies of Srinagar. No Government of Kashmir would ever allow Hindu pilgrims coming to establish township in the Valley.

Let us now examine what exactly was the implication of diversion of 100 acres of land to the Amarnath Shrine Board. Diversion of Forest land to various departments or even private companies has been a routine affair in the State. Thousands of acres of forest land had been so diverted to different agencies — to Reliance and Airtel for putting up communication towers, to PWD and Border roads for construction of roads, to Power Corporation for hydel projects, to education department for university campus and so on When the State Cabinet unanimously approved diversion of forest land to Amarnath Shrine Board, five other such diversion to other agencies were approved. There was no basis for picking on the diversion of land to Amarnath Shrine Board to launch an agitation. Maybe the objection was to the fact that the Shrine Board was a religious institution. Even that argument was not tenable. The State Government had transferred several hundred acres of forest land to Shri Mata Vaishno Devi Shrine Board at Katra in Jammu province and no objection had been raised by anyone. Katra and Baltal were both in the same State and there could not be different set of rules for them.

Much hue and cry was raised regarding damage to ecology due to Amarnath Yatra. Facts were ignored. Not a single tree was cut, no wild life was disturbed nor any permanent accommodation put up by the Shrine Board. The Board had been taking all possible measures to prevent pollution. The Mughal Road under constructions from Poonch to Shopayan in the Valley had led to the cutting of 10,000 trees, shifting of a 25 km long wild life sanctuary and construction of several permanent buildings. Once the highway would get completed, thousands of vehicles would ply every year, polluting the atmosphere with carbon emissions. Yet the Amarnath

Yatra was being targeted for degrading the ecology and environment and a Nelson's eye was turned towards the Mughal road.

There was another point which needs to be stressed. The 100 acre plot of land diverted to the Shrine Board was not to be used for any purpose other than for temporary pre-fabricated shelters for pilgrims going to Amarnath. Perhaps the only occasion when that land was used for another purpose was in September/October 1948 when the army had set up a tactical headquarter to conduct operations. We had used tanks to break through Zojila held by the enemy. This had set a world record for using tanks at that high altitude. At that time, I had stayed in the Tactical Headquaters at Baltal for a couple of days.

It also needed to be brought out that the Government order sanctioning the diversion of the land to the Shrine Board dated 26 May 2008 had laid down that "The proprietary status of forest land shall remain unchanged. The forest land so diverted shall be used only for the purpose for which it has been diverted. It shall not be transferred to any other agency without approval of the forest department". It also stipulated that the land would be used "for prefabricated structures only for camping purpose of pilgrims without going in for construction of permanent structure" and "the forest land so diverted shall return to the forest department free of any encumbrances when it is no longer required by the User Agency". For this diversion of land the Board was required to pay Rs 2.51 crores.

Communal and anti-national elements launched a most vitriolic propaganda arousing communal passions against the diversion of land to the Shrine Board, based on total falsehood. The terms of the diversion of land were suppressed and the totally baseless canard of Hindu Amarnath township to change the demography of the Valley was spread. No attempt was made by the Government or any political party to put facts connected with diversion of Baltal land in their correct perspective. The Goebbelsian technique of constantly repeating the Big Lie and suppress the truth was followed most vigorously. Goebbels had said that this can make the people believe that Hell is Heaven and Heaven is Hell. This was proved true. The communal elements lambasted me for the decision to divert the Baltal land. This case had been processed by two PDP Ministers Mohd Afzal, the Forest Minister and Muzaffar Hussain Beg the Law Minister, for nearly three years. After obtaining clearance from all concerned the Cabinet unanimously approved the diversion of Baltal land to the Shrine Board at its meeting on 20 May, 2008. For a week or so thereafter when objection to this diversion started being raised, Mohd Afzal tried to justify the Government decision. Mufti and his daughter put up the plea that they were not aware that the PDP ministers had been a party to that decision. Even if one accepts their plea, they had to answer why, when they got to know of it, they did not ask their ministers concerned to resign. In early 2006 Mufti had got peeved because of Muzaffar Beg praising Azad at public meetings and had forced him to quit the Cabinet. The fact is that as anticipated by many long back, the PDP was working to its plan of continuing in office till as late as possible to enjoy the fruits of office before finding an excuse to quit on the eve of elections. With elections approaching and the Baltal agitation gaining momentum, Mufti struck. So far as I was concerned, my only connection with the Baltal land issue was that I had asked the Board to request for the land in 2005 for valid reasons. Erecting and dismantling prefabricated shelters caused much damage. I wanted the shelters to remain in situ so that for two months it could be used for Yatra and for two months by Tourist Department for tourists and for winter sports. The remaining eight months the land remains unusable. The State Government examined this request for three years and then took a decision. I was in no way connected with that decision or their decision making process.

I visited the Baltal Base Camp on 17 June. The agitation was building up but had not yet assumed serious proportions. The local MLA of National Conference a much respected person, Mian Altaf, went round the camp with me. He was very satisfied with the arrangements at Baltal and even issued a statement that the Yatra should not be communalised or politicised. About the same time Arun the Chief Executive Officer, took Rafeeq Mir the PDP MLC to the other Base Camp of the Yatra at Pahalgan. He is the local leader of that area. He too was satisfied with the Yatra arrangements. Of course the local media blacked out the visits of Main Altaf and Rafeeq Mir to Baltal and Pahalgam. It came out with the story that permanent helipads had been constructed by Baltal by the Shrine Board without prior government approval. Ghulam Hasan Mir, the Tourism Minister in Mufti's Cabinet who had broken with Mufti's party, issued a statement on his own clarifying what had happened. He stated that the helipad had been constructed by the State Government as approved by Mufti and he as Tourism Minister had inaugurated it.

On 19 June I inaugurated the Sufi Music festival which I used to do every year at the commencement of the Yatra. This year international participation was more than in previous years. We had artists from Pakistan, Egypt, Syria and Uzbekistan besides our own artists participating in the function. The following day I proceeded to Jammu for three days to pack up my baggage at the Raj Bhavan there. Many individuals and institutions were keen to give me a farewell. I could not accept all the invitations I tried to keep them to the minimum. The Army Commander was keen that I visit Udhampur for a farewell from Northern Command. I requested him to excuse me because I just did not have the time to go to Udhampur. I told him that he had organized a grand function for the inauguration of Pirpanjal Hostel for Gujjar Bakkarwal children. That had virtually become a farewell function from Northern Command for me. Jammu was now part of Western Command and the Western Army Commander had come all the way from Chandi Mandir to give me a farewell. I was a founder member of Western Command having joined it on the day it was raised in September 1947. I was perhaps the only living officer who had joined the headquarters on its raising day. Thirty four years later I was Army Commander of Western Command. The present Army Commander was a brother Gorkha Officer with whom I had served in Kashmir, He had commanded the Division I had commanded earlier. He also commanded a Corps in the State, when I was the Governor. They gave me a touching farewell. My other engagement with the Army was a farewell from my battalion, 3/5 Gorkha Rifles, with which I had been associated for over half a century. I had commanded that Battalion for three years including two winters in Ladakh. The battalion gave me a most touching and overwhelming emotional and traditional Army farewell. They presented me a trophy inscribed to "our legendary icon". On the civil side I accepted three functions. A public reception from the Mayor of Jammu with ministers and leading dignitaries of the town attending the function. I also accepted a public farewell from Dogra Sabha and a combined farewell from the three Vice Chancellors of universities around Jammu. Professor Bhim Singh declared at the Dogra Sabha that I would remain the patron-in-chief of the Sabha for life. They instituted a new award called Dogra Ratna. I was the first person to be conferred this award. On return to Srinagar on 23 June I found the situation worsening with agitationists taking to the streets. I declined all invitations for farewell in Srinagar except the formal farewell hosted by the Chief Minster at his residence. All ministers other than the PDP ministers attended this function. The latter as usual were boycotting functions connected with me. Political leaders, judges and senior civil and army officers were present and so was Dr Karan Singh who was on a visit to Srinagar. As usual, Ghulam Nabi Azad and his talented wife Shameem Azad were most gracious and affectionate towards us. Azad in his speech said a lot of nice things about me and so did Justice Kakru the Acting Chief Justice and AR Rather, the Leader of the Opposition. Dr Karan Singh and senior civil and army officers also spoke at the function. Ghulam Nabi Azad sent a charming farewell letter to me on the eve of my departure. He wrote, "As your Excellancy has completed your assignment as the Governer of Jammu and Kashmir and are planing to leave the State on the 25th June 2008, I look back with great satisfaction at the very close, cordial and always inspirational association with you since I took over as the Chief Minister of the State. You have served the State with distinction for five years and your contribution to the development of Jammu and Kashmir would to long remembered by the people here. Personally for me it has been a pleasure working for you. Your intellect, articulation and concern for the public have impressed me a lot"

As the day for my departure was approaching a number of leading people from different walks of life came to Raj Bhavan to bid me farewell. On my last day as governor the police had to open fire against agitators in which one person was killed. The totally unnecessary agitation launched by communal and anti-national elements along with some unscrupulous politicians was becoming like what had happened in the Valley when the holy relic had been stolen from Hazratbal in 1963. I could not help but feel that it was due to a grave failure of information management on our part. Had the Government officially and politically taken up cudgels to rebut all the totally false and vicious propaganda in time, the people would not have been so misled and the voice of the silent majority would not have been suppressed. The communalists also now targeted the Shardapeeth University, calling it a Hindu cultural invasion of the Valley. Their communal mindset was betrayed when they did not raise any objection to two Islamic Universities and ignored the fact that Shardapeeth University was to be a technical University with 40 percent seats reserved for Kashmiri Pandits and 10 percent for Kashmiri Muslims. It was meant to be the first step towards the return of Kashmiri Pandits to the Valley and their rehabilitation in their homes. Of course communal elements which had been responsible for the eviction of Kashmiri Pandits from the Valley could not be happy about the prospect of their return. The Shardapeeth University project got shelved.

The State Government did not have an effective Director of Information. The officer chosen for this appointment, who had been a good PR man, had not joined his post for the last few months due to some bureaucratic hassles about whether his appointment could be Director General or Director. The information department had remained totally silent while the agitation against diversion of land at Baltal was building up. No political leader took any step to politically counter the agitation. Congress had stalwarts like Azad and Wakil, the senior vice-president of the State Congress. The latter is a staunchly nationalist leader who was known for his bold and fearless stand. Azad had personal family problem at that time with his wife suffering a serious ailment requiring treatment and surgery in Mumbai. The guns were heavily loaded against national and liberal forces in the Valley.

On the morning of 25 June my Raj Bhavan staff led by Arun, my two ADCs Sumit and Sanjay, my Deputy Secretary Sunita Anand, my Director Public Relations Madan Mantoo, my Private Secretary Rajnath, the household Manager Harjeet and many others including the waiters and peons overwhelmed me by their affectionate farewell. We had all been like one extended family living together happily for five years. Parting with them was a sweet sorrow.

At the airport I was given a formal guard of honour by J&K police. The Chief Minister, ministers, senior civil and military officers were all present. Both the senior army officer Lt General Mukesh Sabharwal and the DG Police Kuldip Khoda were very warm towards me at the farewell. Kuldeep had been doing excellent work and I had become fond of him. As a policeman by birth and soldier by profession, I was delighted at the army -police cooperation that I had been able to promote. Azad told me that he was holding a Press conference that afternoon, when he would clarify matters and point out that there was no legitimate basis whatsoever for the Baltal land agitation. He was confident that he would be able to turn round the situation. I found his confidence reassuring.

As I got into my aircraft to depart from Srinagar in the forenoon of June 25, I could not help but have grave forebodings. Dark clouds had gathered over the Valley and a cloudburst could take place any moment. Although Azad's confidence had reassured me, I had a nagging feeling that it may now be too late for him to turn the tide. I was now ending my intimate association with the State going back to over sixty years, with the last five years as the Head of the State. It had been a long story of success and failure, happiness and distress and of hope and despair, but throughout that long journey one thing had remained constant. That was my faith in the people of the State and their future. They have had a great past and despite all the trials and tribulations of the present, a glorious future awaits them as the crown of an emerging world power. Although I may no longer be actively associated with the people of the State, my thoughts and prayers will always be with them.

4 AMARNATH CONTROVERSY AND AFTER

1

During the flight from Srinagar to Delhi, I remained deeply immersed in my thoughts. My prime concern was whether Azad would be able to turn round the situation with his Press Conference that afternoon. For the last two weeks the Information Department of the State Government and nationalist leaders had been maintaining a total silence. For want of a nail a kingdom was lost. Would that get repeated in Kashmir? Would the Valley be lost for want of information management? I still had faith in *Kashmiriyat* and the wisdom of the people of Kashmir. The communal and anti-national forces spreading totally false and venomous propaganda continued to have a field day. Their agitation had been fueled by the PDP in a rare act of duplicity. Having been in the Government and their ministers having been the prime actors in sanctioning diversion of land at Baltal, they jumped on to the bandwagon of the agitation against the land transfer. The local Press in the Valley went whole hog to support the communal and anti-national forces. This communal movement based on total falsehood found sympathetic echo in the "secular" media at the national level. However, there were some who felt that even if there had been no diversion of land at Baltal, the communal and anti-national elements would have picked up some other excuse to generate a communal tornado on the eve of the approaching elections to the State Assembly. With sharply deteriorating situation one felt that the communalists had succeeded in Talibanising the Valley.

My thought also travelled to my personal problems. I wondered whether I had taken the right decision to settle in Delhi and not in my home at Patna. Our huge ancestral house built by my grandfather adjacent to Danapur Cantonment in Patna, had a few acres of compound with orchards. It was lying vacant with no one to live there. As a child, I had grown up in that house. I had fond memories of my happy days there. My wife had spent many years in that house when I used to be posted in non-family stations during my Army career. Both of us felt that our home in Danapur would be an ideal place to lead a retired life. With the army close by and with its medical and canteen facilities available to me, we would have been well off living in Danapur. However, there were other considerations which had to be taken into account. All my old friends and old relatives in Patna had passed away, one by one. This would make me lonely if not a stranger in my own home town. Most of my immediate relations had settled in Vasant Kunj in Delhi, where I had also bought a flat. My sister, two brothers, a nephew and a niece were living in Vasant Kunj with all except one, within walking distance from my house. Our children were abroad who found Delhi a more convenient place to visit than Patna. Our son would come to Delhi on posting to his ministry. Apart from the family support that I would have in Delhi, there were also other considerations. There would be much better medical facility, both civil and military, available to us in Delhi. There would also be more scope for me to pursue intellectual activities in Delhi. The decision to settle in Delhi had much to commend itself. Yet my urge to go back to my home in Patna was strong. Emotion had to give way to reason. I could console myself by saying that though we would be living in Delhi, we could frequently visit Patna.

In the seventies, when I was the Adjutant General of the Army, I had started the Army Welfare Housing Organisation for the Army. Our first housing colony was Som Vihar in Ramkrishnapuram, at a prime location in South Delhi. Over four hundred, three bed-room flats were built for serving and retired officers in that colony. I could easily have taken a flat for myself at a concessional price. At that time I had all my friends and relatives living in Patna. I had also built a fairly large house of my own in Patna. Despite my wife being keen that I buy a flat in Delhi, I decided not to do so. I felt that I should not waste my limited funds over a flat in Delhi. In thirty years, conditions had changed drastically. In the changed circumstances I had sold my house in Patna and bought a small flat in Vasant Kunj. For the flat that I now bought, I had to spend forty times more than what I would have spent thirty years earlier for a bigger and a better located flat in Som Vihar. I have always been bad at financial management. I had rented out my flat in Delhi while I was Governor. As my term as Governor was getting over, I had my flat dehired in January 2008. We worked out an ambitions and expensive plan for renovating the flat to make it comfortable for us. We hired an architect and a contractor. My niece, Nilima, undertook to supervise the renovation of the flat. She is knowledgeable and experienced in such work. She had a lot of ideas and made an excellent job of renovating the flat. However, as it often happens, the contractor could not stick to the time schedule. The renovation work was supposed to have been completed in six months by June 2008 when we were due to move out from Jammu and Kashmir. We found that two more months were required to complete the work. Luckily, I had no accommodation problem and the delay of two months would not matter much. My brother, Pranu had his own flat in Delhi which would be vacant as he was to go on one month's leave to his children abroad. He also had a guest house very close to our flat. The guest house was lying vacant. He offered these to us. We initially stayed in his flat for nearly a month and then moved to his guest house for close supervision of the work in our flat, in its final stages.

Engrossed in my thoughts about Kashmir and my personal problems of settling in Delhi, I dozed off to sleep in the aircraft. My wife woke me up as our plane approached Delhi. Both of us were looking forward to the change that was to come in our lives. From *Khas Admi* (VIP) we would now be *Aam Admi* (common person). We would no longer be shackled to protocol and security requirements. We could now roam around freely, going out shopping or to restaurants. We looked forward to a life of freedom.

Our second daughter Minnie had flown in from the USA, within two days of the announcement of the name of my successor. She came to Srinagar and took on the complete burden of packing all our personal belongings spread over in the two Raj Bhavans, at Srinagar and Jammu. Minnie did a tremendous job in packing our belongings. She also disposed off quite a few things. A whole lot of mementos was sent for display in the museum named after me at my Regimental Centre in Shillong. We hardly had anything to do with all the packing as Minnie took care of everything. She accompanied us to Delhi and after some initial unpacking she had to go back to the USA for her commitments there. Luckily, she had to come back to India after a month on an assignment from her university. Our eldest daughter Meena along with her daughter Anjali, came to look after us and to settle us in our new house. They stayed with us for nearly a month and took care of the completion of renovation work in the flat. Meena bought all the furniture and furnishings. She was of immense help. She saw us settled in our new flat. Minnie returned and was with us to ensure that we were fully settled. Thus thanks to our niece, two daughters and granddaughter, we had no problem in making our new three bedroom flat, a very comfortable place to live in. And all this was done for us by our children, without either of us lifting our little finger.

2

The following day after my return to Delhi I paid a courtesy call on Shivraj Patil, the Union Home Minister. As usual, he was very nice and courteous. He told me that he had always valued my advice. I said to myself that if he had really done so, things would have been ever so bad in Kashmir today. Advani asked me to brief the BJP leaders about the situation in Kashmir and the Amarnath controversy. I felt it was my duty to do so. A meeting with some fifty top leaders of the BJP was arranged. I addressed them on the Kashmir situation and the Baltal land controversy. I also praised Ghulam Nabi Azad for his positive role. Some BJP leaders raised their eyebrows. Had the Congress Party invited me to do a similar briefing, I would have been only too glad to respond positively. The situation in Kashmir was worsening and prospects getting very bleak. I expected the Prime Minister or the Home Minister to ask for my views. They did not do so. Antony, the Defence Minister gave an indication to that effect but he did not pursue the matter. I shall presently mention how this happened.

3

Within two days of my return to Delhi, on 27 June 2008, Field Marshal Manekshaw passed away at Wellington in the Nilgiri Hills. I had known Sam, as he was popularly called, for over sixty years. I had first interacted with him in 1946 and thereafter had served under him in various capacities. As a part of what was then called Indianisation, three Indian officers, Lt Col SHFJ Manekshaw, Major Yahya Khan who later became President of Pakistan and I, then in the rank of Captain, were posted to Military Operations Directorate of General Headquarters, redesignated Army Headquarters after Independence. Military Operations Directorate was the crème d' la crème of the Headquarters. Hitherto, it had only British officers. Even the clerks in the directorate were all British. Sam, Yahya and I had been posted to different sections of the directorate but we often met each other. The following year when India became Independent, Sam took over as the Director in the rank of Brigadier. By then I had been promoted to the rank of Major. Within a month of our gaining Independence, a skeleton Command Headquarters was established for restoring law and order in Delhi and Punjab during the Partition holocaust. I was posted as General Staff Officer (Operations) to this newly raised Headquarters. On 26 October 1947, this Headquarters was given the task of conducting operations in Kashmir from the following day. Throughout that over one year long war in Jammu and Kashmir, I was closely interacting with Sam. After the war, Sam and I were part of the Indian delegation that had gone to Karachi. The United Nations Commission for India and Pakistan had convened a conference there, of delegations of both countries for delineating the Cease Fire Line. Sam was a member of the delegation and I was its Secretary. We stayed in Karachi for over a week delineating the 750 kilometer long Cease Fire Line in Jammu and Kashmir. That line was redesignated Line of Control after the 1971 war. I had several other occasions to work under Sam in my Army career. I was an Instructor in the rank of Major when Sam as a Brigadier commanded the School at Mhow, now redesignated Army War College. I worked under him again as an instructor, now in the rank of Lt Col when he as Major General was Commandant of the Staff College in Wellington. Subsequently, he became Army Commander in the East when I commanded a Brigade under him in the North-East. Thereafter, when he became the Army Chief, I served on his staff first as a Brigadier for a while and then as a Major General. When war clouds had gathered in 1971 and it was clear that we would soon be at war with Pakistan, I requested Sam for an active assignment in command of a formation. I told him that when the GSO 1(Lt Col) was going to war with the GSO 2 (Major), the GSO 3 (Capt) should not be left out of battle. I was referring to the pre-partition days when Sam, Yahya and I had served together in Military Operations Directorate. Sam declined my request saying that he needed me more on his staff and he could not spare me. After that war, Sam showed his appreciation for whatever little I had done, by getting me the highest military decoration for distinguished service, the PVSM. On 1 January, 1973 Sam was promoted to the rank of Field Marshal. Fifteen days later, he was to demit the office of Army Chief. I was officiating as Adjutant General at that time and in that capacity, I was the Chief of Personnel of the Army. It fell to me to take up the case of pay, privileges and protocol for him. This was the first time we were having a Field Marshal in our country and there was no past precedent to guide us. I made out a case for Sam on the basis of the practice followed in the UK and other countries in Europe. The USA does not have a Field Marshal. They have a Five Star General instead. The then Defence Minister, Jagjivan Ram, was not too favourably disposed towards Sam, who had been promoted Field Marshal by Indira Gandhi overruling him. The civilian bureaucracy at Delhi as usual was anti-Army in regard to privileges and benefits for Army officers. I had a difficult time getting approval for a Field Marshal's baton for Sam. The bureaucrats considered a few thousand rupees to be spent on a Field Marshal's baton as wasteful expenditure. They argued that a Field Marshal in India could do without one, like the Five Star General in the USA. I quoted examples from history to prove that a baton was a necessary accompaniment for a Field Marshal starting from the time of Frederick the Great of Prussia. I managed to succeed on the baton issue. We had to organize a special investiture ceremony in Rashtrapati Bhavan when the President would present the Baton to Sam. There were protocol hassles raised for the investiture function. The civilian bureaucracy did not want the Field Marshal to have a higher status than the number one civil servant, the cabinet secretary. I worked out a compromise in having a separate seating arrangement for Sam at the function without affecting his relative protocol status with the cabinet secretary, whom in the Army we used to call, the Bara Babu. A Field Marshal never retires and he is entitled to full pay, secretarial staff and other concessions at par with a serving officer throughout his life. Here the civil bureaucracy was miserly and petty. They would not settle on a salary for the Field Marshal. He was given only Rs 400 a month as special pay in addition to the meagre pension of a General.

After retiring from the appointment of Army Chief, in theory, Sam continued to be a serving officer. He settled at Conoor to a busy retired life, refusing any assignment from the Government. He was Director in several companies. While serving in the Army and later as Governor of Assam, and of Jammu and Kashmir, I was often invited to give talks at the Staff College. Whenever I went there, I made it a point to call on Sam, if he was in station. My last meeting with him was a few months before he passed away. Sam was lying terminally ill and was on life support system. He was in the Military Hospital at Wellington and the Army was doing the best that was possible for him. Dr Kalam had visited Sam in Military Hospital a couple of months earlier. On his intervention the Government ultimately took a decision on his salary and gave his arrears of pay as a Field Marshal after 35 long years. This was indeed a poor reflection on the functioning of the Government. The Defence Secretary had gone to Wellington and handed over a cheque of 1.2 crores as arrears to Sam. This had been widely reported in the Press. When I met Sam in the hospital, I realized that it would be our last meeting. Even while on life support system, Sam was fighting his disease valiantly and had all the pep in him. He smiled and cracked jokes. I congratulated him on his getting his arrears. He pulled my leg saying that I had failed to get his salary settled in 1973. And then with a smile added that a Babu had come from Delhi and handed over a cheque of 1.2 crores to him as arrears. He had sent that cheque to his bank but he was not sure whether the cheque would be honoured.

I had been avoiding talking to the media about Kashmir but when several journalists and TV channels wanted to get my views on Sam, I was only too happy to oblige. I told them that we as a Nation had failed to give due honour to Sam after his demise. Government of India was represented by a Minister of State, the Army by its Vice Chief (the Chief was on tour abroad) and the Navy and the Air Force, by officers of two star rank at his funeral. I am told the civilian bureaucracy argued that from protocol point of view that was quite adequate. The Field Marshal did not have a high enough protocol status. The cabinet secretary enjoyed a higher status. In the UK, when their first Field Marshal, the Duke of Wellington, the victor of the Battle of Waterloo, had died, his funeral was attended by several Heads of State, Heads of Government and other top dignitaries. In India, we treated our first Field Marshal and the victor of the Bangladesh War so shabbily. This fueled resentment among the people. A condolence register was put up at India Gate in Delhi and thousands of people went there to put their signatures in that register. I was also one of them.

Tej Sapru as Army Commander Western Command and as President of the Gorkha Brigade, organized a memorial function at Delhi Cantonment. I had during my Army career held both the appointments which Tej Sapru was now holding. Sam was from the 8th Gorkha and I from the 5th Gorkha. Both are sister regiments with a common training centre. Being one of the senior most living Gorkha officers and in view of my long association with Sam, I was invited to be one of the main speakers at the memorial function. In my speech I narrated quite a few humorous and personal anecdotes concerning Sam, including what he had said about the cheque of his 35 years arrears of pay.

Antony, the Defence Minister, was presiding over the function. I had met him a couple of times when he had come on visit to Kashmir. In his presidential remarks, Antony claimed credit for releasing the arrears of pay for Sam, which had been pending for so long. He also paid a compliment to me saying that I had a computer mind. During tea after the function, he told me that he would like to meet me and discuss some things with me. I told him that I would be delighted to meet him, whenever it suited him. I was living in Delhi and his staff could let me know, when he would like to meet me. Obviously, Antony was wanting to discuss the worsening situation in Kashmir with me. I never received a call from Antony or his staff. I did not consider it necessary to ask for an appointment with him. The ruling party was too engrossed with the confidence motion in the Parliament on the nuclear deal and had little time for Kashmir or the views of a former governor of Kashmir.

4

Azad's Press Conference on the afternoon ot 25 June failed to have the desired effect. I read a brief report of it in the national Press. Subsequently, I saw a complete transcript of the Press Release. It gave out in great detail with references and extracts from various documents, how the land diversion order was sanctioned. It clearly brought out that all the prescribed procedures had been duly followed. The two PDP ministers holding the forest and law portfolios, had processed the case and were a party to that decision. It was an impeccable document which would have served its purpose in a court of law or before a judicial commission. It was more of a bureaucratic and legalistic than a political presentation. What had to be countered was that there was nothing wrong *per* se in the diversion of the land. This had been done in the case of various government and private agencies as also Aukaf Board in Kashmir and Mata Vaishno Devi Shrine Board in Jammu. On the day land diversion to Shrine Board was sanctioned, five other such transfers had been sanctioned. The facts that the proprietary right over the land remained with the State Government and the land was to be used by the Board only for the purpose of constructing temporary pre-fabricated shelter for pilgrims and for no other purpose, was not sufficiently highlighted. If the Board failed to comply with this requirement, the land would revert to the State Government. Another very important issue that had to be rebutted, was the ridiculous and absurd canard being spread about Hindu pilgrims being settled at Baltal with a view to change the demography of the

Valley. Possibly, at that stage, even if all this had been done, the tidal wave of communal passions that had been aroused could not be stopped. Be that as it may, Azad's Press Conference fully exposed the duplicity of the PDP in the whole affair. Not long after, crowds in Srinagar were burning effigies of Mufti and other senior PDP leaders. It is surprising that no one brought out that there was nothing wrong nor any impropriety committed in allocating the Baltal land to the Shrine Board. The communalists with the support of the Valley Press conjured the ghost of Hindu cultural and religious invasion of the Valley. The absurd theory about a conspiracy to change the demography of the Valley as Israel had done in Palestine, was widely propagated. It was also propagated that the transfer of land to the Board was an act of grave injustice to the people of Kashmir. Even the national media, ever keen to establish its secular credentials, toed this line without finding out the real facts. Thus, the land controversy was being projected as having arisen due to the machinations of Hindu fundamentalists. In the absence of anyone to contradict this false propaganda and present facts truthfully, this issue erupted like a communal tornado engulfing the Valley. The interests of the communalists and separatists coincided. The whole issue became a raging national controversy. It also got much international publicity. It is only after the strong winds of the tornado started dying down that a realization dawned that a non-issue had been used to fuel communal passion for electoral gains.

Mufti with his influence in Delhi now had a governor of his choice in the State. It appeared that Vohra had been briefed at Delhi to carry out Mufti's agenda. Mufti and Vohra had worked together in 1990, when Mufti was Union Minister and Vohra a Secretary. Soon after his arrival in Kashmir, Vohra went on an overdrive of appeasement. As Chairman of the Shrine Board, he withdrew the request of the Board for the Baltal land. The PDP gave an ultimatum to Azad to revoke the Baltal land allotment order by 30 June 2008. Without waiting for the ultimatum period to expire, the PDP withdrew support from the Azad Government two days earlier, reducing it to a minority. Azad felt that he could carry the day and prove his majority in the Assembly where a trial of strength was scheduled for 7 July 2008. In the meanwhile the land allocation order was revoked. In pursuit of the policy of appeasement, the Government dismantled the Amarnath Shrine Board, which was not even the demand of the agitators. The Chief Executive Officer of the Shrine Board was removed, the members of the Board were asked to resign and the functions of the Shrine Board taken over by the State Government. The Shrine Board was being treated as the foul guy for its "sin" of making a request for the Baltal land for very valid reasons, some three years ago. All this was perhaps done at the instance of Mufti, who had visceral hatred for the Board. The agitation had become very widespread, reminiscent of the agitation when the Prophet's hair had been stolen from Hazratbal. The decision of the Government to revoke the land allotment order and also to dismantle the Amarnath Shrine Board, was widely welcomed in the Valley. Victory processions were taken out by the agitators. There was now a demand for reorganising Mata Vaishno Devi Shrine Board, whose achievements had been an eyesore for some people.

To be fair to the State Government, one must admit that irrespective of the legitimacy or otherwise of the demand for revocation of the land transfer order, there was now no choice but to accept that demand. A democracy has to respect overwhelming popular sentiments of the people. A solution could be found which could douse the agitation and yet not arouse adverse reaction in Jammu. Instead of withdrawing the request for allocation of Baltal land, the Chairman of the Shrine Board could have written saying that the Board was not prepared to pay Rs 2.5 crores demanded from it in the land allocation order. The Government could have then cancelled the land allocation order but at the same time announced that the Board will be allowed the use of the Baltal land for pilgrims, as heretofore. Had this been done, it may possibly have met the demand of the agitators in Kashmir and at the same time may not have aroused any adverse reaction in Jammu. Possibly, the Government felt that there would not be any reaction in Jammu and even if there was, it could be contained easily.

There was much pent up feeling among the people of Jammu against injustice and discrimination being meted out to them for long. They had numerous grievances, both political and economic. For every 66,000 voters in Jammu region there was one MLA as against one MLA for every 49,000 voters in the Valley. Thus for 30 lakh voters Jammu had 37 seats in the State Assembly while the Valley for 28 lakh voters had 46 seats. The long pending demand of Jammu region for delimitation commission had been ignored. The bulk of the revenue earned by the State came from Jammu, yet more funds both from revenue earnings and Central grants were given to the Valley. After the revoking of the Baltal land order and the dismantling of Amarnath Shrine Board, there was now talk of reorganising the Mata Vaishno Devi Shrine Board. While the State Government was denying the diversion of 100 acre of land at Baltal, Government of India was spending hundreds of crores on Haj pilgrimage. No Muslim country, not even Pakistan provides Haj subsidy. At about the same time as Baltal land allocation order was revoked, the Chief Minister of Delhi had laid the foundation stone at Naraina in Delhi for a 22 crore Haj complex. All this lit the tinder box and a massive spontaneous people's movement erupted in Jammu.

On 7 July, 2008 before the vote of confidence could be taken in the State Assembly, Azad tendered his resignation. While doing so, he delivered an admirable fighting speech in the newly constructed excellent Assembly building in Srinagar. This building had been completed in record time with work being done in double shifts, under the directions of Azad. It was one of the symbols of all the development work being done in the State by Azad. It was indeed an irony that he had to resign as Chief Minister on the day of the inauguration of the new Assembly building. Similarly, it was an irony that as soon as we reached the high watermark of promoting Kashmiriyat in late May 2008, a blatantly communal movement was started, soon thereafter, to undo what had been achieved.

While the communalists and anti-nationals in the Valley had been trying to vilify me as a Hindu communalist and the "secularists" at Delhi seemed to be toeing the same line, EI Hadees in the Valley, had the courage to openly say in public that I was secular. Editorials and articles had been coming out in the Press blaming me for all the unfortunate developments. The editor of a national newspaper who had been my friend for many years, wrote that on the eve of my departure from Kashmir, I had issued orders transferring the Baltal Land to the Shrine Board. I clarified to him that I had issued no such order nor is a Governor competent to do so. The land transfer had been unanimously approved by the State Cabinet with PDP Ministers a party to that decision. I had no role whatsoever in sanctioning this transfer beyond making a request to the Government for this land, three years earlier in 2005, for very valid reasons. Despite my clarification, that same newspaper came out with an editorial repeating the falsehood that I had sanctioned the land transfer. The official spokesperson of the Congress Party, Jayanti Natarajan, gave a Press statement that General Sinha created trouble wherever he went. He did so in Assam and he had also done so in Kashmir. Her reference to Assam was in regard to my report to the President on illegal migration of Bangladeshis. This hurt the vote bank politics of her party.

Hitherto, I had avoided talking to the Press about Kashmir. I now felt that I must go all out to place facts before the people. The Conclave of Defence Veterans decided to start annual Field Marshal Manekshaw lectures. I was invited to deliver the first Field Marshal Manekshaw memorial lecture at the India International Centre. I readily accepted the invitation. I chose to talk on the Kashmir problem and the current unfortunate developments there. Considering the fact that Sam and I had been associated with Kashmir from Day One in 1947, Kashmir issue was an appropriate topic for my lecture paying tribute to him. There was a large and distinguished audience including several former governors and retired Generals. My presentation of facts on the ongoing critical situation in Kashmir had a good impact, I felt that I owed it to the Nation to place facts before the people to counter all the false propaganda that had been unleashed. I undertook to give talks on Kashmir at several educational institutions and various non-political forums. I visited various cities, Chandigarh, Ahmedabad, Mumbai, Chennai, Bangalore, Patna and so on. In Delhi I spoke from dozens of platforms. I also appeared on various TV channels to clarify facts and give my views. It was a one man's crusade and I had the satisfaction that it was having some impact.

The Jammu agitation continued unabated. It was a true people's movement led by people one had not heard of before. Such a sustained mass movement for over two mouths had not taken place earlier. As a student, I had seen the Quit India Movement of 1942 from close quarters. It had lasted for about a fortnight. All the leaders were locked up in jail. The army and the police had suppressed the movement by force and soon all was quiet. The Jammu movement continued for over two months. Their three demands were restore Baltal Land to the Amarnath Shrine Board, re-establish the Board and recall the Governor. People in the Valley dubbed this movement as communal and so did our "secularists" at the national level. The fact is that it was the Valley agitation which was communal with not a single Hindu participating in it. The Jammu agitation on the other hand had the participation of a number of Muslim leaders and Muslim organizations. A group of 100 Muslims after offering prayers at Jamma Masjid in Delhi, proceeded to Jammu to express their support for the agitation to restore Baltal Land to the Shrine Board. Yet the leaders in the Valley and the "secularists" at the national level, were all the time trying to dub the Jammu agitation as communal. The BJP fully supported the agitation and so did all the local Congressmen from Jammu. All the MPs and MLAs of the Congress from Jammu, including former ministers in the State Government who had approved of the revocation order, expressed support for the movement.

Two incidents added fuel to the movement in Jammu. Omar Abdullah delivered a brilliant speech in the Parliament during the vote of confidence debate, on the nuclear deal with the USA. A sober and secular person like him with balanced views had got carried away by the disinformation that had been spread. Referring to the Baltal land, he said that he would rather give his life than the land. There was no need for him to have become so emotional on this issue. The land had been traditionally used as a temporary camp for pilgrims for long. This only showed how the disinformation campaign and false propaganda had misguided and misinformed people. Omar's speech had a very adverse impact in Jammu. Kuldeep Dogra who was on hunger strike committed suicide, showing that he could actually give his life for the Baltal land. The police showed disrespect for his body burning it at night with tyres and not allowing his wife and family access to it. This ham handed action greatly inflamed the local people giving further momentum to their agitation. Mehbooba Mufti went to the extent of warning the people of Jammu of retaliatory action. It so happened that within a few days, some terrorists from Pakistan infiltrated into Jammu, killing some civilians and taking a few hostage including children. The Army conducted an operation rescuing the hostages and killing the terrorists. The Army had a very difficult task. It was asked to operate against agitators in the Valley carrying Pakistan flag and demanding that the Army quit Kashmir. While in Jammu it had to deal with agitators carrying the Indian National flag and shouting slogans in praise of the Army. In both instances, the Army acted with complete impartiality and used minimum force.

All Congress MPs and MLAs from the State including Dr Karan Singh, petitioned Delhi to recall the Governor whose effigies were being burnt in Jammu almost every day for two months. No governor in our county had ever faced such hostile protests for so long by so many people of his State. I am glad that Government of India stood firm and refused to recall the Governor. Had this been done, it would have set a wrong precedent of a person holding an apolitical high office being recalled as a result of political agitation. However the Government had to yield on the other two demands made by the people of Jammu. The Baltal land was restored to the Shrine Board and the Shrine Board was revived. The Board was given back its responsibility of managing the Yatra which had been taken over by the State Government.

During the agitation in Jammu Province, vehicle movement on roads got interrupted with calls for "Chakka Jam" (no movement of vehicles). This disrupted supplies coming from Pathankot into the State. Although the agitationists had not announced any economic blockade but as the Valley was entirely dependent on supplies coming by road from Jammu, it amounted to an economic blockade of the Valley. The fact that many parts of Jammu also suffered similar hardship, was not highlighted nor even mentioned in the Press. However, it was natural that disruption of supplies caused much hardship and resentment in the Valley. The separatists exploited the situation and called for a Muzaffrabad Chalo movement. Their rationale was that since supplies were not coming from India, they would obtain supplies from Pakistan through Muzaffrabad. This had obvious political implications, harmful to our national interests. Mehbooba Mufti was quick to announce support for this movement. The PDP has always been hand in glove with the separatists. The Government's reaction to this grave situation in the Valley was slow and left much to be desired. In February-March 2005 Srinagar Valley had been cut off for several weeks due to unprecedented snowfall. We had on that occasion flown in 1000 sorties of AN-32 aircraft of the Air Force from Chandigarh bringing essential supplies. If the Government had woken up and taken similar action in July-August 2008, the suffering of the people of the Valley could have been alleviated and the wind taken out of the sail of Muzaffrabad Chalo movement. The Army was deployed to open the land route of over 300 kilometers to road traffic but that took sometime. Not enough publicity was given to the fact that the Army had cleared the route and vehicle with supplies had started coming by 4 August. The separatists had given a call for Muzaffrabad Chalo. No attempt was made to stop this movement. No curfew was imposed. A sea of humanity numbering a lakh or more, joined the Muzaffrabad Chalo movement. They could not be allowed to proceed to the LoC. The police tried to stop them near Baramulla and had to open fire, in which a separatist leader got killed. This led to widespread protests all over the Valley. A non-violent mass movement began with lakhs of people joining in the protest rallies. Some analysts started writing in newspapers that a new phase of separatist movement had started in Kashmir. Pakistan having failed to secure Kashmir through wars had started a terrorist movement. Terrorism had been losing steam. A new phase of non-violent mass movement had now started which was more dangerous for Indian interests. It would put India in the doghouse before the international community. Some people with bleeding hearts in India like Arunadati Roy and Veer Singhvi started advocating that India should pull out from Kashmir. This was music to the ears of the separatists. They gave wide publicity to the "liberal" views of these well-known personalities. At long last, the authorities decided to take firm action. The Lal Chowk Chalo call was not allowed to materialize by imposing curfew. The situation was gradually brought under control and the impetus for mass rallies in the Valley died down. By October normalcy was restored in the State. The agitation in both Kashmir and Jammu left a bitter trail, completely polarising the people of the two regions. The scars of the summer madness will take a long time to heal.

About sixty people had been killed in both regions of the State. The economy of the State had suffered a loss of over a thousand crores. At the end of it all, things were back to status quo ante. The controversy over the Battal land had been totally unnecessary and misconceived. The realisation of this fact began to dawn on the people as statements issued by prominent Muslim leaders showed. Maulana Mohmood Madani, MP, led 600 clerics from Deobund to Hyderabad for a peace meet in early November. At this meeting in Hyderabad he spoke, "Transferring of land from the Forest Department to the Board did not hurt Muslim interests in any way. There was nothing to oppose. It was unnecessarily made into a political issue by all sides". Fida Iqbal writing in Greater Kashmir of 9 November wrote, " Recent Amarnath land row was the creation of vested political interests in collaboration with other elements of dubious character", Dr Farooq Abdullah stated, "Mufti Mohammad Sayeed's politics had a hidden agenda to erode *Kashmiriyat*. Mufti with his sinister design made all efforts to erode *Kashmiriyat,* a tradition of religious tolerance and brotherhood, with his divisive politics".

During the summer madness of 2008 when widespread agitation had peaked both in Kashmir and Jammu, in my lecture tours and interactions, I maintained that the battle of *Kashmiriyat* may have been lost but the war of *Kashmiriyat* will eventually be won. I used to underscore my faith in the people of Kashmir.

5

I had been in the thick of the controversy raging over the Amarnath dispute during the first few months of my retirement in Delhi, from July to September. By October the controversy was dying down and I could now afford to relax. Golf gives me relaxation, I resumed playing golf in Delhi.

My father had been a very good sportsman. He was a polo player of national standing. He was also a good tennis player. He was one of the few police officers who played football and hockey with his men. In his later years, he had taken to golf. He was a little disappointed in me because I had not inherited his talent in sports. I played all games but I was not too good in any. In my youth I played a reasonable game of squash. I picked up golf in my later years. In my young days in the Army, golf was considered an old man's infirmity.

After I quit the Army and returned home to Patna, I started playing golf regularly. My father was the President of Patna Golf Club. I succeeded him in that appointment and he was happy to see me keen on golf. As Governor in Assam and in Jammu and Kashmir, I had ample opportunity and facility to play Golf. In Jammu and Kashmir, I had presented two trophies, one each to the Army and the Police for organising Army versus Police tournaments. This was done with a view to promoting friendly relations between officers of the two forces. The Army Commander and the Corps Commanders were all golfers. Kuldeep Khoda took over as DC Police in 2006 and he too was a good golfer. I used to play alternately for the army and the police in these tournaments. The fact that I would play 18 holes at my age in these tournaments was much appreciated. I recall a unique foursome one year in the tournament organised at Nagrota by the Army. The foursome comprised Ghulam Nabi Azad the Chief Minister, Bashir Khan the Chief Justice, Deepak Kapoor, the Army Commander who later became the Army Chief, and I. On this occasion, I was playing for the Army.

When I had respite from all the controversy about Amarnath land row over which I was being constantly sniped at, I resumed playing golf. I had a stroke of rare good luck. A hole-in-one is a bit of a miracle. The best of players playing golf for decades, do not manage to get one. Much to my own surprise and the surprise of my two brothers, Jyoti and Chakru who were playing with me, I managed a hole in one on the 13th hole at the Army Golf Course in Delhi. I was told that it was a record for someone above 80 to get a hole-in-one. This was of much satisfaction to me. The situation in Jammu and Kashmir was settling down. I said to myself that the hole-in-one is a Divine message to me to boost my morale and assure me that the war for *Kashmiriyat* will eventually be won in Jammu and Kahsmir. There was also a remarkable coincidence. My son, Yash, serving as India's Ambassador in Venezuela, got a hole-in-one at Caracas, the previous week. My youngest brother Chakru, who is an outstanding and a very regular golf player, had scored a hat-trick, getting his third hole-in-one. I am sure my father in Heaven, must be very happy to see his progeny doing well in golf.

6

Elections to the State Assembly were due in September-October 2008. After the fall of the Azad Government in June, the State had been placed under Governor's rule. There was divided opinion about holding State election in November-December 2008 or in the summer of 2009. After the widespread disturbances from July to August, many thought that it may be prudent to defer election till the following summer. All the political parties, except the PDP were for holding election in the winter of 2008, to ensure the early restoration of democracy in the State. As always, the separatists called for a boycott. The PDP was also toying with the idea of boycotting the election, along with the Hurriyat, with whom they had always been close. At the last minute, the PDP also decided to join the election fray, fearing that if they did not do so, then the Election Commission may derecognize them as a political party and withdraw their election symbol.

The Election Commission after much deliberation decided to take the risk and took the hard decision of holding the election in the State in seven phases in November - December 2008. According to newspaper reports, there was divided opinion in the Commission on the timing of the election. The Chief Election Commissioner in a statement expressed concern that the voter turnout may be low. The National Conference also expressed similar concern.

I was keenly watching the start of electioneering. I had no idea that an attempt would be made to drag my name again in a controversy during electioneering. Tareeq Hamid Qarra who was fully exposed for his involvement in the multi-crore forest scam by the Kundal Committee made baseless allegation of corruption against the Shrine Boards, indirectly targeting me. He had done so earlier too during the Amarnath land row. I decided to ignore his insinuation with the contempt it deserved. All his antics like introduction of Pakistan currency and so on did not help him much. He was one of the few top leaders of his party who could not retain his seat in the Assembly election.

Mufti Mohammad Sayeed though always hostile to me had always maintained decorum. Surprisingly, a senior leader like him who had been India's Union Home Minister, tried to indulge in street level politics. He issued a statement to the Press that I was close to Dayanand Pandey one of the accused in Malegaon blast case. He even accused me of entertaining him to dinner in Raj Bhavan and having put him up in Raj Bhavan as my guest. The PDP had been playing the communal card for some time. The mischievous canard that he was trying to spread had a dual motive. He wanted to tarnish my image by trying to link my name with the Malegaon blast and at the same time get electoral mileage from exposing Hindus involved in the terrorist explosion at Malegaon.

It is surprising that despite having been Chief Minister, Mufti did not realilse that Raj Bhavan is a semi-public place where no one can stay without the knowledge of a hundred or more staff, comprising security personnel, personal staff including ADCs, secretarial and household staff. A record is kept of guests staying in Raj Bhavan. So far as Dayanand Pandey was concerned as far as I remember, I had never even met him. I issued a statement that I was considering filing a libel suit against Mufti. Thereafter, Mufti did not repeat this allegation. However, Prithviraj Chauhan a Union Minister of State on a visit to Srinagar issued a statement that the matter should be investigated. This was of course in line with the well-known policy of his party to pamper to minority sentiments.

Mufti also made allegations against Omar Abdullah on the basis of a photograph of Omar at a meeting being addressed by Dayanand Pandey. He further alleged that Omar had been going to Hardwar to meet Dayanand Pandey. By roping in Omar like this, Mufti was only eroding his own credibility. Omar threatened to sue him for 1 crore as damages. The allegation against Omar was not repeated again.

Professor Bhim Singh, President of the J&K Panthers Party launched a tirade against Mufti. He issued a Press statement saying that the terrorists who had attacked the Akshardham temple at Gandhinagar in Gujarat, had hatched their plot at the house of Zargar in Kashmir. At that time, Zargar was a senior PDP minister serving in Mufti's cabinet. Bhim Singh also stated that one of the terrorists was a former cook of Mufti who had served him for a few months. I was aware of this allegation because in my early days as Governor, there was a demand for the removal of Zargar from the Cabinet. Mufti gave him a clean chit and the police investigation was closed. I was not aware that one of the terrorists was a former cook of Mufti.

Time Now, a leading TV news channel organised a programme on Mufti's sensational allegation against me which had not only been reported by national newspapers but had also been picked by some international newspapers. Dr Farooq Abdullah, Chandan Mitra, the Editor of the Pioneer, Jayanti Natarajan, the spokesperson of the Congress Party and I participated in this programme, which was anchored by Arnab Goswami. I emphatically rebutted the allegation and said that I did not remember ever meeting Dayanand Pandey. I only came to know of him, when his name appeared in the newspapers linking him to the Malegaon blasts. I also mentioned that Mufti's allegation against me was as absurd as mine would be, if I were to accuse him of having met Osama Bin Laden during his foreign tours. Jayanti Natarajan was quick to react. In pursuit of her party's policy of championing the minority cause, she alleged that I was being communal in talking about Osama Bin Laden. Of course for her it was nothing communal in Mufti linking me with Dayanand Pandey. Chandan Mitra gave an effective reply saying that there was nothing communal in what I had said. I had only given an example to emphasise my point. I did not feel it appropriate to get involved in a slanging match with Jayanti Natarajan. I was aware of the allegation in connection with the attack on Akshardham temple. I considered it not in keeping with my dignity to mention this allegation and score a point. Besides Chandan Mitra, Dr Farooq Abdullah and the anchor were all supportive of me. Jayanti Natrajan was isolated during the discussion.

At a public meeting in Rajouri, Ghulam Nabi Azad rubbished the charge made by Mufti against me. He said that it had been made because of Mufti's longstanding enmity with me. Knowing Congress culture, I admired Ghulam Nabi Azad for his courage and honesty. He had taken a stand against the line being toed by his party's spokesperson and a Union Minister.

On the eve of elections, some political leaders indulge in all sorts of unbecoming antics. I did not expect a senior political leader of Mufti's eminence to indulge in such gutter politics. After creating a cheap sensation for a while, Mufti's allegation against Omar and me died down. It was given a fitting burial. In any case, the allegation had not been taken seriously by the people. It was dismissed by them as an election stunt.

7

Two serious terrorist attacks occurred in the country outside Jammu and Kashmir, in the run-up to elections in that State. The first was on 30 October in Assam. Over 80 innocent people were killed in serial blasts. This was the biggest such attack in Assam. Police investigations revealed that Hizb-ul-Jihadi-al Islam (HUJI) comprising Bangladeshi religious fundamentalists was behind this heinous act. Yet this incident did not give a wake up call to the Congress Party to whom vote bank politics was so dear. However, the second big terrorist attack, the most high profile such attack in the country jolted the entire Nation causing much angry outburst against the UPA Government. Under the UPA Government, India had become a very soft State. The terrorists have been merrily attacking one city after another and the Government frozen in inaction with its leaders voicing inane platitudes. The terrorists seem to be following Lenin's Maxim, "Probe with a bayonet; if you meet steel, stop; if you meet mush then you push". The Mumbai carnage exposed a failed Government in India. Ten terrorists who had come from Pakistan, about whom prior intelligence was available, held the city of Mumbai and the country to ransom for 62 hours. This was fully highlighted on the TV channels and was watched helplessly by the entire Nation. It exposed the total incompetence of our Governmental machinery. The Nation was seething with rage. About 180 innocent people had been killed and 300 injured in the terrorists attacks at Taj Hotel, Strident Hotel, Nariman House (a Jew religious centre) and Chhatrapati Sivaji Terminus. Among the killed were, a number of foreigners from the USA, Europe and Israel. At Narriman House the Rabi, his wife and some Jews were killed. The Jews were mercilessly butchered. The international community and the top leaders of the world condemned this barbaric act. Pakistan's involvement in this horrific deed came out loud and clear. One of the Pakistani terrorists had been captured alive and he gave a wealth of information to our intelligence agencies as also to the intelligence agencies of the USA and Israel. The only silver lining in the national humiliation of 26 November, 2008 was the exemplary bravery shown by our soldiers, policemen and firemen.

26/11 was a repeat of what had happened to us in October-November 1962. The comparison was very stark. Both were avoidable humiliations brought about on the Nation. In 1962 Prime Minister Nehru had to admit that he was living in a world divorced from reality and in 2008 Prime Minister Manmohan Singh had to apologise to the Nation. In 1962 Defence Minister Krishna Merion had to quit and in 2008 Home Minister Shivraj Patil had to do so. Law and order is a State subject. The Congress Government in Maharashtra stood exposed for its incompetence. The Chief Minister was only seen after the critical three days, on a sight seeing tour of Taj Hotel with his film actor son and a film director. The Deputy Chief Minister had the audacity to dismiss the Mumbai carnage as a small incident that happens in a big city. This was an insult to the memory of the large number of martyrs. Both the Chief Minister and the Deputy Chief Minister had to be shown the door. In 1962, the Army Chief and the Corps Commander had to quit but in 2008 no heads of any official responsible for monumental lapses, rolled. The National Security Adviser and various officials continue to flourish, despite their lapses coming to light during the Mumbai outrage. In Pakistan, the National Security Adviser was sacked for a minor indiscretion but in India the National Security Adviser was exonerated of his grave culpable negligence leading to a great national tragedy. Apart from the Government not acting on available intelligence, the crisis was not handled appropriately. The Crisis Management Group never met. The NSG took nine hours to reach Mumbai as aircraft was not readily available to transport them.

After 9/11, the United Nations Security Council had asked member countries to enact stringent laws against terrorism. The UPA Government on coming to power, immediately scrapped POTA for vote bank considerations. While city after city in the country was being subjected to terrorist attacks the UPA Government remained adamant in its stand that there was no need for any special law to deal with the menace of terrorism. The Moily Commission set up by the Government, under the chairmanship of a former Congress Chief Minister had recommended a stringent law against terrorism. The Government had been sleeping over that recommendation. The Mumbai calamity forced the Government out of its slumber and at long last a legislation was enacted on the lines of POTA except that confession before a police officer was not to be treated as legal evidence. A National Investigating Agency was also set up in the wake of the Mumbai disaster. It remains to be seen how far the new laws are implemented on the ground and how far the NIA is allowed to function without political interference. The blatant manner in which the UPA Goverment has misused the CBI, holds out little hipe of it allowing the NIA to function inpartially. I recall one of our most distinguished civil servants, B K Nehru telling me that in the British days, there were too few laws and they were all implemented strictly. After Independence we have framed too many laws and we do not implement them.

At the political level reactions of the UPA Government to terrorism have been bizarre. Cabinet ministers have been speaking in different voices. Two Cabinet ministers and Samajwadi Party leaders opposed the banning of SIMI, a well-known outfit sponsoring terrorism. The Supreme Court had to do the needful. One Cabinet minister demanded that all illegal Bangladeshi immigrants be given Indian citizenship, when it is well known that on several occasions, they have been involved in acts of terrorism. One minister justified use of government funds allocated to a university to defend students in court, who are being prosecuted for involvement in the terrorist incident at Batla House in Delhi. Another minister advocated an inquiry into this incident to determine if the whole thing had been faked by the police. A minister went to the UN to represent India and forgot to mention that among the killed in Mumbai carnage were Jews and 20 percent of the victims were Muslims. He later apologized for his omission in the Parliament. Yet another minister issued a statement insinuating that Hemant Karkare, the ATG Chief, was killed on 26/11 as a result of conspiracy by Hindus and not by Pakistani terrorist. The Prime Minister condoned this, saying that to err is human. And in this theatre of the absurd, a senior Congress general secretary allowed his imagination to run wild. To score a point over the BJP which had surrendered to terrorist demand to save the lives of nearly 200 passengers of Indian Airlines plane held hostage at Kandahar, he claimed that the UPA Government did not yield to terrorist demand in Mumbai to release Afzal Guru. This was despite the fact that no communication had ever taken place with the terrorists in Mumbai.

The Mumbai carnage took place in the wake of elections in Jammu and Kashmir. Separatist and anti-national leaders tried to toe the Pakistan line regarding that tragic episode. The people of Kashmir did not allow themselves to be misguided. Election results in the State amply proved this.

8

The huge and unprecedented voter turnout in Jammu and Kashmir took everyone by surprise. The odds were so much against this happening that no one could forecast this. In the wake of Amarnath land row, the separatist and communal elements seemed to have caught the imagination of the people of the Valley. Their massive participation in the Muzaffarabad Chalo movement and subsequent mass rallies were indicative of the separatists having a complete hold over the people in the Valley. And when the separatists called for a boycott of the polls, it was expected that the people of the Valley will abide by that call. As mentioned earlier, the Chief Election Commissioner while taking the decision to hold early polls was apprehensive of low voter turnout. There was another important factor likely to affect voter turnout. The elections were due in September-October. They had to be postponed to November-December, when the mercury goes down considerably, specially in the Valley. Extreme cold of the winter would deter the voters lining up in large numbers at the polling booths. The Kashmiri voter defied all these considerations. The pessimistic forecasts about voter turnout was rubbished by him.

The voter turnout in the State as a whole was 62% which was higher than the national average. In 2002 Assembly election the voter turnout was 43%. In the Valley the voter turnout had shot up from 29% to 55%. Srinagar City has been the hotbed of separatists. Voter turnout in the city had increased three times from the 2002 figures.

Apart from the remarkable large voter turnout, there was also another very significant fact. The 2008 election saw the lowest level of poll violence and minimal complaints of poll rigging or coercion of voters. In 2002 election, 63 people had been killed and 84 injured in 114 incidents of violence. Among the killed were 48 political activists including a minister. In 2008 there were 21 incidents of violence with five fatalities. No political activist was killed in this election. The credit for all this must go largely to J&K Police under the dynamic leadership of Kuldeep Khoda, the DG Police of the State. The police apprehended three terrorists in Jammu City. They had come from Pakistan with the intention of disrupting the election. One of them was a regular soldier of Pakistan Army in civilian clothes.

Various analysts have been giving divergent reasons for the large voter turnout. The common refrain of the separatist and their sympathisers has been that the people voted for development and good governance. The large turnout had nothing to do with the people's views on the resolution of the long festering Kashmir problem. However, the hard core separatist leader, Syed Ali Shah Geelani was stunned. He stated, "Times change and with it the situation changes". He was hopeful that the situation will change again. Sajjad Lone admitted that this had been a big setback requiring revision of strategy. Mirwaiz Omar Farooq harped on this election not being a true reflection of the views of the people of Kashmir. It would not be out of place to mention that his views on elections are often not in line with reality. In 2007 when the people of Pakistan were almost unanimous in opposing Musharraf's rigged re-election to Presidency and the international community condemned it, Mirwaiz and his supporters were firing crackers to express their jubilation over Musharraf's re-election. Yasin Mallik declined to give any comment on the State Assembly election. It is obvious that the separatists were in disarray. Notwithstanding this, the Valley Press continued with its venomous anti-India articles and editorials, belittling the success of the Assembly election. It was being asserted that this election was for bread and butter and had no political relevance in regard to the Kashmir problem. Even if we accept this, the fact is that these elections convincingly established that the separatists do not have much following among the people. Like the Emperor seen having no clothes the separatists swimming in the high tide of communal wave were seen to have no clothes after the tide ebbed. If they really had much support among the people, such a high voter turnout would not have taken place. In 1983 during the students' movement in Assam, the leaders of that movement called for a boycott of the Assembly election. The voter turnout was a mere 3 percent, an all time low in the history of Indian democracy.

9

As already mentioned earlier, I was planning for a free and fair election with a large voter turn out, with international diplomatic community and international media provided free access to observe the elections. In 2006 by-elections in four key constituencies in Baramulla and in Doda the voter turnout was 70% despite boycott by terrorists. With Azad concentrating on development, the security forces successfully combating violence reducing average daily killings from 10 to 1 and I doing my bit for Kashmiriyat and other psychological initiatives, I was hopeful that we would achieve the desired goal in 2008 Assembly election. The best laid plans can get derailed due to unforeseen developments. That is exactly what happened during the summer madness of 2008 in Jammu and Kashmir. It was a great setback and it appeared that we had lost the battle for Kashmiriyat. Even so, I still had faith in the people of Kashmir and kept repeatedly asserting that the battle for Kashmiriyat may have been lost but the war for Kashmiriyat will eventually be won. The high voter turnout in 2008 Assembly election augurs well for the ultimate triumph of Kashmiriyat. Apart from a road map for 2008 Assembly election, I also had a road map for the ultimate resolution of the Kashmir problem. I was convinced that it had to be more economic than political. All of us should be partners in the fight against our common enemies of poverty, ignorance and disease. Europe which had been the originator of the concept of Nation State had become an international economic community in which national borders had lost much relevance. That was a model which all of us should work for. An economic union of South Asia on the lines of European Union in which national boundaries will not be of much consequence will provide a win-win situation for all—the people of India, the people of Kashmir and the people of Pakistan.

In the context of the 2008 Assembly election, one may reflect on the report of the 2002 Mori Poll in the Valley conducted under the patronage of Lord Avebury, a known protagonist of Pakistan. The results of that poll were interesting. 61% of the people wanted to stay with India, 6% wanted to go to Pakistan and 37% were undecided. In early nineties the slogan raging in the Valley was "Kashmir Banega Pakistan" (Kashmir will become part of Pakistan). There was widespread belief at that time that this would happen very soon. After a decade, the view on this appeared to have changed. The sentiment for Azadi (Independence) now appeared very strong. Only future can tell whether the 2008 election will be a harbinger of a further change. If Kashmiri Muslims get their so called "Azadi" from India, would'nt non-Kashmiri Muslims and non-Muslims want their "Azadi" from them? Of course the communalists often say that two and a half districts (referring to Hindu majority area which has now more districts) may secede if they want to. In that case Ladakh which constitutes the largest land space of the State, will also secede. Another division on the basis of the two nation theory will bring back the spectre of 1947 Partition holocaust. The majority of the people including the separatists do not want that the present territorial contour of the State be altered.

The electorate has given a fractured mandate for the 87 member State Assembly. National Conference has again emerged as the single largest party retaining 28 seats, as in 2002. The PDP is at number 2 position with a tally of 21 having appreciably improved its position from 16 in 2002. The Congress lost seats in Jammu which used to be its citadel. Its tally has dropped from 20 in 2002 to 17 in 2008. The BJP was a big gainer. Its share of seats in the Assembly has gone up from 1 to 11. There are 10 others mostly independents. This includes 3 of Panther's Party, much opposed to the PDP. The PDP was able to increase its numbers from 16 to 21 using the communal card while opposing Amarnath land transfer to the Shrine Board and enlisting the support of the Jamait and Islamists. BJP became a beneficiary of the Amarnath controversy and was able to achieve a spectacular rise in its seat tally. The election results put Congress in the position of Kingmaker.

Given the past history of relationship between the Congress and the PDP in the State coalition government, the Congress would have found it very difficult to go for coalition with the PDP. The PDP had acted as the opposition within the coalition when it was being headed by the Congress. A few months before the election, the PDP stabbed the Congress in the back leading to the fall of the Azad Government. Further, the PDP was virtually aligned with the separatist. It had floated the idea of dual currency in Kashmir, accepting Pakistan currency as legal tender. Its President Mehbooba Mufti, on a visit to Pakistan had announced at the Pugwash Conference in 2007 that Kashmir should be placed under the joint control of India and Pakistan. She talks of Kashmir's geographical and sentimental links with Pakistan. The Pakistani flag was seen fluttering on Pakistan's Independence Day (14th August) in 2008 on the house of a former PDP Minister Qazi Mohammad Afzal in Gandarbal. Given these facts it was surprising how some leaders in the Congress were in favour of an alliance with the PDP. Politics is a strange game, where one can have strange bed fellows.

Mufti Mohammad Sayeed was desperately wanting to revive the Congress-PDP alliance to again somehow manage to be in power in the State. It reminded me of October 2005 when he had so desperately tried to get his term as chief minister extended. He wanted the Congress then to forego its claim in his favour. With his links with the Congress high command, Mufti nearly succeeded. At the last minute the Congress decided not to forego the chief minister's appointment for the next three years. The 2008 situation was a repeat of what had happened in 2005. Perhaps Mufti hoped that his strong links with Congress high command would be able to defy the logic of numbers and the memory of the bad blood during the last Congress-PDP coalition. Things went awry for him and the PDP was left out in the cold. The National Conference and the Congress agreed to form an alliance with Omar Abdullah as the

Chief Minister for a full six year term. There would be no rotational Chief Minister this time. This was the most sensible arrangement in the circumstance. Omar from generation next, has undoubtedly been a good choice. Mufti in a statement to the Press protested that in spite of the old alliance between the Congress and PDP, the Congress had concluded an alliance with National Conference without consulting him. This statement caused amusement among many and Mufti was held to ridicule. One wondered as to how the PDP expected to be consulted when it had brought down the Azad Government in July 2008 without consulting the Congress. Mufti walked out of the UPA alliance at the Centre and he showed his resentment by not attending the function of Omar Abdullah's swearing in as chief minister. The Congress Party now seemed to have changed its stand regarding Amarnath land row and its pursuit of appeasement policy in regard to that controversy. Manish Tewari the official spokesman of the Congress Party stated on 30 December 2008, "what happened in July-August (Amarnath land issue) was completely avoidable. Those who contributed to polarization on Amarnath land issue should introspect whether it was worth it". It was obvious that he was having a dig at both the PDP and the BJP.

After Mufti had lost the levers of power in the State and his party its presence in Rajya Sabha at Delhi, he was keen to have his party's presence in Lok Sabha to retain national relevance. In an attempt to woo the voters in Jammu, he issued a statement that he was always against revocation of the order alloting the land at Baltal to the Amarnath Shrine Board. This flew in the face of facts. He was the master mind behind the Baltal land agitation and had repeatly opposed the allotment of that land to the Board. Political somersaults by politicians on the eve of elections is common in our country.

Omar Abdullah has struck the right note by issuing a statement that he would create the environment required for the return of Kashmiri Pandits to the Valley. He has announced that a commission would be constitued to look into the grievance of the people of the three regions and ensure equitable distribution of funds and resources to all regions.

10

2008 was a year of much success and much tragedy for our Nation. We had our share of success in the spectacular launch of

Chandriyan to the moon which was overshadowed by the Mumbai carnage of 26 November 2008. The Mumbai killings benumbed the nation.

With all the dark clouds enveloping our national security there are some silver linings. The Mumbai terrorist attack was condemned all over the world. Pakistan stands isolated. She had been blackmailing the USA by threats to withdraw her troops from her western border and blackmailing India with her nuclear weapons. Her bluffs has been called by the new regime in the USA. It has put the squeeze on her. Musharraf had to quickly buckle down when the Americans threatened to bomb Pakistan to the Stone Age. The present regime in Pakistan, has shown that it cannot resist pressure from the USA. However we have to solve our problems with Pakistan on our own. We should not rely on others to take the chestnuts out of the fire for us. Nor can we rely on any agreement with Pakistan nor on any promise made by Pakistan. That country has a long history of flouting written agreements starting from Standstill Agreement to the Cease Fire Agreement, the Tashkent Agreement, the Shimla Accord and the Lahore Declaration. Pakistan always has initially been in denial mode and later admitting to its complicity. These have been numerous such instances. Initially, Pakistan denied its hand in the tribal invasion of 1947 and later admitted that she had moved her Army into Kashmir. In 1965 it stated that there was an internal uprising in Kashmir. It had moved its troops into Kashmir only when the Indian Army crossed the LoC in Kashmir. In this case, the lie was exposed by the then Pakistan Army Chief General Mohammad Musa in his book, *My Version*. In the nineties, Pakistan maintained that what was happening in Kashmir was a freedom struggle and it was only providing moral and political support. There was no cross-border terrorism. The lie to this version was given by a former ISI Chief, Lt Gen Javed Ashraf Qazi who as a minister in his statement in Pakistan National Assembly confirmed Pakistan's involvement in terrorist activity in Kashmir. Musharraf first maintained that there was no cross-border terrorism in Kashmir. Then he promised that he would not allow Pakistan controlled territory to be used for cross-border terrorism. This implied that this had been happening. Five times he repeated this assertion but this meant nothing. Cross-border terrorism from Pakistan continued. The same story of denial and subsequent admission was repeated during the Kargil conflict. In the case of the Mumbai terror attack Pakistan started off with total denial, then talked of non-State actors. Initially, Pakistan denied that Kasab, the captured terrorist in Mumbai, is a Pakistani but later accepted that he is. Given this long track record of Pakistan of obfuscation, denial and prevarication, India must be very careful in dealing with that country. Written agreements or any promises should not be taken at their face value. We should not be satisfied with anything less than credible and actual action on the ground.

The recent developments in Bangladesh have been favourable and are a silver lining in the dark cloud. The return of Sheikh Hasina to power with a thumping majority and the defeat of Islamist forces hold hope for the future. During her previous term Sheikh Hasina had not been able to do much to curb Indian militant activities from Bangladesh but that does not mean that we should presume her inability to do anything, in the present changed circumstances.

The unexpected and astounding course of elections in Jammu and Kashmir has perhaps been the most welcome development in Kashmir since the Maharaja's accession to India and Sheikh Abdullah's endorsement of the same. Despite the summer madness of 2008 when all appeared lost in the wake of Amarnath controversy, there is more than a ray of light in Kashmir recalling the Mahatma's famous remark in 1947. The new dispensation of a coalition of nationalist forces keeping anti-national elements out of the Government is an encouraging development. One can hope that the State under a young and progressive chief minister would apply a balm on polarization that took place in the State, during the summer of 2008.

The UPA Government has woken up after the Mumbai tragedy and has been endeavouring to do some course correction in its last 100 days. However its inability to take hard decisions and its ministers speaking in different voices in its pursuit of the policy of appeasement do not inspire much confidence. A cabinet minister's outrageous insinuations in regard to the killing of Hemant Karkare and some leaders trying to defend him, only shows that the ruling party like a leopard but cannot change its spots.

Parliamentary elections are round the corner. I hope the Indian electorate will be mature enough to elect a Government which can effectively meet the grave national security challenges we face today. India is emerging as a great power and our human resource material has shown its high calibre in our outstanding achievements in various fields. All those gains can be lost if we do not successfully overcome the national security challenges, underscored so dramatically by the tragedy of 26/11 in Mumbai. Our electorate which is known to have shown great maturity after the Emergency in 1977 and again in 1980 after the failure of the Janata a experiment, must rise to meet the challenges we face in 2009. Irrespective of which party wins the forthcoming 2009 election, we need to have a strong Government at the Centre, preferably not a coalition, which tends to be weak. Even if a coalition is unavoidable, we need a Government capable of taking hard decisions and not pursuing vote bank politics at the cost of national security. Neither the policy of appeasement nor a communal agenda should mar the image of the new Government that gets elected in 2009. The new Government must go all out to lift the Government and the society from the quagmire of corruption and feudal democracy enshrined in dynasticism and courtier culture. In the evening of my life after having rendered service to the Nation for over sixty years, that is the wish I ardently nurture for my country. I conclude my memoirs which I have penned in this book with that earnest hope and with Jai Hind on my lips.

Index